THE OXFORD SHAKESPEARE

General Editor · Stanley Wells

The Oxford Shakespeare offers new and authoritative editions of Shakespeare's plays in which the early printings have been scrupulously re-examined and interpreted. An introductory essay provides all relevant background information together with an appraisal of critical views and of the play's effects in performance. The detailed commentaries pay particular attention to language and staging. Reprints of sources, music for songs, genealogical tables, maps, etc. are included where necessary; many of the volumes are illustrated, and all contain an index.

PETER HOLLAND, the editor of *A Midsummer Night's Dream* in the Oxford Shakespeare, is Director of the Shakespeare Institute and Professor of Shakespeare Studies at the University of Birmingham.

THE OXFORD SHAKESPEARE

Currently available in paperback

The rest of the plays and poems are forthcoming

OXFORD WORLD'S CLASSICS

WILLIAM SHAKESPEARE

A Midsummer Night's Dream

Edited by
PETER HOLLAND

Oxford   New York
OXFORD UNIVERSITY PRESS

Oxford University Press, Great Clarendon Street, Oxford OX2 6DP

Oxford New York

*Athens Auckland Bangkok Bogota Bombay Buenos Aires
Calcutta Cape Town Dar es Salaam Delhi Florence Hong Kong Istanbul
Karachi Kuala Lumpur Madras Madrid Melbourne Mexico City
Nairobi Paris Singapore Taipei Tokyo Toronto Warsaw*

*and associated companies in
Berlin Ibadan*

Oxford is a trade mark of Oxford University Press

*First published by the Clarendon Press 1994
First published as a World's Classics paperback 1995
Reissued as an Oxford World's Classics paperback 1998*

*British Library Cataloguing in Publication Data
Data available*

*Library of Congress Cataloging in Publication Data
Data available*
ISBN 0–19–812928–9 (hbk.)
ISBN 0–19–283420–7 (pbk.)

3 5 7 9 10 8 6 4 2

Printed in Spain by Book Print S.L.

PREFACE

As it has been for so many thousands of other people, *A Midsummer Night's Dream* is the first Shakespeare play that I can remember seeing. My parents took me to Peter Hall's production at Stratford in 1959 when I was eight. My memories are restricted to Mary Ure's white dress as Titania and Ian Holm, as Robin, popping up out of a trapdoor and sticking his tongue out at the audience; of Charles Laughton as Bottom I remember nothing and none of the photographs of the production I have looked at while working on this edition have any resonances in my memory. But then my memories of *Othello* with Paul Robeson the same season are similarly restricted.

As an undergraduate I was confronted by *A Midsummer Night's Dream* as a set play, 'a pappy play' as a friend dubbed it. Noel Purdon's supervisions opened my eyes to the play's mythological complexities, Anne Barton's lectures to the full range of the play's brilliance. No intellectual discovery as an undergraduate excited me more than realizing that this play was as dizzyingly wonderful as they showed it to be.

When Stanley Wells offered me the chance to edit *A Midsummer Night's Dream*, there was no play I would rather have worked on. Stanley's tolerance and guidance as deadlines for delivery came and went have been a model of editorial patience and tact. Other people have patiently listened to me talking about the play at conferences in Limoges (thanks to Pierre Iselin), Rome (thanks to Giorgio Melchiori, Viola Papetti and Paola Faini), Stratford (thanks again to Stanley Wells), UCLA (thanks to Reg Foakes) and at various seminars in Cambridge. Two wonderful months at the Huntington Library in San Marino as a Visiting Fellow in 1989 and 1992 pushed the work along at the breathless pace that that scholarly paradise makes possible: my warmest thanks to Martin Ridge and Roy Ritchie for the election to those fellowships and to all the Readers Services staff there for their unfailing kindness, and, of course, to the many Huntington readers whose lunchtime conversations gave me so much help. The Cambridge

University Library has, as ever, demonstrated that an enormous library has the resources to make research easy as well as fruitful and its staff has, as ever, demonstrated that great libraries need not be frustrating. Work at the Shakespeare Centre Library in Stratford has been similarly pleasant. But much of the research in the secondary literature would have been impossible without the help of the fine annotated bibliography for the play edited for the Garland Shakespeare Bibliographies by D. Allen Carroll and Gary Jay Williams (1986), their work a model of accuracy and fair-mindedness. When an extremely archaic computer was dying, its dinosaur disks incompatible with my new lap-top, Laura Thorp kindly typed large chunks of the introduction and commentary into their new format.

Many friends and colleagues have, over the years, read parts of the introduction, sent helpful clippings and suggestions and generally put me much in their debt. I name some and apologize to any others who may feel slighted: Anne Barton, Jonathan Bate, Warren Boutcher, Al Braunmuller, Jean Chothia, Michael Cordner, Liz Goodman, Victoria Hayne, Russell Jackson, John Kerrigan, Jeremy Maule, Louis Montrose, Stephen Orgel, Adrian Poole, Robert Smallwood, Gary Taylor, David Wiles, Gary Jay Williams, Lynn Wolf. I apologise particularly to Michael Cordner for not finding space to mention in any detail Benny Hill's performance as Bottom. My debt to the play's many editors, especially its most recent, Harold Brooks and Reg Foakes, is immeasurable; the acknowledging of this debt often seems a gesture of academic courtesy but here is genuine and heartfelt.

Frances Whistler at OUP has gently but firmly extracted the typescript from me at crucial stages. Christine Buckley's copy-editing was exemplary and her marvellous help on various matters botanical is most gratefully acknowledged.

The love and support of Angela Ritter made me finish the work, at a point when I was beginning to despair of ever completing it. But I remember most, at the end of the work, my parents, Cissie and Alf, whose love of theatre infected me from the first.

PETER HOLLAND

CONTENTS

LIST OF ILLUSTRATIONS

INTRODUCTION

OF all the commentators on Shakespeare, perhaps the oddest is Ulrich Bräker, a Swiss weaver, who in 1780 finished writing his thoughts on the plays under the title *A Few Words about William Shakespeare's Plays by a poor ignorant citizen of the world who had the good fortune to read him*. Bräker did not like much of *A Midsummer Night's Dream*:

I don't want to run down your dream, but I just can't make it out. The whole tone of the piece doesn't appeal to me. If I ever dreamt of entering a community where affairs are conducted in this tone then I'd leap out of bed, I'll be bound, without even waking up! A certain Theseus, a certain Lysander, every fairy in fact, is busy spouting his own wooden verses. I don't know what fairies are like, and if I did, I'd make a point of not mixing with them—they'd be too quick for me.[1]

Only the workers appealed to this Swiss Bottom: 'The characters of the interlude in this dream—they're the ones for me!' (p. 29).

I doubt if there are many who would agree with Bräker. *A Midsummer Night's Dream* is probably the most performed of all Shakespeare's plays, not least because, in schools, it is so often the way children first encounter Shakespeare. It has always seemed to me a play peculiarly perfect, ideally compact and coherent in its form. At this early stage in his career, in *A Midsummer Night's Dream* as in *The Comedy of Errors*, Shakespeare's approach to comic form is to transmute the enormous range and divergent nature of the materials that lie behind the play into a surface of disarming simplicity.

Like the work of Freudian analysts of genuine dreams, critics considering *A Midsummer Night's Dream* find that the play has a 'manifest' level behind which lurks their own version of the 'latent dream'.[2] For Freudians, dreamers change

[1] Ulrich Bräker, *A Few Words about William Shakespeare's Plays*, ed. Derek Bowman (New York, 1979), p. 29.

[2] Among the many texts on modern dream-theory, I have found the following most helpful: Sigmund Freud, *The Interpretation of Dreams*, Penguin Freud Library, 4 (Harmondsworth, 1976); C. G. Jung, *Memories, Dreams,*

their dreams as they remember them, this 'dream-work' transforming the latent dream through a process of distortion involving four techniques, identified as condensation, displacement, representation and symbolisation. The task of the critic should then be to uncover the dream-work that has made the 'real' subject of the play, its anxieties and repressions, acceptable.[1] The childlike world of the play is then, along such a line, part of its attempt to avoid the repressed conflict or to resolve it through the fantasy of fictitious solutions 'that are marked by infantile characteristics ānd are often contradictory among themselves'.[2]

For Jungians, this approach to decoding the secrets of a dream is mistaken. There is for Jung no latent dream since the manifest dream is not a disguise: 'dreams are a part of nature, which harbours no intention to deceive our eyes, but expresses something as best it can'.[3] Our problem, as spectators and critics, is then to learn how to read the dream. If we cannot understand the text, the fault lies in the reader, not the text, since 'the dream attempts to reveal rather than conceal'.[4]

But modern scientific analysis of dreams has moved from the psychoanalytic to the psycho-physiological, finding the source of dreams in neural activity. The most delightful surprise in such research turns out to be its emphasis on the pleasure of dreaming. Dreams can be seen as a form of entertainment and their function a form of relaxation. As Hobson argues: 'Why can't we accept the autocreative function of dreams as something given to us . . . for our own pleasure?'.[5]

This introduction will sometimes try to uncover the latent in *A Midsummer Night's Dream*; it will more often accept that

---

Reflections (1963); James A. Hall, *Clinical Uses of Dreams* (New York, 1977); James L. Fosshage and Clemens A. Loew, *Dream Interpretation: A Comparative Study* (New York, 1978); David Foulkes, *A Grammar of Dreams* (Brighton, 1978); Charles Rycroft, *The Innocence of Dreams* (1979); Liam Hudson, *Night Life: The Interpretation of Dreams* (1985); J. Allan Hobson, *The Dreaming Brain* (New York, 1988).

[1] For a full-blown psychoanalytic reading see James L. Calderwood, *A Midsummer Night's Dream* (Hemel Hempstead, 1992).

[2] Angel Garma in Fosshage and Loew, p. 28.

[3] Jung, p. 185.

[4] Edward Whitmont, 'Foreword' to Hall, p. xv.

[5] Hobson, p. 297.

the play reveals rather than conceals; and it will, I hope, always try to keep in the foreground the pleasure of watching or reading the play. The opening sections of the introduction set out a late sixteenth-century context for dreams and dreaming. Since dreams, even dramatic ones like *A Midsummer Night's Dream*, are constructed out of odd scraps of different material, the next sections explore the play by setting out from the 'day-residue', the sources which fed this particular dream. The last section provides the traditional stuff of introductions, considering the play's date and the nature of the text.

Dreams

Dreams and Dreaming. Wittgenstein, worrying how to pinpoint his sense of disliking Shakespeare, tried comparing his work to dreams:

Shakespeare and dreams. A dream is all wrong, absurd, composite, and yet at the same time it is completely right: put together in *this* strange way it makes an impression. Why? I don't know. And if Shakespeare is great, as he is said to be, then it must be possible to say of him: it's all wrong, things *aren't like that*—and yet at the same time it's quite right according to a law of its own . . . [Shakespeare] is completely unrealistic. (Like a dream.)[1]

There is no evidence to indicate whether Wittgenstein knew *A Midsummer Night's Dream* and yet this passage could in so many ways be an anxious paraphrase of the exchange between Theseus and Hippolyta at the opening to Act 5. Wittgenstein's description of a dream as 'all wrong, absurd' belongs firmly within the rationalist framework of Theseus's 'More strange than true' (5.1.2); his awareness that it can also be 'composite' and 'completely right' shares Hippolyta's understanding that, however strange it may be, it 'grows to something of great constancy' (5.1.26). Theseus wants it to 'be possible to say of' the events of the night in the wood that 'things *aren't like that*' but the night-world has, as the audience by this stage is well aware, laws of its own that he does not understand. Indeed, like a dream, which has its own

---

[1] L. Wittgenstein, *Culture and Value*, ed. G. H. von Wright, trans. P. Winch (Oxford, 1980), p. 83e.

internally consistent sense of realism, an awareness of reality that communicates itself to the dreamer, or that the dreamer creates in creating the dream, the play as a whole is both 'completely unrealistic' and yet 'at the same time ... quite right'.

How true the play is, *how* far it can be described as 'quite right' I shall come back to frequently. But, however much *A Midsummer Night's Dream* is 'like a dream', it is not one.[1] It contains only one description of something that may unequivocally be taken to be a dream, one 'real' dream, Hermia's dream of the serpent:[2]

> Help me, Lysander, help me! Do thy best
> To pluck this crawling serpent from my breast!
> Ay me, for pity. What a dream was here?
> Lysander, look how I do quake with fear.
> Methought a serpent ate my heart away,
> And you sat smiling at his cruel prey.
>
> (2.2.151–6)

Everything else that is recounted by mortals or fairies as having been part of a dream is not a dream at all. The experiences have been turned into dream, experienced as if they were dream—but they were not. Titania, waking, tells Oberon 'what visions have I seen' but her 'love', the image she ascribes to her dream of an ass she had fallen in love with, lies rather solidly beside her (4.1.75, 77). The lovers return 'back to Athens' assuming that 'all this derision' that they experienced in the wood is perhaps, as Oberon promises, nothing more than 'a dream and fruitless vision' (3.2.370–1), though they worry about whether it is indeed fruitless. Bottom wakes having had what he without hesitation describes as 'a dream past the wit of a man to say what dream it was' (4.1.202–3). Robin even gives the whole audience the option of considering the entire play as a dream in his epilogue:

[1] For approaches to the play in the context of dream see Marjorie B. Garber, *Dream in Shakespeare* (1974), pp. 59–87, and John Arthos, *Shakespeare's Use of Dream and Vision* (1977).

[2] For a discussion of different performances of Hermia's dream see H. R. Coursen, *Shakespearean Performance as Interpretation* (Newark, Del., 1992), pp. 74–84.

> If we shadows have offended,
> Think but this, and all is mended:
> That you have but slumbered here,
> While these visions did appear
>
> (5.1.414–7)

If we wish to dismiss the play, we can choose to treat it as a 'weak and idle theme, | No more yielding but a dream' (5.1.418–19). This is the final, largest-scale version of this recurrent device in the play, reducing vision to dream or reaccommodating an accurate perception of experienced reality into the more comfortable framework provided by dream.

Oberon and Robin make it possible for the other characters—and the audience—to see the play as a dream, not, that is, *like* a dream but as a dream itself, a true dream experience not a similitude. This extraordinary ability to transform experience into dream needs to be placed against an understanding of what dream was, where it came from and what it signified.

Oneiro-criticism, to give it its pedantic title, was a standard and important part of classical divination. Only one major account of early Graeco-Roman interpretation has survived: the *Oneirocritica* by Artemidorus of Daldis, written in the second century AD.[1] Artemidorus emphasizes throughout that dream-analysis must not only take into account what happens in the dream but also the name of the dreamer, his or her occupation, habits and attitudes. His method is non-superstitious and he scrupulously refuses to distinguish between dreams sent by the gods and dreams that are products of the dreamer or even to indicate whether dreams could be so divided.[2]

Artemidorus is, from the start, concerned to classify dreams, providing a system of significance within which all dreams may be easily placed.[3] The process of classifying a dream-

[1] Artemidorus, *The Interpretation of Dreams: Oneirocritica*, trans. R. J. White (Park Ridge, N. J., 1975): references are by chapter and section; see also S. R. F. Price, 'The Future of Dreams: From Freud to Artemidorus', *Past and Present*, 113 (1986), pp. 3–37.

[2] See Ruth Padel's review of White's ed. of Artemidorus, *TLS*, 23 April 1976, p. 494.

[3] See further A. H. M. Kessels, 'Ancient Systems of Dream-Classification', *Mnemosyne* (4th series), 22 (1969), pp. 389–424.

experience, pigeon-holing it conveniently or troublingly, is central to the way that characters in *A Midsummer Night's Dream* relate to their forms of dream and Artemidorus' system is fundamental to Western thinking about dreams until well after the date of Shakespeare's play. His basic distinction is between a predictive dream, which he terms *oneiros*, and a non-predictive one, termed *enhypnion*. The latter are simply 'anxiety-dreams and petitionary dreams' (1.6). There is for him nothing at all interesting in the fact that a lover may dream of the beloved, hungry people dream of food and thirsty people dream of drink. Such dreams, clearly generated by what will later be termed 'day-residue', are not for interpretation. These dreams, belonging with apparitions and phantasmata, lie outside his professional concerns. Dreams of the past and present are necessarily less interesting to his clients; they will also lie outside the concerns of most subsequent dream-analysis.

But if *enhypnion* dreams can be disregarded as insignificant or irrational fantasies, *oneiroi* matter enormously. These dreams or visions, occurring to people who are not anxious, are the stuff of his analysis, the raw material on which he can work, using his simple technique: 'the interpretation of dreams is nothing other than the juxtaposition of similarities' (2.25). Such proper dreams can be further subdivided into two groups: direct or theorematic and indirect or allegorical. Direct dreams show without metaphor what will occur: a dream of a shipwreck may indeed mean that the next day the dreamer will be shipwrecked. Allegorical dreams signify by replacement. A dream is, for Artemidorus, a claim by the mind; 'in a way it cries out to each of us', he writes, 'look at this and be attentive, for you must learn from me as best you can' (1.2).

His attempts to categorize dreams are full and inventive. Some features of a dream are treated as tightly defined within their range of meanings. Other dream-features may have multiple possibilities. A serpent such as appeared to Hermia could signify a king, because of its strength, or time, because of its length and skin-changing, or wealth, because it often guards treasure, or any of the gods who use it as a symbol of their sacredness. A serpent is not the same as a snake:

snakes signify sickness or an enemy; if a man dreams that his wife has a pet snake which she keeps in her bosom it signifies that she is adulterous. Artemidorus even analyses the different meanings for watersnakes and blindworms.

At the same time he is concerned to emphasize that the same dream may have different meanings according to the circumstances of the dreamer. He gives examples of seven women who had the same dream, during pregnancy, of giving birth to a serpent. In each case the relationship between the serpent of the dream and the son varied. One child became a famous public speaker, because speakers share with serpents the advantages of forked tongues. One son became a priest because the serpent is a sacred animal and the dreamer was a priest's wife. A prostitute's son was wanton because a serpent is slippery. A bad woman's son was a thief and beheaded because serpents are beheaded when caught. A slave woman's son became a runaway slave because serpents do not follow a straight path. Artemidorus does offer a precise explanation for Hermia's dream; dreaming that a serpent is 'entwined about someone and binds him . . . foretells imprisonment' and 'portends death for the sick' (2.13).

There were sixteenth-century translations of Artemidorus into Latin, Italian, French and German. A fairly full English translation by Robin Wood—from the French translation of the Latin translation—was first published in 1606 as *The Judgement or Exposition of Dreams* and had reached its twenty-fourth edition by 1740.[1]

The major late-classical statement on dreams is by Macrobius, part of his enormous commentary on the dream of Scipio in Cicero's *De Re Publica* written around AD 400.[2] The popularity of Macrobius ensured that his dream-classifications became the basis of much early medieval dream-theory. Hence Chaucer includes a lengthy summary of the dream of Scipio in *The Parliament of Fowls* (ll. 29–112) and it is to Macrobius that Chauntecleer turns in 'The Nun's Priest's

---

[1] Price, p. 32.
[2] See Macrobius, *Commentary on the Dream of Scipio*, trans. W. H. Stahl (New York, 1952). The *somnium Scipionis* itself was available in English translation in, e.g., Thomas Newton's translation of *Fowre Severall Treatises of M. Tullius Cicero* (1577).

Tale' (ll. 3123–6).[1] Macrobius plainly derives his ideas from Artemidorus and translates his divisions and classifications into Latin. *Oneiros* dreams are broken down into three types: *somnium*, *visio* and *oraculum* (enigmatic, prophetic and oracular). These are for Macrobius, as for Artemidorus, the only significant kinds of dream. *Enhypnion* dreams are divided into *insomnium* and *visum* (nightmare and apparition); neither is prophetic.

But medieval writers were less concerned with a classificatory system for a Macrobian typology of dreams than with the means to decode those dreams that could be seen as visionary, oneiric or somnium dreams; the means to do it acquired greater sophistication. There were four types of medieval dreambooks: chancebooks often used with psalters, physiological dreambooks defining dreams as indications of physiological ailments, dream-lunars which (intriguingly for *A Midsummer Night's Dream*, a play recurrently and almost obsessively concerned with the moon) interpreted dreams differently according to the day of the lunar month and hence the phase of the moon, and alphabetical dreambooks.[2]

It is the last category that were most common, particularly the *Somnia Danielis*, the dreams of Daniel. Known in hundreds of different manuscripts from the ninth century to the fifteenth, the *Somnia Danielis*, an alphabetical list of dream topics, is 'a library of ancient dream topoi',[3] far more reliable as a guide to medieval use of dream topoi than Artemidorus whose work was at that stage only available in Greek and Arabic. In different versions of the *Somnia*, Hermia's serpent most often indicated enemies, conquered or victorious accord-

---

[1] See also *The Book of the Duchess*, ll. 284–9; Alison Peden is however sceptical about the extent of the influence of Macrobius on Chaucer: see her 'Macrobius and Medieval Dream Literature', *Medium Aevum*, 54 (1985), pp. 59–73, esp. pp. 67–9.

[2] See Steven R. Fischer, 'Dreambooks and the Interpretation of Medieval Literary Dreams', *Archiv für Kulturgeschichte*, 65 (1983), pp. 1–20; his *The Dream in the Middle High German Epic* (Bern, 1978) and his edition of the *Somnia Danielis* as *The Complete Medieval Dreambook* (Bern, 1982); see also Lynn Thorndike, 'Ancient and Medieval Dreambooks' in her *A History of Magic and Experimental Science* (1923), vol. 2, pp. 290–302, and Jacques Le Goff, 'Dreams in the Culture and Collective Psychology of the Medieval World', in his *Time, Work and Culture in the Middle Ages*, trans. A. Goldhammer (Chicago, 1980), pp. 201–4.

[3] Fischer, 'Dreambooks', p. 7.

ing to what happened to the dream-serpent, though it could also indicate deception by a woman.[1] To dream of an ass usually signified hard work.[2]

What the long tradition of dream-theory suggests above all is that the indecipherability of dreams, the ambiguity of their sources, underlines the danger for the dreamer. As Steven Kruger comments,

> The dreamer stands in a precarious position . . . The realm of dreams, poised between truth and fiction, is also torn between good and evil; it provides a ground . . . in relation to which human beings must make complicated decisions—decisions with crucial implications for their moral lives.[3]

But the tradition also emphasized, particularly in late medieval theory, the extent to which dreams underline the humanity of the dreamer: 'The dream stands . . . in a quintessentially human position: between brute animals on the one hand and God and the angels on the other; between the mundane and divine, body and idea, deception and truth'.[4] Bottom and the other 'dreamers' are all the more human for having dreamed, Theseus, in his rejection of the dream-world, all the more limited.

Renaissance Dreams. English Renaissance texts on dreams, their causes or interpretations, are rarely original. They derive their classificatory systems and their analysis of causality from the kind of works I have already referred to, as well as such sources as Aristotle's brief studies of dream in the *Parva Naturalia* and Aquinas's distinction between inward and outward causes. The conventionality of Renaissance thinking on the subject provides the framework within which the experiences within *A Midsummer Night's Dream* and that of the whole play by the audience would have been understood. How the lovers understand their dream or the audience the play depend on reconciling the experience with the forms of dream with which Oberon (for the lovers) or Robin (for the audience) align the action.

[1] Fischer, *Complete Medieval Dreambook*, pp. 134–5.
[2] Ibid., p. 27.
[3] Steven F. Kruger, *Dreaming in the Middle Ages* (Cambridge, 1992), pp. 52–3.
[4] Ibid., p. 82.

Thomas Hill, in *The Most Pleasant Art of the Interpretation of Dreams* (1576), made perhaps the most coherent attempt in the period to provide an orthodox presentation of dream-science in English, deriving his work from Averroës, Aristotle, Artemidorus and Aquinas, filtered through Italian sources. For Hill, true dreams 'only happen to such, whose spirits are occupied with no irrational imaginations, nor overcharged with the burthen of meat or drinks, or superfluous humours, nor given to any other bodily pleasures' (sigs. [A] 2^{r-v}). Any others are, as we would expect, 'vain dreams, no true signifiers of matters to come but rather showers of the present affections and desires of the body' (sig. [A]2^v). Hill provides four categories according to whether the causes are bodily or not and new or not; causes can be categorized as food, humours, anxieties and, the most important group, those 'which frame the superior cause come unto the soul' or are divinely caused (D7^r). But all natural dreams, inwardly caused, are generated by the soul; as Wood's Artemidorus states, 'a dream therefore is a motion or fiction of the soul in a diverse form' (p. 1). They are created through the operation of the imagination, one of the three internal senses of the sensitive part of the soul, on material provided by the other two internal senses (common sense and memory) or by the 'vegetative' soul, while the external senses are quiescent. The memory provides images derived from the events that immediately preceded falling asleep; the vegetative soul provides images from the state of the body during sleep, for example, cold, thirst, sexual desire.[1] Thomas Nashe, the most contemptuous of Renaissance commentators on dream-theories, puts it even more forcefully:

A dream is nothing else but a bubbling scum or froth of the fancy, which the day hath left undigested; or an after-feast made of the fragments of idle imaginations . . . our thoughts intentively fixed all the daytime upon a mark we are to hit, are now and then overdrawn with such force, that they fly beyond the mark of the day into the confines of the night.[2]

---

[1] Neatly summarised by Sears Jayne, 'The Dreaming of *The Shrew*', *SQ* 17 (1966), pp. 41–56, esp. pp. 43–4. See also Thomas Lodge's distinction beween bodily and mental causes in 'To Master W. Bolton, Epistle 2', in *A Fig for Momus* (1595), sig. E4^r.

[2] Thomas Nashe, *The Terrors of the Night* (1594), sig. C3^v.

Such dreams are unlikely to be true, or as Nashe puts it, 'there is no certainty in dreams',[1] since the soul is working without the active support of the external senses; as Vandercleeve suggests, in *The Wisdom of Doctor Dodypoll*, an anonymous play of 1600, 'these present our idle fantasies | With nothing true, but what our labouring souls | Without their active organs, falsely work' (D2ʳ). But, as Alphonso answers Vandercleeve, there is always the other category of dream:

> My lord, know you, there are two sorts of dreams,
> One sort whereof are only physical,
> And such are they whereof your Lordship speaks,
> The other hyper-physical: that is,
> Dreams sent from heaven, or from the wicked fiends,
> Which nature doth not form of her own power,
> But are extrinsicate, by marvel wrought,
> And such was mine.[2]

Wood's Artemidorus and Hill's accumulation of fragments of Renaissance theory are, as one would expect, full of curiosities, such as the belief that dreams dreamed 'in the hour of the full moon or change' will come true 'within 15 days after'.[3] But, however fascinating such a timetable may be for *A Midsummer Night's Dream*, it seems less significant than, for instance, the confident assertion of that sense of true understanding that comes through the dream. As Hill puts it, 'And a man also doth more comprehend in his dream than waking in the day-time, because in a dream is more resolved than that in the day which is troubled through the doings of the outward sense' (B2ᵛ). Or, as Timothy Bright will later phrase it, 'in sleep our fantasy can perceive those truths which are denied to it when we are awake'.[4] All one then has to do is to recall the dream: Wood recognises that 'before the attempting

---

[1] Ibid., sig. F2ʳ.

[2] There are exceptions to this general theory, of course. See, e.g., Stephen Bateman's notion that 'the air is the cause of dreams' (S. Bateman, *Batman uppon Bartholome* (1582), sig. 2F5ʳ) or Christopher Langton's straightforward approach, as befits the author of *An Introduction into Physicke* [1547]: 'A dream is nothing, but an imagination made in the sleep' (quoted by Carroll Camden, 'Shakespeare on Sleep and Dreams', *Rice Institute Pamphlets*, 23 (1936), p. 121).

[3] Hill, sig. E2ʳ.

[4] Quoted by Camden, p. 122.

to interpret he willeth that one should have perfect remembrance of the beginning, the middle, the end, and all the circumstances of his dream' (A6ᵛ). As Demetrius will say in Act 4 of *A Midsummer Night's Dream*, 'And by the way let us recount our dreams' (4.1.197). Similarly, Nashe's venom for dream-interpreters matters less than his sense of dreams as part of the curative function of sleep: 'You must give a wounded man leave to groan while he is in dressing: Dreaming is no other than groaning, while sleep our surgeon hath us in cure' (C2ʳ). But even Nashe carefully preserves the distinction between the impenetrability and untrustworthiness of dream, Artemidorus's *enhypnion* or Macrobius' *insomnium*, compared with the power of vision, *oneiros* or *somnium*, even while he is lambasting Artemidorus and others:

Could any man set down certain rules of expounding of Dreams, and that their rules were general, holding in all as well as in some, I would begin a little to list to them, but commonly that which is portentive in a King is but a frivolous fancy in a beggar . . . Some will object unto me for the certainty of dreams, the dreams of *Cyrus*, *Cambyses*, *Pompey*, *Caesar*, *Darius and Alexander*. For those I answer that they were rather visions than dreams, extraordinarily sent from heaven to foreshow the translation of Monarchies. (D4ʳ)

Lodge, too, is reminded to prove that

> spirits either good or bad,
> In forms, and certain apparitions clad,
> Can further force, or else infuse by right,
> Unfeigned dreams, to those that sleep by night. (F1ʳ)

His reminder is Apollo, for, as Wood states, 'dreams and their interpretations seem particularly to agree and belong to poets, because that to their Apollo . . . is attributed and dedicated, not only the art of Poetry, but also the knowledge and interpretation of dreams' (A2ᵛ–A3ʳ), a more sympathetic insight into the poet's imagination than that offered by Theseus.

Not all dreams have such divine sources. Hermia's dream appears to have a straightforward and direct cause. When Hermia and Lysander prepare themselves for sleep, Lysander is determined to be as close to Hermia as possible, while she, modestly and accurately, distrusts his intentions and wants to be sure he keeps his distance. Tired and lost though he may be, Lysander sees the opportunity of being alone with Hermia in the woods as too good to pass up. For all the elegant virtuosity of his reasoning (2.2.47–52) it is clear he has sex al fresco in mind and Hermia has to be fairly insistent in giving him the verbal equivalent of a goodnight peck on the cheek (2.2.62–7). Most Lysanders, however, manage to find in 'Here is my bed' (2.2.70) a certain begrudging indication of just how uncomfortable that spot of the stage is.

Eighteenth-century productions had difficulty with this part of the scene. Francis Gentleman, in 1774, marked the lines for omission, for, 'though founded in delicacy, they may raise warm ideas'.[1] The Morality of the moment was troubling: how could Lysander, a gentleman, be seen to be suggesting pre-marital sex and how could Hermia, a virtuous maid, understand what he had in mind? In the version David Garrick prepared with George Colman the Elder in 1763, the passage is substantially rewritten. Barely into his stride, Lysander's attempt at seduction is halted by Hermia's firm request and he offers to stand guard:

> My honor is the best security for thine.
> Repose thee, love; I'll watch thee thro' the night,
> Nor harm shall reach thee—
> Sleep give thee all his rest.[2]

Garrick's Robin has to produce some fairy music to 'throw this youth into a trance', a 'sweet enchanting harmony' that Lysander cannot resist. Shakespeare's awkward morality is rendered acceptable and a convenient opportunity for music found in the process, cultural adjustment combined with theatrical efficiency.

But such rewriting removes the primary source of the dream. It did not need Freud to identify the serpent of Hermia's dream as a phallic threat. Lysander has presented Hermia with the problem of his sexual desire, and her dream enacts her anxiety about it. At the same time the dream represents Hermia's careful disjunction of Lysander as phallic

---

[1] *Bell's Shakespeare* (1774), viii. 159.
[2] David Garrick, *The Plays*, ed. Harry W. Pedicord and Frederick L. Bergmann (Carbondale, Ill., 1980–2), iv. 199. I have corrected their 'reach the' to 'reach thee', the clear reading of the MS (Folger prompt-book MND 6).

serpent from Lysander himself, who sits smiling and separate
from the actions of his penis, thereby ensuring that the phallic
threat from Lysander is dissociated from the 'person' Lysander
to some extent. A Freudian reading of the dream would find
in the object of the phallic attack, Hermia's breast and heart,
a displacement from her vagina. Lysander, in this reading of
the dream, is both passive and complicit, accepting, in effect,
the sexual desire that Hermia has for him but that she has
refused to acknowledge.[1] In Alexandru Darie's production for
the Comedy Theatre of Bucharest (1991), it was only with
great difficulty that Hermia kept her modesty and her clothes
on, so strong was her desire for Lysander.

But Hermia offers her own explanation of the dream when
she wakes. Accusing Demetrius of having murdered Lysander
she turns him into a serpent:

> And hast thou killed him sleeping? O brave touch!
> Could not a worm, an adder do so much?
> An adder did it, for with doubler tongue
> Than thine, thou serpent, never adder stung.
>
> (3.2.70–3)

Demetrius has, in effect, eaten Hermia's heart out by killing
her love Lysander. In her comparison with the adder and its
double tongue, Demetrius' protestations of innocence, which
she sees as lies, intensify his status as serpent. Rather than
facing the problem of her repressed desire and Lysander's
sexuality as represented by the dream, she displaces the fear
of Lysander into fear *for* Lysander and fear *of* Demetrius. The
dream is now somehow Demetrius' fault.

This is grotesquely and comically unfair to Demetrius for,
if Hermia's dream has obvious cause in the events preceding
sleeping, it is also oneiric in its warning of an event taking
place as Hermia dreams: for Lysander, drugged by Robin, has
transferred his affections from Hermia to Helena and is therefore the classic betrayer, smiling on another. Lysander is, of
course, a passive actor in this change and his passivity in

---

[1] For Freudian readings of this dream see, among many, M. D. Faber,
'Hermia's Dream: Royal Road to *A Midsummer Night's Dream*', *Literature and
Psychology*, 22 (1972), pp. 179–90, and Norman N. Holland, 'Hermia's
Dream', in Murray M. Schwartz and Coppélia Kahn, eds., *Representing Shake-
speare* (1980), pp. 1–20.

Hermia's dream seems to mimic this. The dream is then also an inner experience for Hermia reflecting the action that takes place during her sleep.

But this does not quite explain why Hermia should dream of a serpent. Where in effect does the dream come from? There seems to be something about the place where Hermia dreams that makes a dream about a serpent both likely and richly resonant. The bank where Titania sleeps has been defined by the fairies' lullaby as a place to be guarded against snakes: 'You spotted snakes with double tongue' (2.2.9). Oberon had already defined it as a place where 'the snake throws her enamelled skin' (2.1.255), defining this beneficial snake that is a source of fairy clothes ('Weed wide enough to wrap a fairy in', l. 256) as female. This useful female snake contrasts with the male snakes/serpents elsewhere in the play. Lysander as the serpent of the dream and Demetrius as the serpent of Hermia's accusation belong with the spotted snakes of the lullaby.

Demetrius is accused by Hermia of having a 'doubler' tongue than an adder; he has also, in Act 1, been accused by Lysander of being 'spotted and inconstant' (1.1.110) for changing from Helena to Hermia. The line links 'spotted' with inconstancy; the lullaby links 'spotted' with snakes. Hermia's dream turns Lysander into a serpent at the very moment that he is being 'spotted and inconstant'. The atmosphere around Titania's bank is full of links back to the world of Theseus' court. It is a place full of suggestions sufficient to generate the precise terms of Hermia's dream.

The richness of this suggestiveness even allows the dream to transfer from one person to another. When Hermia does find Lysander again, now changed and spotted, she hangs on to him as he tries to shake her off: 'Hang off, thou cat, thou burr; vile thing, let loose, | Or I will shake thee from me like a serpent' (3.2.260–1). He has now turned her into a serpent entwined around him. Hermia has not had a chance to tell Lysander her dream; the dream seems to have caught him, entwined him into it. His first line here contains an odd and magical echo of Oberon, half-heard by a character who could not have heard it at all. Oberon's spell on Titania conjures up her possible objects of desire: 'Be it ounce, or cat, or bear,

| Pard, or boar with bristled hair' (2.2.36–7). 'Or cat, or bear' has now become for Lysander 'thou cat, thou burr'. The echo is imprecise, as echoes are wont to be. The effect is of sounds and serpents inhabiting the place, the language and the minds of characters who stray near there.

Dramatic Dreams. Hermia's dream may, from this perspective, be a rich *oneiros* such as Artemidorus would have been proud to interpret, a dense enigma to be read across the whole play. But the whole play, of course, calls itself a dream. The fascination with dream as an overarching device, an embedding form for poetry is an immense and powerful tradition in English medieval poetry.[1] It may indeed be because the Chaucerian form of dream-vision was so overwhelmingly successful, so broad in its imaginative sweep and magnificent in its application of literary form to its concerns, that the device is comparatively rarely used in the Renaissance. Dream is, in any case, a mode no longer to be comfortably trusted. Thomas Churchyard's poem 'A Dream', in *Churchyard's Challenge* (1593), rehearses all the warnings about dreams as the product of 'the roving thoughts of idle braine', ending uncertainly,

> Well, be thy visions good or bad,
>   or swevens [dreams] of the night:
> Such idle freaks as fancy had,
>   now shall you hear aright. (p. 179)

before going on to give a serious dream-warning about death, vanity and the deceptiveness of the world.

Dream-poetry and dream-narrative seem, however, to have been of particular recurrent interest only to Robert Greene, in works like *A Quip for an Upstart Courtier* (1591), 'A Maiden's Dream' (1591), *Greene's Vision* [1592], 'A most rare and excellent dream' (in *The Phoenix Nest*, 1593), and, published after the date of *A Midsummer Night's Dream*, *Greene's*

---

[1] See for example A. C. Spearing's brilliant study, *Medieval Dream Poetry* (Cambridge, 1976); for Chaucer see B. A. Windeatt, *Chaucer's Dream Poetry: Sources and Analogues* (Cambridge, 1982) and Piero Boitani, 'Old Books Brought to Life in Dreams: the *Book of the Duchess*, the *House of Fame*, the *Parliament of Fowles*', in Piero Boitani and Jill Mann, eds., *The Cambridge Chaucer Companion* (Cambridge, 1986), pp. 39–57.

Orpharion (1599.[1]) At his best he considers the paradoxes of dream in terms worth considering alongside Shakespeare's play:

> Why art thou not (O dream) the same you seem?
> Seeing thy visions our contentment brings;
> Or do we of their worthiness misdeem?
> To call them shadows that are real things?
> And falsely attribute their due to wakings?[2]

Dream-plays had always been a much less common device. Robin's offer to the audience to consider the whole play as something that has taken place while they have been asleep (5.1.414–19) had been made twice before in plays by John Lyly. For *Sapho and Phao* (1584), Lyly offered an apologetic prologue for performance at court, speaking directly to the Queen:

Whatsoever we present, whether it be tedious (which we fear) or toyish (which we doubt), sweet or sour, absolute or imperfect, or whatsoever, in all humbleness we all, and I on knee for all, entreat, that your Highness imagine yourself to be in a deep dream, that staying the conclusion, in your rising your Majesty vouchsafe but to say, *And so you awaked.*[3]

Lyly's elaborate humility is an artful piece of modesty. While *Sapho and Phao* has some passages on dreams there is no need to consider the whole play as a dream, except as a means of excusing its weaknesses. The dramatic device is no more than a conventional ritual of excuse. In *The Woman in the Moon* (performed *c.*1591–3), Lyly uses the prologue to extend the notion of dream from an excuse for the experience of the play in performance to an excuse through a recognition of the play's origin:

> Our Poet slumbering in the Muses' laps,
> Hath seen a woman seated in the moon, . . .

---

[1] *Greene's Orpharion* was entered in the Stationers' Register on 9 February 1590. Thomas H. McNeal, in 'Studies in the Greene Shakspere Relationship', *Shakespeare Association Bulletin*, 15 (1940), pp. 210–18, argued unconvincingly for Greene's poems as an object of Shakespeare's satire in Bottom's dream.

[2] 'A most rare, and excellent Dreame' in *The Phoenix Nest* (1593), p. 43 (ed. H. E. Rollins (Cambridge, Mass., 1931), p. 51).

[3] Lyly, *Works*, ii. 372.

> This, but the shadow of our Author's dream,
> Argues the substance to be near at hand: ...
> If many faults escape her discourse,
> Remember all is but a Poet's dream.[1]

The entire play is now a product of the poet's dream 'in *Phoebus*'s holy bower'[2] and the audience's tolerant response is to be the result. But Lyly does not combine the two ploys, treating the performance as a dream and recognizing the poet's work as the product of a dream.

The most intriguing version of a dream-play, not least because of its vexed relationship to Shakespeare, is the ending of *The Taming of A Shrew* (1594), the play that is somehow connected with Shakespeare's *The Taming of The Shrew*.[3] Shakespeare's Induction has Sly who has fallen drunkenly asleep found by a Lord who, for fun, has Sly carried off, transformed into a gentleman and made to sit and watch a play. At a point equivalent to Shakespeare's 5.1.102 *A Shrew*'s Sly falls asleep again. When the play performed for him is over, the Lord has Sly changed back into his own clothes and put back 'in the place where we did find him' (passage D, l. 4).

As in the experience of the mortals who enter the wood in *A Midsummer Night's Dream*, the play's events can be taken to be nothing more than a dream, in this case a dream of metamorphosis of social status that is subordinated in the play to the dream-play that is presented for Sly. Unlike Bottom, Sly is only too keenly aware of the person he was (is) outside this 'dream'-experience: 'What, would you make me mad? Am not I Christopher Sly—old Sly's son of Burton Heath' (Induction 2.16–17). Only as the others insist does he convince himself that this state is true reality and his previous existence only a dream in its turn:

---

[1] Lyly, *Works*, iii. 241, ll. 1–2, 12–13, 16–17.

[2] Ibid., l. 18; compare the bowers of Oberon and Titania (3.1.186, 3.2.6–7 and n., 4.1.60).

[3] The precise relationship of *A Shrew* and *The Shrew* is irrelevant here but I share Oxford's assumption that the additional Sly passages, present in *A Shrew* and not in *The Shrew*, could have existed in some form in a version of Shakespeare's text; certainly productions of Shakespeare's play have often very successfully incorporated the other Sly comments and particularly the ending. I use the text of the passages printed as Additional Passages to Oxford's text of *The Shrew*.

> Am I a lord, and have I such a lady?
> Or do I dream? Or have I dreamed till now?
> I do not sleep. I see, I hear, I speak.
> I smell sweet savours, and I feel soft things.
> Upon my life, I am a lord indeed,
> And not a tinker, nor Christopher Sly.
>
> (Induction 2.67–72)

Sly, of course, much prefers this new reality and 'would be loath to fall into my dreams again' (Induction 2.123).

The Lord had assumed that the experience will be for a reawakened Sly nothing more than 'a flatt'ring dream or worthless fancy' (Induction 1.42). But, as Sly explains to the Tapster who wakes him up at the end of the play, this dream, 'The bravest dream . . . that ever thou | Heardest in thy life' (passage E, ll. 11–12), will have unexpected results:

TAPSTER

> Ay, marry, but you had best get you home,
> For your wife will curse you for dreaming here tonight.

SLY

> Will she? I know now how to tame a shrew.
> I dreamt upon it all this night till now,
> And thou hast waked me out of the best dream
> That ever I had in my life. But I'll to my
> Wife presently and tame her too,
> An if she anger me.
>
> (passage E, ll. 14–21)

Sly's assumption that he can put the dream-play into effect against the unseen stereotype of the wife waiting for the drunken husband with the Elizabethan equivalent of the rolling-pin may be comic bravado. But in *A Midsummer Night's Dream* the question of what will be the consequence of the dream-play in the woods is far from simply comic. Where in *A Shrew* the events after awaking from the 'dream' occupy a brief epilogue scene, in *A Midsummer Night's Dream* there is the whole of Act 5 to come. The reaccommodation of the people to the post-dream world is now not only comic but also complex and worrying.

We would expect that a play with the word 'dream' in its title would make fairly frequent use of the word. But Shakespeare seems to have been particularly interested in the word at this stage of his career: nearly a third of all Shakespeare's usages of the word 'dream' occur in only three plays, *Richard III*, *Romeo and Juliet* and *A Midsummer Night's Dream*, plays written close in time to each other.

In *Romeo and Juliet*, written, most probably, immediately before *A Midsummer Night's Dream*,[1] Shakespeare makes the matter of dreams Mercutio's and places it in the world of Queen Mab. Romeo, trying to quiet the wild exuberance of Mercutio's description of Mab, advises him 'Thou talk'st of nothing' (1.4.96) but Mercutio turns the nothing of dreams into its own fantasy:

> True. I talk of dreams,
> Which are the children of an idle brain,
> Begot of nothing but vain fantasy,
> Which is as thin of substance as the air,
> And more inconstant than the wind
> (ll. 96–100)

Dream, that nothing that is so powerfully something, may be mocked and belittled—throughout *A Midsummer Night's Dream* it often is—but it strikes back at those who mock it. Lysander defines true love as 'short as any dream' (1.1.144) but the play will make the true love of Lysander and Hermia endure much longer than a night of adventures in the wood. Hippolyta reassures Theseus that 'Four nights will quickly dream away the time' (1.1.8) before their wedding but the time will be dream in senses other and far richer than her lines suggest. Oberon may say of the lovers, 'When they next wake, all this derision | Shall seem a dream and fruitless vision' (3.2.370–1); yet his next line suggests that this dream is not a fruitless vision at all, since the result will be that 'back to Athens shall the lovers wend | With league whose date till death shall never end' (ll. 372–3), exactly the same contrast between the supposed empty brevity of the nothing of the dream and the enduring consequences that hover over Lysander's 'short as any dream'. Viewed in this light, Oberon's line suggests a different emphasis: it is not that the derision *is* a dream, but that it should *seem* so.

[1] See below, p. 110.

Oberon's line has combined dream and vision. If the lovers may find the experience a 'fruitless vision', for Bottom it was 'a most rare vision' (4.1.202). Even Robin advises the audience that it has seen 'visions' (5.1.417). The audience can choose to take them as trivial, 'No more yielding but a dream' (5.1.419), but, if we have responded to the play fully, we will share with Bottom the sense of vision, of something revealed from out there, from the world of fairy, not the false or trivial world of dream but a revelation of another reality. The obligation on the audience is to treat the play as a benevolent *oneiros*, a true prophetic dream. This dream is an attempt to resolve the great puzzle of dream-theory, the source of dreams, for this dream is not the product of the dreamer's imagination or the reformulation of the experiences of the day but a phenomenon generated by extra-human forces. Such dreams matter greatly.

Fairies

At a climactic moment of J. M. Barrie's *Peter Pan*, when Tinkerbell lies dying, having drunk the poison that Captain Hook intended for Peter Pan himself, Peter turns to the audience for their help:

Do you believe in fairies? Say quick that you believe! If you believe, clap your hands! (*Many clap, some don't, a few hiss . . . But* TINK *is saved*.)[1]

For adults in the audience it is a moment of nostalgia and embarrassed sadness, nostalgia for a time when they could believe in fairies and clap their hands in a desperate need to participate in the magic of the fairy's resurrection, embarrassed sadness because they no longer believe and cannot easily pretend to any longer for the sake of a theatrical trick. For them the mechanics of theatre, not least the fact that Tinkerbell only exists as a theatrical spotlight dancing around the stage, inhibit belief. Fairies are for children and the history of productions and illustrations of *A Midsummer Night's Dream* has been bedevilled by the assumption that a fairy-play was essentially a childish piece of magic gossamer.

[1] *Peter Pan*, in J. M. Barrie, *Plays* (1928), p. 72.

For Reginald Scot, belief in fairies was similarly something that belonged both to a past time when 'your grandam's maids were wont to set a bowl of milk before.... Robin Goodfellow'[1] and to childhood:

But in our childhood our mothers' maids have so terrified us with an ugly devil . . . and they have so fraied us with bull beggers, spirits, witches, urchins, elves, hags, fairies, satyrs [and 25 other named 'bugs'] . . . that we are afraid of our own shadows.[2]

Scot's switch to the present tense at the end of this colossal listing of the things that go bump in the night suggests the extent to which these childhood experiences cannot be completely dismissed, however much the rational, educated and enlightened adult might wish to do so. At *Peter Pan* we still clap. E. K., glossing Spenser's *Shepheardes Calendar*, identifies fairy belief as 'very old, yet sticketh very religiously in the myndes of some' before denouncing it, in terms of which Scot would have approved, as a popish trick, explaining the words 'elf' and 'goblin' as corruptions of Guelphs and Ghibellines.[3]

Scot places the full belief two generations ago but belief in the fairies always appears to have belonged to previous generations.[4] Chaucer's Wife of Bath, talking of the time of King Arthur when

> Al was this land fulfild of fayerye.
> The elf-queene, with hir joly compaignye,
> Daunced ful ofte in many a grene mede.
> This was the olde opinion, as I rede;
> I speke of manye hundred yeres ago.
> For now kan no man se none elves mo,
>   (ll. 859–64)

before going on to compain that clerics have been so busy blessing everywhere that 'This maketh that ther ben no fayeryes' (ll. 872).

Popular belief in fairies is notoriously difficult to document, in spite of the work of the two great scholars of Elizabethan

[1] Reginald Scot, *The Discovery of Witchcraft* (1584), Bk. 4, ch. 10, p. 85.

[2] Ibid., Bk. 7, ch. 15, pp. 152–3.

[3] E. K.'s gloss to June, l. 25.

[4] See Keith Thomas, *Religion and the Decline of Magic* (Harmondsworth, 1978), p. 726.

fairies, Minor White Latham and Katharine Briggs,[1] but it seems reasonable to sum up what can be taken as normal rural Elizabethan assumptions about fairies as a widespread acceptance of a body of traditional belief that fairies existed. In particular there was the group of fairies dubbed 'trooping fairies'[2] who shared with their Celtic ancestors certain characteristics: an interest in riding, hunting, dancing and feasting; abilities to shift size and shape, fly and become invisible; generosity with presents to mortals and equal generosity with punishments, particularly pinching and the removing of human children as changelings.

What the 'normal' size of such fairies was has been the subject of inordinate controversy,[3] but it seems safest to accept that fairies varied in size from rare appearances at full adult height through frequent manifestations as small children to occasional sightings as tiny creatures down to the size of ants.[4] Shakespeare's fairies in *A Midsummer Night's Dream* and elsewhere belong firmly and comfortably within this tradition. His fairies' size seems to shift unpredictably and fluidly. They are small enough to wear snake-skins (2.1.255–6), creep into acorn cups (2.1.31) and risk being covered with one bee's honeybag (4.1.15–16). Their names, similarly, suggest their small size: Peaseblossom, Cobweb, Mote, Mustardseed. At the same time Titania is large enough to hold an undiminished Bottom in her arms (4.1.39) and both she and Oberon accuse each other of having had human lovers before (2.1.65–80).

This fluidity may have been reflected in the casting of the four fairies. Oberon is usually argued to have been played by an adult male actor but it is often thought that Titania's fairies were played by boys (and therefore that the play was performed under the kind of special auspices in which a large number of boys might have been available). The assumption

---

[1] Minor White Latham, *The Elizabethan Fairies* (New York, 1930); K. M. Briggs, *The Anatomy of Puck* (1959), *The Fairies in Tradition and Literature* (1967), *A Dictionary of British Folk-Tales* (1971), *A Dictionary of Fairies, Hobgoblins, Brownies, Bogies and Other Supernatural Creatures* (1976).

[2] Briggs, *Anatomy*, pp. 13–15.

[3] Latham argues that Shakespeare invents diminutive fairies, pp. 180–1, but Briggs firmly rejects such a belief, *passim*.

[4] Conveniently assembled by Brooks, pp. lxxi–lxxv.

is a logical extension of our belief that fairies are always small. If they are of variable height there is no need for the actors to be small. As William Ringler shows the pattern of appearance of the fairies and the workers (leaving out Bottom) makes it practicable for actors to take a role in each group. Proposing that 'the four fairies are played by the same large lumbering adult actors who take the parts of four rude mechanicals', he goes on to suggest that

the visual effect that Shakespeare intended to be conveyed by the fairies was not one of literal diminutive beauty . . . Instead he appears to have intended an effect either of bulky grotesquerie or of something quite different from and more subtle than productions in our time have indicated.[1]

Ringler's doubling pattern seems to be corroborated by the droll of *The Merry Conceited Humours of Bottom the Weaver* (1661) in which the cast-list recommends that Snout, Snug and Starveling 'likewise may present three Fairies'.[2] My own experiments with doubling patterns suggest that this is a necessary double if the cast is to be reduced to the normal size for a Shakespearian company. What I cannot see is why the actors should be characterized as 'lumbering'; this is to confuse actor and role—though I am not sure that the workers are lumbering either. The result need have nothing to do with 'grotesquerie', only with the metamorphic world shared by the fairies and the practice of theatre itself. Adult fairies, as Peter Brook's production showed, can be disconcertingly strange and threatening; they need not be in the least awkward.

Presenting the fairies, finding a style for the fairies, is perhaps the most acute problem for any modern director of the play. As Hazlitt commented, on the adult fairies in Reynolds's version in 1816,

We have found to our cost, once and for all, that the regions of fancy and the boards of Covent-Garden are not the same thing . . .

---

[1] William A. Ringler, Jr., 'The Number of Actors in Shakespeare's Early Plays', in G. E. Bentley, ed., *The Seventeenth-Century Stage* (Chicago, 1968), p. 134.

[2] Sig. [A]2ᵛ; for a modern edition see J. J. Elson, ed., *The Wits or, Sport upon Sport* (Ithaca, N. Y., 1932).

Fancy cannot be represented any more than a simile can be painted; and it is as idle to attempt it as to personate Wall or Moonshine. Fairies are not incredible, but fairies six feet high are so.[1]

The history of the play in performance can be defined in terms of the treatment of the fairies on-stage. At the Royal National Theatre in 1992, the fairies were adults, half-naked, dressed in black and prone to slither through the muddy pond that dominated the set. That unmitigatedly sinister version is about as far as one can get from the long saccharine tradition of the fairies attending Titania appearing as a full-scale female *corps de ballet* dressed in white.[2] That style of performance has an extremely long history: Frank Benson's production at the Globe Theatre in 1889 included for Act 2 24 dancing girls and 12 dancing boys arranged two by two and later supplemented by 16 ladies in green;[3] further back, Charles Kean's production in 1858 at the Princess's Theatre (see fig. 1) included 54 fairies to sing a chorus to the sleeping lovers at the end of 3.2 and, in Act 5 when the mortals left the stage, Snout's earlier attempt to metamorphose into a wall paled beside the spectacle of the whole back wall of the set sinking to 'discover Oberon, Titania and Fairies grouped all over the stage' with nearly 90 fairies going up and down the staircases.[4]

Brook apart, there have been three significant attempts this century to find a new way of presenting the fairies.[5] Peter Hall's film version (1969) took the tradition of children playing fairies but turned the sentimentality into something rougher and muddier; his fairies, accompanying Titania (Judi Dench), naked with her modesty covered by a long wig, were dirty urchins covered in mud. George Devine's 1954 production at Stratford, designed by Motley, resisted Lilian Baylis's dictum,

---

[1] William Hazlitt, *Complete Works*, ed. P. P. Howe (1930–4), vol. 5, pp. 274–6.

[2] See, for example, the illustrations of the play in 1937 and 1949 in Foakes, pp. 18 and 19.

[3] See prompt-book in the Shakespeare Centre, Stratford-upon-Avon.

[4] See prompt-book in the Harvard Theatre Collection, MND 250.

[5] Benjamin Britten, in his opera *A Midsummer Night's Dream*, Op. 64 (1960), found an intriguing vocal solution to the problem of Oberon, using a counter-tenor, still an unusual sound when the opera was composed, to represent the male but magical qualities of his Oberon.

1. Troops of fairies: 2.1 in Charles Kean's production, Princess's Theatre, 1858.

'I like my fairies gauzy', and searched for a different model from 'the dainty midget, the tutu fairy, the decorative butterfly of recent tradition';[1] his fairies were 'beaked and feathered, Titania with white eye-streaks from crown to bill that gave her the air, light, bright and ferocious, of a falcon' (see fig. 2).[2]

Granville Barker's fairies, at the Savoy in 1914, were the most controversial of all (see fig. 3). As *The Times* commented, 'Is it Titania's Indian Boy that has given Mr. Barker his notion of Orientalizing Shakespeare's fairies? Or is it Bakst? Anyhow they look like Cambodian idols and posture like Nijinsky in *Le Dieu Bleu*.'[3] Almost all the fairies were adult, dressed in exotic costumes and with their faces and hands gilded with

[1] Richard David, 'Plays Pleasant and Plays Unpleasant', *SS 8* (Cambridge, 1955), p. 138; see also Michael Mullin and David McGuire, 'A "Purge on Prettiness": Motley's Costumes for *A Midsummer Night's Dream*, Shakespeare Memorial Theatre, Stratford-upon-Avon, 1954', *Shakespeare Studies* (Shakespeare Soc. of Japan, Tokyo), 27 (1989), pp. 65–77.

[2] David, p. 138.

[3] Quoted in Gary Jay Williams, '*A Midsummer Night's Dream*: The English and American Popular Traditions and Harley Granville-Barker's "World Arbitrarily Made" ', *Theatre Studies*, 23 (1976/7), p. 44.

2. Motley's costumes for George Devine's production, Stratford-upon-Avon, 1954.

'hair like gold wood shavings, beards like golden rope, and metallic-looking moustaches'.[1] Desmond MacCarthy, initially astonished by these 'ormolu fairies, looking as though they had been detached from some fantastic, bristling old clock', found that 'the very characteristics which made them at first so outlandishly arresting now contribute to making them

[1] Christine Dymkowski, *Harley Granville Barker: A Preface to Modern Shakespeare* (Washington, 1986), pp. 60–2.

3. Oriental Fairies and an English Robin: Granville Barker's production at the Savoy, 1914.

inconspicuous . . . It is without effort we believe these quaintly gorgeous metallic creatures are invisible to human eyes'.[1]

What the theatre history suggests is a reflection of a problem present at the moment of writing the play: the changing pattern of belief over fairies. Briggs charts implicitly the way in which, through the sixteenth century, fairies 'proved no longer so formidable as they had been, and fairy-lore could be used for delight and ornament'; as an apparent corollary, 'general belief in fairies declined'.[2] Seen as harmless or at least less threatening, fairies no longer deserved believing. I suggested that Elizabethan belief was rural; certainly fairy-lore has always been tightly associated with the countryside, with farming and village communities. Ben Jonson brings the fairy queen to London in *The Alchemist* but plays that use fairies, as much as folk-tales and other accounts, restrict their appearances to the world beyond the city, a world 'out there'

[1] Desmond MacCarthy, *Theatre* (1954), p. 53; see also Trevor Griffiths, 'Tradition and Innovation in Harley Granville-Barker's *A Midsummer Night's Dream*', *TN* 30 (1976), pp. 78–87.
[2] Briggs, *Anatomy*, p. 19.

where such creatures may exist but which can also be, with anxious patronizing assurance, dismissed.

At the same time one of the major changes was the gradual appearance of fairies in drama associated with court performance and entertainment. Robert Weimann suggests that 'the fact that the seriousness of the belief in such airy creatures was more and more widely undermined made their playfully imaginative treatment in the public theater possible'[1] but the evidence clearly shows that it was not in the public theatres that fairies were seen. With the single exception of Robert Greene's *The Scottish History of James the Fourth* (published 1598 but probably written *c.*1590), all the stage fairies were seen in court contexts.

The entertainments offered to Elizabeth at Woodstock in 1575 included a moment when 'Her Majesty thus in the middest of this mirth might espy the Queen of the Fairy drawn with six children in a waggon of state'.[2] The Fairy Queen approached, spoke to Elizabeth and presented her and her ladies with gifts of gowns, verses and nosegays. The entertainments devised by Thomas Churchyard for Elizabeth in Suffolk and Norfolk in 1578 included a scene when he decided it would be a good idea to dress seven boys 'like Nymphs of the water' and they played 'by a device and degrees like fairies, and to dance (as near as could be imagined) like the *fairies*'.[3] The Queen of Fairies drew attention to their unusual appearance in public:

Though clean against the *fairies*' kind, we come in open view,
(And that the Queen of *Fairies* here, presents herself to you)[4]

On the fourth day of the Elvetham entertainments of 1591 the Fairy Queen, named as Aureola, appeared yet again, dancing with her maids, presented Elizabeth with a garland of flowers, 'Given me by *Auberon* the *Fairy* King' and sang and danced so successfully that Elizabeth 'desired to see and hear it twice over'.[5]

---

[1] Robert Weimann, *Shakespeare and the Popular Tradition in the Theater* (Baltimore, 1978), p. 193.

[2] A. W. Pollard, ed., *The Queen's Majesty's Entertainment at Woodstock* (1575) (Oxford, 1903 and 1910), sigs. B4ᵛ–C1ʳ.

[3] Thomas Churchyard, *A Discourse of The Queenes Maiesties Entertainment in Suffolk and Norfolk* (1578), sig. G2ᵛ.

[4] Ibid., sig. G3ᵛ.

[5] Lyly, *Works*, i. 449–50.

Apart from these events, all significantly including the fairy queen, fairies also made a very brief and silent entrance in Lyly's *Gallathea* (1592), 'dancing and playing and so, Exeunt'.[1] In his *Endimion* (1591), they made a slightly more substantial appearance, dancing, singing and pinching Endimion who falls asleep:

> Pinch him, pinch him, black and blue,
> Saucy mortals must not view
> What the Queen of Stars is doing,
> Nor pry into our Fairy wooing.[2]

Fairies offered a convenient excuse for songs and dances—it is difficult to see their momentary manifestation in *Gallathea* in any other light—and Shakespeare responded fully to the opportunities they provided. But the fairy queen of these entertainments offered other much more resonant symbolic import. Though a fairy king is mentioned at Elvetham, he does not appear. The concept of a fairy realm with a single female monarch had obvious analogies and conceptually it is not far from this to Spenser's *Faerie Queene*, however far it may be in artistic achievement. As Dr Johnson sums it up, in his observations on *A Midsummer Night's Dream* in his edition of 1765, 'Fairies in his time were much in fashion; common tradition had made them familiar, and Spenser's poem had made them great'. In effect, Shakespeare is combining two markedly separate traditions, one in which the fairy kingdom is ruled by a fairy queen alone and another in which there is a joint and equal power-sharing monarchy of king and queen. This latter tradition is frequently linked to the presentation of Pluto as 'kyng of Fayerye' with Prosperpina as 'his wyf, the queene' in Chaucer's 'Merchant's Tale' (ll. 2227 ff.). This showed rulers, dissenting, like Shakespeare's Oberon and Titania, over mortals and, like them too, instrumental in creating a moderately happy solution to the problem. Chaucer's choice of names is part of a tradition, of which Shakespeare makes extraordinary use, of combining the classical and the popular traditions.

[1] Ibid., ii. 442.
[2] See C. L. Barber, *Shakespeare's Festive Comedy* (Cleveland, 1959), pp. 119–21.

While the fairy queen is usually nameless, the fairy king is more usually named as Oberon. Though briefly mentioned in Spenser's poem and at Elvetham, Oberon is a much less potent figure than the fairy queen. Fully described and actively involved in the action of the colossal romance *The Book of Duke Huon of Bourdeaux* (translated by Lord Berners, 1533–42), this fairy king who controls a wood 'full of the Fairy and strange things'[1] shares with Shakespeare's Oberon a delight in hunting and great magical power (particularly the ability to conjure up the illusion of extremely localised storms). This Oberon is only three feet high but this is solely a result of his growth having been halted by a curse.

For the fairy queen to be connected with court entertainments was inevitable but Shakespeare appears to have taken some notice of the appearance of the fairy king in Greene's *James IV*. His Oberon is an observer of the action who agrees to help Slipper when needed, as Oberon had helped Huon in the later parts of the romance. He and his subjects are identified as small: the fairies who dance on are, according to Bohan, 'puppits that hopped and skipped' and Oberon himself 'lookest not so big as the King of Clubs'[2] and is a 'little king'.[3] As usual the fairies most often appear as dancers, at gaps in the action. Like Titania's fairies in *A Midsummer Night's Dream*, these fairies sing a lullaby.[4]

But Greene's Oberon, like so many fairies, is restricted to the world of night:

> The rising sun doth call me hence away;
> Thanks for thy jig, I may no longer stay....[5]

Shakespeare's Oberon is making an extremely unusual and powerful claim for the extent of his power and influence by calming Robin's fears at the imminence of the dawn: 'But we are spirits of another sort' (3.2.388).

It is, though, in naming his fairy queen Titania that Shakespeare is most disruptive of the isolable native fairy tradition.

---

[1] Ed. S. L. Lee (EETS, 1882), ch. 21, p. 63.

[2] Robert Greene, *The Scottish History of James the Fourth*, ed. Norman Sanders (1970), Induction, ll. 12–18.

[3] Ibid., Chorus 1.1.

[4] Ibid., Chorus 5.14.0.2.

[5] Ibid., Chorus 5.11–12.

James VI of Scotland, in his attack on devils 'conversing in the earth', a specific rebuttal of the dangerously sceptical views of Reginald Scot, identifies 'the fourth kind of spirits' as those who 'by the gentiles was called *Diana*, and her wandering court, and amongst us was called the *Phairie*',[1] though he also described and mocked the belief that 'there was a King and Queen of *Phairie*, of such a jolly court and train as they had . . . how they . . . did all other actions like natural men and women'.[2] Shakespeare derives his choice of name, Titania, directly from Ovid's *Metamorphoses*, where it appears five times, including once for Diana in the narrative of Actaeon (3. 173). It never appears in Golding who always uses phrases like 'Titan's daughter'. Golding's translation is accurate, hence Ovid's use of the same name for Pyrrha (1. 395) and Latona, Diana's mother (6. 346), and for Circe (14. 382 and 14. 438), the great metamorphoser whose ability to turn men into pigs may be relevant to *A Midsummer Night's Dream*.[3]

Shakespeare's use of an Ovidian name is, in effect, a mirroring of Golding's incorporation of English fairies in his translation of Ovid, a deliberate part of Golding's Englishing of Ovid. Ovid's classical nymphs become fairies with remarkable frequency: an oread becomes 'a fayrie of the hill' (8. 178); naiads and dryads become 'the Fairies which | Reported are the pleasant woods and water springs to haunt' (6. 579–80); where nymphs dwelt is now 'the fayres bowre' (14. 586). But it also allows him to invoke and use extensively the complex associations of Diana and Titania.

When, at the end of the play, Robin identifies himself and the others as 'we fairies that do run | By the triple Hecate's team' (5.1.374–5) he gestures at the multiplicity of the nature of Diana: as George Sandys noted in a marginal note in his translation of Ovid, '*Hecate*: called *Cynthia* in Heaven, *Diana* on earth, and *Proserpina* in hell: from whence she received the name of *Trivia*'[4]. As Cynthia, the goddess is associated

[1] James VI, *Daemonologie* (Edinburgh, 1597), pp. 57 and 73.

[2] Ibid., p. 74.

[3] See A. D[avenport], 'Weever, Ovid and Shakespeare', *N & Q* 194 (1949), pp. 524–5.

[4] George Sandys, *Ovid's Metamorphosis Englished* (1632), p. 233.

with the moon, causing lunacy and change; as Diana, with hunting and chastity; as Proserpina, with the seasons. *A Midsummer Night's Dream* and Titania in particular connect with all of these aspects.[1] The play is dominated by moonshine, associated with Diana's bow when Hippolyta the Amazon warrior-huntress first describes it (1.1.9–10). The restorative drug will be 'Dian's bud' (4.1.72), the culmination of the play's transformation of Diana from her opening status as the goddess of the 'cold fruitless moon' (1.1.73) into the goddess of married chastity as well as virginity. Titania describes the result of her quarrel with Oberon as the disruption of the seasons, the concern of Proserpina. The lovers, in the wood by moonlight, experience madness and inconstancy. The list is endless. Shakespeare's fairy queen, through her name, carries the classical tradition with her unstoppably. The play's war of deities is as much between Diana and the unrestrained desire of Venus and her acolyte Cupid as between Oberon and Titania.

Shakespeare's view of fairies in the rest of his work is both uniform and unlike the fairies of *A Midsummer Night's Dream*. In *The Comedy of Errors*, for instance, when Antipholus of Syracuse and his Dromio find themselves invited to dinner with Adriana, Dromio turns to popular folk-lore:

> This is the fairy land. O spite of spites,
> We talk with goblins, oafs, and sprites.
> If we obey them not, this will ensue:
> They'll suck our breath or pinch us black and blue.
>
> (2.2.192–5)

Dromio's expectation of being pinched seems perfectly reasonable: that is what fairies do. They sang about it when they appeared in Lyly's *Endimion*. The pretend fairies that torment Falstaff at Herne's Oak at the end of *The Merry Wives of Windsor* pinch him mercilessly: 'Pinch him, fairies, mutually. | Pinch him for his villainy' (5.5.98–9). Throughout fairy-lore they were held to be particularly inclined to punish, as well as willing to reward a few lucky mortals.

But the fairies of *A Midsummer Night's Dream* are not tormenting, pinching, punishing elves at all. Robin apart, the

---

[1] See Noel Purdon, *The Words of Mercury: Shakespeare and the English Mythography of the Renaissance* (Salzburg, 1974).

fairies, from their rulers downwards, seem remarkably, conspicuously and consistently benevolent towards mortals. Oberon's one concern, when he realizes what Robin has done, is to put things right. Everything the play indicates of the fairies' direct relations to humans is of a piece with this benign intent. Only in their effect on the weather, a result of their internal wrangling, are they indirectly harmful to mortals and Titania pities this effect. Comically human in their passions though they may be, Oberon and Titania meet in this wood near Athens only because both are drawn by love of Theseus and Hippolyta to come to 'give their bed joy and prosperity' (2.1.73).

This emphasis on fairy benevolence seems to have been Shakespeare's invention. Their dissociation from the ghosts and damned spirits is reassuring in its metamorphosis of the tradition. Even the changeling, one of the darkest and most disturbing features of fairy-lore, the notion of the healthy child removed and replaced by a weak fairy child,[1] is here changed into an expression of friendship and delight, a cherished reminder of Titania's dead friend, a mortal who shared jokes with Titania as Bottom will; the changeling is brought up 'for her sake' (2.1.136). Indeed, since there is no mention of a fairy child left with the boy's father, it may be that he is a 'changeling' only because he has exchanged the human world for the world of fairies.

Shakespeare's fairy-world is more than an adjunct and parallel reality with its own rules and activities. It is also a source of our actions. The blessings of Oberon and Titania are more than the well-wishes of some fascinating Eastern princelings; they are a genuine benediction from a source of power and influence, a benediction all the stronger for our recognition of the harm they could do if they chose.[2]

---

[1] Compare Henry IV's desperate desire, 'O, that it could be proved | That some night-tripping fairy had exchanged | In cradle clothes our children where they lay' (*1H4* 1.1.85–7) or the darker picture, when Tom a Lincoln is removed from his mother and King Arthur makes her believe 'that some night-tripping fairy had bereaved | her infant from her' (*Tom a Lincoln*, ed. G. R. Proudfoot, Malone Society Reprints (Oxford, 1992) ll. 201–2).

[2] David Bevington's argument that the fairies' 'chief power to do good lies in withholding the mischief of which they are capable' is a recognition of fairy power to harm but underrates the blessings at the end of the play; see ' "But we are spirits of another sort": the Dark Side of Love and Magic in *A Midsummer Night's Dream*', *Medieval and Renaissance Studies*, 7 (1975), p. 84.

Robin

As far as Reginald Scot was concerned, Robin Goodfellow was no longer believed in:

Heretofore Robin Goodfellow and Hobgoblin were as terrible, and also as credible to people as hags and witches be now: and in time to come, a witch will be as much derided and condemned, and as plainly perceived, as the illustration and knavery of Robin Good-fellow.[1]

For Scot, Robin belonged to a previous time when he 'kept such a coil in the country'[2] but he 'ceaseth now to be much feared, and popery is sufficiently discovered'.[3] Certainly by the 1590s Robin's place in popular culture had been transformed.

Robin Goodfellow, hobgoblins and pucks all belonged to the same group of fairies, a class of rough, hairy domestic spirits characterized by their mischievousness. Scot lists all three as distinct and separate types of 'bugs' with which 'our mothers' maids have so terrified us'.[4] Nashe describes the 'Robin Good-fellows, Elves, Fairies, Hobgoblins of our latter age, which idolatrous former days and the fantastical world of Greece ycleped *fawns, Satyrs, Dryads and Hamadryads*' who 'did most of their merry pranks in the night'.[5] Shakespeare alone combines the three into a single spirit, Robin Goodfellow the puck, also known as 'hobgoblin' (2.1.40).

As Katharine Briggs shows, puck was a generic name, a potent genre of small devil: '*Puckle*, a small puck, comes from the same root which gave us Pixy, Phooka, Tom Poker, Bogles, Bugs and Boggarts'.[6] In his more demonic form, Puck appears as Pug, 'the lesse divell' of Ben Jonson's *The Devil is an Ass* (1616).[7] Similarly, later dramatic appearances of Robin

[1] Reginald Scot, *The Discovery of Witchcraft* (1584), Bk. 7, ch. 2, p. 131.

[2] Ibid., Bk. 7, ch. 15, p. 152.

[3] Ibid., sig. B2ᵛ.

[4] Ibid., Bk. 7, ch. 15, pp. 152–3.

[5] Thomas Nashe, *The Terrors of the Night* (1594), sig. B2ᵛ.

[6] K. M. Briggs, *The Anatomy of Puck* (1959), p. 21; see also Winifried Schleiner, 'Imaginative Sources for Shakespeare's Puck', *SQ* 36 (1985), pp. 65–8.

[7] Jonson, *Works*, vi. 162; Shakespeare's character is called Pugg throughout *The Merry Conceited Humors of Bottom the Weaver* (1661), an adaptation of *A Midsummer Night's Dream*.

Goodfellow, in *Wily Beguiled* and *Grim the Collier of Croydon* linked him closely to hell and devils (see note to 2.1.34).

Pucks, poukes, pookas, puckles and plucks were still widely feared and invoked in popular culture. Pamphlets about the witches of Warboys name one of their familiars Pluck.[1] In a different cultural world, Spenser's *Epithalamion* (1595) fervently, though patronisingly, hopes:

> Ne let the Pouke, nor other evill sprights,
> Ne let mischivous witches with theyr charmes,
> Ne let hob Goblins, names whose sence we see not,
> Fray us with things that be not.
>
> (ll. 341–4)

Even Golding used the name to describe the '*Chymaera* that same pooke' with 'Goatish body, Lions head and brist, and Dragons tayle' (9. 766–7). Identifying Robin Goodfellow as 'the puck' of *A Midsummer Night's Dream* is automatically to underscore the more diabolic of his antecedents.

But, in any case, Robin as 'the best-known and most often referred to of all the Hobgoblins of England in the 16th and 17th centuries . . . seemed to swallow all others and their names were nicknames of his'.[2] If hobgoblins and pucks were fairly universally feared, the attitude to Robin was more ambivalent. Samuel Rowlands, in *More Knaves Yet* (1613), describes him as 'a good fellow devil, | So called in kindness, cause he did no evil'.[3] Yet the only early illustration of Robin, on the title-page of *Robin Good-Fellow, His Mad Pranks and Merry Jests* (1628) shows a figure with devil's horns and phallus (see fig. 4). If he could be summed up as occupying 'the unique position of the national practical joker',[4] his victims may not have been so amused. The 1628 pamphlet's narrative of his pranks and tricks is prefaced by the language of fairy-tale, balancing his pranks and his blessings:

Once upon a Time, a great while ago, . . . About that time (when so ere it was) there was wont to walk many harmless Spirits called Fairies, dancing in brave order in Fairy Rings on green hills . . .

[1] Schleiner, p. 67.

[2] K. M. Briggs, *A Dictionary of Fairies, Hobgoblins, Brownies, Bogies and other supernatural creatures* (1976), p. 341.

[3] Quoted by Briggs, *Anatomy*, p. 72.

[4] Minor White Latham, *The Elizabethan Fairies* (New York, 1930), p. 223.

4. Title-page of *Robin Good-Fellow, His Mad Pranks* (1628).

(sometime invisible) in divers shapes; many mad pranks would they play, as pinching of sluts black and blue, and misplacing things in ill ordered houses, but lovingly would they use wenches that cleanly were, giving them silver, and other pretty toys ... (sig. A4ʳ)

The pamphlet belongs to the sudden efflorescence of interest in Robin in the 1620s and 1630s[1] but earlier commentators narrated similar tricks. Robin was a country spirit, operating

---

[1] See also *The Mad-merry Prankes of Robbin Good-fellow* (*c.* 1625), *The Merry Puck, or Robin Goodfellow* (*c.* 1633) and Drayton's poem 'Nimphidia' (1627), heavily dependent on *A Midsummer Night's Dream*. 'Puck-hairy, Or Robin-Good-fellow' also appears as the witch's servant in Act 3 of Ben Jonson's *The Sad Shepherd* (1637), defined as 'her Devil' (3.1.7), 'my lov'd Goblin' (3.5.16); Jonson's argument for Act 3 mentions the 'delusions of Puck' (7.43). Like Shakespeare's Robin, Jonson's Puck-hairy has to search the wood: 'I must go dance about the forest, now, | And firk it like a Goblin, till I find her'

indoors and out in rural communities. His principal area of work was in the house, working to help tidy and hardworking maids with housework, 'sweeping the house at midnight' (hence his depiction with a broom) and grinding 'malt or mustard',[1] and working equally hard to create more chaos for those who did not leave him out his reward of a bowl of milk and white bread. William Tyndale, in his commentary on the First Epistle of St John (1531), describes one of Robin's other outdoor tricks: 'The scripture . . . is become a maze unto them, in which they wander as in a mist, or (as they say) led by Robin Goodfellow, that they cannot come to the right way.'[2] There is a massive body of reference to Robin throughout the sixteenth and seventeenth centuries but the tricks and pranks do not differ substantially. Even the groupings of stories, like *Robin Good-Fellow His Mad Pranks*, add nothing to the range of Robin's activities. His place in popular culture seems to have been remarkably well defined.

There is only one significant exception. In a group of pamphlets of the 1590s Robin is conjured up in connection with popular satire and the clowns of the theatres. *Tarlton's News out of Purgatory* (1590) is spoken in the character of the ghost of Tarlton, the great clown actor of the 1580s; the introduction to the satire promises that 'sith my appearance to thee is in a resemblance of a spirit, think that I am as pleasant a Goblin as the rest, and will make thee as merry before I part, as ever *Robin Goodfellow* made the country wenches at their Creambowls' (sig. A3ᵛ). The reply to this pamphlet, *The Cobbler of Canterbury* (1590), opens with an epistle from Robin Goodfellow himself, describing the lack of hospitality he now finds in the country, for 'where he was wont to find a mess of cream for his labour, he should scarce get a dish of float milk' (sig. A4ʳ), and vowing that he will no longer 'say as I was wont: What Hemp and Hamp, here will I never more grind nor stamp' (sig. A4ᵛ).[3]

(3.1.14–15). Jonson's witch, though not Puck-hairy, is a shape-changer and able to create sudden local fogs, like Shakespeare's Robin.

[1] Scot, Bk. 4, ch. 10, p. 85.

[2] Quoted by Tilley, R47.

[3] See also Robert Weimann, *Shakespeare and the Popular Tradition in the Theater* (Baltimore, 1978), pp. 192–4.

The use of Robin in pamphlets reappears in *Tell-Truth's New-year's Gift* (1593) where, as the title-page promises, he brings 'news out of those countries, where inhabits neither charity nor honesty'. This Robin, 'one who never did worse harm than correct manners, and made diligent maids' (sig. A2^r), as well as inveighing against jealousy, is concerned to help young women to marry as they wish, against the wishes of authoritarian parents who 'do not match them with the mates their children's eyes have chosen, but with the men their own greedy desire have found out' (p. 6).[1] The pamphlet makes Robin a helper against an army of Egeuses. For the first time in published texts Robin is involved in problems of love and marriage, shifted away from his normal ground of domestic chores and misleading night-travellers.

Robin belongs firmly and almost exclusively to a popular and folk-lore tradition; only at one point does he appear to have made contact with the court. In Thomas Churchyard's 'A Handful of Gladsome Verses', presented to Elizabeth I at Woodstock in 1592, his recurrent interest in fairies as a useful device for royal entertainments led him to include mention of Robin Goodfellow:

> A further sport fell out,
> When they to spoil did fall:
> Rude *Robin* Goodfellow the lout,
> Would skim the milk bowls all.[2]

Churchyard and the pamphlets of 1590 and 1593 cumulatively witness the extent of Robin's new visibility in a variety of unexpected cultural forms at exactly the point at which Shakespeare was writing *A Midsummer Night's Dream*. But the conjunction of Robin and the other fairies, the redefinition of Robin as also puck and hobgoblin and the decision to put Robin on-stage at all were entirely new.

Shakespeare may have found a partial dramatic source for the energetic elf, more or less obedient to his master's commands, in the character of Shrimp in Anthony Munday's *John*

---

[1] See also Jeff Shulman, '*Tell-Trothes New-years Gift* (1593): Another Source of *A Midsummer Night's Dream*', *Theatre Journal*, 33 (1981), pp. 391–2.

[2] Thomas Churchyard, 'A Handful of Gladsome Verses', sig. B4^v, in W. C. Hazlitt, ed., *Fugitive Tracts First Series 1493–1600* (1875).

a Kent and John a Cumber. The problem here is that the date of Munday's play is unclear and the manuscript ends with a note in Munday's hand that might refer to 1590 or to 1596[1] (though even if it is 1596 the play could just have been written and performed before Shakespeare wrote *A Midsummer Night's Dream*). Munday's play, incoherent and repetitive in its dramatic form, as each magician tries to outdo the cunning of his rival, certainly does not appear to have learnt anything from the structural brilliance of Shakespeare's play. Nevill Coghill has summarized the two plays' shared elements of plot:

> Lovers in flight from parental opposition to their love. Moonlit woods through which they flee to join their lovers. A mischievous fairy imp, in service to a master of magic. A crew of clowns who organise buffoonish entertainments, in honour of their territorial overlord, on the occasion of a double wedding. Contention for the leading part. Malapropisms. Young men led by an invisible voice until they fall exhausted. A 'happy ending' with True Lovers properly paired and wedded.[2]

Munday's play has a few just possible verbal echoes from a number of characters. But it is the similarity of Shrimp to Robin that is most intriguing. Shrimp shares four significant characteristics with Shakespeare's Robin: he is always rushing off the stage at high speed ('I fly Sir, and am there already'[3]); he crows at his success ('Why, now is Shrimp in the height of his bravery, | That he may execute some part of his master's knavery'[4]); he is most often invisible to the other characters on-stage as he leads them up and down false trails; he frequently comments in asides about what he intends to do ('Nay pause awhile, I'll fetch ye company'[5]).

While Shrimp may be a dramatic source, Shakespeare also used a massive iconic source, for Robin is in many respects

[1] I. A. Shapiro, 'The Significance of a Date', *SS* 8 (Cambridge, 1955), pp. 100–5; William B. Long accepts the 1590 date in '*John a Kent and John a Cumber*: An Elizabethan Playbook and its implications', in W. R. Elton and William B. Long, eds., *Shakespeare and Dramatic Tradition* (1989), pp. 125–43.

[2] Nevill Coghill, *Shakespeare's Professional Skills* (Cambridge, 1964), p. 52.

[3] Anthony Munday, *John a Kent and John a Cumber*, ed. M. St C. Byrne, Malone Society Reprints (Oxford, 1923) l. 989. He also enters in a way characteristic of Shakespeare's fairies, 'Enter Shrimp skipping' (l. 1012); compare Titania's instruction, 'Fairies, skip hence' (2.1.61).

[4] Ibid., ll. 577–8.

[5] Ibid., l. 589.

the play's Cupid. As Leonard Barkan suggests, when 'Helena characterizes Cupid as winged, blind, hasty, lacking in judgment, and juvenile...[it] is a veritable program for the actions of Puck'.[1] Oberon's description of 'Cupid, all armed' in flight (2.1.155–65) makes it clear that Robin cannot in any way be wholly identified with Cupid. His own relish of Cupid's activities may be nothing more than the approval of a professional rival: 'Cupid is a knavish lad | Thus to make poor females mad' (3.2.440–1). But his dramatic function aligns him closely with Cupid in the play's mythological schema, the spirit responsible for creating irrational affection and the one responsible for transforming it into a harmonious and socially acceptable desire. The Renaissance debates on the meaning of Cupid find frequent echo in the implications of Robin's activities.

If Robin is indeed a form of dramatic Cupid then one would expect the role to have been played by a boy. Certainly Shrimp was a boy in Munday's play but there is no suggestion that the Robin Goodfellow of folk-lore was anything other than adult, even if in such matters size is rarely a guide. The phallic Robin of the woodcut (Fig. 4) is clearly no child.

There is nothing in the text of *A Midsummer Night's Dream* to clarify the problem. At the end of *Merry Wives* the fairies who tease Falstaff at Herne's Oak include Mistress Quickly disguised as the Fairy Queen and looking, I suspect, rather like Titania; the group also includes a figure described as a 'hobgoblin' in the Folio text and as 'Puck' in the Quarto. The part was played either by Sir Hugh Evans (in quarto) or by Pistol or by the actor who had played Pistol earlier in the play.[2] This hobgoblin or puck was certainly played by an adult male; it might suggest that Robin was as well.

When Robin first appears Titania's fairy is not entirely sure who he is and has certainly only heard of him, never met him:

> Either I mistake your shape and making quite
> Or else you are that shrewd and knavish sprite
> Called Robin Goodfellow.
>
> (2.1.32–4)

---

[1] Leonard Barkan, *The Gods Made Flesh* (New Haven, 1986), p. 254.
[2] See Oxford's n. to *Wives* 5.5.41, etc.

5. Frontispiece to Nicholas Rowe's text of *A Midsummer Night's Dream* in his edition of Shakespeare's *Works* (1709).

The Fairy's lines suggest that Robin looks distinctly different from the other fairies, even the ones in Oberon's train. But it is far from clear what Robin looked like. The costumes worn by Robin in *Wily Bequiled* and *Grim the Collier of Croydon* (see note to 2.1.34) suggest too strongly a diabolic and perhaps mummers' play[1] reference.

For most of the play's history the dominant images of Robin have been derived from illustrations to the play rather than

---

[1] Briggs, *Anatomy*, pp. 76–7.

performances. Robin is not specifically identifiable in the two illustrations to Rowe's editions of 1709 (fig. 5) and 1714 but in François Gravelot's engraving for Theobald's 1740 edition, 'a very English and Elizabethan'[1] Robin appears squeezing the juice into Lysander's eyes, dressed in a broad-collared Elizabethan shirt and wearing a jester's cap, plainly suggesting his position with Oberon, 'I jest to Oberon, and make him smile' (2.1.44).

In Boydell's Shakespeare Gallery there were paintings of Robin by Sir Joshua Reynolds and Fuseli, engraved and published in Boydell's *Graphic Illustrations of the Dramatic Works of Shakespeare* in 1802 (figs. 6 and 7). Reynolds's *Puck*, 'an ugly little imp' according to Horace Walpole,[2] is clearly Robin as sentimentalized cherub with pointed ears. It is intended to be endearing but dissociates the character from the play, in spite of the depiction of Bottom and Titania in the background, encouraging the twee fairy mythology that would later envelop productions and reach its apotheosis in the tradition of illustrations of the play in the work of Arthur Rackham. The illustration becomes indeed a resource for designers working on the play and the mushroom on which Reynolds's Robin is seated is used for the first appearance of Robin in 2.1 by Madame Vestris for her production at Covent Garden in 1840,[3] by Charles Kean in 1856 (with Ellen Terry, aged eight, as Robin)[4] and by Augustin Daly's New York production in 1888.[5] Such theatrical traditions were not restricted to mushrooms: Shaw fulminated against Daly's casting of an actress as Oberon, another device in which Daly was following Madame Vestris.[6]

[1] Kenneth Garlick, 'Illustrations to *A Midsummer Night's Dream* before 1920', *SS* 37 (Cambridge, 1984), p. 43 and fig. 3; see also W. Moelwyn Merchant, '*A Midsummer Night's Dream*: A Visual Recreation', in John Russell Brown and Bernard Harris, eds., *Early Shakespeare*, Stratford-upon-Avon Studies, 3 (1961), pp. 165–85.

[2] Quoted by Garlick, p. 45.

[3] See Trevor Griffiths, 'A Neglected Pioneer Production: Madame Vestris' *A Midsummer Night's Dream* at Covent Garden, 1840', *SQ* 30 (Cambridge, 1979), p. 390.

[4] Gary Jay Williams, 'Madame Vestris' *A Midsummer Night's Dream* and the Web of Victorian Tradition', *Theatre Survey*, 18.2 (1977), p. 18.

[5] 'Enter a FAIRY, plucking flowers. With her wand she switches at a mushroom-growth near C., and from it PUCK appears' (SD in Daly's edition of the play (1888), 'Arranged for production at Daly's Theatre').

[6] George Bernard Shaw, *Our Theatres in the Nineties* (1932), I. 178.

6. Sir Joshua
Reynolds, *Puck*,
engraving
published 1802.

7. Henry Fuseli, *Puck*,
engraving published
1802.

Fuseli's *Puck* is extraordinarily different. A violent semi-human figure, causing a night-traveller to fall off his horse in a river by a mere gesture, this Robin is demonic and powerful, uncaring in his actions. There is nothing gleeful and laughing, only mockery, a cynical echo of Robin's pleasure in 'those things ... That befall prepost'rously' (3.2.120–1). This is perhaps the most disconcerting of all representations of Robin, the most complete denial of anything sympathetic and endearing.

In the theatre Robin was entangled in the stage machinery, complete with flying, dummies, and even flying dummies. Not until Granville Barker's production (Savoy, 1914) was Robin transformed—and grounded! Barker recognized the extent to which Robin's separation from the other fairies needed to be visualized on stage. Where the other fairies were covered in exotic, vaguely eastern gold (see above, p. 000), Robin was recognized as 'a genuine English "hobgoblin" ', dressed in scarlet, with red berries in bright yellow hair which streamed 'like a comet behind him'.[1] Robin was, for Barker, 'as English as he can be' while the other fairies were 'undoubtedly foreign'[2] and he therefore wore an Elizabethan costume of doublet, breeches, tights and slippers. Barker's casting of Donald Calthrop was another break with theatrical tradition: though not the first male Robin since the eighteenth century, Calthrop seems to have been the first *adult* professional male to play the role,[3] a reversion perhaps to Shakespeare's own practice.

In the structure of separate worlds that Shakespeare formed in *A Midsummer Night's Dream* Robin's position is more oddly isolated than anyone else. Apart from his opening dialogue with Titania's fairy in 2.1 he is only able to speak directly to one other character for the whole of the rest of the play, Oberon. It is a technique that fascinated Shakespeare and he returned to it in, for example, *Othello*, where Roderigo is almost completely restricted to dialogue with Iago, and, with

[1] Dymkowski, p. 63.

[2] Quoted by Dymkowski, p. 63.

[3] Crosse, who saw a male Robin at Oxford in February 1899, thought him so good that the part should 'never be played by a girl again' (vol. 2, p. 73). Crosse disliked Calthrop, for making Robin 'a sort of affected half-wit, with a squeaky voice' (vol. 5, p. 167).

distinctly comparable effect, in *The Tempest*, where Ariel, clearly a metamorphosis of Robin, talks directly in his own voice only to Prospero while all his speeches to other characters are either a virtuosic extension of Robin's ventriloquism in 3.2 or a form of role-playing, as, for example, a harpy (3.3.53–82).

For large sections of the play the action is watched by Robin, an observer and commentator, a participant through his invisibility, a doubly disturbing presence in that he both disturbs the action and disturbs our reactions to it. As Alexander Leggatt recognizes, in both *Wily Beguiled* and *Grim the Collier of Croydon*,

> Robin Goodfellow not only appears to mortals, but is on neighbourly terms with them. Shakespeare's Puck, for all his mischief, is far more detached than this, appearing to mortals—when he appears at all—in an assumed shape.[1]

This detachment allows for and justifies Robin's amusement at human activity. Titania is concerned at the effect of her quarrel with Oberon, saddened at its consequences for mortals: 'The human mortals want their winter cheer. | No night is now with hymn or carol blessed' (2.1.101–2). But 'the mazèd world' (2.1.113) that she pities is for Robin an infinitely various source of enjoyment. The chaos he has generated is comic: 'Then will two at once woo one. | That must needs be sport alone' (3.2.118–19). Human behaviour is nothing more than a series of tableaux of folly, put on for Robin's enjoyment, a spectacle with fairies the only members of the audience: 'Shall we their fond pageant see? | Lord, what fools these mortals be!' (3.2.114–15).

In production Robin's invisibility generates opportunities for him to create this comedy himself. At times it can be a response to the text's implications: Robin may show something of the pursuit and torment of the workmen that he promises after Bottom's transformation (3.1.101–6). In Granville Barker's production, for instance, the stage business is carefully charted:

> During this Flute gets LC with Snout and Puck pinches them, Flute runs twice round mound, Puck follows him once . . . Meanwhile

---

[1] Alexander Leggatt, *Shakespeare's Comedy of Love* (1974), p. 107 n. 11.

Snout has gone up mound LC, being tripped up by Puck as he chases Flute.[1]

But at other times the business becomes busy-ness, the introduction of extraneous comedy. Barker's Robin was given too ample an opportunity to become an 'actor' in the workers' play, leaving the rehearsal too far behind:

[Robin] tickles Quin with wand; ditto Bot, then Snout, Starv and Snug. Then Snout again who thinking it is Star pushes him over ... Puck tickles Bot's legs 3 times, he thinking it is a fly tries to catch it, Puck buzzes, all rise and try to catch it.[2]

The interconnection of the discrete worlds of *Dream* is an interlocking network of comic contrasts. As Leggatt suggests, 'Each group, so self-absorbed, is seen in a larger context, which provides comic perspective. Each in turn provides a similar context for the others.'[3] But these comic perspectives cannot include Robin who travels so freely across the play, constrained only by Oberon's orders and Oberon's anger. Indeed he travels more freely than he at first appears to know, for he is not, as he thinks, restricted to the world of night and threatened by the arrival of the dawn: as Oberon so categorically informs—or, perhaps, reminds—him, 'we are spirits of another sort' (3.2.388).

Robin's air-travel makes him the play's importer, bringing into the play the flowers Oberon describes, changing the description into the object. Harold Bloom goes as far as calling Robin 'a kind of flying metalepsis or trope of transumption ... what the rhetorician Puttenham called a far-fetcher'.[4] But such a rhetorical device seems irrelevant. What Robin has above all is the ability to be the agent of metamorphosis, to transform himself and others. He 'exemplifies the spirit of

[1] Barker's prompt-book, quoted by Trevor Griffiths, 'Tradition and Innovation in Harley Granville Barker's *A Midsummer Night's Dream*', *Theatre Notebook*, 30 (1976), p. 82.

[2] Ibid.

[3] Leggatt, p. 91.

[4] Introduction to Harold Bloom, ed., *William Shakespeare's A Midsummer Night's Dream* (New York, 1987), p. 5; to be entirely accurate, Puttenham calls *metalepsis* 'the *farfet*': see George Puttenham, *The Arte of English Poesie*, ed. Gladys Doidge Willcock and Alice Walker (Cambridge, 1936), p. 183.

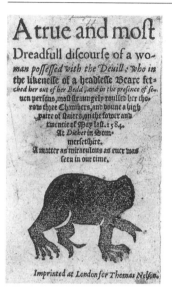

8. Headless Bears: *A true and most dreadful discourse* (1584).

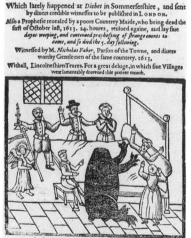

9. *A Miracle of miracles* (1614).

metamorphosis for its own sake'.[1] Even his name is unfixed: he is 'Robin Goodfellow ... hobgoblin ... Sweet puck' (2.1.34, 40). He can change himself into 'a filly foal' (2.1.46), 'a roasted crab' (2.1.48), a 'three-foot stool' (2.1.52), 'a horse ... a hound, | A hog, a headless bear, sometime a fire' (3.1.103–4), Lysander or Demetrius (3.2.360 ff.). Robin belongs to and creates a world of flux and instability, where a stool may be a stool or a metamorphosed goblin. Robin inhabits this place of shifting surfaces, of endless and almost uncontrollable transformability. It is, of course, his stage, a theatre where he is simultaneously playwright and actor and audience.

Theseus and Hippolyta

In Chaucer's 'Knight's Tale' in *The Canterbury Tales*, Shakespeare found a number of details he used in *A Midsummer Night's Dream*; Chaucer alone gave Theseus the title of Duke and identifies as the initiating moment for his narrative his return to Athens with his new bride, Hippolyta. Though other details of Theseus' life were taken from North's translation of Plutarch's 'Life of Theseus', paired with Romulus, in *The Lives of the Noble Grecians and Romans* (1579), North was unsure whether the Amazon Theseus married was named Hippolyta or, as most evidence suggested, Antiopa. Shakespeare makes Antiopa one of the long list of women Theseus seduced and abandoned (2.1.80).

Neither Chaucer nor North has much to say about Amazons. Though Chaucer's Emelye is Ypolita's sister and has no desire to marry, there is little else about her that suggests her nationality. In Chaucer the name of the Amazon's country, 'Femenye', seems to evoke a perfect realm of women. Theseus conquers their kingdom outside the Knight's narrative, after a 'grete bataille' (l. 879) and siege, ambiguously and simultaneously a siege of Ypolita as an individual woman besieged by a lover and conquered into marriage and a siege of her as queen with her kingdom conquered into subjection. North records the great war waged by the Amazons against Athens, with the women here besieging Athens itself and peace made

[1] William C. Carroll, *The Metamorphoses of Shakespearean Comedy* (Princeton, N. J., 1985), p. 173.

by Hippolyta, later, according to some sources, 'slain (fighting on *Theseus*'s side) with a dart' (p. 15). For North the war 'methinks was not a matter of small moment, nor an enterprise of women' (p. 15). Both do no more than gesture towards the threat of the self-sufficient women's kingdom that the realm of the Amazons represented, a kingdom needing to be brought within the normal and 'natural' constrictions of patriarchy.

Amazons appeared throughout the range of Elizabethan writing,[1] embodying a range of characteristics threatening men: female sexual desire, self-mutilation, the rejection and subjugation of men, disobedience to male dominance through their effective self-governance, uncontrolled female will, female strength and success in the male skills of war.[2] Their traditional dress, armed with axes and shields, wearing buskins and with one breast exposed or amputated, specified their intrusiveness from a distant land into accepted conventions of male control.[3] Even the location of their country was significant; it was usually placed close to Scythia, a byword for barbarism. Shakespeare's references to Scythia associate it directly with infanticide,[4] in the same way that Amazons were often reported to murder their sons—or at least make them do work more usually associated with women.[5] Significantly, some association was clearly made between amazons and fairies: Caelia in the anonymous play *Tom a Lincoln* is queen of fairyland and her subjects are women armed with bows and arrows who have killed their husbands for refusing to come home from war for sex.[6]

The Amazonian inversion of gender hierarchy has been resolved before *A Midsummer Night's Dream* begins and the blessing on future children at the end of the play does not in the slightest suggest that their mother is an infanticidal threat.

---

[1] See Celeste Turner Wright, 'The Amazons in Elizabethan Literature', *SP* 37 (1940), pp. 433–56.

[2] See Simon Shepherd, *Amazons and Warrior Women* (1981).

[3] On Hippolyta's costume see n. to 1.1.1 and Spenser's description of his Amazon warrior in *The Faerie Queene*, 5.5.2–3.

[4] *Titus* 1.1.131 and *Lear* 1.1.116.

[5] See Montrose, p. 66.

[6] *Tom a Lincoln*, ed. G. R. Proudfoot, Malone Society Reprints (Oxford, 1992), esp. ll. 1168–86.

Hippolyta has been conquered, defeated into marriage. Theseus is well aware that his courtship has been entirely military
but his language leaves unclear whether she has simply
agreed through defeat or whether she is now in love with
him: 'Hippolyta, I wooed thee with my sword, | And won
thy love doing thee injuries' (1.1.16–17). Her 'love' may be
nothing more than enforced and constrained consent.

Productions have varied greatly in their representations of
the degree of her consent. Traditionally she has been seen as
calmly acquiescent, an image of the perfect queen. But more
recently she has registered a sense of captivity. In John
Hancock's production for the Actors Workshop Company in
San Francisco in 1966 she was brought on stage in a cage
without her usual accompaniment of female attendants.[1] Elijah Moshinsky's production for BBC television opened with a
shot of Hippolyta pacing to and fro 'restlessly, even angrily';[2]
Theseus spoke his first lines while still wearing armour, con-
fronting her with a marked space between them.

Chaucer's Ypolita is silent; Shakespeare's Hippolyta is
allowed one speech in the scene, a speech ambiguously of
reassurance to Theseus at the rapid passage of time or reluctant recognition that the time of her independence has nearly
ended. In either case Hippolyta as an image of female monarch defeated and subject to a man is unlikely to have
appealed to Elizabeth.[3] The subject monarch Hippolyta, a
duchess through her marriage, will be opposed by the play's
complex representation of female monarchical independence
in Titania whose powers are emphatically equal to Oberon's,
for all his triumph over her in the course of the play.

Theseus' second expression of male power over female marriage, in respect of Hermia, is explicitly made through a
recognition of the established legal rights of the father to
control the daughter. Though he offers some form of apology
for the necessity of his own obedience to the law, 'Which by
no means we may extenuate' (1.1.120), he fully adumbrates

[1] See Shirley Nelson Garner, '*A Midsummer Night's Dream*: "Jack shall have
Jill;/Nought shall go ill" ', *Women's Studies*, 9 (1981), p. 52. For set and
costume designs and some photographs of the production, see Jim Dine,
Designs for A Midsummer Night's Dream (New York, 1968).

[2] Philip C. McGuire, *Speechless Dialect* (Berkeley, 1985), p. 10.

[3] Montrose, *passim*, esp. pp. 75–85.

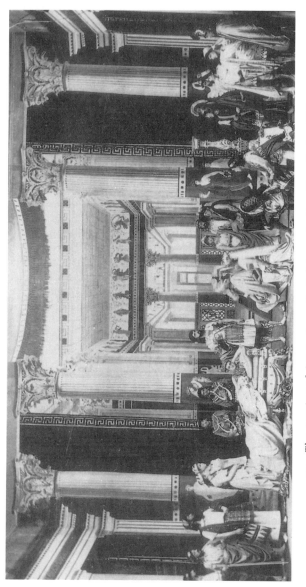

10. The opening of Act 1, Augustin Daly's production, New York, 1888.

and accepts the notion of paternal power that the law frames
in its punitive form:

> To you your father should be as a god,
> One that composed your beauties, yea, and one
> To whom you are but as a form in wax,
> By him imprinted, and within his power
> To leave the figure or disfigure it.
>
> (1.1.47–51)

Theseus' antagonism towards virginity, a state that denies
male power, is expressed in the implications that keep bur-
sting through his attempts to praise, with appropriate religious respect, the lot of the nun, a life of barrenness and
withering, 'Chanting faint hymns to the cold fruitless moon'
(1.1.73).

Hippolyta constitutes in Act 1 an unrealized or at least
unsuccessful opposition to the principles of male power that
Theseus so completely embodies. There is only the implicit
antagonism to male power that the audience's conventional
approval of Hermia allows it to extend towards Hippolyta,
denying, however implicitly, the complex of pejorative associations that cluster around the image of the Amazon. Significantly, Elizabeth's own expression of her power, so intensely
predicated on the notion of her virginity, rarely made use of
the apparatus of Amazonianism;[1] Spenser's approving image
of the warrior maiden in *The Faerie Queene* is Britomart, not
the Amazon Radigund. By the end of Shakespeare's play,
however, in the complex balances of judgement that the two
characters express, the balance of approval, if not of power,
shifts.

But the play has already had to negotiate the complex
problem represented by Theseus himself. There are few clues
in Chaucer to the traditions of doubt and disapproval that
cluster around Theseus. North, however, in the comparison
between Theseus and Romulus heavily emphasizes the problem of Theseus' relationships with women:

Theseus's faults touching women and ravishments, of the twain, had
the less shadow and colour of honesty because *Theseus* did attempt

---

[1] Montrose, pp. 75–7; see also Winifried Schleiner, 'Elizabeth I and Amazons', *SP* 75 (1978), pp. 163–80.

it very often: for he stole away *Ariadne, Antiopa,* and *Anaxo* the Troezenian ... Then his taking of the daughters of the Troezenians, of the Lacedaemonians, and the Amazons ... did give men occasion to suspect his womanishness was rather to satisfy lust, than of any great love ... The Athenians contrariwise, by Theseus's marriages, did get neither love nor kindred of any one person, but rather they procured wars, enmities, and the slaughter of their citizens. (p. 43)

Theseus' successive abandonment of women he had raped and/or married is, for North, an example of his bad government, belonging with his gradual degeneration into 'a very tyrant' (p. 42). For all the virtue of his exploits as a young man, the older Theseus represents a figure to be rejected, not approved. Certainly Theseus' character was widely documented and denounced for his 'dissolute and vicious living'[1] in medieval and Elizabethan literature, building on such classical models as the complaints by Ariadne[2] and others, mentioning his 'lechery and treachery',[3] in Ovid's *Heroides*.

It is easy to see how the Theseus whose first speech dismisses women as irritating obstacles to a young man's enjoying his inheritance, 'Long withering out a young man's revenue' (1.1.6), belongs in this tradition. But it is equally easy to overemphasize his sins. When Theseus acknowledges that he had intended to talk to Demetrius about his treatment of Helena but had forgotten to get round to it, 'being over-full of self affairs' (1.1.113), this is not the same thing as 'an inversion of ideal lordship; he has allowed private vice to destroy public virtue'.[4] I cannot see that those 'self affairs', which presumably centre on Hippolyta, are anything as culpable as a sin. It is also distinctly unfair to assert, as Pearson does, that Theseus is wrong not to approve of Hermia's choice of Lysander in Act 1 and equally wrong when he does approve of it in Act 4.

[1] Quoted by D'Orsay W. Pearson, ' "Unkinde" Theseus: A Study in Renaissance Mythography', *ELR* 4 (1974), p. 288.

[2] Julia, in *The Two Gentlemen of Verona*, had performed 'a lamentable part. | Madam, 'twas Ariadne, passioning | For Theseus' perjury and unjust flight' (4.4.163–5).

[3] Pearson, p. 287.

[4] Ibid., p. 294; see also his 'Male Sovereignty, Harmony and Irony in *A Midsummer Night's Dream*', *The Upstart Crow*, 7 (1987), pp. 24–35.

Whatever the extent of the play's doubts about Theseus, in Act I his denial of Hermia's wishes both respects the law and, above all, enables the play's action to begin; this may be comedy's complicity with authority but it also establishes the block the action needs to remove. The doubts about the character are redirected in Act 5 into the problem of Theseus' limited imagination. For the rational Theseus who rejects the imaginative irrationalities of the lunatic, the lover and the poet is, quite simply, wrong. The experience of the wood has been both strange and true, not 'More strange than true' (5.1.2). The man who mocks 'antique fables' (5.1.3) is a character from one. The man who thinks himself wittily imaginative when he warns ' 'tis almost fairy-time' (5.1.355) after having disparaged 'fairy toys' (5.1.3) does not stay on stage long enough to see fairies really arrive in his own palace.[1] Theseus' painfully and comically limited perspectives, the range of vision of rationalist daylight scepticism, are grotesquely inadequate to the experiences the play has shown. For him, 'whatever is not "out there" for reason to contemplate, comprehend and categorise does not exist';[2] for us there is by the end of the play known to be far more out there than he can begin to suspect, let alone accept.

In the adaptation of the play into *The Fairy Queen* in 1692, the final great pageant of the opera is presented by the fairies directly to Theseus. No sooner has Theseus scorned the lovers' account of their night in the wood than he hears 'strange Musick warbling in the Air' and Oberon appears and announces,

> 'Tis Fairy Musick, sent by me;
> To cure your Incredulity.
> All was true the Lovers told,
> You shall stranger things behold. (p. 47)

The Fairy Queen's Theseus is educated out of his mistake by being shown the fairy world; Shakespeare's Theseus remains in his ignorant scepticism. *The Fairy Queen*'s Bottom is excluded

---

[1] I am fond of Harriett Hawkins's comment, 'Theseus flatly says he doesn't believe in fairies, but do we *really* believe in Theseus?' ('Fabulous Counterfeits: Dramatic Construction and Dramatic Perspectives in *The Spanish Tragedy*, *A Midsummer Night's Dream*, and *The Tempest*', *Sh Studs* 6 (1972), p. 54).

[2] Graham Bradshaw, *Shakespeare's Scepticism* (1987), p. 39.

from the sight of the fairies here; Shakespeare's Bottom alone perceives what has happened.

More than a little smug in his attempt, patiently, to explain to Hippolyta all these complex ideas that are, as far as he is concerned, way beyond her intelligence, he is unable to hear her argument, to realize that the play has shown something that has transfigured the lovers' minds, whether he can make sense of it or not. His 'dogmatic and positivistic scepticism'[1] cannot compete with her vision of constancy, for all its strangeness. When David Young dubs him 'Poor Theseus'[2] I share the sympathetic pity in the label.

Confronted with the prospect of 'Pyramus and Thisbe' Hippolyta is inordinately worried: 'I love not to see wretchedness o' ercharged, | And duty in his service perishing' (5.1.85–6). But this interlude is not the same as the pageant of the Nine Worthies at the end of *Love's Labour's Lost*. Where those performers are humiliated into silence and forced to rebuke their audience for their hurtful contempt, the workers of 'Pyramus and Thisbe' are not, in most productions, put out by their audience's comments as much as by their own difficulties with managing their props and costumes. Only Starveling, as Moonshine, grinds to a halt, angry at the mockery. Theseus' judgement is, for once, fair and accurate: 'If we imagine no worse of them than they of themselves, they may pass for excellent men' (5.1.214–15). Theseus' generosity towards those who offer him artistic and rhetorical tributes, lengthily and honourably expressed (5.1.89 ff.), has an undercurrent of private sneering, suggesting a gap between the public pleasure and the private mockery that is a little disconcerting: 'Our sport shall be to take what they mistake' (5.1.90).

Hippolyta, alone of the three brides, speaks during Act 5. Initially she joins in the game of witty comments in which

[1] Ibid., p. 42. Barbara Mowat has drawn out the intriguing parallels between Theseus' scepticism and Reginald Scot's in *The Discovery of Witchcraft* (1584): Scot, like Theseus, doubts poets' accounts of witchcraft and fairies, including Ovid's *Metamorphoses*, and repeatedly mocks imagination as a delusion (Barbara A. Mowat, ' "A local habitation and a name": Shakespeare's text as Construct', *Style*, 23 (1989), pp. 344–6).

[2] David P. Young, *Something of Great Constancy* (New Haven, 1966), p. 139.

the men indulge so freely and unconcernedly (at 5.1.122–3, for example). But her open mockery of it, 'This is the silliest stuff that ever I heard', produces an exchange with Theseus that marks both a certain slight antagonism towards him and a disagreement on the nature of art:

THESEUS The best in this kind are but shadows, and the worst are no worse if imagination amend them.
HIPPOLYTA It must be your imagination, then, and not theirs.

(5.1.209–13)

It appears easy to sum up the balanced implications of such an exchange: Howard Nemerov suggests, for example, that 'the excess of Theseus is to declare that art is entertainment; the excess of Hippolyta, to declare that art is mystery'.[1] But it would be truer to say that Hippolyta recognizes art is both.

For a man of such limited imagination as Theseus to evoke the usefulness of imagination in responding to a play is hardly encouraging.[2] Theseus's description of the best actors as 'shadows' is both limiting and accurate: limiting in that for him it constitutes a limitation of the scope of the unreal world of theatre, the similitude rather than object which he sees as the sole truth; accurate in that the word extends far beyond his version of it, responding with a full imagination to the possibility of shadows in both its meanings in the play, the shadow world of the fairies combined with the shadow world of performance, the shadow of another reality unrecognized by the realist model superimposed with the shadow world of poetic truth which, beyond the reaches of visible reality, recognizes and reproduces this other form of reality. Robin has already referred to Oberon as 'king of shadows' (3.2.347) and, at the end of the play, he will make 'shadows' embrace both the world of fairy and the world of performance in a way that Theseus's limited usage of the word cannot envisage: 'If we shadows have offended' (5.1.414).

[1] Howard Nemerov, 'The Marriage of Theseus and Hippolyta', *Kenyon Review*, 18 (1956), p. 641.
[2] On imagination see R. W. Dent, 'Imagination in *A Midsummer Night's Dream*', *SQ* 15 (1964), pp. 115–29; William Rossky, 'Imagination in the English Renaissance: Psychology and Poetic', *Studies in the Renaissance*, 5 (1958), pp. 49–73; and, particularly, Young, pp. 109–66.

Hippolyta's response sounds accusatory but also recognizes the need of our imaginative engagement with those things, those forms, to which imagination can testify: the success of a performance depends far more on the audience's imaginations than on the performers; the acceptance of the fairy world depends on our awareness, not their existence. It leads her to make her subsequent comments partly in gentle mockery of Theseus; she worries about the performance's realism ('How chance Moonshine is gone before Thisbe comes back and finds her lover' 5.1.306–7) and she recalls, in her own boredom with the interlude, Theseus' opening lines in Act 1 ('I am aweary of this moon. Would he would change', 5.1.246–7).

But her understanding also leads her to praise the actors' work, generously identifying their engagement of her imaginative affective sympathies with their creation: 'Beshrew my heart, but I pity the man' (5.1.284). Where the others can only mock, she expresses something of the seriousness that the matter of 'Pyramus and Thisbe' represents, a play of death, isolation and loss. Comic though Bottom is, Hippolyta can still pity Pyramus.

If imagination is to 'amend' the work of these actors, then it must be nearer Hippolyta's form of it than the men in the audience, for their mockery amends nothing, subjecting the amateur actors' efforts to ever more extreme mockery. Theseus may enunciate a theory of audience collaboration but the practice of Theseus, Lysander and Demetrius is antagonistic to the performance, a display of their own self-regarding wit which consistently denies the world of dramatic shadows the respect it deserves.

For Theseus the interlude promised to be a useful way to fill up time and proved successful in that aim: 'This palpable-gross play hath well beguiled | The heavy gait of night' (5.1.358–9). But as he leaves the play for bed, the appearance of Robin mocks his mockery of 'fairy time'. Hippolyta had envisaged something more.

A Midsummer Night's Dream ends with the fairies' blessing on the best bride bed and the promise that the 'issue there create | Ever shall be fortunate' (5.1.396–7). But the child of Theseus and Hippolyta casts a strange shadow over the end of the play. The child of Theseus and his Amazon bride will be Hippolytus, the man whose name carries the form of his own death, 'destroyed by horses'; the child's name means that Hippolyta's name is a back-formation, a name passed back from son to mother. Oberon's careful listing of the 'blots of nature's hand' which 'Shall not in their issue stand' (ll. 400–1) was right:

> Never mole, harelip, nor scar,
> Nor mark prodigious such as are
> Despisèd in nativity,
> Shall upon their children be (402–5)

for Hippolytus was unquestionably a stereotypically gorgeous macho man. But the result of this physical beauty is Phaedra's sexual obsession with him and Theseus' responsibility for his own son's death. It is as if the Theseus myth of unfaithfulness and destruction has one further trick to play on the characters of the play.[1]

The Lovers

Shakespeare had numerous resources to call on for the lovers. The complex interlocking of two pairs of lovers in a pattern of chaos and confusion is a staple of romance. He would have come across it in the tangle achieved by Philoclea, Zelmane, Basilius and Gynecia in Sidney's *Arcadia*.[2] He might well have known the way Cinthio set out the same kind of problems in a tale in his *Hecatommithi* (ninth novella, second decade), a work which Shakespeare used as his prime source for *Othello* some time later. Cinthio's treatment of his lovers is certainly closer to *A Midsummer Night's Dream* than any of the other suggestions: in Cinthio, love is an involuntary attraction amongst indistinguishable lovers who are trying to evade parental authority and whose escape is disrupted by a certain amount of supernatural intervention.[3] But there is little even here that was not widely available, almost as a formula, elsewhere.

[1] See my article, 'Theseus' Shadows in *A Midsummer Night's Dream*', *SS 47* (Cambridge, 1995), pp. 139–51.

[2] See Irving Ribner, 'A Note on Sidney's *Arcadia* and *A Midsummer Night's Dream*', *Shakespeare Association Bulletin*, 23 (1948) pp. 207–8.

[3] See Hugh M. Richmond, 'Shaping *A Dream*', *Sh Studs* 17 (1985), pp. 49–60.

More problematic is Shakespeare's possible use of Jorge de Montemayor's *Diana* (1559) and Gil Polo's continuation and re-examination of the romance in *Diana Enamorada* (1564). Bartholomew Yong's translation was not published until 1598 though it had probably been completed by 1582.[1] Shakespeare made use of Montemayor for *The Two Gentlemen of Verona*, either reading the Spanish original or relying on the French translation by Nicolas Collin (1578, 1587) or possibly through reading a manuscript copy of Yong's version.[2] A number of features of the two romances seem to be echoed by Shakespeare in *A Midsummer Night's Dream*: the dominance of the goddess Diana who 'is seen as devoted not primarily to chastity, but to finding a happy solution to lovers' problems',[3] the use of a love-juice to restore the lovers to their rightful pairs, the recurrent tension between reason and love[4] and the lovers' sense of their experiences after they wake up.[5] Cumulatively the arguments for Shakespeare's use of the romances are strong and I am less surprised than many seem to be by the idea that Shakespeare should return to a previously used source or carry into a later play echoes or memories from a work he seems to have known well when writing an earlier play. But that is not the same as suggesting that Shakespeare might have 'gained the entire conception of confused lovers from the Spanish pastoral'.[6]

Since, after all, he was working with Chaucer's 'Knight's Tale' close at hand he need only have squared the triangle of Palamon, Arcite and Emelye.[7] The onset of love is in

[1] See Judith M. Kennedy's outstanding edition of Yong, *A Critical Edition of Yong's Translation of George of Montemayor's 'Diana' and Gil Polo's 'Enamoured Diana'* (Oxford, 1968).

[2] Bullough, i. 206.

[3] Kennedy, p. xlviii.

[4] For example: 'true lovers for the most part fall to hate and neglect themselves, which is not only contrary to reason, but also to the law of nature. And this is the cause why they paint him blind, and void of all reason' (Montemayor, Book 4; Kennedy, pp. 156–7); compare Helena at 1.1.234–5.

[5] As they recover from enchanted sleep, they 'were all astonished at the sight one of another, and verily thought they were in a dream, standing like enchanted persons, and not believing their own eyes' (Gil Polo, Book 4; Kennedy, p. 376); compare 4.1.186–97.

[6] T. P. Harrison, Jr., 'Shakespeare and Montemayor's *Diana*', *Texas Studies in English*, 6 (1926), p. 102.

[7] On the link to Chaucer see particularly Larry S. Champion, *The Evolution of Shakespeare's Comedy* (Cambridge, Mass., 1970), pp. 47–59; Ann Thompson,

Chaucer as obsessive and immediate as it is under the influence of Oberon's drug and Lysander and Demetrius come to hate each other with a comic version of the fierce enmity of Palamon and Arcite. The latter's close friendship is transferred to Hermia and Helena, something recalled only when lost.

The crucial change is to Emelye. While Chaucer's two men are, as far as Emelye is concerned, essentially interchangeable, Hermia and Helena are absolutely and constantly clear which of the two men they love. The men may change Hermia for Helena or Helena for Hermia, following that notion of indistinguishability that the names suggest in their echo of Ovid's comment in *Ars Amatoria*: 'Scilicet Hermionen Helenae praeponere posses' ('Would you be able to prefer Hermione to Helena?', 2. 699). Emelye's commitment to chastity leaves her effectively passive as the narrative unfolds, forced to acquiesce in the process of choice that is made for her. In Shakespeare chastity is transmuted: it is both the threat of enforced virginity, Hermia compelled to become a nun, and also the possibility of chastity through marriage. What both Hermia and Helena deny, particularly when their lovers manifest it, is the notion of male promiscuity and inconstancy, the trait that Theseus, above all, embodies.

Alongside the sources in Chaucer and romance, though, the lovers need to be set against the courtship world of Elizabethan England. For the only crucial difference between the processes that confront the lovers in the play and those that would have confronted almost all the young people in the audience at the Globe lies in the vehemence and absolute nature of Egeus' interdiction. The initiative with establishing a couple, the definition of a relationship leading towards marriage, lay with young people in all but the very highest reaches of early modern English society.[1] They were subject to the advice and consent of parents and kin, their 'friends',[2]

Shakespeare's Chaucer (Liverpool, 1978), pp. 88–91; John S. Mebane, 'Structure, Source, and Meaning in *A Midsummer Night's Dream*', *Texas Studies in Literature and Language*, 24 (1982), pp. 255–70; E. Talbot Donaldson, *The Swan at the Well: Shakespeare Reading Chaucer* (New Haven, 1985), pp. 30–48.

[1] The best guide to courtship practices is John Gillis, *For Better, For Worse* (Oxford, 1985), chs. 1–3, esp. pp. 11–54.

[2] See 1.1.139 and n.

but the consent was rarely withheld, provided there was no financial or class impediment (as Lysander makes clear there is not, 1.1.99–100). Night-visits, like those Lysander makes to Hermia's window, were the standard way for couples to get to know each other better and would involve the exchange of gifts.[1] Such meetings were usually but by no means always conducted with parents' knowledge. They mark the transition from friendship to being defined, socially as well as privately, as lovers, as a couple moving slowly through the complex procedures that would lead to marriage. Lysander's anger and surprise at Egeus' actions would match comfortably with Elizabethan conventional behaviour.

With marriages usually taking place when individuals were well into their twenties, the move to defining a couple is a move from two forms of behaviour. First came the homosocial world of peer-group friendship, of the kind that Hermia and Helena had enjoyed. Rather than referring back to a childhood friendship, their relationship had begun early and would normally have continued until the development of particular heterosexual relationships disrupted it, as, from the beginning of the play, Hermia's friendship with Lysander takes her away from Helena.

The second was the remarkably innocent forms of heterosexual contact, the 'innocent polygamy' of kissing-games.[2] It is striking how much this sort of game is associated with festivals like St Valentine's Day or Maying, both of which are central to *A Midsummer Night's Dream*. Lysander met both Hermia and Helena to 'do observance to a morn of May' (1.1.167); it is not a private activity for a couple but a social celebration for a group, a time for friendship without too much intimacy, for in practice such events were remarkably chaste, whatever reformers may have argued. As Gillis sums it up, 'In game, festival, and dance, young single persons were able to transcend, if only for a moment, those boundaries, social as well as sexual, that dominated ordinary life' (p. 23). The courtship rituals of the play, the dance of the couples as they try to form themselves into fixed, unalterable pairs, were remarkably unremarkable. By the end of the play they have

---

[1] See Gillis, pp. 30–4.   [2] Gillis, p. 23.

made the final move: 'courtship created a personal relationship; wedding made a public institution'.[1] The events of the
wood finalize that transition, the distinctions between the men
and women that the lovers must sort out for themselves.

While audiences are encouraged to distinguish between
Helena and Hermia, since Shakespeare specifies the difference
in height for the two performers, they often find it difficult to
separate Lysander from Demetrius. Ralph Berry suggests that
the play's 'best epigraph, perhaps, is H. L. Mencken's. "Love:
the illusion that one woman is any different from another" '.[2]
But the play makes it far more difficult to tell that one man
is any different from another. Though, as Joan Stansbury
has shown,[3] the lovers are carefully distinguished by their
language, particularly in their forms of address, it is not an
effect that seems to matter all that much in production.[4] It
is another aspect of the play's investigation of love that the
loved object is completely self-sufficient and unique for the
lover. Neither Hermia nor Helena comments on the other's
choice of loved one but there is no moment at which either
of them could imagine exchanging their choice of men or
making sense of the men's willingness to do so. The influence
of the drug seems, in effect, an extension of normal male
practice, a habit of inconstancy that is ironically displaced
from its conventional place as an attribute of women. The
moon, a female deity, emblematizes inconstancy as its prin-
ciple, a process of endless change to which the frequency of
the menstrual cycle seemed to link women. But in the wood
dominated by the moon in *A Midsummer Night's Dream* it is
the men who manifest inconstancy.

The men do not even have that nostalgia of friendship
which Helena conjures up. Contradicted though it may be by
Helena's warning about Hermia, 'She was a vixen when she

[1] Gillis, p. 81.

[2] Ralph Berry, *Shakespeare's Comedies: Explorations in Form* (Princeton,
1972), p. 101.

[3] Joan Stansbury, 'Characterization of the Four Young Lovers in *A Midsummer Night's Dream*', SS 35 (Cambridge, 1982), pp. 57–63.

[4] Alexandru Darie's production for the Comedy Theatre of Bucharest (1991)
distinguished between a bearded, leather-clad, darkly evil Demetrius and a
wimpish Lysander whose attempts at being macho once drugged were extremely funny as well as a fine exploration of the modes of masculinity. But
the distinction seemed too strong for the text.

went to school' (3.2.324), Helena's long description, in the otherwise frenetic pace of the four-sided quarrelling of 3.2, of the shared childhood of the two women has an innocence that cannot quite be disrupted:

> So we grew together,
> Like to a double cherry: seeming parted,
> But yet an union in partition,
> Two lovely berries moulded on one stem.
>
> (3.2.208–11)

It echoes the strength of the bond between Titania and the changeling's mother, suggesting, fiercely, that the all-female bond has a perfect adequacy, a fulfilment that is disrupted by men:

> And will you rend our ancient love asunder,
> To join with men in scorning your poor friend?
>
> (3.2.215–16)[1]

The play's suggestions of disruption to patriarchal values lies strongly in such moments, a strength of friendship that the men have never had, other than in their clubbability in Act 5.

The effect of indistinguishability that all the lovers manifest from the outside and that the men are made to manifest from the inside is obviously enhanced by the lovers' substantive restriction by verse-form. It seems at times as if they are turned into puppets by their couplets, made to speak in particularly limited ways by the style imposed upon them. The kind of metrical virtuosity enjoyed by Robin is not available for them; instead it seems that even when their language moves into elaborate stanzaic forms (at 3.2.122–33, for instance) the very elaboration marks out the narrow and effectively trite emotional range they are usually forced to speak. The exceptions, like Hermia's dream, Helena's account of their friendship or her sad exhaustion ('sleep . . . | Steal me a while from my own company', 3.2.435–6), characteristically belong to the women and mark all the more emphatically how much of their language is designedly unlike this. When in the BBC production lengthy parts of 3.2 were spoken overlappingly,

[1] See Shirley Nelson Garner's argument that 'men need . . . to sever women's bonds with each other' (*'A Midsummer Night's Dream*: "Jack shall have Jill;/Nought shall go ill" ', *Women's Studies*, 9 (1981), p. 60).

all four lovers speaking at once at a number of points, the reason lay, I suspect, less with the offered explanation of the lovers' 'understandable confusion and ... to raise the comic tone of the scene still higher',[1] or with the apparent gain in a species of televisual realism but in directorial distrust of the length and evenness of the scene.

As well as this linguistic constriction the lovers are restricted by the action itself, forced to go through a series of permutations—twenty-three according to one count[2]—so that, as David Young comments, 'almost any discussion of them is apt to resort to diagrammatic figures'.[3] More sympathetically and marginally less mathematically the whole action of the play can be viewed as dance:

The plot is a pattern, a figure, rather than a series of events occasioned by human character and passion ... This dance-like structure makes it almost inevitable that the lovers should be as devoid of character as masquers or masque-presenters.[4]

This formalization of pattern has curious consequences for the audience's reaction to the events. Viewed as pattern the complications have the classic ambience of farce: a dispassionate and amused observation of events that are painful for the participants and painless for the observers. In effect the audience reproduces in its reaction to the lovers the male lovers' own reaction to the version of their story depicted as 'Pyramus and Thisbe'; in both cases the action is seen as 'subjectively painful, objectively comic'.[5] This quality of farce has often seemed to some critics overdone in production: Shaw complained, of Daly's production in 1895, that Ada Rehan, as Helena, 'condescends to arrant clowning';[6]

---

[1] David Snodin, 'The Text', in *A Midsummer Night's Dream: The BBC TV Shakespeare* (1981), p. 30.

[2] Mary E. Comtois, 'The Comedy of the Lovers in *A Midsummer Night's Dream*', *Essays in Literature*, 12 (1985), p. 21.

[3] David P. Young, *Something of Great Constancy* (New Haven, 1966), p. 94.

[4] Enid Welsford, *The Court Masque* (Cambridge, 1927), pp. 331–2.

[5] Trevor Griffiths's introduction to his translation of A. Chekhov, *The Cherry Orchard* (1978), p. vi; see also Alan Bellringer's analogy with 'the painless violence of filmed cartoons; they are shocks that will do no harm, but provide acceptable opportunities for recovery' ('The Act of Change in *A Midsummer Night's Dream*', *English Studies*, 64 (1983), p. 203).

[6] George Bernard Shaw, *Our Theatres in the Nineties* (Standard edition, 1932), i. 181.

Gordon Crosse complained of the lovers in Frank Benson's company in 1900 'there was rather too much farce & horse-play' (vol. 2 p. 110); and John Russell Brown complained of Peter Hall's production at Stratford in 1959, 'The presentation of young love held little interest for Peter Hall: he was content to direct the quartet to be young, foolish and clumsy . . . Their actions are consistently clownish'.[1] Significantly Hall cut all the lovers' lines after the exit of Theseus and the others (4.1.186–97), 'their quartet of amazement and determination' (see fig. 11).[2]

By contrast, Granville Barker's production at the Savoy in 1914 did away with the nineteenth-century tradition in which the men 'were a kind of pair of Dromios or Antipholuses' and the women 'quite too literally, two lovely berries moulded on one stem'.[3] This contrast between male farce and fair young English women at least recognized a difference in the play's treatment of the genders.

The farce of the lovers and the comedy of male inconstancy has, for the men at least, the excuse of the drug. Lysander's ability to understand what has happened is hampered by the way his adventures are a dream-state imposed on him by Robin. Demetrius is in an even odder state: a dream-state that has led him from mistaking to truly taking. For many critics and audiences, there is a residual unease about the fact that Demetrius does not receive an antidote. The waking state that he is in on the following morning leaves him still under the influence of the charm and some have felt that he is therefore not 'properly' in love with Helena. If the play moves from the world of Cupid to that of Diana ('Dian's bud o'er Cupid's flower', 4.1.72), Demetrius appears to stay in the world of Cupid, still charmed by the 'Flower of this purple dye, | Hit with Cupid's archery' (3.2.102–3).

But something has happened to the juice of the flower between its second and third applications; its properties have changed. Earlier it has had the same effect on both Lysander and Titania: each must immediately fall in love with whom-

[1] John Russell Brown, 'Three adaptations', *SS* 13 (Cambridge, 1960), p. 143.

[2] Ibid., p. 144.

[3] Review in *The Outlook*, quoted Dymkowski, p. 72.

11. The lovers watched by Oberon and Robin in Peter Hall's production, Stratford-upon-Avon, 1959.

soever they next see. Awake they would (and do) refuse the object of love created arbitrarily by the charm. But Demetrius' spell is different:

> When his love he doth espy,
> Let her shine as gloriously
> As the Venus of the sky.
> When thou wak'st, if she be by,
> Beg of her for remedy.

(3.2.105–9)

Demetrius' emotion changes because his loved object will now appear as Venus. The charm makes Helena appear to him glorious; it does not alter the object of his affection. The random effects of the drug on Lysander and Titania have become focussed to make Demetrius more intensely in love with the person with whom he is actually, in love. He had acquiesced in Egeus' wish that he should marry Hermia but his true love is Helena. The charm leaves him in an intensified state of his previous affection, not in a new state of unwanted and unwonted desire. As Demetrius will make clear to Theseus, he was actually betrothed to Helena before he saw Hermia (4.1.171) and was therefore, in English law, unable to marry Hermia in any case. His love for Helena is, as comedy prescribes, his 'natural taste' (4.1.173).

When Hermia leaves to follow the duke 'and my father' (4.1.194) she has spoken her last line in the play. Helena's voice has stopped after the recognition of Demetrius as 'Mine own and not mine own' (l. 191). Throughout Act 5 the women will never speak. Jonathan Goldberg, noting that after the night in the woods 'they return to Athens as bodies, married, barred from discourse', also emphasizes that the play

marks, but does not necessarily condone, their place in patriarchal culture. And in the last act, Hippolyta, also married, is hardly silent, and the fullness, range, complexity, and diversity of her vocality must be read in counterpoint to the silence of Hermia and Helena.[1]

Hippolyta's rich perception has to be set against the boorishness and patrician arrogance of Hermia's and Helena's husbands. Lysander and Demetrius share with Theseus an intellectual snobbishness that we are right to find distasteful; indeed, the feebleness and, at times, opacity of their wit underlines the extent of our sympathies with the workers. The lovers have been given the chance to apply their experience to 'living within the city once again, and this they do by reassuming the city's standards'.[2] The experience of the woods can lead the lovers towards each other but it cannot necessarily transform them in the cold light of normal social practice

[1] Jonathan Goldberg, 'Shakespearean Inscriptions: the Voicing of Power', in Patricia Parker and Geoffrey Hartman, eds., *Shakespeare and the Question of Theory* (1985), p. 134.

[2] Stephen Fender, *Shakespeare: 'A Midsummer Night's Dream'* (1968), p. 33.

in Theseus' court, as they take their cue from their ruler. The law against lovers has been set aside but the dream and its potency have been too quickly forgotten. We would like the lovers to recognize how far 'Pyramus and Thisbe' mirrors the tragic potential of their experience. But it is characteristic of dreams and their healing power that they can be quickly forgotten. The lovers can only be reunited in the terms defined by Robin, a folkloric pattern that turns the women into animals:

> Jack shall have Jill,
> Nought shall go ill,
> The man shall have his mare again,
> And all shall be well.
>
> (3.2.461–4)

The dream has consequence, the marriages have taken place, but the pattern of patriarchy has not altered.

Bottom

In *A Midsummer Night's Dream*'s transmutation of the residue of materials into its dream-world, no part of the plot has caused the adrenalin to pump through source-hunters' veins with the same thrill as Bottom's transformation at the hands of Robin. The search for men changed into asses, whether wholly or in part, has become a quest in which the notion of a single precise and fully adequate source becomes the critics' Holy Grail. But Shakespeare, as usual, transmutes a variety of 'sources', turning materials into contexts, structures of association which the play can choose to play with, develop and differ from, in its own particular pursuit of the meaning of Bottom's translation. As Deborah Baker Wyrick comments on asses, 'Shakespeare had at his disposal a tantalizingly slippery word, the connotations of which ranged from the sacred to the scurrilous'.[1]

The most obvious source is probably Lucius Apuleius' *The Golden Ass* in William Adlington's translation of 1566.[2]

---

[1] Deborah Baker Wyrick, 'The Ass Motif in *Errors*, and *A Midsummer Night's Dream*', *SQ* 33 (1982), p. 439.

[2] See, particularly, Sister M. Generosa, 'Apuleius and *A Midsummer Night's Dream*: Analogue or source, which?', *SP* 42 (1945), pp. 198–204; DeWitt

Lucius' transformation, by a mistaken use of an ointment, from man to ass is the consequence of his sexual desire as well as his curiosity. Adlington is concerned to moralize Lucius' change and, by terming his version 'the Metamorphosie', associate it firmly with the massive tradition of moralized commentaries on Ovid's *Metamorphoses*. As Adlington says in his preface,

Verily under the wrap of this transformation, is taxed the life of mortal men, when as we suffer our minds so to be drowned in the sensual lusts of the flesh, and the beastly pleasure thereof: (which aptly may be called, the violent confection of witches) that we lose wholly the use of reason and virtue (which properly should be in man) and play the parts of brute and savage beasts.[1]

But Adlington's moralizing tendencies and his occasional tendency to bowdlerize Apuleius' text cannot disguise the novel's gentle and genial fascination with the pleasures Lucius finds when transformed. His encounters with women, even when, as with the 'noble and rich Matron' of Corinth, the women's sexual fascination with the massive phallus of the ass might be paramount, have a tenderness and affection that is remarkably similar to Titania's words to Bottom in 4.1. While Lucius is worried about how to embrace the woman and whether she can accommodate his massive penis, conjuring up recurrently the encounter of Pasiphae and the bull that resulted in the conception of the Minotaur, her language comes from an alien world to his:

And I verily thought if I should hurt the woman by any kind of mean, I should be thrown out to the wild beasts: But in the mean season she kissed me, and looked on me with burning eyes, saying, 'I hold thee, my cony, I hold thee, my nops, my sparrow', and therewithall she eftsoons embraced my body round about, and had her pleasure with me . . .[2]

T. Starnes, 'Shakespeare and Apuleius', *PMLA* 60 (1945), pp. 1021–50; Annie-Paule Mielle de Prinsac, 'Le métamorphose de Bottom et *L'Ane d'Or*', *Études Anglaises*, 34 (1981), pp. 61–71; J. J. M. Tobin, *Shakespeare's Favorite Novel* (Lanham, Md., 1984), pp. 33–40. James A. S. McPeek has argued effectively for the resonance of the Cupid and Psyche episode in Apuleius with many aspects of Shakespeare's play ('The Psyche Myth and *A Midsummer Night's Dream*', *SQ* 23 (1972), pp. 69–79).

[1] William Adlington, *The xi Bookes of the Golden Asse* (1566), sigs. A2ᵛ–A3ʳ.
[2] Ibid., sig. 2F3ʳ.

Similarly when Lucius rescues a damsel in distress she re-
wards him in the way Titania and her fairies treat Bottom:

I will bravely dress the hairs of thy forehead, and then I will finely
comb thy mane, I will tie up thy rugged tail trimly, I will deck thee
round about with golden traps, in such sort, that thou shalt glitter
like the stars of the sky, I will bring thee daily in my apron the
kernels of nuts, and will pamper thee up with dainty delicates, I will
set store by thee ...[1]

There are other significant links between Adlington's Apuleius
and *A Midsummer Night's Dream*, particularly the resonances
between the myth of Cupid and Psyche and the events of the
fairies and the wood. But Lucius' ordeal—for, for all the
pleasant interludes, his experience of transformation is an
ordeal of beatings and humiliation—ends with his finally
eating the roses (a flower that appears frequently in *A Midsummer Night's Dream*) that will transform him back again to
a man after the intervention of the goddess Isis, who appears
to him in a dream. Adlington's description of her 'odoriferous
feet'[2] is temptingly reminiscent of Bottom's problems with
'odours' and 'odious' (3.1.77–9). Lucius ends as a servant of
the goddess; the experience of the transformation brings him
a sense of religious awareness and obligation.

In this final transformation, a transformation of Lucius'
moral and religious sense, the ass connects powerfully with
the long tradition of the Feast of the Ass, a recurrent and
significant form of serious mockery of the mass, found
throughout the whole gamut of European medieval church ceremonies.[3] Once such a tradition is invoked, together with the
image of the '*asinus portans mysterium*', the stupid ass carrying
a religious statue and assuming itself, not the statue, to be
the object of veneration,[4] Bottom's vision becomes immensely
portentous.

There are two major problems with treating Apuleius as a
complete and sufficient source: Lucius is completely trans-

---

[1] Ibid., sig. S1ᵛ.
[2] Ibid., sig. 2H1ᵛ.
[3] See, for example, E. K. Chambers, *The Medieval Stage*, 2 vols. (Oxford,
1903), i. 13–15; Enid Welsford, *The Fool* (1935), p. 200; Mikhail Bakhtin,
Rabelais and His World, trans. H. Iswolsky (Cambridge, Mass., 1968), p. 78;
Beryl Rowland, *Animals with Human Faces* (1974), p. 22.
[4] See Deborah Baker Wyrick, p. 433.

formed whereas Bottom only wears an ass's head and Lucius is all too painfully aware of his transformation whereas Bottom is not. Both features are common in productions of the play. Robert Lepage's version at the Royal National Theatre in 1992, for instance, gave Bottom four hooves. When, in Elijah Moshinsky's production for the BBC Shakespeare, his Bottom (Brian Glover) looks in a lake and is horrified when he sees his reflection, the whole subsequent course of the play is altered. Something similar happens when James Cagney as Bottom in the Reinhardt–Dieterle film (1935) is so upset by his awareness of the transformation that he collapses against a tree weeping. But Bottom always treats his change as something natural and unworrying; he shows, quite simply, no awareness that anything has changed. He does not need to adapt to his new circumstances and has no memory of once being more normally and completely human. He will, of course, be aware when he wakes up in 4.1 that he *was* different during the night ('Methought I was, and methought I had', 4.1.205 and note)—Cagney's Bottom, terrified by his memories, checked his reflection in a pond and was hugely relieved to see his normality—but, while transformed, no awareness of a different past self troubles Bottom's placidity.[1] Those critics, of whom Jan Kott has been the most influential,[2] who see the transformation as reflecting above all the phallic associations of the ass, or those productions which turn the scene into a phallic celebration build on something the text never begins to suggest,[3] make their own associations

[1] De Prinsac neatly contrasts 'conscience de Lucius, naiveté de Bottom' (p. 69).

[2] Kott affirms categorically that 'Oberon openly announces that as a punishment Titania will sleep with a beast' and that 'in this nightmarish summer night, the ass does not symbolize stupidity. Since antiquity and up to the Renaissance the ass was credited with the strongest sexual potency and among all the quadrupeds is supposed to have the longest and hardest phallus' ('Titania and the Ass's Head' in *Shakespeare Our Contemporary* (1967), pp. 182–3). Kott's ideas are far from dead: see, for example, W. Thomas MacCary's extraordinary notion that Shakespeare 'restores . . . the essential concern of the original story: the insatiable sexual desire of women, their preference for beasts with huge phalluses to men' (*Friends and Lovers* (New York, 1985), p. 142).

[3] Peter Brook turned Titania's exit with Bottom at the end of 3.1 into a massive parodic wedding, accompanied by Mendelssohn's wedding march (written for the weddings in Act 5), with Bottom's ass stimulated to a huge

dominate anything apparent in the naïve and unsexual way Bottom's language actually suggests he behaves. As William Empson chooses to emphasize,

As to whether it is 'bestiality' to love Bottom, many a young girl on the sands at Margate has said to her donkey, unblamed: 'I kiss thy fair large ears, my gentle joy.' If the genital action is in view, nobody denies that the genitals of Bottom remain human.[1]

What is so remarkable about Titania's night with Bottom is not a subdued, suppressed sexual bestiality that has only been properly uncovered in the twentieth century but rather the innocence which transforms something that might so easily have been full of animal sexuality into something touchingly naïve. It is no more erotic than Oberon, 'in the shape of Corin', 'Playing on pipes of corn, and versing love | To amorous Phillida' (2.1.66–8). The innocent tradition of productions of *A Midsummer Night's Dream* as the school-play Shakespeare *par excellence* does not need subverting. Whatever Shakespeare's awareness of the phallic ass, the association is never allowed to blossom in the play. In this dream, sexuality is diminished rather than intensified.

There are, though, many candidates as sources for partial transformations.[2] Reginald Scot narrates a number of different transformations into asses in *The Discovery of Witchcraft* (1584), a work with a number of references to Robin Goodfellow. Scot, prejudging his readers' scepticism, announces

If I affirm that with certain charms and popish prayers I can set a horse or an ass's head upon a man's shoulders, I shall not be believed ... And yet if *J. Bap. Neap.* experiments be true, it is no difficult matter to make it seem so. (Bk. 13, ch. 19, p. 315).

Scot goes on to give the recipe for boiling an ass's head and instructs the reader to 'anoint the heads of the standers-by, and they shall seem to have ... ass's heads'. He adds that 'if

erection represented by an actor's arm. Moshinsky's Bottom was scratched to a heaving, hee-hawing orgasm in 4.1, a curious notion of the masturbatory efficacy of scratching.

[1] William Empson, *Essays on Shakespeare* (Cambridge, 1986), p. 229.

[2] In the prose Faust-book, *The History of the Damnable Life and Deserved Death of Doctor John Faustus* (1592), Faustus 'made that every one had an Asses head on, with great and long eares' (ch. 43) as part of a banquet entertainment. I cannot see this as a significant resonance for Shakespeare.

that which is called *Sperma* in any beast be burned, and anybody's face therewithal anointed, he shall seem to have the like face as the beast had' (pp. 315–16). Significantly Scot's emphasis is on a seeming transformation, not an actual one, placing the metamorphosis in the spectator's vision, not in an empirical reality.

More intriguing is his discussion of the story he narrates of the young Englishman turned into an ass by a witch for three years while on Cyprus. Scot worries 'where was the young man's own shape all these three years' (Bk. 5, ch. 4, p. 97) and answers his own question in the margin: 'His shape was in the woods: where else should it be?', an evocative suggestion remembering the location of Bottom's change. This man-ass is also like Bottom in that he 'must either eat hay, or nothing' (p. 99).

But Scot also follows Bodin in believing that '(his reason only reserved) he was truly transubstantiated into an ass; so as there must be no part of a man but reason remaining in this ass' (p. 99). This concern about the human faculty of reason and its irrelevance to an ass connects not only to Bottom's sage comments on reason and love while he is at least part-ass but is also central to the whole tradition of asses and folly. In Brant's *Das Narrenschiff*, the main source for the 'ship of fools' tradition, there was an engraving of a wheel of fortune showing men changing into asses and ironically placing the full ass as a triumphant figure at the pinnacle of the wheel.[1] As Barclay, Brant's translator, asserts, 'ass's ears for our follies a livery is'.[2]

The most brilliant exploration of this notion of the ass and folly is in Erasmus' *Praise of Folly*, the pinnacle of the *encomium moriae* tradition. Erasmus' Folly turns his whole audience into people as asinine as Midas, inviting them

to bestow on me your ears a while. I mean not those ears ye carry with you to sermons, but those ye give to players, to jesters, and to fools, yea those (hardly) wherewith my friend *Midas* whilom hearkened to the rural god *Pan*.[3]

---

[1] See fig. 12 (from Sebastian Brant, *Ship of Fools*, translated by James Barclay (1509), fol. 77ʳ).

[2] Barclay, quoted Wyrick, p. 436.

[3] Sir Thomas Chaloner's 1549 translation as *The Praise of Folly*, ed. Clarence H. Miller (EETS, 1965), p. 8.

10 ¶ Dayly proue by example and euydence
That many be made folys mad and ignorant
By the brode worlde/puttynge/trust and confydence
In fortunes whele vnsure and inconstant
Some assay the whele thynkynge it pleasant
But whyle they to clym vp haue pleasour and delyte
Theyr fete them faylyth so fall they in the myre

12. Sebastian Brant, *Ship of Fools*, translated by James Barclay
(1509).

Erasmus is recurrently concerned with the ass-ness of men;
one segment of society after another is described as 'ass-like'.[1]
He is also, particularly in Chaloner's translation, concerned
with plays; Erasmus' '*publicos ludos*' become 'a midsummer
watch, or a stage play'.[2] Not least, as a link, Erasmus quotes
the same passage of I Corinthians that Bottom mangles
synaesthetically in awakening from his vision.[3] Erasmus' intellectual pyrotechnics convince the reader of the folly of
wisdom and the wisdom of folly. It is the wise fool who will
truly understand both the reality of the world and the other
reality of divine truth, Bottom who may have the clearest
conception of the human and divine experience the mortals

[1] Ibid., p. 45.   [2] Ibid., p. 33.   [3] Ibid., pp. 127–8.

undergo during the night. Erasmus' virtuoso mental paradoxes, his Folly's twistings and turnings are as subtle as the
paradoxes that surround Bottom and frequently seem, at the
least, analogous or parallel.[1]

Erasmus' celebratory mockery of Folly frequently associates
human folly with Midas whose acquisition of ass's ears[2] for
preferring the music of Pan over Apollo stood both as an
association of the ass with bad musical taste[3] and as the
iconic epitome of bad judgement.[4] Like Bottom, whose taste
in music runs no higher than 'the tongs and the bones'
(4.1.29), Midas cannot see the worth of Apollo's music.
Shakespeare dramatizes the contrast in the successive musics
of 4.1, the change from this 'Rural music' (4.1.29.1) to the
'still music' (4.1.82.1) and dance music (4.1.84) which the
fairies choose.

Midas' plight had been narrated in Ovid's *Metamorphoses*
(Golding, 11. 94–216) and had been the subject of a play by
Lyly (performed 1590, published 1592).[5] Lyly's Midas is only
too painfully aware of the partial nature of the change: 'Ah
Mydas, why was not thy whole body metamorphosed, and
there might have been no part left of *Mydas*?',[6] an awareness
of change like Lucius', but again unlike Bottom's.

By this point it should be clear that the notion of finding a
particular, defined and adequate source is far less important
than seeing how the associative resonances of the concept of
an ass and of transformation into one might function in

[1] See also Thelma N. Greenfield, '*A Midsummer Night's Dream* and *The Praise of Folly*', *Comparative Literature*, 20 (1968), pp. 236–44.

[2] Unlike Bottom, Midas only acquires ears, not a whole head, but Titania's kissing Bottom's ears at 4.1.4 might just remind an audience of Midas' more limited metamorphosis.

[3] See Helen Adolf, 'The Ass and the Harp', *Speculum*, 25 (1950), pp. 49–57 .

[4] Wyrick gives an example from Whitney's emblem-book as '*Perversa judicia*', p. 434.

[5] Lyly's hunting scene in *Midas* has at least one passage that seems to prefigure the hunting scene in *A Midsummer Night's Dream*: 'Such as you are unworthy to be hounds, much less huntsmen, that know not when a hound is fleet, fair flewed, and well hanged, being ignorant of the deepness of a hound's mouth, and the sweetness' (*Works*, iii. 147; compare Theseus at 4.1.118–25). It is most likely that they share a common source in Golding's Ovid.

[6] *Works*, iii. 144.

relation to the play. Two further suggestions rich in suggestion meet here.

Along one track Bottom's transformation into a half-man,
half-animal figure is reminiscent of a character never referred
to directly in the play but closely tied to the play's mythological context, the Minotaur.[1] While many of the constituent
parts of the myth are present, Shakespeare never offers a
direct link to Theseus' killing of the monster at the heart of
the Cretan labyrinth. The play talks directly of 'mazes'
(2.1.99) but they are turf mazes, not the one Daedalus constructed. Ariadne is mentioned as one of Theseus' abandoned
lovers (2.1.80) but that is hardly enough in itself to evoke
her help to Theseus in finding his way out of the labyrinth.
Bottom's transformation is into a half-ass, not a half-bull.

The myth of the Minotaur can then only function as a
structure of analogy and difference, glimpsed fleetingly in the
play but never sufficient to structure and control it. Seeing
the wood as labyrinthine, as it plainly is for the lovers, does
not mean therefore that the monster at its centre must be
murdered. Invoking the Minotaur, even for a sensitive critic,
is to see the myth itself paradoxically and perhaps mockingly
transformed: 'Bottom is both the monster of this labyrinth
and the thread leading the way out of it'.[2] The terror and
destructiveness that surrounds the image of the Minotaur is
only too glaringly irrelevant to the benign and gentle harm-
lessness of Bottom. Even the terror of the labyrinth itself is
only superficially similar to the terrors of the labyrinth of the
wood, a maze which proves beneficial to the individuals who
tread its paths. Yet it seems both permissible and even necessary to see how one of Theseus' greatest exploits is so partially,
so inadequately evoked by the play, even a play that mentions
some of his other adventures (for example, at 5.1.44–5). The
marginalization of the Minotaur could define how our attention is really to be directed.

[1] See David Ormerod, '*A Midsummer Night's Dream*: the Monster in the
Labyrinth', *Sh Studs* 11 (1978), pp. 39–52; M. E. Lamb, '*A Midsummer Night's
Dream*: The Myth of Theseus and the Minotaur', *Texas Studies in Literature and
Language*, 21 (1979), pp. 478–91; on mazes, see also T. M. Evans, 'The
Vernacular Labyrinth: Mazes and Amazement in Shakespeare and Peele',
Shakespeare-Jahrbuch (West) (1980), pp. 165–73.

[2] Lamb, p. 481.

The second track sees Bottom's transformation, a type of change which Adlington was quite happy to dub a metamorphosis, as some sort of second-level metamorphosis, a metamorphosis of a metamorphosis, in some ways the play's apotheosis of its fascination with and delight in transformability, the possibilities of metamorphic change. When Leonard Barkan suggests that 'the meeting of Bottom and Titania . . . is the fullest example in Renaissance literature of the Diana and Actaeon story',[1] the suggestion, superficially ridiculous, seems, precisely through its oddity, to express the miraculous nature of the change Shakespeare explores in the play. Ovid had narrated the metamorphosis of Actaeon into a stag, torn apart by his own hounds, punished by Diana for the accident of seeing her naked while bathing, in Book 3 of *Metamorphoses* (Golding, 3. 160–304). The narrative is one of the occasions on which he uses the name Titania, 'Titan's daughter', here a name for Diana herself (Ovid, 3. 173).

Bottom, as the ultimately versatile actor, is himself a shape-changer, a master of metamorphosis; he can become Pyramus, Thisbe or a lion at will, at least to his own satisfaction. Unlike Ovid's luckless hunter, Shakespeare's Actaeon is metamorphosed before he sees his Titania. He has already become a dramatized visual metaphor for his own stupidity. But, in this wood of transformations already transformed, the hounds are safely transferred to Theseus, marking the ending of the night's dream-world with their cry, a concord of discord.

There is a further resource on which Shakespeare calls, the theatre itself. Wearing animal masks has a long folk-tradition behind it. As Muriel Bradbrook suggests, Bottom's ass's head is 'the usual masque for a country "antic"; he is properly disguised for a "rite of May" '.[2] This rural practice has other versions in medieval theatre. Willis, recalling seeing an interlude, *The Cradle of Security*, in the 1570s, describes a king sung to sleep and being transformed with 'a vizard like a swine's snout upon his face'.[3] Other interludes include trans-

---

[1] Leonard Barkan, 'Diana and Actaeon: the Myth as Synthesis', *ELR* 10 (1980), pp. 317–59.

[2] M. C. Bradbrook, *Shakespeare: The Poet in his World* (1978), p. 115.

[3] R. Willis, *Mount Tabor or Private Exercises of a Penitent Sinner* (1639), p. 111; see also n. to 3.1.97.1.

formations during sleep: in *The Marriage of Wit and Science* (1569), Wit's clothes are changed with Ignorance while he sleeps; in *A Marriage of Wit and Wisdom* (1579), Wit, again lulled asleep by women singing, has a fool's bauble put on his head and his face sooted.[1] In the Cappers' play in the Chester Mystery Cycle, Balaam rides on his ass and, as the stage-direction states, '*hic oportet aliquis transformiari in speciem asinae*', somebody has to appear in the shape of an ass.[2] Animal masks were common in other forms of European medieval theatre, in entertainments by mummers and in parades. These masks, the pictorial evidence suggests, were either whole-head masks or, more often, masks that allowed part or all of the face to be seen, often through the gaping mouth.[3] Later Inigo Jones, too, found a need for a costume with an ass-head.[4]

In performance the ass-head is carefully placed as one of three masks which are used by the workers: Flute is reassured by Quince that he can play Thisbe in a mask (1.2.45); Snug as Lion is usually equipped with some sort of head-piece in performance, with 'half his face . . . seen through the lion's neck' (3.1.33–4). Bottom's is a theatrical mask which becomes the actor's head, a role that cannot be put off at will. One of the earliest records of a performance of the play connects the ass-head and the actor, denying the disjunction of actor and role in the forms of punishment: when, in 1631, the play was performed on a Sunday for the Bishop of Lincoln, the actor

[1] See J. R. Moore, *The Transformation of Bottom*, Indiana University Studies, 13 (1926), p. 46.

[2] *The Chester Mystery Cycle*, ed. R. M. Lumiansky and David Mills (EETS, 1974), p. 88. In Thomas Nashe's *Summer's Last Will and Testament* (performed in 1592), a play whose interest in the cycle of the seasons recalls Titania's speech, Bacchus enters 'riding upon an ass trapped in ivy' (*Works*, ed. McKerrow, iii. 264), though there is no indication whether this ass is human or animal.

[3] See Meg Twycross and Sarah Carpenter, 'Masks in Medieval English Theatre: the Mystery Plays', *Medieval English Theatre*, 3 (1981), pp. 7–44 and 69–113, esp. fig. 4 (animal-headed mummers, Flemish, *c.*1340), fig. 5 (lion parade helmet, Aragonese, 1460s) and fig. 6 (mummers with bird-heads, French, *c.*1540), and their 'Materials and Methods of Mask-making', *Medieval English Theatre*, 4 (1982), pp. 28–47.

[4] Audrey Yoder, *Animal Analogies in Shakespeare's Character Portrayal* (New York, 1947), p. 89; for Jones's design for 'an ass like a pedant' in *Tempe Restored* (1632) see Stephen Orgel and Roy Strong, *Inigo Jones: The Theatre of the Stuart Court* (1973), fig. 229, p. 492.

who played Bottom 'and did in such a brutish manner act the same with an Ass's head' was put in the stocks,

attired with his ass head, and a bottle of hay set before him, and this subscription on his breast:

> Good people I have played the beast
> And brought ill things to pass:
> I was a man, but thus have made
> Myself a silly Ass.[1]

In most productions the ass-head is usually little more than a comic prop: Gordon Crosse praised Mr Weir as Bottom with 'a most mirth-provoking ass's head with rolling eyes, wagging ears, and moving jaws'[2] and an unnamed Oxford student who 'was most amusing when, safely hidden away under the mechanical ass's head, he let that act for him'.[3] But for Samuel Phelps as Bottom in the 1860s it was much more: 'the movements of the head were not used to provoke laughter, but only to aid in the actor's expression of character'.[4] In a letter to his wife while on tour to Liverpool in 1867 he wrote,

I am very glad I have brought the Donkey's head, for though they have a new one it is not good. It is a most *impudent* looking ass instead of the *stupid* sleek thing it should be for Bottom. It looks impossible that it should *sleep*. I should be dreadfully annoyed if I had to wear it.[5]

There is a risk that Bottom becomes wholly identified with his transformation, nothing but the man metamorphosed into an ass. It would, of course, be wrong to take Bottom at his self-valuation, though, as Theseus advised, 'If we imagine no worse of them than they of themselves, they may pass for excellent men' (5.1.214–15). But the reductiveness of assuming Bottom to be only an ass is a patronizing contempt that

---

[1] See E. K. Chambers, *William Shakespeare*, 2 vols. (Oxford, 1930), ii. 348–50. There is some doubt about the exact date and whether the play was indeed *A Midsummer Night's Dream* but no other play with an ass-head has been proposed.

[2] For Frank Benson's company, January 1890, vol. 1, p. 2.

[3] February 1899, vol. 2, p. 74.

[4] Shirley S. Allen, *Samuel Phelps and Sadler's Wells Theatre* (Middletown, Conn., 1971), p. 185.

[5] Ibid.

belongs with many of the other comments made about the performers in 'Pyramus and Thisbe'. Bottom is foolish, vain, and arrogant; he is also gentle, lovable and admirable. The comedy lies in the disjunction between himself and the circumstances in which he finds himself, his existence beyond the bounds of his own competence. After all, we never see any of the Athenian workers at work, though Peter Brook's Snug the Joiner displayed his carpentry talents in the manufacture of the lion's mask, a neat cupboard with two doors to reveal his face. Bottom may be a bad actor but then, unlike the actor who plays the part of Bottom, he is not a professional.

As J. B. Priestley commented, in the most brilliant and sympathetic description of Bottom, this is a man with a 'passion for the drama itself . . . the creative artist is stirring in the soul of Bottom'.[1] Bottom's confidence may be 'so gigantic that it becomes ridiculous' but he has an artist's vision ('vanity and a soaring imagination are generally inseparable'[2]): 'There was a poet somewhere in this droll weaver and so he came to a poet's destiny'.[3] Through Priestley's genuine admiration for the character, the comedy of disjunction is fully realized: Bottom is 'a trades-unionist among butterflies, a ratepayer in Elfland. Seen thus, he is droll precisely because he is a most prosaic soul called to a most romantic destiny'.[4]

It is precisely this prosaic quality, his down-to-earth ordinariness, that makes Bottom so naturally an ass. Whatever the loading of referential meaning which the ass-head may invoke, this ass is primarily concerned to munch hay, have his head scratched, fall asleep. Bottom, as an ass, is suddenly devoid of ambition. He is too busy being an ass to be a symbol. The experience is a comfortable one: 'To Bottom, as to Shakespeare, all these beings, fairy, heroic or human, are equally congenial'.[5] The man-ass who becomes so quickly unconcerned to find himself loved by the queen of the fairies is also the man who turns to speak to Duke Theseus himself in a

---

[1] J. B. Priestley, *The English Comic Characters* (1925), p. 8.
[2] Ibid., p. 11.
[3] Ibid., p. 16.
[4] Ibid., p. 5.
[5] John Palmer, *Comic Characters of Shakespeare* (1947), p. 93.

self-confident and unabashed spirit of helpful correction, even while his fellow-performers, in many productions, are in paroxysms of terror at the presumption of answering the Duke back: 'No, in truth, sir, he should not. "Deceiving me" is Thisbe's cue . . . You shall see, it will fall pat as I told you' (5.1.182–5). Bottom achieves, after all, an ambition of which many have dreamed.

One of the dreamers, ambitious for a fairy queen, was Chaucer's Sir Thopas, the comic knight of Chaucer's own parodic Canterbury tale:

> Me dremed al this nyght, pardee,
> An elf-queene shal my lemman be
>   And slepe under my goore.
>   An elf-queene wol I love, ywis,
> For in this world no womman is
>   Worthy to be my make
>   In towne
>
> ('Sir Thopas', ll. 787–93)

Chaucer's 'Sir Thopas' and Shakespeare's 'Pyramus and Thisbe' share a number of characteristics: 'in either case, a master of literary form makes fun of old-fashioned and primitive examples of that form while he is himself engaged in writing it, and then assigns his parody to the most naive and most naively self-confident of artists'.[1] Bottom, the artist rather than the hero of the parody, achieves the elf-queen that Sir Thopas only dreamed of.

But Bottom is not sure when he awakes whether what he experienced was a dream. Shakespeare's generosity towards Bottom makes him the one who remembers the 'dream' best. If his attempts to make tentative sense of his vision are comic, it is a comedy in which the audience shares his wonder. Though we know more than he does—or at least more clearly—we are not superior to him, even envying him the experience which he has undergone and is struggling to recall.

It is, however, dangerously easy to overvalue this 'rare vision' (4.1.202). Frank Kermode, the most influential exponent of the visionary critics, sees Bottom's dream as the exact opposite of the lovers' experience:

[1] E. Talbot Donaldson, *The Swan at the Well: Shakespeare Reading Chaucer* (New Haven, 1985), pp. 9–10.

this is the contrary interpretation of blind love; the love of God or of Isis, a love beyond the power of the eyes. To Pico, to Cornelius Agrippa, to Bruno . . . this exaltation of the blindness of love was both Christian and Orphic . . . Bottom is there to tell us that the blindness of love, the dominance of the mind over the eye, can be interpreted as a means to grace as well as to irrational animalism; that the two aspects are, perhaps, inseparable.[1]

It is not the strange and exalted nature of Bottom's vision that gives me pause so much as the assumption of its connection with religious experiences and the manifestation of grace. When Erasmus' Folly quotes from St Paul, he shares 'the essential outlines of . . . these comic-Christian perspectives on faith and folly'.[2] Faith and folly and the unspeakable nature of the revelation of the divine are closely allied in Christian thought and both St Paul's Epistles to the Corinthians are full of passages pinpointing the links. Erasmus' description of the state of mind of those who return to normality, having tasted 'this said felicity', has strong resonances with the experiences of both the lovers and Bottom:

In sort that when a little after they come again to their former wits, they deny plainly they wot where they became, or whether they were then in their bodies, or out of their bodies, waking or sleeping: remembering also as little, either what they heard, saw, said, or did than, saving as it were through a cloud, or by a dream[3]

But Bottom does not simply quote St Paul at 1 Corinthians 2: 9–10, he garbles the biblical text: 'The eye of man hath not heard, the ear of man hath not seen, man's hand is not able to taste, his tongue to conceive, nor his heart to report what my dream was' (4.1.207–10). The garbling may be taken, of course, as the complex synaesthetic experience of the mystic who sees visions but it is more likely to be the kind of mistake to which Bottom and his fellow-workers are prone. There is comedy here as well as vision. In any case, Bottom's vision has not been of Christian grace but of a night with an Ovidian

[1] Frank Kermode, 'The Mature Comedies', in John Russell Brown and Bernard Harris, eds., *Early Shakespeare*, Stratford-upon-Avon Studies, 3 (1961), p. 219.

[2] R. Chris Hassel, Jr., *Faith and Folly in Shakespeare's Romantic Comedies* (Athens, Ga., 1980), p. 15.

[3] Erasmus, trans. Chaloner, p. 128.

fairy-queen. The invocation of grace to describe Bottom's experience is excessive and misguided, making religious something that is equally miraculous in its genuine form: a union with another world, a union of top and bottom, a union of ease and comfort.

'Pyramus and Thisbe'

Whatever else Shakespeare may or may not have been reading while he was writing *A Midsummer Night's Dream*, he was certainly reading Golding and Chaucer and in both he found ample narrative material for the plot of 'Pyramus and Thisbe'. But he also needed a style or styles to parody and his sources for that have always seemed problematic. There has been no shortage of suggestions but no clear idea of what a suggested source should provide.

It may be that, for instance, the French tradition of Pyramus and Thisbe stories places greater emphasis on the role of the lovers' parents[1] but there is no indication why Shakespeare should have gone to such obscure sources when his own work on *Romeo and Juliet* had made him only too aware of the relationship between parents and tragic young lovers. George Pettie had, in any case, already linked the two narratives in his collection *A Petite Palace* (1576), warning that 'such presiness [compulsion] of parents brought *Pyramus and Thisbe* to a woeful end, *Romeo* and *Julietta* to untimely death'.[2] Similarly the long series of articles for and against Shakespeare's use of an obscure poem by Thomas Moffett, *The Silkworms and their Flies* (published in 1599, after *A Midsummer Night's Dream* was written),[3] rarely troubled to answer

[1] W. G. Van Emden, 'Shakespeare and the French Pyramus and Thisbe Tradition, or Whatever Happened to Robin Starveling's Part?', *Forum for Modern Language Studies*, 11 (1975), pp. 193–204.

[2] Quoted by Kenneth Muir, *The Sources of Shakespeare's Plays* (1977), p. 68.

[3] The source was first proposed by Margaret L. Farrand, 'An Additional Source for *A Midsummer Night's Dream*', *SP* 27 (1930), pp. 233–43; rejected by Douglas Bush, 'The Tedious Brief Scene of Pyramus and Thisbe', *MLN* 46 (1931), pp. 144–7; supported by A. S. T. Fisher, 'The Source of Shakespeare's Interlude of Pyramus and Thisbe: A Neglected Poem', *N & Q* 194 (1949), pp. 400–2, by Kenneth Muir, 'Pyramus and Thisbe: A Study in Shakespeare's Method', *SQ* 5 (1954), pp. 141–53, and in his *The Sources of*

Douglas Bush's point, early in the argument: 'Would a popular dramatist incorporate in a play a burlesque of a poem which he and a few others knew in manuscript?'[1]

The answer is, of course, that he would not have done if the comedy depended on the audience's recognition of the source parodied, if, that is, the parody itself was the object. But he might well have done so simply because the resultant parodic form was itself funny. Few critics, as they search for sources, seem to remember or care that modern audiences laugh almost unfailingly at 'Pyramus and Thisbe'[2] without having read either Golding or Chaucer, let alone Thomson, Moffett, French narratives or any of the other suggestions. In addition, audiences appear to have less difficulty than scholars in recognizing that 'Pyramus and Thisbe' has a complex and powerful meaning within *A Midsummer Night's Dream*, far more important than any local parodic effect.

Golding's dedicatory epistle, bringing to bear the whole massive tradition of '*Ovide moralisé*', emphasizes the usefulness of all the books of the *Metamorphoses* for moral understanding:

> . . . in all are pithy, apt and plain
> Instructions which import the praise of virtues and the shame
> Of vices, with the due rewards of either of the same.
>
> (Epistle, ll. 64–6)

Golding's summary of the moral of Pyramus and Thisbe warns

> The piteous tale of Pyramus and Thisbe doth contain;
> The heady force of frantic love whose end is woe and pain.
>
> (Epistle, ll. 109–10)

George Sandys's emphasis, in a later translation of *Metamorphoses* (1621) but one whose notes are densely responsive to the corpus of Ovidian commentary, is primarily on the lesson for parents: the lovers 'whose wretched ends upbraid those

---

Shakespeare's Plays (1977), pp. 73–6; and finally laid to rest by Katherine Duncan-Jones who proved in 'Pyramus and Thisbe: Shakespeare's Debt to Moffett Cancelled', *RES*, NS 32 (1981), pp. 296–301, that Moffett's poem was not written until after *Dream*.

[1] Bush, p. 144.

[2] Elijah Moshinsky's BBC production managed to make the performance less funny than anyone else, a drably over-serious event which emphasized sympathetically the performers' serious intentions at the expense of representing their comic results.

parents, who measure their children's by their own out-worn and deaded affections; in forcing them to serve their avarice or ambition in their fatal marriages ... more cruel therein to their own, than either the malice of foes or fortune'.[1] For Sandys and his sources the responsibility lay with parents who, like Egeus, attempt to control children. Along such a line 'Pyramus and Thisbe' would have warned what might have happened had Egeus not been overruled. But Shakespeare's concern is with the actions of the lovers, not their parents.

As usual with Ovid, the metamorphosis takes place at the end of the narrative: Pyramus' blood turns the mulberry-tree's leaves black and its berries a 'deep dark purple colour' (Golding 4. 252) and, ever after, 'when the fruit is throughly ripe, the Berry is bespecked | With colour tending to black' (Golding 4. 199–200). Golding's translation of the blood-bath is only slightly more comic than Ovid's Latin: 'the blood did spin on high | As when a conduit pipe is cracked, the water bursting out | Doth shoot it self a great way off and pierce the air about' (4. 147–9). But Shakespeare rejected this opportunity for comedy—though a production might well try a trick fountain at this point—primarily because his approach to this metamorphosis had already been completed. The botanical colour change to purple is copied directly but is now the result of Cupid's bad aim, as Oberon narrates in 2.1, when his arrow hits 'a little western flower', turning the milk-white pansy to one 'purple with love's wound' (2.1,166–7). As Leonard Barkan brilliantly suggests,

Like many Renaissance Ovidians, Shakespeare is more interested in transformation as a cause than transformation as an effect. So he transfers the metamorphosis from the end of the story to the beginning: instead of a memorial via the oozing blood of the dead lovers, he offers a cause for the passionate blood of the living lovers. The now-purple flower is itself an emblem of metamorphosis by love and, more important, it becomes the inspiration for the metamorphoses of passion.[2]

---

[1] George Sandys, *Ovid's Metamorphosis Englished, Mythologized, and Represented in Figures*, ed. Karl K. Hulley and Stanley T. Vandersall (Lincoln, Nebr., 1970), p. 202.

[2] Leonard Barkan, *The Gods Made Flesh* (New Haven, 1986), p. 257.

Whatever else Golding offered, the metamorphosis is itself metamorphosed.

Golding certainly offered considerable resource for the comedy of archaic, inappropriate and awkward language of the type that 'Pyramus and Thisbe' could use. Shakespeare does not need to be trivializing or undervaluing his much-loved Golding to find that, for instance, his repeated use of 'did' is a stylistic tic worth imitating to represent the lurches of Quince's verse-style when Lion

> The trusty Thisbe coming first by night
> Did scare away, or rather did affright;
> And as she fled, her mantle she did fall,
> Which Lion vile with bloody mouth did stain.
>
> $(5.1.139–42)^1$

However much Shakespeare may have admired Golding, at moments such as the lovers' apostrophes to the wall, 'O thou envious wall' (4. 91), Golding is both comic in himself and an echo of earlier or other comic moments in versions of the story. Chaucer's 'Legend of Thisbe', in *The Legend of Good Women*, is as much source here, 'Alas, thou wikkede wal!' (l. 756), though Shakespeare ignores the rich comic possibility given by Chaucer's Pyramus' apostrophe to Thisbe's 'wympel' (ll. 847–9).

Muir claims 'Shakespeare took very little from Chaucer . . ., the only [version] which was not in some way ludicrous'.[2] But the tone of Chaucer's version is notoriously difficult to judge: 'he somehow manages to leave it more open to the possibility of ridicule than Ovid had'.[3] There is an implicit

---

[1] For the parallel, see Muir, *Sources*, p. 70. For an argument of the importance of Golding as source of the parody, see Robert F. Willson, Jr., 'Golding's *Metamorphoses* and Shakespeare's Burlesque Method in *A Midsummer Night's Dream*', *ELN* 7 (1969), pp. 18–25; for an over-elaborate defence of Golding against the charge that Shakespeare might have found him at all funny, see Anthony Brian Taylor, 'Golding's Ovid, Shakespeare's "Small Latine", and the Real Object of Mockery in "Pyramus and Thisbe" ', *SS 42* (Cambridge, 1990), pp. 53–64. For Shakespeare's use of Ovid in Latin see Niall Rudd, 'Pyramus and Thisbe in Shakespeare and Ovid', in D. West and T. Woodman, eds., *Creative Imagination and Latin Literature* (Cambridge, 1979), pp. 173–93.

[2] Muir, *Sources*, p. 72.

[3] E. Talbot Donaldson, *The Swan at the Well: Shakespeare Reading Chaucer* (New Haven, 1985), p. 21; see also Ann Thompson, *Shakespeare's Chaucer*

recognition in Chaucer of the potential of the events to be treated or seen as comic in their excess: 'the lovers' charming innocence threatens at any moment to become mere incompetence'.[1] This dangerous and controlled balancing act between tragic events and nearly comic method seems to me Chaucer's most important offering to Shakespeare from this source.[2]

But if the idea of a naïve comic hero falling in love with an elf-queen is something that Shakespeare might have developed from Chaucer's 'Sir Thopas' in *The Canterbury Tales*, he is likely to have found Chaucer's parodic style in that poem a useful model for his own burlesque in 'Pyramus and Thisbe'.[3] Chaucer's description of Sir Thopas, in particular, seems to have fed Thisbe's lament over Pyramus's corpse as well as Quince's desperate padding rhyme of 'certain' (5.1.129)—Chaucer, after all, makes use of Quince's preferred rhythm of 'eight and six' (3.1.22):

> Sire Thopas wax a doghty swayn;
> Whit was his face as payndemayn,
>   His lippes rede as rose;
> His rode is lyk scarlet in grayn,
> And I yow telle in good certayn,
>   He hadde a semely nose.
>
>   (ll. 1914–19)

Shakespeare certainly made use of at least one more version of the Pyramus and Thisbe story, finding hints in I. Thomson's 'A New Sonnet of Pyramus and Thisbe'[4] and possibly in 'The History of Pyramus and Thisbe truly translated'.[5]

(Liverpool, 1978), p. 93 and, more extreme on Chaucer as satiric, James W. Spisak, 'Pyramus and Thisbe in Chaucer and Shakespeare', in E. Talbot Donaldson and Judith J. Kollmann, eds., *Chaucerian Shakespeare: Adaptation and Transformation* ([Detroit], Michigan, 1983), pp. 81–95.

[1] Donaldson, p. 21.

[2] The collocation, in Chaucer's prologue to 'The Legend', of the month of May and dreaming in an arbour seems, however, quite potent in connection with Shakespeare's play, see Prologue, G text, ll. 89–90.

[3] See Donaldson's comment, 'Shakespeare actually awarded to Bottom the elf-queen that Sir Thopas only dreamed of possessing' (p. 9); for other suggestions of echoes from 'Sir Thopas' see esp. pp. 7–17.

[4] From Clement Robinson and others, *A Handful of Pleasant Delights* (1584), reprinted in Bullough, i. 409–11.

[5] From *A Gorgeous Gallery of Gallant Inventions* (1578), ed. Hyder E. Rollins (Cambridge, Mass., 1926).

None of the sources I have mentioned so far were dramatic but Shakespeare's burlesque object must surely be in part a dramatic style, some form of performance method. While the sources may have been mostly poetic rather than dramatic, surely the workers' method ought to relate as burlesque to some current or recent mode of play production. Ironically the most certain source of mockery is Shakespeare himself. Bottom's endlessly repeated cries of 'O' (5.1.168–74 and note) may owe something to Gascoigne's version of Euripides' *Jocasta* (1566) but they owe at least as much to the Nurse's lament over the 'dead' body of Juliet, an event which suggests some similarities with other events in 'Pyramus and Thisbe' as a comic character mistakes living for dead. Laments are, of course, always liable to seem excessive and hence comic; Leo Salingar has suggested, by paralleling Thisbe's lament with Neronis's speech in *Sir Clyomon and Sir Clamydes*, which was the sort of play Flute at first hoped Thisbe was in (1.2.41 and note), that Shakespeare 'and his audience had heard a number of passages in the same strain'.[1] I am sure they had but the object of the burlesque does not appear to be straightforwardly the work of rival companies or indeed of Shakespeare's own.[2]

There were certainly plenty of plays from the 1580s and earlier with paradoxical titles like the one Quince announces for 'Pyramus and Thisbe'. Indeed *Romeo and Juliet* would be published as 'The Most Excellent and Lamentable Tragedy' in 1599. Theseus' exclamations at 5.1.58 can be rewritten for plenty of better plays: 'excellent' *and* 'lamentable' for *Romeo*, 'tragical' *and* 'comedy' for Lyly's *Campaspe* (1584). Many older plays had abstract characters more exotic than Wall and Moonshine: *Cambyses* (published *c.* 1570) can boast Counsel, Shame, Commons' Complaint, Trial, Proof and Execution and many more. Shakespeare may well be burlesquing such a dramatic style, together with such characters' habitual

---

[1] Leo Salingar, *Shakespeare and the Traditions of Comedy* (Cambridge, 1970), p. 70.

[2] G. E. P. Arkwright's suggestion that the death speeches of Pyramus and Thisbe parody court drama is based on the weak notion that they parody songs in Richard Edwardes's *Damon and Pythias* (1582), though treating them as songs might well be comic ('The Death Songs of Pyramus and Thisbe', *N&Q*, May 1906, pp. 341–3 and 401–3).

announcement of their identity at their first appearance: 'Commons' Complaint I represent' (4.33), 'I, Proof' (4.59), 'I, Trial' (4.65)—compare 'I, one Snout by name, present a wall' (5.1.155), Snug's excuse for playing Lion (5.1.217 ff.) and Starveling's explanation of himself as 'the man i'th' moon' (5.1.240).

What seems lacking, though, is evidence for the kind of performance by workers at an aristocratic celebration that takes place in *A Midsummer Night's Dream*. For Quince and his company are complete amateurs[1] performing a type of classical play unlike anything their Elizabethan counterparts seem to have played.[2] The nearest parallel is the payment of four shillings by the Earl of Cumberland's steward in 1606 to 'young men of the town being his lordship's tenants and servants, to fit them for acting plays this Christmas'.[3] Whenever Elizabeth went on progresses she was liable to find herself presented with an entertainment, usually learned and allusive and often involving amateur performers of variable abilities. But such works were presented by aristocrats as lavish displays. Groups of workers neither wrote nor initiated such shows,[4] though Turnop and his crew in *John a Kent and John a Cumber*[5] perform a welcoming emblematic display in which Turnop corrects and improves the speeches written by Hugh the Sexton with asides to the noble audience (ll. 372–404) and they plan a wedding entertainment, again written by Hugh, mocking John a Kent (ll. 1033–8).

Workers had performed biblical drama in cycle-plays generated by guilds like those of the crafts that some of Quince's

[1] J. W. Robinson's useful study of the plays burlesqued misses the point of the workers' status as rank amateurs by arguing that Shakespeare is mocking 'the previous irregularity of his own profession' ('Palpable Hot Ice: Dramatic Burlesque in *A Midsummer Night's Dream*', *SP* 61 (1964), p. 197).

[2] For comments on workers' performances see Clifford Davidson, ' "What hempen home-spuns have we swagg'ring here?": Amateur Actors in *A Midsummer Night's Dream* and the Coventry Civic Plays and Pageants', *Sh Studs* 19 (1987), pp. 87–99.

[3] John Tucker Murray, *English Dramatic Companies 1558–1642*, 2 vols. (1910), ii. 255.

[4] Bullough suggests that 'Pyramus and Thisbe' 'laughs at the entertainments and the amateur acting presented by humble subjects to the Queen in her Progresses or to her Lords on their estates' (i. 374) but the evidence of progresses does not bear his assertion out at all.

[5] See above, p. 40, for the problem of the date of this play.

actors represent: carpenters, weavers, joiners. Elizabeth had seen some of the cycle plays when she visited Coventry in 1566 though all performances of cycle-drama throughout the country had ceased by the time of *A Midsummer Night's Dream*. They performed folk-plays at festive seasons or, as at Kenilworth in 1575, had brought their traditional show to an aristocratic entertainment when local people enacted for the Queen a bridal procession and 'certain good harted men' of Coventry brought 'there olld storiall sheaw', a Hock Tuesday dance and a battle between the Danes and the English,[1] though the show had been banned from performance in Coventry after 1568.[2] Montrose argues that the play is alluding to the diminution over the previous thirty years of popular civic play forms, often suppressed by the state, and their replacement by celebrations of such events as the Queen's accession,[3] a shift from agrarian or religious year calendar to aristocratic celebration. A performance at a wedding might, then, be a deliberate mark of the transformation of the occasion for proletarian performance. Certainly the social significance of the kind of native popular performance so recently vanished is far from the significance of the entertainment Theseus wants, a convenient way of filling the gap before bedtime, a consumerist approach that belongs firmly within an ethos of professional theatres like the Globe.

But, even so, workers seem never to have acted classical Ovidian plays like 'Pyramus and Thisbe'. The nearest parallel I can find is, predictably, in Shakespeare himself when, in *The Two Gentlemen of Verona*, Julia describes to Silvia a performance she took part in:

> at Pentecost,
> When all our pageants of delight were played,
> Our youth got me to play the woman's part, . . .
> For I did play a lamentable part.

[1] Robert Laneham, *A Letter* (1575), p. 32; see also C. L. Barber, *Shakespeare's Festive Comedy* (Princeton, 1959), p. 33.

[2] See Louis Montrose, 'A Kingdom of Shadows: Theatre, State, and Society in Shakespeare's *A Midsummer Night's Dream*', in *The Theatrical City: London's Culture, Theatre and Literature*, ed. David L. Smith, Richard Strier and David Bevington (Cambridge, forthcoming).

[3] See, e.g., R. W. Ingram, ed., *Records of Early English Drama: Coventry* (Toronto, 1981), p. 286.

> Madam, 'twas Ariadne, passioning
> For Theseus' perjury and unjust flight
> $(4.4.155-7, 163-5)^1$

Presumably Julia's performance was a version of Ariadne's famous lament, her letter of complaint to Theseus, which forms Book 10 of Ovid's *Heroides*. Such a juxtaposition of festive drama ('Pentecost') and classical material has no direct analogy before Quince and his actors. When Barber describes Julia's performance as 'an entirely familiar sort of Ovidian elaboration on native ground-work',[2] he seems to me to be suggesting a more harmonious blend between aristocratic and proletarian forms of drama than ever seems to have been the case. The blend was never accomplished, only, as at Kenilworth, a juxtaposition. Hence Bottom and his fellows are trespassing into an area of performance usually the exclusive preserve of university students and comparable groups of educated amateur actors or the preserve of educated authors. Their trespass is part of the comedy: nothing like a bunch of workers attempting their own adaptation of a play on 'Pyramus and Thisbe' had ever been seen in England, let alone Theseus' Athens.

In a footnote C. L. Barber suggested '*Pyramus and Thisby* almost amounts to a developed jig which has been brought into the framework of the play instead of being presented as an afterpiece, in the usual fashion'.[3] Though the history of jigs is still hazy, they seem to have been the normal conclusion to Elizabethan public theatre performances. A combination of song and dance jigs were beginning in the 1590s to acquire greater and greater narrative complexity, becoming small-scale parodic, almost anarchic, dramas. Their subject matter was primarily a farcical action of sexual relations, usually adulterous; as Baskervill makes clear, the jigs' emphasis on farce was so persistent 'that we may be sure the jig dealt with love less often romantically than in burlesque or vulgar fashion'.[4] The increasing success of jigs in the

---

[1] Compare Oberon on Theseus, 2.1.79–80.

[2] Barber, p. 34.

[3] Barber, p. 154 n. 25.

[4] C. R. Baskervill, *The Elizabethan Jig and Related Song Drama* (Chicago, 1929), p. 189; Baskervill's work is still the only substantial analysis of the form.

1590s was closely tied up with the success of Will Kemp, the chief clown of Shakespeare's company and, most probably, the actor who played Bottom.[1] The four surviving Kemp jigs

are all written as vehicles for a clown, who ends up paired with a lady. The clown always starts in a mood that is explicitly 'sad' or full of 'woe' in order to offset the mirth that follows. He starts the jig in a predicament, and the audience's pleasure consists in seeing how he extricates himself.[2]

'Pyramus and Thisbe' is built around Bottom, the clown who has, in the play, ended up 'paired with a lady'. It also occupies, thanks to the strange shape of *A Midsummer Night's Dream*,[3] the position after the end of the narrative action usually occupied by the jig. But where the jig treats parodically anything that other forms of drama might see as romantic, 'Pyramus and Thisbe' treats seriously that tragic romantic love that the main action of the play has found by turns farcical and comedic. The parodic form of 'Pyramus and Thisbe' rests not in its material but in its manner and it is precisely the guying of the methods of conventional theatre that allows its on-stage audience to manage to disregard the commentary it threateningly offers on the potential tragedies of the night in the woods the lovers have just survived. If the jig is a form of inversion then 'Pyramus and Thisbe' offers inversion both of the matter of the rest of the play (into tragedy) and the manner (into farce). To perceive only one side of this inversion is to lose the force of the jig.[4]

[1] On Kemp's career see David Wiles, *Shakespeare's Clown* (Cambridge, 1987).

[2] Wiles, p. 52.

[3] On the relationship between action and form, see below, pp. 95–110.

[4] In an interesting article François Laroque has reached for another dramatic form to describe 'Pyramus and Thisbe', seeing it as a form of antimasque, contrasting and distorting the material of the rest of the play. His argument depends on underlining the masque-like elements of the rest of the action but it also runs against the structural relations of masque and antimasque in which the latter always precedes the former and is replaced by or integrated with the masque itself. In any case this two-part form is essentially a development by Ben Jonson in a series of masques all later than *A Midsummer Night's Dream*. (See François Laroque, 'Masque et antimasque dans *A Midsummer Night's Dream*', in Pierre Iselin and Jean-Pierre Moreau, eds., *Trames. Actes des Journées Shakespeare 9–11 Décembre 1988* (Limoges, 1989), pp. 113–36).

In the current critical enthusiasm for combining Barber's kind of festive theory with the potent analyses of carnival in the work of Bakhtin and others,[1] 'Pyramus and Thisbe' has come to be associated with the forms of threat and social disruption which strongly marked artisan discontent in the 1590s.[2] Underlining the potential threats in the play and the workers' sharp awareness of the dangers they were running in presenting a lion and a drawn sword, such an approach sees their search for dignity in tension with their desire to accommodate themselves to aristocratic demands. As Leinwand observes, 'Their pride in their manhood, as well as their anxiety, is merely patronized by Theseus'.[3] Over and over again, the workers are concerned with their self-definition as men, for, as Bottom suggests, Snug must tell the audience 'I am a man, as other men are' (3.1.40). The workers fear for their lives; their ambitions rise no higher than a pension for life of 'sixpence a day' (4.2.18–19).

But what Bottom has already achieved, before 'Pyramus and Thisbe' can be performed, is to rise beyond his class. Titania, from her first words to him, has consistently defined Bottom as 'gentle' (3.1.130), a word that suggests 'gentility' much more than 'gentleness'; to her fairies, she calls him 'this gentleman' (3.1.155). The drug has made her confuse his status, made him a fit match for a fairy queen but, even as Pyramus, he will be a gentleman and a lover. Flute, whose ambition was to play 'A wandering knight' (1.2.41), will be, at worst, a lady, and Thisbe's death, while farcical, can also in performance have a moving pathos that recalls the exhausted sadness of Helena and Hermia as they fall asleep at the end of their night of confusions. After all, with the silencing of Helena and Hermia in Act 5, Hippolyta and Thisbe are the only mortal women to speak.

'Pyramus and Thisbe' contains and controls the kind of social unrest that workers were demonstrating. But it also

[1] See, for example, M. Bakhtin, *Rabelais and His World* (Boston, 1968) and Peter Stallybrass and Allon White, *The Politics and Poetics of Transgression* (1986).

[2] See Theodore B. Leinwand, ' "I believe we must leave the killing out": Deference and Accommodation in *A Midsummer Night's Dream*', *Renaissance Papers* 1986, pp. 11–30, and Annabel Patterson, *Shakespeare and the Popular Voice* (Oxford, 1989), pp. 52–70.

[3] Leinwand, p. 23.

gives the workers a chance of metamorphosis, a change in status of the kind that only the theatre can confer. For all its farcical business—and in modern productions 'Pyramus and Thisbe' has often become overloaded with business—the workers' play has a seriousness of purpose and a seriousness of matter that is in deliberate tension with the mockery their clumsiness provokes. The end of this dream has to find a way of accommodating both.

Shapes

Dreams have peculiar shapes. Bizarre and illogical though they may appear when recalled on waking, the experience of the dream to the dreamer is of a logical and coherent form. Dream-narratives are condensed and compacted—hence the Herculean labours of expansion Freudian dream-analysis demands—but that concision is not opposed to shapeliness. Dreams seem to take place extraordinarily quickly in waking time ('short as any dream' as Lysander puts it (1.1.144)) but can contain massive, epic and complex actions in that space. A night's dreaming may contain many different dreams but for Freudian analysts the dreams of a night cohere, the separate parts converge, as the separate parts of *A Midsummer Night's Dream* converge and cohere in the play's wholeness. As a Freudian analyst describes:

Since the traumatic conflicts reactivated by the day's events are not resolved by dreaming they continue to be active in the mind of the individual and thus present themselves in each of the successive dreams during the same period of sleep. Thus all the dreams of the same night contain the same latent meaning. Accordingly it usually occurs that each dream approaches, disguises and even seemingly solves the common genetic traumatic conflicts in a different way.[1]

A Midsummer Night's Dream, too, has a compacted and shapely form but one that is, like any dream, notoriously difficult to unpick and lay out coherently. Formally structured, conscious of the artifice of its own shaping, the play seems to draw attention to its own formalism, making its audience

[1] Angel Garma in James L. Fosshage and Clemens A. Loew, *Dream Interpretation: A Comparative Study* (New York, 1978), p. 22.

aware of its own sequence. As Strindberg wrote of *A Dream Play* (1907), his own attempt to find the dramatic forms that would reflect dreams:

the Author has sought to reproduce the disconnected but apparently logical form of a dream ... on a slight groundwork of reality, imagination spins and weaves new patterns made up of memories, experiences, unfettered fancies, absurdities and improvisations. The characters are split, double and multiply; they evaporate, crystalize, scatter and converge.[1]

One of the ways in which sixteenth-century drama created structural form was through significant doubling of roles,[2] a way of reflecting Strindberg's description of characters multiplying and converging. The audience's recognition of an actor was used to underline the interconnectedness of a series of roles he performed in a play, often defining the structure of the moral argument of the work. In *A Midsummer Night's Dream*, this possibility has most often been pursued through the potential for doubling Oberon and Theseus, Titania and Hippolyta.

Discussion of this pair of potential doubles is bedevilled by the rules assumed by analysts of the casting of Renaissance plays. Since Theseus and Hippolyta enter in 4.1 immediately on the exit of Oberon and Titania, it is assumed that the double is impossible.[3] But as Stephen Booth comments, its use in Peter Brook's production in 1970 'was so spectacularly workable and so spectacularly successful as to have since become a theatrical fad among less grand companies'.[4] Though its modern use probably began with Frank Dunlop's production in 1967,[5] the idea was present, even though the problem in 4.1 was not, as early as 1661 when the adapter

[1] August Strindberg, *Six Plays*, trans. Elizabeth Sprigge (New York, 1955), p. 193.

[2] See David M. Bevington, *From 'Mankind' to Marlowe* (Cambridge, Mass., 1962).

[3] See, for example, William A. Ringler, Jr., 'The Number of Actors in Shakespeare's Early Plays', in G. E. Bentley, ed., *The Seventeenth-Century Stage* (Chicago, 1968), p. 133.

[4] Stephen Booth, 'Speculations on Doubling in Shakespeare's Plays', in Philip C. McGuire and David A. Samuelson, eds., *Shakespeare: The Theatrical Dimension* (New York, 1979), p. 107.

[5] Nicholas Shrimpton, 'Shakespeare Performances in Stratford-upon-Avon and London, 1982–3', *SS 37* (Cambridge, 1984), p. 169.

of *A Midsummer Night's Dream* into *The Merry Conceited Humours of Bottom the Weaver*, a shortened version of the workers' scenes performed by apprentices, suggested in the list of characters that Oberon 'likewise may present the Duke' and Titania 'the Dutchesse' (sig. [A] 2ᵛ). This early evidence at least suggests the possibility that it was pre-Restoration practice.

But this evidence only suggests that the economy of the size of company necessitates doubling. It does not indicate the interpretative meaning which an audience might attach to the double. If these doubles were in use in Shakespeare's company—and the size of the company necessitated extensive doubling in every single performance, far more than in twentieth-century practice—then the theatrical need did not prescribe either a specific meaning to the connection of characters or even that a meaning should be perceived at all. Not all doubling is meaningful. Yet the performance exists outside the company's control and the double could have been perceived as interpretative whether intended so or no.

Brook's interest in the double was seen as a celebration of theatrical virtuosity, the actors' delight in the quick change as 'apparent triumph at the transparent theatricality of their physically minimal metamorphosis'.[1] But it was also seen as arguing that the scenes in the forest were 'the subconscious experience of the daytime characters'.[2] Though Alan Howard, playing Theseus and Oberon, indicated that he had avoided the suggestion that the play was 'a *dream* of Theseus's . . . as far as we could',[3] he also describes the two characters as if they amounted to a single individual: 'Theseus/Oberon has somehow got to explain *his* case'.[4] This coalescence of the two characters dissolves the boundaries between the worlds to a disproportionate extent. It suggests no more than that Theseus metamorphoses into Oberon and then back into himself; it denies the separate and parallel existence of Oberon's world alongside Theseus' own.

---

[1] Booth, p. 107.

[2] Shrimpton, p. 169.

[3] Glenn Loney, ed., *Peter Brook's Production of William Shakespeare's 'A Midsummer Night's Dream'* (1974), p. 26.

[4] Ibid., p. 41; the italics are his, the emphasis on the significance of the singular pronoun mine.

Graham Bradshaw has suggested that the doubling enhances precisely this contrast:

> Theseus is lord of one realm, Oberon of the other; doubling their roles makes excellent dramatic, psychological and symbolic sense, because they are the respective representatives of reason and of those life mysteries which reason cannot encompass or control.[1]

But I remain unconvinced that the doubling would emphasize contrast over similarity. Rather, it allows for a slippage from similarity towards superimposition: James Calderwood, in the course of an elaborate argument about the way Oberon 'evokes' Theseus and vice versa, finding the one character 'invisibly present' in the other, moves, at one revealing moment, to finding an 'identification' between the pairs.[2]

It is significant too that such approaches give such dominance to Oberon/Theseus (as in the title of Calderwood's article). In the theatre the only resistance has been provided by Bill Alexander's production for the RSC in 1986 which, by doubling Hippolyta and Titania but not Oberon and Theseus, turned the play into Hippolyta's dream, a dream in which, on her wedding night, once the fairies had to appear at the end of Act 5, Hippolyta seemed to leave her husband for her fairy lover.

The problem of the doubling, the stress on interpretation it provides, suggests the extent to which its dominance in a production subsumes other elements of the play, other more prominent and basic structures. *A Midsummer Night's Dream* depends for its form on the equal importance it attaches to each of its segments, aristocrats, workers and fairies. In particular, the stage history of *A Midsummer Night's Dream* demonstrates how complex is the interrelationship of the different sections of the play's cast, the different groupings of the characters.

Between 1661 and Frederick Reynold's adaptation in 1816, the theatre history of *A Midsummer Night's Dream* is almost entirely one of fragmentation and abbreviation, a continual reflection of the sheer difficulty of assimilating the disparate

---

[1] Graham Bradshaw, *Shakespeare's Scepticism* (Brighton, 1987), p. 69.

[2] James Calderwood, '*A Midsummer Night's Dream*: Anamorphism and Theseus' Dream', *SQ* 42 (1991), pp. 409–30, esp. p. 414 n. 13.

parts of the text within the narrowing of culture.[1] Apart from Pepys's visit to a performance in 1662, when he described it as 'the most insipid ridiculous play that ever I saw in my life',[2] there are no records of the play being performed complete. Instead, over and over again, one or more of the play's groups were omitted so that the adaptation could focus on the others. *The Merry Conceited Humours of Bottom the Weaver* (1661), a version which had been used for amateur performance by a group of apprentices, cut out anything extraneous to the action involving the workers. The unknown adapter of *The Fairy Queen* (1692) cut the text by half to leave space for Purcell's brilliant reinterpretation of the action in the masque-like entertainments attached to each act.[3] By the early eighteenth century the text was being further fragmented to produce material for satiric attacks on the fashion for Italian opera in Richard Leveridge's *The Comic Masque of Pyramus and Thisbe* (1716) and in John Frederick Lampe's *Pyramus and Thisbe: A Mock-Opera* (1745).

David Garrick's first adaptation of *A Midsummer Night's Dream, The Fairies* (1755), cut the text even more savagely than *The Fairy Queen* had required, leaving barely a quarter of Shakespeare's lines in order to leave space for the many new songs transposed from Shakespeare, Milton and others that this operatic treatment required.[4] The dignity of high opera meant that the workers were eliminated completely in favour of preserving the action of the lovers and the court, leaving no space for parody so that only two and a half lines

---

[1] I have explored this period of the play's stage history at length in '*A Midsummer Night's Dream*, 1660-1800: Culture and the Canon' in P. Faini and V. Papetti, eds., *Le forme del teatro: Saggi sul teatro elisabettiano e della Restaurazione* (Rome, 1994), pp. 201-46.

[2] Samuel Pepys, *The Diary*, ed. R. Latham and W. Matthews, 11 vols. (1970-83), entry for 29 September 1662. There is no certainty that Pepys did see the play performed unadapted but equally no evidence for an adaptation at this date.

[3] See, in particular, Robert Savage, 'The Shakespeare–Purcell *Fairy Queen*', *Early Music*, 4 (1976), pp. 201-21, and Curtis A. Price, *Henry Purcell and the London Stage* (Cambridge, 1984), pp. 320-57.

[4] On Garrick's adaptations, see George Winchester Stone, Jr., '*A Midsummer Night's Dream* in the hands of Garrick and Colman', *PMLA* 54 (1939), pp. 467-82; the texts of Garrick's versions are reprinted in Harry William Pedicord and Frederick Louis Bergmann, eds., *The Plays of David Garrick*, 7 vols. (Carbondale, 1980-2).

of Shakespeare's Act 5 remained. Garrick's second attempt to restore *A Midsummer Night's Dream* to the stage, in 1763, resulted in a version further adapted by George Colman the Elder when Garrick left for a visit to Europe. This version survived only a single disastrous performance but a reviewer's praise of the fairy action as 'most transcendently beautiful' [1] may have spurred Colman to salvage something from the wreckage by producing a two-act afterpiece performed only three days later as *The Fairy Tale*. This eliminates the lovers and court completely to focus on the fairies, leaving only so much of Bottom as was needed to link the fairy plot together. The workers, the lovers, and finally the fairies each provided the single focus necessary for productions in this period; each reduction demonstrates the fullness and complexity of Shakespeare's original. [2]

This awareness in *A Midsummer Night's Dream* of a dramatic form which marks the separation of its groups, allowing them rare and carefully controlled points of interaction, is something Shakespeare may well have derived from the work of John Lyly. Again and again, Lyly's plays demonstrate this form, 'balancing a number of self-contained groups, one against the other'. [3] *A Midsummer Night's Dream* shares with Lyly's style this sense of parallelism as a means of shaping a debate-structure, setting out, for instance, 'a clearly exposed debate subject of moonlight versus daylight or imagination versus reason, which all the groups sound out in turn'. [4] Leah Scragg has, indeed, argued that Lyly's *Gallathea* constitutes a fully adequate source for Shakespeare's dramatic method in *A Midsummer Night's Dream*, [5] finding in it a movement from daylight to a forest at night, four groups of characters, a world ruled by 'emotional deities whose passions bring disorder to the human frame but whose purposes to

[1] Quoted Stone, p. 480.

[2] Something similar to this process happens in Benjamin Britten's opera *A Midsummer Night's Dream* (1960) where Act 1 vanishes completely and Theseus and Hippolyta only survive as parts of the audience for 'Pyramus and Thisbe' in Britten's Act 3.

[3] G. K. Hunter, *John Lyly: The Humanist as Courtier* (1962), p. 318.

[4] Ibid., p. 319.

[5] See, for example, Leah Scragg, 'Shakespeare, Lyly and Ovid: The Influence of *Gallathea* on *A Midsummer Night's Dream*', *SS* 30 (Cambridge, 1977), pp. 125–34.

man are ultimately benign' (p. 126), and an interest in metamorphosis, as well as numerous claimed verbal echoes, variably convincing. The case is interesting but it again only demonstrates the brilliance of the form Shakespeare created in the play.

Whatever the considerable virtues of Lyly's *Gallathea*, it serves here only as a foil to set off *A Midsummer Night's Dream* the brighter. The convergence of the different segments of *A Midsummer Night's Dream* is barely visible in *Gallathea* whose components seem mostly to underline their complete isolation from each other, making it possible for a critic as sympathetic as Hunter almost entirely to ignore one major strand. It is quite likely that Shakespeare found in Lyly an abstract of dramatic shape, particularly the potentials of a multi-levelled form, that might well have appealed, but *A Midsummer Night's Dream*'s virtuosity, its showy cleverness, is unprecedented.

Eighteenth-century responses to *A Midsummer Night's Dream* are, again and again, troubled by the play's plot. Francis Gentleman, editing the play for Bell's Shakespeare in 1774, condemned its 'puerile plot, an odd mixture of incidents, and a forced connection of various styles'.[1] Edmond Malone was appalled to find 'the fable thus meagre and uninteresting'.[2] The theatrical forms of abbreviation also involved a rearrangement of the play's action. In *The Fairy Queen*, for instance, the final sequence of music, the explanation to Theseus of the world of fairy, depends on the exclusion of the lower classes and the elimination of 'Pyramus and Thisbe'; hence the workers perform as much of their play as they are ever going to during the rehearsal in the woods and Bottom, after being reunited with his friends (Shakespeare's 4.2), simply vanishes from the play. A similar rearrangement happens in Reynolds's version (1816) where Theseus watches the rehearsal in the wood; in Reynolds's last act, just as the couples are leaving for the temple to be married, a trumpet announces the arrival of Theseus' army and a parade displays '*A Grand Pageant, commemorative of the Triumphs of* Theseus' (p. 57). Again there is no room for Bottom; instead Reynolds appears to be responding to Malone's complaint about Shakespeare's play:

---

[1] Bell's *Shakespeare* (1774), vol. 8, p. 137.   [2] Malone, i. 285.

'Theseus, the associate of Hercules, is not engaged in any adventure worthy of his rank or reputation',[1] as well as producing the military display appropriate for the year after the battle of Waterloo.

Such rearrangements of the play continued into the nineteenth century, even though by then most of Shakespeare's text had been restored to the performing tradition. What is particularly problematic at this stage seems to have been the sequence of the sections that make up 4.1, the move from fairies to aristocrats to Bottom. From Madame Vestris's production at Covent Garden in 1840 onwards it became conventional to play Bottom's awakening (4.1.198–215) immediately after the departure of the fairies (at l. 101), follow it with Bottom's reunion with his friends (4.2), though this brief scene was often omitted completely, and only then play the scene between the lovers and Theseus (ll. 102–97).[2] This change allowed for spectacular scenic transformation. In Augustin Daly's production in New York in 1888, for instance, Bottom's awaking and exit was followed by a dawn sequence:

After a strain of music daybreak begins to appear. The sun rises. The glen and tangled wood disappear, as the mists ascend and discover the lovers asleep as before. Music is heard, and a pleasure-barge appears in the background bearing THESEUS, HIPPOLYTA, EGEUS, PHILOSTRATE and others. It pauses at the C., and THESEUS and the others descend.[3]

After the scene is finished, all the characters go back on to the barge (see fig. 13) and 'As the barge begins to move off the picture changes, showing the passage of THESEUS to his capital'.[4] Such a spectacle, dependent on a moving panorama,[5] echoes the grand transformation scenes so beloved of nineteenth-century theatre, as well as creating a stage picture to accompany Mendelssohn's music.

[1] Malone, i. 284.

[2] See Gary Jay Williams, 'Madame Vestris' *A Midsummer Night's Dream* and the Web of Victorian Tradition', *Theatre Survey*, 18.2 (1977), p. 12.

[3] *A Midsummer Night's Dream*, 'Arranged for representation at Daly's Theatre, by Augustin Daly' (1888), p. 63.

[4] Ibid., p. 64.

[5] Reproduced in Charles H. Shattuck, *Shakespeare on the American Stage*, vol. 2 (Washington, 1987), illustrations 46–9.

13. The start of the journey back to Athens in Augustin Daly's production, New York, 1888.

It also denies the structure Shakespeare had aimed to create. *A Midsummer Night's Dream* has a neat and symmetrical scenic form. Acts 1 and 5 take place in Athens, Acts 2 to 4 in the wood. Immediately preceding the move to the wood comes the casting scene for Quince, Bottom and company (1.2); Bottom is reunited with the others immediately after the wood scenes (4.2), before the full Athenian splendours of the court in Act 5. Mark Rose describes this shape as 'a double frame around the central panel',[1] emphasizing the central moment of the play as the union of extremes, Titania and Bottom, at the end of 3.1, the point at which modern productions almost always place the interval.

As Rose also shows, the whole play consists of only seven scenes, fewer than any other Shakespeare play.[2] Two scenes

---

[1] Mark Rose, *Shakespearean Design* (Cambridge, Mass., 1972), p. 19.

[2] Rose, pp. 88–9 and p. 182 n. 7. Rose rightly counts 2.2 and 3.1 as a single scene and 3.2 and 4.1 as another, noting the on-stage sleepers. Oxford, noting that the stage clears, marks new scenes at 3.2.413 and 5.1.362; see my commentary at these points. Neither clear stage seems to me to suggest

in Athens, three in the wood and then two in Athens again adds up to a structure of almost ostentatious simplicity, a form of visible shapeliness and formal discipline. Such scenic restraint contains and controls the opulent movement of the different groups of characters as their worlds flow and blur and collide in the wood. It also intensifies the perception of the double frame, a feature intensified in modern production by the three sets the play has conventionally been given: the court for 1.1 and 5.1, Quince's house for 1.2 and 4.2, the wood for the central panel.

To some extent, the movement of the play from city to country and back again is tied to the play's interest in May Day and its associated festivities. It was in the wood that Lysander once met Hermia with Helena, 'To do observance to a morn of May' (1.1.167), just as Theseus will mockingly suggest that the presence of the four lovers in the wood is because 'No doubt they rose up early to observe | The rite of May' (4.1.131–2).[1] As Barber saw, at the beginning of his outstanding analysis of the significance of popular festivity for the play, 'the May game, everybody's pastime, gave the pattern for his whole action'.[2] Maying and its other games need not take place only at May Day, hence its appearance in a play explicitly linked in its title to Midsummer Eve. The best description of May games is the attack on them by Phillip Stubbes in *The Anatomy of Abuses* (1583):

Against May, Whitsunday, or other time all the young men and maids, old men and wives, run gadding over night to the woods, groves, hills, and mountains, where they spend all the night in pleasant pastimes . . . I have heard it credibly reported (and that *viva voce*) by men of great gravity and reputation, that of forty, three-score, or a hundred maids going to the wood over night, there have scarcely the third part of them returned home again undefiled.[3]

anything as strong as a scene division suggests on the page; certainly in performance there is no suggestion of a time-gap—there is no change of fictive place in either case.

[1] See also Hermia's insulting of Helena as 'thou painted maypole' (3.2.296).

[2] C. L. Barber, *Shakespeare's Festive Comedy* (1959), p. 119.

[3] Quoted Barber, pp. 21–2.

Others put the figures even higher: 'I have heard of ten maidens which went to fetch May, and nine of them came home with child'.[1]

This rustic celebration of fertility combines neatly with the pleasures of sex in the woods that Hermia resists when Lysander proposes it (2.2.45–71).[2] But its presence in the play is set against the notion of Midsummer itself, strongly associated with bonfires, watches, magic and carnival parades.[3] Midsummer Eve, one of the oldest of all festivals in its celebration of the summer solstice, the turning point of the year, was particularly a time when spirits were abroad, when particular plants must be gathered and when one might see one's future true love in the fires or through other magic.[4] Spenser's *Epithalamion* (1595) also suggests links between Midsummer and marriage. But Shakespeare makes the two festivals, Midsummer and May, into a blur, refusing to limit the associations of the two holidays in order to create 'a more elusive festival time'.[5]

Such blurring of two calendrical events is echoed in the problems of the formal shape. The play's abstract design with its symmetries and balances is in tension with two aspects of the dramatic action in Act 5, the movement necessary to balance Act 1 and the completion of the outermost frame. In effect, with the solution of the problems and obstacles to the marriages of the lovers, the action of *A Midsummer Night's Dream*, the action that conventionally marks the process of comedy towards marriage, is complete by 4.1.197. Titania has been reconciled with Oberon, the mortal lovers paired off.

[1] Robert Fetherston, *Dialogue against Light, Lewde and Lascivious Dauncing* (1582), quoted by François Laroque, *Shakespeare's Festive World* (Cambridge, 1991), p. 113.

[2] On May celebrations see also David Cressy, *Bonfires and Bells* (1989), pp. 21–3, and Laroque, pp. 110–20.

[3] See Cressy, pp. 25–8; Laroque, pp. 140–1; Barber, pp. 123–4 and Anca Vlasopolos, 'The Ritual of Midsummer: A Pattern for *A Midsummer Night's Dream*', *Renaissance Quarterly*, 31 (1978), pp. 21–9.

[4] See David P. Young, *Something of Great Constancy* (New Haven, 1966), pp. 20–3.

[5] Young, p. 24; see also Laroque, p. 217: 'Shakespeare played on the similarity between the festivities of May Day and those of Midsummer, deliberately confusing them as if they were more or less equivalent'. The third festival the play conjures briefly into existence to add to this blend is St Valentine's Day: see my note on 4.1.138–9 and Laroque, pp. 105–7.

Indeed, at 4.1.183–4, Theseus speaks what in any other play would have sounded suspiciously like a final couplet: 'Away with us to Athens. Three and three, | We'll hold a feast in great solemnity.' As Anne Barton notes,

This couplet has the authentic ring of a comedy conclusion. Only one expectation generated by the comedy remains unfulfilled: the presentation of the Pyramus and Thisby play before the Duke and his bride. Out of this single remaining bit of material, Shakespeare constructs a fifth act which seems, in effect, to take place beyond the normal plot-defined boundaries of comedy.[1]

The exploration of art and artifice as reflection and revaluation that constitutes 'Pyramus and Thisbe', the exploration of the nature of theatre that constitutes the workers' performance of their play and the exploration of social assimilation that constitutes the reactions of the male members of the on-stage audience, have no place in the conventional structures of comedy. In many ways, as my discussion of 'Pyramus and Thisbe' as jig has already suggested, Act 5 is formally extraneous to the action of the drama, however essential it may be to the formal shaping of the structure.[2]

This tension between dramatic action and abstract form reaches its culmination in *A Midsummer Night's Dream* late in Act 5, for neither the formal shape nor the dramatic action prescribes that anything should follow the exit of the aristocrats. Again Theseus 'is given a couplet which sounds like the last lines of a play' (5.1.360–1);[3] again the play proves not to have ended. The arrival of Robin and then the rest of the fairies, another opportunity in nineteenth-century productions for grand transformations and spectacle, must be unexpected. Just as, when Pyramus is dead, Bottom leaps up, resurrected, to offer an epilogue or a dance (5.1.345–6), so the play will offer both an epilogue and the spectacle of the fairies dancing and singing.[4] For once 'Pyramus and Thisbe'

---

[1] Introduction to *A Midsummer Night's Dream*, in G. Blakemore Evans, ed., *The Riverside Shakespeare* (Boston, 1974), p. 219.

[2] See Brooks's comment, in his consideration of the play's 'design', that 'the plot is completed . . . before the start of Act V' (p. xcix).

[3] Barton, p. 220.

[4] It has often been argued, particularly by those critics who believe that *A Midsummer Night's Dream* was written first for performance at an aristocratic

proves predictive as well as retrospective in its relation to *A Midsummer Night's Dream.*

Wherever Robin comes from, the audience cannot have assumed that he would enter the world of the palace, move from wood to court, from country to city. Even though from the first the presence of the fairies near Athens has been caused by the royal wedding, with Oberon 'Come from the farthest step of India, | . . . To give their bed joy and prosperity' (2.1.69, 73), even though Oberon has announced that they 'will tomorrow midnight solemnly | Dance in Duke Theseus' house, triumphantly' (4.1.87–8), the play's form had seemed to trap them in the forest, just as Robin has assumed that they are trapped by the hours of night (3.2.378–87). The final arrival of the fairies, as the mortals go off to make love and to sleep, is the audience's privilege: even more than Bottom, the audience is granted a 'most rare vision'.

This structural peculiarity, this deliberate transformation of dramatic form and expectation is one of the great glories of the play. But the play has also posed dramatic difficulties in its central sequence in the wood. No other Shakespeare play creates the potential awkwardness of leaving members of the cast inconveniently around on stage in such profusion, immobile because asleep. From the moment of Titania's falling asleep at 2.2.30 to Bottom's awaking in 4.1, the problem is frequently repeated. Titania stays asleep till 3.1.122, over 250 lines of text. Hermia and Lysander sleep from 2.2.71 to 109 (Lysander) and 151 (Hermia). Demetrius sleeps from 3.2.87 to 137. All four of the lovers start to fall asleep from 3.2.420, staying asleep till 4.1.137 (over 170 lines). Titania and Bottom fall asleep at 4.1.44; she wakes up at 4.1.75, he sleeps on till 4.1.198. At one point six different characters are asleep on stage at once, presumably in two distinct groupings. No wonder that nineteenth-century productions, as they

wedding, that Q1 incorporates two alternative endings for the play, the fairies' song and dance for the wedding and an epilogue by Robin which would have replaced their 'masque' at the Globe. There is no evidence at all to support such an argument; I can see no reason why both 'endings' should not have been used both at the wedding entertainment (in the improbable event that the play was written for one) and in the public theatre performances. See the rebuttal by Stanley Wells, 'A Midsummer Night's Dream Revisited', *Critical Survey*, 3 (1991), pp. 17–18.

displayed various parts of the wood, often let the lovers disappear from sight, bringing them back on, as Daly did, only when the mists clear. Fussy modern sets always leave plenty of corners for sleepers; Peter Brook's bare white box, designed by Sally Jacobs, deliberately highlighted the problem, marking the emphatic visibility of the giant scarlet feather suspended in mid-air on which Titania and later Bottom slept (see fig. 14).

In a play about dream we should not be surprised that the stage shows us sleepers. But *A Midsummer Night's Dream* also makes of sleep the mark of a series of crucial transitions in the play. Titania asleep is drugged and will wake to fall in love with Bottom, Lysander and Demetrius undergo similar transformations as they sleep. Hermia wakes, having dreamed, to find Lysander gone. Titania wakes again to find 'My Oberon' (4.1.75); the four lovers will wake from sleep into that wonderfully ambivalent state of half-waking half-dreaming that they describe so wonderingly in 4.1;[1] Bottom wakes to try, like them, to recall his dream.

The 'visions' Titania had in which 'I was enamoured of an ass' (4.1.75–6) can be changed, by being proved no dream, into something loathsome: 'O, how mine eyes do loathe his visage now' (l. 78). The mortals' experience, once they have recounted their dreams 'by the way' (l. 197) both to each other and to Theseus and Hippolyta, is much more complex, for they will never be able to see that their visions were no dreams at all, thanks to Oberon's kindness in turning all 'this night's accidents' into 'the fierce vexation of a dream' (4.1.67–8). All the lovers will have, apart from finding each other, will be their curiously coinciding dreams, 'all their minds transfigured so together', as Hippolyta puts it (5.1.24). She perceives it as 'something of great constancy' (l. 26), as Bottom will find his dream something he cannot begin to explain but whose awesome scale he is only too well aware of.

---

[1] It is a moment brilliantly and magnificently explored in Britten's opera when the four lovers each take up their own version of 'I have found Demetrius like a jewel' (4.1.190), repeating the line over and over (one of the very few moments of repetition of a line of libretto in the whole opera), emphasizing the wondering magic of the discovery.

14. Oberon and Robin watch Titania and Bottom in Peter Brook's production, Stratford-upon-Avon, 1970.

Throughout this introduction one of my major concerns has been the metamorphic processes of the play.[1] *A Midsummer Night's Dream* is endlessly fascinated by the possibilities of transformation and translation within its action and by its metamorphoses of its materials. The richness of its fascination has been finely explored by Barkan and others. But where in Ovid metamorphosis is the final consequence of the narrative, in *A Midsummer Night's Dream* it initiates action. Barkan's emphasis that 'Shakespeare is more interested in transformation as a cause than transformation as an effect'[2] is reflected in the significance of sleep as the greatest, the most profound and unknowable of all transformative states. Carroll's

---

[1] See also Leonard Barkan, *The Gods Made Flesh* (New Haven, 1986), esp. pp. 251–70; William C. Carroll, *The Metamorphoses of Shakespearean Comedy* (Princeton, 1985), esp. pp. 141–78; Jonathan Bate, *Shakespeare and Ovid* (Oxford, 1993).

[2] Barkan, p. 257.

recognition that 'the metamorphs in the play notice nothing'[1] is epitomized by this state of sleep. We cannot consciously know that we are asleep, though we can be strangely aware that we are dreaming. Sleep in *A Midsummer Night's Dream* is the embodiment for unknowing metamorphosis, dream the most complete state of transformed existence that we ever, let alone nightly, undergo.

It is in the process of recall of metamorphosis that *A Midsummer Night's Dream* distinguishes between the mortals. As Carroll observes, 'Only Bottom experiences metamorphosis, finally, by *remembering* it, though he was unaware of it at the time; the four lovers shrug it off like a hangover'.[2] Yet even the hangover involves transfiguration, as Hippolyta recognizes. Living with one's dreams is never an easy process.

Date

A Midsummer Night's Dream was written and first performed in 1595 or 1596. The exact date is unknown and impossible to establish more precisely. A reference to the play in the list of Shakespeare's work mentioned by Francis Meres in *Palladis Tamia* (1598) provides the latest possible date; the assumption that the problem over the lion relates to an event at the Scottish court in August 1594 (see note to 1.2.70–1) provides an earliest date. Stylistically the play fits with the other plays of the same date, especially *Romeo and Juliet*.[3]

Determining whether *A Midsummer Night's Dream* preceded or followed *Romeo and Juliet* is difficult. The weight of opinion tends towards seeing *A Midsummer Night's Dream* as the later,[4] though Oxford is more cautious, placing *Dream* before *Romeo*. I have, at a number of points in the Commentary, indicated possible reasons for thinking that *Dream* followed *Romeo* but, in the final analysis, all that matters is that the two plays were clearly being worked on at roughly the same moment.

[1] Carroll, p. 149.

[2] Carroll, p. 157.

[3] For recent consideration of internal tests for Shakespeare chronology see Oxford, *Textual Companion*, pp. 93–109.

[4] See, for example, G. Blakemore Evans's edition of *Romeo* (Cambridge, 1984), pp. 4–6; Foakes, pp. 1–2; Amy J. Reiss and George Walton Williams, ' "Tragical Mirth": From *Romeo* to *Dream*', *SQ* 43 (1992), pp. 214–18.

A Midsummer Night's Dream's place in the canon does not, in any case, help very much to determine the date further. To do that editors have relied on supposed allusions in the text. Such allusions have included the bad weather of which Titania speaks so eloquently (2.1.88–114) or the exact identity of someone who might fit 'the death | Of learning, late deceased in beggary' (5.1.52–3). The problem is that there are always more candidates than one might desire: in England, predictably, the weather is often bad and the lines could apply just as easily to 1594, 1595 or 1596;[1] poor scholars regularly die, not only Robert Greene (died 1592). It is not even clear that such passages are direct allusions to recent events.

Much more common have been attempts to fix on the exact date of the first performance of the play by assuming that the play must have been performed at the celebrations for a particular noble wedding and that the play's references to the phases of the moon, particularly Theseus' opening reference to a new moon, describe the exact state of the moon on the night of that performance.[2] Such arguments are often combined with assumptions that, since the play includes a direct reference to Queen Elizabeth as 'a fair vestal thronèd by the west' (2.1.158), the Queen must have been present at the first performance.

As W. J. Lawrence pointed out in 1922, the first play, rather than masque-like entertainment, certainly written specifically for a wedding celebration was Daniel's pastoral *Hymen's Triumph* in 1614.[3] In any case, arguments from the particular nature of the play and its supposed casting demands fail to take into account the certain fact that, as the title-page of Q1 makes clear, the play was performed on the public theatre stage as well and must therefore have been within the normal capabilities of the Lord Chamberlain's Men. As Lawrence comments, 'no private play ... ever found its way to the

---

[1] See, for example, Sidney Thomas's advocacy of 1596 in 'The Bad Weather in *A Midsummer Night's Dream*', *MLN* 64 (1949), pp. 319–22.

[2] See, for one example out of many, William B. Hunter, *Milton's 'Comus': Family Piece* (1983), pp. 95–101 and his 'The First Performance of *A Midsummer Night's Dream*', *N&Q* 230 (1985) pp. 45–7.

[3] W. J. Lawrence, 'A Plummet for Bottom's Dream', *The Fortnightly Review*, NS 3 (1922), p. 834.

regular stage . . . the players gave no play publicly that had not been written for public use'.[1]

Of the eleven weddings proposed, the most popular candidate is the marriage of Sir Thomas Berkeley to Elizabeth Carey in February 1596[2] but the detailed contemporary family history makes no mention either of the Queen's presence or of the performance of any play, let alone one especially written for the event.[3] There is no better evidence for any other of the suggested weddings. The wedding occasion theory appeals to critics who like the concept of a site-specific play, with fairies running through the noble house to bless the real wedding of members of the audience, and to those who wish to rescue the play from the clutches of the popular theatre audience. I fail to see the need to want either.

The Text

A Midsummer Night's Dream presents probably fewer textual problems than any other Shakespeare play published both as a quarto and as a part of the Folio of 1623. There has been such widespread agreement about the nature of the copy for both quarto texts and such convincing arguments analysing the slightly more difficult problem of the Folio copy that there is comparatively little for me to do other than rehearse, briefly, what has been much more extensively discussed elsewhere.[4]

[1] Ibid.

[2] See, for example, for an argument finding further allusions to the family in the play, Steven May, '*A Midsummer Night's Dream* and the Carey–Berkeley Wedding', *Renaissance Papers 1983*, pp. 43–52, and David Wiles's vigorous support for the wedding theory in *Shakespeare's Almanac* (1994). I am grateful to David Wiles for letting me read his typescript.

[3] See Marion Colthorpe, 'Queen Elizabeth I and *A Midsummer Night's Dream*', *N&Q* 232 (1987), pp. 205–7; the neatest rebuttal of the wedding occasion theory is still Wells's comments in his edition, pp. 12–14. See also Stanley Wells, '*A Midsummer Night's Dream* Revisited', *Critical Survey*, 3 (1991), pp. 14–18. I am grateful to Gary Jay Williams for letting me read the typescript of his full-scale demolition of the occasion theory, the first chapter of his forthcoming stage history of the play, *Our Moonlight Revels*.

[4] See, in particular, W. W. Greg, *The Shakespeare First Folio* (Oxford, 1955), pp. 240–7; Brooks, pp. xxi–xxxiv; Foakes, pp. 135–43; Oxford, pp. 279–87.

Q1. 1600. The first Quarto (Q1) of *A Midsummer Night's Dream* was published by Thomas Fisher in 1600. The play had been entered in Fisher's name in the Stationers' Register on 8 October 1600 in the regular fashion:

Tho. Fyssher   Entred for his copie vnder the handes of m^r Rodes and the Wardens. A booke called A mydsomer nightes dreame.

It was the first work to be entered for Fisher whose career as a publisher seems to have been fairly brief. The work was almost certainly printed by Richard Bradock, a regular printer of play quartos at the time. Its title-page makes clear that, whatever other auspices the play may have been acted under, it had been performed 'sundry times' by Shakespeare's company: 'as it hath been sundry times publicly acted by the Right Honourable the Lord Chamberlain his Servants'. The only major study of the printing of Q1 argued for setting by formes.[1] But Turner's argument has been questioned by Blayney[2] and there is insufficient evidence as yet to establish the setting-order. No one has yet undertaken a full collation of the extant copies of Q1 in search of press-variants, though Oxford found one at 2.2.49. That tedious search still remains to be done.

There is more than enough evidence, according to the canons of bibliographical proof, to show that the copy for Q1 was autograph foul papers.[3] In other words, Bradock's compositor(s) worked from a manuscript in Shakespeare's hand, effectively his rough draft, while the fair copy made from the draft stayed with the Lord Chamberlain's Men. The evidence for this is derived from a number of features of Q1:

(i) Q1's stage directions are both incomplete and inconsistent. It lacks a number of necessary entries (e.g. for Robin at 3.1.97, for Lysander at 3.2.412) and even more exits. Its speech prefixes vary for a number of characters: Robin is sometimes *Puck* and sometimes *Rob* or *Robin*;[4] Titania is often

---

[1] Robert K. Turner, Jr., 'Printing Methods and Textual Problems in *A Midsummer Night's Dream* Q1', *SB* 15 (1962), pp. 33–55.

[2] Peter W. M. Blayney, *The Texts of 'King Lear' and their Origins. Volume 1: Nicholas Okes and the First Quarto* (Cambridge, 1982), pp. 92–3.

[3] See further Brooks, pp. xxii–xxviii, and Foakes, pp. 135–6.

[4] These variants were a major part of the evidence used by Wilson, pp. 86–100, to argue for a series of layers of revision in Q1, in 1592, 1594 and 1598. The theory has never commanded general assent. For revision of Act 5 see the Appendix, pp. 257–68.

Que⟨en⟩; in Act 5 Theseus and Hippolyta become *Du⟨ke⟩* (at 107 and from 205) and *Dutch* (from 209); Bottom is *Clowne* in 4.1. Entrances often indicate who is included only in a general way: Q1 reads '*Enter the Clownes*' at the beginning of 3.1 and '*Enter* Theseus *and all his traine*' at 4.1.101.3–4; at the opening of 4.2 the direction '*Enter* Quince, Flute, Thisby *and the rabble*' manages both to confuse Flute and his role and to cover Starveling and Snout as 'the rabble'. Helena is wrongly included in the entry at 1.1.19, presumably because Shakespeare was thinking of all four lovers as a group. Shakespeare could afford such abbreviated terms for groups or varied descriptions for a character like 'Titania, Queen of the Fairies'; the bookholder, or prompter, at the theatre would have needed to be more exact.

(ii) While Elizabethan compositors often varied the spelling of words, a number of the more unusual spellings in Q1 agree with the spellings used by Hand D in the manuscript of the play of *Sir Thomas More*, a handwriting usually held to be Shakespeare's own. In particular Hand D and Q1 share a preference for using 'oo' (in, for instance: prooue, hoord, boorde, shooes, mooue), for 'ea' (in, for instance: pearce, vneauen) and for 'z' (in, for instance: practiz'd, mouzd).

All the evidence makes Q1 an unusually authoritative text and all modern editions take it as copy-text, while incorporating some of Folio's corrections and variants. The only problematic feature of the text, the mislineations in Act 5, is discussed in the Appendix (pp. 257–65).

Q2. 1619. Though its title-page carries the date 1600 and the name of the printer as 'James Roberts', Q2 belongs to a group of quartos that were printed for William Jaggard in 1619. Q2 is effectively a page-for-page reprint of Q1, except for the first five pages of sheet G where the changes in the number of lines of type per page in Q1 seem to have been a response to problems in the copy (see Appendix, p. 258). Q2 took the opportunity here to restore some of the mislined verse. That apart, Q2 repeats numerous errors in Q1, managing to correct a few of the more obvious ones (e.g. 'wanes' for 'waues' at 1.1.4). There is nothing in Q2's corrections to suggest that the compositor had any other authority to consult, all its emendations being pretty obvious from the context. Inevitably Q2 managed to include a few errors of its own. There is nothing in this text to give it any authority for an edition.

F1. 1623. A Midsummer Night's Dream next appeared in the first collected edition of Shakespeare's works, the First Folio of 1623, put together primarily by John Heminges and Henry Condell, two fellow-members of Shakespeare's company, the King's Men (as the Lord Chamberlain's Men had become). It was the eighth play in the section devoted to the comedies, occupying pp. 145–62.[1]

F1 was set up from a copy of Q2, repeating many of its corrections and errors. But it is clear that the copy for F1 was prepared by an editor by checking Q2 every so often against some other authority. The changes are by no means complete enough to suggest anything very systematic in the checking but their source is generally accepted to have been a playhouse prompt-book.

Most of these alterations and additions affect stage directions. The most important change, assigning Philostrate's speeches in Act 5 to Egeus, I discuss in the Appendix, pp. 265–8. Many of the others are helpful clarifications of stage business. Q (that is, both Q1 and Q2) had, for instance, failed to include any entrance for the transformed Bottom at 3.1.97; the Folio not only adds the entrance but specifies the necessary prop: '*Enter Piramus with the Asse head.*' But F1's additions are occasionally made without the necessary and corollary deletions: after Quince's prologue, F1 added a direction '*Exit all but Wall*' (5.1.150.1) but failed to remove Q's direction three lines later, '*Exit* Lyon, Thysby, *and* Mooneshine'. At other moments the collator's enthusiasm seems to have got the better of him: seeing a line of names at 3.1.153, '*Pease-blossome, Cobweb, Moth,* and *Mustard-seede?*', he interpreted it as a stage direction, rather than Titania's summoning her four fairies by name; Q's direction '*Enter foure Fairyes*' was incorporated as '*and foure Fairies*', leaving a direction that

---

[1] On the typesetting of *A Midsummer Night's Dream* in F1 see Charlton Hinman, *The Printing and Proof-Reading of the First Folio of Shakespeare*, 2 vols. (Oxford 1963), ii. 415–26.

brings eight fairies on to the stage. Sometimes F1 adds a degree of helpful specificity: for example, '*Manet Lysander and Hermia*' at 1.1.127 after the '*Exeunt*' for Theseus and his court; '*solus*' for Oberon's entry at 3.2.0, removing Q's entrance for Robin with him at this point and putting '*Enter Pucke*' at 3.2.3; '*Quince*' as a marginal addition to explain Q's '*Enter the Prologue*' at 5.1.107 (also giving the playhouse instruction '*Flor. Trum*' for the flourish of trumpets to accompany this entry).

Two of the changes are particularly intriguing: at 3.1.49 F1 gives an entry for Robin well before Q's entry at 3.1.71 but duplicates Q's entry as well; at 4.1.0 F1 copies Q's direction for Oberon to enter '*behinde them*' but also indicates an entry for Oberon at 4.1.44. Both suggest substantially different stagings from Q, an earlier entry for Robin in 3.1 and a later one for Oberon in 4.1. The latter may however also be parallel to the entry F marks at 3.2.344, '*Enter Oberon and Pucke*', when they have never left the stage but have been on stage observing the action. Foakes wonders where Oberon and Robin stood 'aside' after 3.2.116 and where Oberon stood 'behind them' at 4.1.0 (p. 141) and hence whether they were far enough removed to necessitate a call for an entry when they were to return to the main part of the stage, leaving its trace in the stage direction; but neither case gives any indication of using the gallery or a tarras at the back of the stage and there is ample space on stage for concealment.

A further new stage direction may give a slight indication of the period in which this new staging was implemented. At the end of Act 3 F1 includes a direction '*They sleepe all the Act.*' In spite of Foakes's argument that this means the section of the play that follows (pp. 141–3) it seems most likely that it relates to a pause between the acts in performance (see my note). F1, in line with its editor's general intentions, divides the play into acts throughout. But this stage direction seems on balance to suggest a playhouse practice of act-divisions, dating this direction—and by implication perhaps other stage directions varying from Q1—no earlier than about 1609.[1]

At 5.1.125.1 F1 adds '*Tawyer with a Trumpet before them*' before Q's stage direction for the entrance of the workers. This is the earliest reference to William Tawyer who was buried as 'Mr Heminges man' in 1625 and was included in a list of 'Musitions and other necessary attendantes' of the King's Men in 1624;[1] this might suggest that the prompt-book consulted for F1 contains performance practice for the period close to the printing of F1 but, given the paucity of references to individual actors, many years could have passed between the date of the performances the prompt-book reflects and 1623.

F1's variants in the dialogue fall into two broad categories: a significant number of new errors of substitution, transposition or misreading which seem likely to have no authority; a small but important group of corrections or alterations which seem to rely on some other authority than the compositor's or editor's ingenuity. The correction of Q2's 'Minnock' (Q1 Minnick) to 'Mimmick' (3.2.19) might just be a lucky guess but it is difficult to see in that light such changes as, for instance: 'merit' for 'friends' at 1.1.139; the addition of 'passionate' at 3.2.220 where a word is clearly missing; the alteration of Q's 'knit now againe' to 'knit up in thee' (5.1.190) or of 'Moon vsed' to 'morall downe' (5.1.205). If some of these are inadequate corrections (see, for example, notes at 1.1.139 and 5.1.205) they certainly cannot be disregarded. In weighing these, editors have come to treat F1 as an important indicator of new evidence; they have been more reluctant to pay the same serious attention to F1's significant evidence for stage movements even if some of these may have been introduced after Shakespeare's death.

[1] See G. E. Bentley, *The Jacobean and Caroline Stage*, 7 vols. (Oxford, 1941–68), ii. 590.

EDITORIAL PROCEDURES

THE text of *A Midsummer Night's Dream* does not leave the editor tearing out his/her hair in anguish. My practice in preparing the text of this edition has been fairly straightforward and, I find, proves largely to agree with, though never, I hope, slavishly follow, the text prepared by Gary Taylor and John Jowett for the Oxford edition. The editorial procedures I have followed are helpfully set out by Gary Taylor in his edition of *Henry V* (Oxford, 1982) and the principles for modernizing Shakespeare's spelling, treating asides and verse indentation by the General Editor in Stanley Wells and Gary Taylor, *Modernizing Shakespeare's Spelling, with Three Studies in the Text of 'Henry V'* (Oxford, 1979).

Q1 has been used as control-text and departures from Q1 are detailed in the collations. Some of these departures derive from F1, particularly the treatment of the opening of Act 5 and a number of stage directions. Adopting F1's directions is not simply the 'quixotic' practice George Walton Williams describes:[1] while F1's directions are indeed largely undatable there is no reason to assume as he does that an edition that incorporates them is attempting to recreate production methods in, say, 1595. Rather my edition at least aims to use such information as significant early evidence of production practices for the play, practices to which Q1 is no reliable witness, since its derivation from foul papers may mean that the text has not had its staging clarified in the way that the rehearsal and production processes made necessary. Early stage solutions seem to me to be at least as interesting as Shakespeare's first thoughts before the experience of rehearsal and bear witness to the genuinely collaborative experience of production in the theatre in which Shakespeare willingly participated.

[1] 'It is quixotic, at least, to argue that the act divisions . . . and Tawyer's name . . . should be detached from the undatable directions so that these latter may be thought to be early and taken as evidence for original production in 1595': George Walton Williams, reviewing the Oxford edition, *Cahiers Elisabéthains*, 35 (1989), p. 107.

119

In accordance with the principles of the series, I have used broken brackets (⌐ and ¬) for stage directions whose form, placing, or inclusions are open to doubt. Productions regularly find themselves limited by their assumption that the text is a bible which may be abbreviated but not altered. Many entrances and exits can be easily moved, many characters might or might not appear at particular moments, all of which produce the potential for different effects and different meanings. In the more unstable world of Shakespeare's text that the attention to revision has revealed, productions should feel freer to recognize the varying potentials concealed behind the holy writ of an edition.

The collations do not record minor modernizations and only give Q or F spellings where the connection with the modernized form might otherwise be unclear. Hence

marvellous] Q1 (maruailes)

indicates that Q1's spelling has been modernized to 'marvellous' and that this does not, in my view, constitute an emendation necessitating the inclusion of later authority. Similarly collations only record changes to Q1's punctuation where the change produces significant syntactic reorganization. I have not included variants in Q2 and F that I have rejected, in the same way that I have not included rejected emendations proposed or included by subsequent editors, except in a very few cases where my preferred emendation for a passage or my acceptance of Q1's version is a choice between options that seem to me reasonably equally valid or where my note includes discussion of other solutions. Lists of rejected Folio variants can be conveniently found in Oxford, pp. 286–7. In the collations Q indicates agreement between Q1 and Q2; QF indicates agreement between Q1, Q2 and F1.

The only further material that the collation includes relates to adaptations of the play. At a significant number of points in the text clarifications of stage movement or stage business or emendations of the spoken text were first made in adaptations of the play, antedating, often by a very considerable period, the incorporation of the same alteration in any edition of Shakespeare's text. Adaptations constitute reasonable and valid authority but I have also included in such cases reference to the first 'normal' edition to make the change. At 2.1.61, for instance, *The Fairy Queen* emended QF's 'Fairy' to 'Fairies' well before Theobald's edition. At 2.2.32.2–3 my stage direction was first used by Oxford, a version of it first appeared in Hanmer's edition and a different version was used on stage well before that in Cox's droll printed in 1661, all of which deserve record.

References to other editions, listed in the 'Editions', p. oo, are printed in capitals in the collations; references to conjectures noted by editors are in normal form. Hence at 2.1.109 'HALLIWELL (*conj.* Tyrwhitt)' indicates that the emendation is a conjecture by Tyrwhitt incorporated by Halliwell in his edition.

In the Introduction and in the Commentary all quotations have been cautiously modernized except in the cases of Chaucer, Spenser and Laneham (whose extraordinary spelling defies any tampering).

Both introduction and notes require, I hope, few other explanations:

(i) References to other Shakespeare plays are to *The Complete Works*, ed. Stanley Wells, Gary Taylor, *et al.* (Oxford, 1986). I have, however, stuck to some traditional forms for titles, preferring, for example, *3 Henry VI* to *Richard Duke of York*.

(ii) Abbreviations are clarified in the list of 'Other Works' at pp. 124–6.

(iii) References to *OED* should be self-explanatory to anyone who has used the great work and will quickly become apparent to anyone who has not.

(iv) As in any edition, notes often reproduce previous editors' wording but I have only attributed the note where the previous editor's contribution deserves recognition for its discoveries or felicities. In many cases there are, after all, only a limited number of ways something can be said and my similar form often owes as much to the practices described by Borges in his great short story 'Pierre Menard, Author of the *Quixote*' as to any disreputable borrowing on my part. As usual, I apologise for any slights on the brilliance of their work and make no claim for the originality of my own.

Abbreviations and References

This list includes only those editions referred to in the Collation and Commentary.

Q1	*A Midsommer nights dreame* (Thomas Fisher, 1600)
Q2	*A Midsommer nights dream* (James Roberts, 1600 [1619])
F, F1	*Comedies, Histories, and Tragedies* (1623)
F2	*Comedies, Histories, and Tragedies* (1632)
F3	*Comedies, Histories, and Tragedies* (1663)
F4	*Comedies, Histories, and Tragedies* (1685)
Andrews	*A Midsummer Night's Dream*, ed. John F. Andrews, Everyman Shakespeare (1993)
Brooks	*A Midsummer Night's Dream*, ed. Harold F. Brooks, new Arden Shakespeare (1979)
Cambridge	*Works*, ed. W. G. Clark and W. A. Wright, Cambridge Shakespeare, 9 vols. (Cambridge, 1863–6)
Capell	*Comedies, Histories, and Tragedies*, ed. Edward Capell, 10 vols. (1767–8)
Chambers	*A Midsummer Night's Dream*, ed. E. K. Chambers, Warwick Shakespeare (1897)
Collier	*Works*, ed. John Payne Collier, 8 vols. (1842–4)
Collier 1853	*Plays* (1853)
Collier MS	Manuscript emendations, probably by Collier, in his copy of F2
Cox	*The Merry Conceited Humours of Bottom the Weaver* (1661)
Cunningham	*A Midsummer Night's Dream*, ed. H. Cunningham, Arden Shakespeare (1905)
Dyce	*Works*, ed. Alexander Dyce, 6 vols. (1857)
Fairy Q	*The Fairy Queen* (1692)
Foakes	*A Midsummer Night's Dream*, ed. R. A. Foakes, New Cambridge Shakespeare (Cambridge, 1984)
Furness	*A Midsommer Nights Dreame*, ed. H. H. Furness, New Variorum (Philadelphia, 1895)
Halliwell	*Works*, ed. James O. Halliwell [-Phillipps], 16 vols. (1853–65)
Hanmer	*Works*, ed. Thomas Hanmer, 6 vols. (Oxford, 1743–4)
Johnson	*Plays*, ed. Samuel Johnson, 8 vols. (1765)

Kittredge	*Works*, ed. George Lyman Kittredge (Boston, 1936)
Lampe	John Frederick Lampe, *Pyramus and Thisbe: A Mock-Opera* (1745)
Leveridge	Richard Leveridge, *The Comick Masque of Pyramus and Thisbe* (1716)
Malone	*Plays and Poems*, ed. Edmond Malone, 10 vols. (1790)
Oxford	*Complete Works*, ed. Stanley Wells and Gary Taylor (Oxford, 1986). Textual notes in their *William Shakespeare: A Textual Companion* (Oxford, 1987)
Pope	*Works*, ed. Alexander Pope, 6 vols. (1723–5)
Pope 1728	*Works*, ed. Alexander Pope, 10 vols. (1728)
Rann	*Dramatic Works*, ed. Joseph Rann, 6 vols. (Oxford, 1786–94)
Reynolds	*A Midsummer Night's Dream*, adapted Frederick Reynolds (1816)
Rolfe	*A Midsummer Night's Dream*, ed. W. J. Rolfe (1877)
Rowe	*Works*, ed. Nicholas Rowe, 6 vols., 1st edn. (1709)
Rowe 1709	*Works*, ed. Nicholas Rowe, 6 vols., 2nd edn. (1709)
Rowe 1714	*Works*, ed. Nicholas Rowe, 8 vols. (1714)
Staunton	*Plays*, ed. Howard Staunton, 3 vols. (1858–60)
Steevens 1778	*Plays*, ed. Samuel Johnson and George Steevens, 10 vols. (1778)
Steevens–Reed 1793	*Plays*, ed. George Steevens and Isaac Reed, 15 vols. (1793)
Theobald	*Works*, ed. Lewis Theobald, 7 vols. (1733)
Theobald 1740	*Works*, ed. Lewis Theobald, 8 vols. (1740)
Warburton	*Works*, ed. William Warburton, 8 vols. (1747)
Wells	*A Midsummer Night's Dream*, ed. Stanley Wells, New Penguin Shakespeare (Harmondsworth, 1967)
White	*Works*, ed. Richard Grant White, 12 vols. (Boston, 1857–66)
White 1883	*Comedies, Histories, Tragedies and Poems*, ed. Richard Grant White, 3 vols. (Boston, 1883)
Wilson	*A Midsummer Night's Dream*, ed. John Dover Wilson and Sir Arthur Quiller-Couch, New Shakespeare (Cambridge, 1924)
Wright	*A Midsummer Night's Dream*, ed. W. Aldis Wright, Clarendon Shakespeare (1877)

Laroque	François Laroque, *Shakespeare's Festive World* (Cambridge, 1991)
Linthicum	M. Channing Linthicum, *Costume in the Drama of Shakespeare and his Contemporaries* (Oxford, 1936)
Lyly	John Lyly, *The Complete Works*, ed. R. Warwick Bond, 3 vols. (Oxford, 1902). References by volume and page.
McGuire	Philip C. McGuire, *Speechless Dialect: Shakespeare's Open Silences* (1985)
MLN	*Modern Language Notes*
MLR	*Modern Language Review*
Montrose	Louis A. Montrose, ' "Shaping Fantasies": Figurations of Gender and Power in Elizabethan Culture', *Representations*, 1 (1983), 61–94
Muir	Kenneth Muir, *The Sources of Shakespeare's Plays* (1977)
Nashe, *Works*	Thomas Nashe, *The Works*, ed. R. B. McKerrow, revised F. P. Wilson, 5 vols. (Oxford, 1958)
North	Plutarch, *The Lives of the Noble Grecians and Romanes Compared*, translated by Sir Thomas North (1579)
N&Q	*Notes and Queries*
Pepys, *Diary*	Samuel Pepys, *The Diary*, ed. Robert Latham and William Matthews, 11 vols. (1970–83)
Proc. Brit. Acad.	*Proceedings of the British Academy*
RES	*Review of English Studies*
RSC	Royal Shakespeare Company
Rydén	Mats Rydén, *Shakespearean Plant Names: Identifications and Interpretations* (Stockholm, 1978)
SB	*Studies in Bibhiography*
Scot	Reginald Scot, *The Discovery of Witchcraft* (1584)
SD	stage direction
Selbourne	David Selbourne, *The Making of Peter Brook's 'A Midsummer Night's Dream'* (1982)
Seng	Peter J. Seng, *Vocal Songs in the Plays of Shakespeare* (Cambridge, Mass., 1967)
ShStuds	*Shakespeare Studies*
Sisson, *New Readings*	Charles J. Sisson, *New Readings in Shakespeare*, 2 vols. (Cambridge, 1956)
SP	speech prefix

SP	*Studies in Philology*
Spenser	Edmund Spenser, *Poetical Works*, ed. J. C. Smith and E. De Selincourt (Oxford, 1970)
Sprague and Trewin	A. C. Sprague and J. C. Trewin, *Shakespeare's Plays Today* (Columbia, S.C., 1970)
SQ	*Shakespeare Quarterly*
SS	*Shakespeare Survey*
Styan, *Reinhardt*	J. L. Styan, *Max Reinhardt* (Cambridge, 1982)
Tilley	M. P. Tilley, *A Dictionary of the Proverbs in England in the Sixteenth and Seventeenth Centuries* (Ann Arbor, 1950)
TN	*Theatre Notebook*
Warren	Roger Warren, *A Midsummer Night's Dream* (1983)

A Midsummer Night's Dream

THE PERSONS OF THE PLAY

THESEUS, Duke of Athens
HIPPOLYTA, Queen of the Amazons
EGEUS, father of Hermia
HERMIA, daughter of Egeus, in love with Lysander
LYSANDER, in love with Hermia
DEMETRIUS, suitor to Hermia
HELENA, in love with Demetrius
PHILOSTRATE, one of Theseus' lords
Other lords attending Theseus

Peter QUINCE, a carpenter
Nick BOTTOM, a weaver
Francis FLUTE, a bellows-mender
Tom SNOUT, a tinker
SNUG, a joiner
Robin STARVELING, a tailor

OBERON, King of Fairies
TITANIA, Queen of Fairies
ROBIN Goodfellow, a puck
PEASEBLOSSOM ⎤
COBWEB ⎥ fairies of Titania's
MOTE ⎥
MUSTARDSEED ⎦
TWO OTHER FAIRIES of Titania's
Other fairies attending Oberon

A Midsummer Night's Dream

1.1 *Enter Theseus, Hippolyta, and Philostrate, with others*

THESEUS

Now, fair Hippolyta, our nuptial hour

Draws on apace. Four happy days bring in

1.1.0.1 *and Philostrate*] THEOBALD; *not in* QF

1.1.1 **Hippolyta** was, according to Chaucer, the 'faire, hardy queene' of 'Femenye' | That whilom was ycleped Scithia' ('Knight's Tale', ll. 882, 866–7); after a battle between the Athenians and the Amazons and a siege, Theseus conquered her kingdom and brought her to Athens. Shakespeare, like Chaucer, opens his narrative with this marriage. In North's Plutarch, Hippolyta is the name of the Amazon who finally made peace when the Amazons who came 'valiantly to assail the city of Athens', camping within the city precincts and repulsing the Athenians on one wing during the battle though overrun on the other (Bullough, i. 386–7). But some Renaissance writers saw the Amazons as victorious; see, for example, Anthony Gibson's comment '*Hippolita* dissipated the troops of great *Theseus*, dismounting himself in the fight, yet afterward (on mere grace) made him her husband' (*A Woman's Worth* (1599), fol. 5ʳ). One of Plutarch's authorities therefore transferred the name to Theseus' Amazon bride in place of the more common name Antiopa, captured by Theseus on his expedition against the Amazons (see 2.1.80 and n.). Spenser describes the costume of an Amazon going out to battle as a light chemise of purple silk embroidered with silver, ankle-length but able to be tucked up to enable her to run, a coat of mail, buskins on her feet

(see n. to 2.1.71), a scimitar at her belt and with a shield like a moon (*The Faerie Queene*, 5.5.2–3) but a defeated Amazon might well lack the weapons and moon-shaped shield.

While traditional theatre productions of *A Midsummer Night's Dream* showed a Hippolyta perfectly content with the marriage, more recent productions have worried about the captive Amazon queen: John Hancock's production for the San Francisco Actors' Workshop in 1966 brought Hippolyta on as a captive animal wearing black body make-up and a leopard-skin bikini in a bamboo cage, her lines snarled with biting sarcasm. In the Reinhardt–Dieterle film (1935), which opened with a grand triumphal procession for Theseus and his army, Hippolyta was later seen isolated and moody, turning their dialogue into a private scene, rather than the public, court occasion that QF suggest. See also McGuire, pp. 1–18.

2 **Four happy days** There are problems over reconciling this with the play's apparent time-scale of two days with one intervening night, ending at midnight again. The four days underline and intensify Theseus' impatience here. Theseus' comment to Egeus at 4.1.134–5, 'is not this the day | That Hermia should give answer of her choice?', suggests a return to a longer duration but, though commentators have anguished over the discrepancy,

Another moon—but O, methinks, how slow
This old moon wanes! She lingers my desires
Like to a stepdame or a dowager   5
Long withering out a young man's revenue.
HIPPOLYTA
Four days will quickly steep themselves in night;
Four nights will quickly dream away the time;
And then the moon, like to a silver bow
New bent in heaven, shall behold the night   10
Of our solemnities.
THESEUS   Go, Philostrate,
Stir up the Athenian youth to merriments.

4 wanes] Q2, F; waues Q1   10 New] ROWE; Now QF

it is effectively invisible in performance. For an extreme example of the
ingenious explanations offered for the
problem, see Anne Paolucci, 'The Lost
Days in *A Midsummer Night's Dream*',
SQ 28 (1977), pp. 317–26.

3 **moon** The very first of the dozens of
references to the moon dominating the
play.
4 **lingers** delays, postpones
5–6 A stepmother or a widow with title
to even a part of her late husband's
estate would prevent the young man
enjoying the full income from what
he would see as his inheritance. The
vicious image is emphasized by 'withering out', suggesting both the long-
drawn-out consumption of the estate
and the withering old woman; Theseus
uses the word again at 1. 77. See
Lysander's very different description of
his kind aunt, also a 'dowager | Of
great revenue', at ll. 157–8 who, unlike Theseus, will enable the fulfilment
of this young man's desires.
6 **revenue** Accented, unusually for the
period and unlike l. 158, on the first
syllable.
7–11 Hippolyta's speech is ambiguous: it
could be an attempt to reassure Theseus that the wedding day they both
long for will soon come or an expression of anxiety that the wedding day
which will cost the defeated Amazon
the last vestiges of her independent

selfhood will come only too soon (see
also McGuire, pp. 2–3).
7 **steep** bathe in sleep (*OED v.*[1] 3a, quoting Spenser, *Virgil's Gnat*, l. 245, 'In
quiet rest his molten heart did steep')
8 **quickly dream** The association of dream
and brevity of time is made here for
the first of many times in the play; cf.,
for example, 'short as any dream'
(1.1.144).
9 **silver bow** An attribute of Diana, the
goddess of the moon and chastity, in
her favourite activity as patroness of
hunting. See also 4.1.101.3 ff.
10 **New** Rowe's emendation corrects a
probable compositorial misreading
affected by 'then' at l. 9. The new
moon will mark the new state of marriage at the end of the play. Arguments for retaining Q1's 'Now' are
possible but unconvincing; best perhaps is Andrews's suggestion that 'the
Moon is already "bent" like a "Bow"
on the verge of dispatching the arrow
that will signify nuptial consumma-
tion'.
11 **solemnities** solemn ceremonies and
celebrations, perhaps echoing Chaucer:
'And broghte hire hoom with hym in
his contree | With muchel glorie and
greet solempnytee' ('Knight's Tale', ll.
869–70).
Philostrate Arcite's assumed name
when disguised ('Knight's Tale', l.
1428).

Awake the pert and nimble spirit of mirth.
Turn melancholy forth to funerals—
The pale companion is not for our pomp.   15
⌈*Exit Philostrate*⌉
Hippolyta, I wooed thee with my sword,
And won thy love doing thee injuries.
But I will wed thee in another key—
With pomp, with triumph, and with revelling.
Enter Egeus and his daughter Hermia, and Lysander
and Demetrius

15.1 *Exit Philostrate*] THEOBALD; *not in* QF   19.1 *Lysander*] F; Lysander *and* Helena, Q1;
Lysander, Helena, Q2

13 **pert** lively, brisk (*OED a.* 6)
15 **companion** fellow, used contemptu-
ously (*OED sb.* 4). See also *2 Henry IV*
2.4.19–20 'scurvy companion'.
19 Since 'pomp' meant a celebration and
triumphal procession or pageant (*OED
sb.* 1 and 2), it is not clear how different this is from a 'triumph'.
19.1 **Egeus** The name of Theseus' father
('Knight's Tale', l. 2838); given the
play's interest in metamorphoses, Shakespeare may be recalling Egeus' knowledge in Chaucer of 'this worldes
transmutacioun, | As he hadde seyn
it chaunge both up and doun, | Joye
after wo, and wo after gladnesse' (ll.
2839–41). But he may also have been
interested, given his Egeus' willingness
to have his daughter put to death, in
the story that Egeus, egged on by
Medea, nearly killed Theseus because
he did not recognise his son (Golding,
7.510–43). The name is also connected to Egeon, the father of the Antipholus twins in *The Comedy of Errors*,
who is himself under sentence of death
for much of the play.
Hermia The name is uncommon. It is
possibly derived from Hermione,
daughter of Helen of Troy, and hence
linked to Helena; Ovid juxtaposes the
names in *Ars Amatoria*, 'Scilicet Hermionen Helenae praeponere posses'
(2.699, 'Would you be able to prefer
Hermione to Helen?')—a teasing comment in view of the choices made by
Demetrius and Lysander throughout
the play; indeed Lysander's line 'Not

Hermia but Helena I love' (2.2.119) is
in effect an answer to Ovid's question.
Hermia was also supposedly a 'most
filthy whore' with whom Aristotle was
in love and 'after her death, did sac-
rifice unto her as a great goddess and
made hymns in her praise' (John Bale,
*The Acts or Unchaste Examples of the
English Votaries* (1560) part 2, sig.
A7ʳ), often mentioned by Greene (see,
e.g., *Works*, ix. 123 and xi. 138); this
Hermia was often paired with Helen of
Troy as examples of unchaste women
(see Nashe, *Have with you to Saffron-
Walden* (1596) in *Works*, ed. McKerrow, iii.111 and iv. 357 n.), a possible
ironic background for Shakespeare's use
of both names here (see J. J. M. Tobin,
'The Irony of "Hermia" ', *AN&Q* 17
(1979), p. 154).
Lysander A version of Alexander (another name for the Paris of Troy who
stole Menelaus' Helen as Lysander
will, in a way, attempt to steal Helena
from Demetrius when under the
magic's influence), perhaps also linked
to Leander, Hero's lover (see 5.1.195
and n.). Nathaniel and others pro-
nounce the name of Alexander the
Great as Alisander in *LLL* 5.2.561.
19.2 **Demetrius** Spencer ('Three Shakespearean Notes', *MLR* 49 (1954), pp.
46–8) suggested that its connotations
as a 'vile name' (2.2.113) derive from
the cruel and lascivious Demetrius
Poliorcetes who is the parallel life to
Antony in North's Plutarch; Wells
(*Cahiers Elisabéthains*, 10 (1976), pp.

EGEUS

Happy be Theseus, our renownèd Duke.   20

THESEUS

Thanks, good Egeus. What's the news with thee?

EGEUS

Full of vexation come I, with complaint

Against my child, my daughter Hermia.—

Stand forth Demetrius.—My noble lord,

This man hath my consent to marry her.—   25

Stand forth Lysander.—And, my gracious Duke,

---

24 Stand forth Demetrius.] FAIRY Q, ROWE (*Stand forth* Demetrius). QF *italicize and centre on separate line.*   26 Stand forth Lysander.] FAIRY Q, ROWE (*Stand forth* Lysander). QF *italicize and centre on separate line.*

67–8) more probably offered a piece of Shakespearian self-reference, the name carrying an echo of the character of the murderous rapist, son of Tamora, in *Titus Andronicus*, twice referred to as 'vile' in the play. But neither reference is likely to be picked up quickly enough by an audience to justify Lysander's comment. Much the most likely Demetrius to be called vile is, as Elsie Duncan-Jones has suggested privately, the silversmith of Ephesus who led a crowd of his fellow-workmen in an attack on St Paul and his companions because their preaching was damaging trade (Acts of the Apostles, 19: 24–41). This Demetrius made 'silver shrines for Diana' (19: 24), a goddess of great significance for *Dream* and whose temple at Ephesus was supposedly built by Amazons (see, e.g., Nashe, *Works*, iii. 29). Shakespeare had previously been interested in a *gold*smith of Ephesus, Angelo, in *Errors*.

The inclusion of Helena in the entry in QF indicates what appears to have been Shakespeare's common practice in foul papers of indicating in a massed entry all who will appear in the scene.

Egeus' intervention here, disrupting Theseus' ceremonial progress, parallels the interruption of his triumphal homecoming with Hippolita in 'Knight's Tale' (l. 893 ff.), later dramatized by Shakespeare and Fletcher in *The Two Noble Kinsmen* 1.1.24.1 ff., as well as numerous other disrupted processions in Shakespeare (e.g. Henry VI's funeral in *Richard III* 1.2). The forcefulness of the disruption of normal order is, perhaps, best shown by Reynolds's polite introduction of an Officer announcing 'My liege, Egeus, and his daughter Hermia, | Intreat an audience' (p. 6). In Moshinsky's BBC production the action shifted to another room without Hippolyta's awkward presence, suggesting the transition from public state affairs to a more private legal decision requiring Theseus' judgement; but the action is precisely a public call on Theseus as a duke.

24, 26 **Stand forth Demetrius ... Stand forth Lysander** These instructions are usually held to be set out as SDs in QF though, as Turner points out ('Printing Methods', p. 54), the names are set in italics, not in roman as would have been the usual form for names appearing in SDs in Q1, and may therefore have been intended to be set as part of the speech but lineated oddly as in the printer's copy. Honigmann ('Re-enter the Stage Direction: Shakespeare and some Contemporaries', *SS 29* (Cambridge, 1976), p. 124) defends QF as representing SDs, adducing parallel examples, but the defective metre supports the emendation first made in *The Fairy Queen*. (Rowe, by printing 'Stand forth' in italics, seems to have been unsure of the words' status.)

This hath bewitched the bosom of my child.
Thou, thou, Lysander, thou hast given her rhymes,
And interchanged love tokens with my child.
Thou hast by moonlight at her window sung   30
With feigning voice verses of feigning love,
And stol'n the impression of her fantasy
With bracelets of thy hair, rings, gauds, conceits,
Knacks, trifles, nosegays, sweetmeats—messengers
Of strong prevailment in unhardened youth.   35
With cunning hast thou filched my daughter's heart,
Turned her obedience, which is due to me,
To stubborn harshness. And, my gracious Duke,
Be it so she will not here, before your grace,
Consent to marry with Demetrius,   40
I beg the ancient privilege of Athens:
As she is mine, I may dispose of her—
Which shall be either to this gentleman
Or to her death, according to our law
Immediately provided in that case.   45

27 This] F2; This man QF

27 **This** QF's 'this man', parallelling l. 25,
produces an extra-syllabic line. Sisson's argument for F2's emendation as
also 'more marked and dramatic' is
convincing (*New Readings*, i. 125).
31 **feigning . . . feigning** Shakespeare puns
on two senses of 'feigning' ('singing
softly', *OED v.* 12 and 'deceitful,
sham', *ppl. a.* 4) and on 'faining' ('affec-
tionate, longing, wistful', *OED*; 'love-
sick', Furness).
32 'stamped his image on her imagination by secret trickery' or 'captured
her imagination by making a secret
impression on it'
33 **gauds** showy toys or ornaments (*OED
sb.²* 2); see also 4.1.166.
conceits fancy articles (*OED sb.* 9),
though the link with 'fantasy' (l. 32)
also suggests 'fanciful notions' (*OED
sb.* 8)
34 **Knacks** knick-knacks, trinkets, as in
Dowland's song 'Fine knacks for
ladies'. Florizel disparages Autolycus'
'knacks', as Polixenes calls them,

as 'trifles' (*Winter's Tale* 4.4.347,
355).
35 **prevailment** power to gain influence or
dominance (first example in *OED*)
unhardened first example in *OED*;
'hardened' also suggests 'hard-hearted'
36 **filched** stolen
39 **Be it so** if it is the case
42 **As she is mine** See *Romeo* 3.5.191
where Capulet tells his daughter Juliet
'An you be mine, I'll give you to my
friend' and Shakespeare's source for
Romeo, Arthur Brooke's *Romeus and
Juliet*: 'what power upon their seed the
fathers had by law | . . . if children did
rebel, | The parents had the power, of
life and sudden death' (Bullough, i.
336, ll. 1952, 1954–5). This use of
Brooke might suggest that *A Midsummer Night's Dream* was written after
Romeo; see Introduction, p. 110.
45 **Immediately provided** as laid down,
allowing nothing to intervene between
sentence and execution

THESEUS

  What say you, Hermia? Be advised, fair maid.

  To you your father should be as a god,

  One that composed your beauties, yea, and one

  To whom you are but as a form in wax,

  By him imprinted, and within his power   50

  To leave the figure or disfigure it.

  Demetrius is a worthy gentleman.

HERMIA

  So is Lysander.

THESEUS   In himself he is;

  But in this kind, wanting your father's voice,

  The other must be held the worthier.   55

HERMIA

  I would my father looked but with my eyes.

THESEUS

  Rather your eyes must with his judgement look.

HERMIA

  I do entreat your grace to pardon me.

  I know not by what power I am made bold,

  Nor how it may concern my modesty   60

  In such a presence here to plead my thoughts,

  But I beseech your grace that I may know

  The worst that may befall me in this case

  If I refuse to wed Demetrius.

THESEUS

  Either to die the death, or to abjure   65

---

48 **composed** formed, framed

49 **a form in wax** See Tilley and Dent W136, 'Soft wax will take any impression', a proverb particularly often used of children. Theseus is outlining a conventional but still brutal view of the father's power; 'disfigure' (l. 51) suggests 'maiming'.

54 **in this kind** in this sort of matter
wanting lacking
voice vote, approval, as Coriolanus has to seek the plebeians' 'voices' in *Coriolanus* 2.3.

56–7 The significant opposition of sensory judgement (eyes) and reason (judgement) emerges here for the first time in the play.

60 **concern** affect, relate to

61 **presence** either a place prepared for a ceremonial presence (*OED* 2c), suggesting the location of the scene, or the group of people assembled with Theseus (*OED* 3)

62–3 **know | The worst** Proverbial (Tilley W915).

65 **die the death** be put to death (*OED v.*[1] I. 2c)

65–6 **or . . . men** Theseus reveals an alternative to death not mentioned by Egeus. Does Egeus know of this and has concealed it? Or is it news to him? Theseus' palliation of the choice alters the mood of the scene—Hippolyta, who belonged to a race that had ab-

For ever the society of men.
Therefore, fair Hermia, question your desires,
Know of your youth, examine well your blood,
Whether, if you yield not to your father's choice,
You can endure the livery of a nun,   70
For aye to be in shady cloister mewed,
To live a barren sister all your life,
Chanting faint hymns to the cold fruitless moon.
Thrice blessèd they that master so their blood
To undergo such maiden pilgrimage;   75
But earthlier happy is the rose distilled
Than that which, withering on the virgin thorn,
Grows, lives, and dies in single blessedness.

HERMIA

So will I grow, so live, so die, my lord,
Ere I will yield my virgin patent up   80
Unto his lordship, whose unwishèd yoke
My soul consents not to give sovereignty.

THESEUS

Take time to pause, and by the next new moon—

jured 'the society of men', might well
respond strongly to this option.

68 **Know of** ascertain from
blood feelings, 'the supposed seat of
emotions' (*OED sb.* 5)

69 **Whether** One syllable, *if* the metre is
regular.

70 **livery of a nun** nun's habit. Nuns may
appear anachronistic but North re-
names Vestal Virgins and other
women associated with religious practice as nuns: Egeus 'went unto the City
of Delphes, to the Oracle of Apollo:
where by a Nun of the temple, this
notable prophecy [of Theseus' birth]
was given him' (p. 2).

71 **mewed** caged; hawks were mewed at
moulting time, aptly describing Theseus' view of Hermia's future as a nun.

73 **cold fruitless moon** Diana was patroness of chastity. Shakespeare uses
'cold' in the sense of 'void of sexual
passion' in *Complaint* l. 315, 'He pre-
ached pure maid and praised cold
chastity'.

fruitless barren

76 **distilled** plucked and distilled for per-
fume; see Lyly, *Euphues*, 'the Damask
Rose which is sweeter in the still
than on the stalk' (i. 234). Marriage,
for Theseus, distils and refines the
essence of the maiden's sweetness; as
far as he is concerned, virginity may
be blessed but it also withers the
beauty of the rose. His speech
awkwardly balances praise of the
nun's state and a male disapproval of
female virginity.

78 **single blessedness** blessed state of celi-
bacy. Brooks suggests that 'single'
could carry overtones of 'attenuated,
feeble'.

80 **virgin patent** entitlement to virginity
(*OED, patent, sb.* 5)

81 **his lordship** Demetrius' dominion,
which he would hold over her as her
husband; 'his' is stressed here—Gordon Crosse was particularly annoyed
by the number of Hermias who
stressed 'lordship' (e.g. Old Vic, November 1931, vol. 13, p. 28).

The sealing day betwixt my love and me
For everlasting bond of fellowship—   85
Upon that day either prepare to die
For disobedience to your father's will,
Or else to wed Demetrius, as he would,
Or on Diana's altar to protest
For aye austerity and single life.   90

DEMETRIUS
  Relent, sweet Hermia; and, Lysander, yield
Thy crazèd title to my certain right.

LYSANDER
  You have her father's love, Demetrius;
Let me have Hermia's. Do you marry him.

EGEUS
  Scornful Lysander, true, he hath my love;   95
And what is mine my love shall render him,
And she is mine, and all my right of her
I do estate unto Demetrius.

LYSANDER ⌈*to Theseus*⌉
  I am, my lord, as well derived as he,
As well possessed. My love is more than his,   100
My fortunes every way as fairly ranked,
If not with vantage, as Demetrius';
And—which is more than all these boasts can be—
I am beloved of beauteous Hermia.
Why should not I then prosecute my right?   105
Demetrius—I'll avouch it to his head—
Made love to Nedar's daughter, Helena,

---

84 **sealing** The image of sealing a 'bond'
(l. 85) is strongly legalistic, suggesting
a business agreement as much as a
marriage.

89 **protest** vow

90 **aye** ever

92 **crazèd title** flawed claim, but 'crazèd'
also suggests 'mad'

98 **estate unto** settle upon as heir; Hermia
becomes one part of Egeus' wealth to
be disposed of.

99 **as well derived** of as good family. It
is not clear whether Lysander's speech
is directed to Theseus or, possibly,
Egeus.

100 **As well possessed** possessing as good
an estate, as much wealth

102 **with vantage** rather better (Foakes)

106 **avouch it to his head** assert it to his
face

107 **Made love to** wooed
    Nedar The name is Shakespeare's in-
vention though it might be a transmutation of Tyndarus, father of Helen of
Troy, often mentioned in Ovid (see
T. W. Herbert, *Oberon's Mazèd World*
(1977), p. 19). It is usually assumed
that Nedar is Helena's father but
Terence Hawkes has suggested that
Nedar is just as likely to have been

And won her soul, and she, sweet lady, dotes,
Devoutly dotes, dotes in idolatry,
Upon this spotted and inconstant man.   110
THESEUS
I must confess that I have heard so much,
And with Demetrius thought to have spoke thereof;
But, being over-full of self-affairs,
My mind did lose it. But, Demetrius, come,
And come, Egeus. You shall go with me.   115
I have some private schooling for you both.
For you, fair Hermia, look you arm yourself
To fit your fancies to your father's will,
Or else the law of Athens yields you up—
Which by no means we may extenuate—   120
To death or to a vow of single life.
Come, my Hippolyta; what cheer, my love?
Demetrius and Egeus, go along.
I must employ you in some business
Against our nuptial, and confer with you   125
Of something nearly that concerns yourselves.

Helena's mother (*Meaning by Shakespeare* (1992), pp. 11–15), though the form 'old Nedar' would be unusual for a woman. He also points out that the word is an anagram of Arden and that Arden was Shakespeare's mother's family name.

109 **dotes in idolatry** See *Romeo* 2.2.81–2: '*Romeo* Thou chidd'st me oft for loving Rosaline. | *Friar Laurence* For doting, not for loving, pupil mine.'

110 **spotted** morally blemished (*OED a.* 2b); see also the 'spotted snakes' at 2.2.9.

113 **self-affairs** private matters, his own concerns (*OED self-* 5)

114 **lose** lose sight of (Brooks)

117 **arm** prepare

119–20 According to North's Plutarch, Theseus reformed the state into 'a commonwealth, and not subject to the power of any sole prince, but rather a popular state. In which he would only reserve to himself the charge of the wars, and the preservation of the laws' (p. 13). Theseus clearly intends to try

to talk Egeus and Demetrius out of their insistence (l. 116) and he may want to clarify the extent of Demetrius' commitment to Helena (as he had previously intended to do, ll. 111–12) but his responsibility to the law is paramount here, even though he had himself been negligent (l. 113) in dealing with the matter, presumably as a result of Hippolyta—many actors playing Theseus glance at Hippolyta at l. 113.

120 **extenuate** mitigate

122 Hippolyta has been silent since l. 11, though Theseus has referred to her (e.g. ll. 84–5). Her reaction to Hermia's situation, which in many ways could be seen as so similar to her own, marriage under compulsion, varies widely in production from placid acquiescence to furious rejection of Theseus and Athens' treatment of women (see McGuire, pp. 1–18).

124 **business** Three syllables here.

126 **nearly that concerns** that closely concerns

EGEUS

With duty and desire we follow you.

                    Exeunt all but Lysander and Hermia

LYSANDER

How now, my love? Why is your cheek so pale?

How chance the roses there do fade so fast?

HERMIA

Belike for want of rain, which I could well   130

Beteem them from the tempest of my eyes.

LYSANDER

Ay me, for aught that I could ever read,

Could ever hear by tale or history,

The course of true love never did run smooth,

But either it was different in blood—   135

HERMIA

O cross!—too high to be enthralled to low.

LYSANDER

Or else misgrafted in respect of years—

HERMIA

O spite!—too old to be engaged to young.

LYSANDER

Or merit stood upon the choice of friends—

127.1 *Exeunt all but Lysander and Hermia*] F1 (*Exeunt | Manet Lysander and Hermia*);
Exeunt Q   136 low] THEOBALD; loue QF   139 merit] OXFORD; else, it QF   friends] Q; merit F

131 **Beteem** grant (*OED v.*[1] 1) with the additional sense of 'teem' with rain

135 **blood** parentage, rank (Brooks compares the well-known story of King Cophetua and the beggar-maid that Shakespeare refers to in *Romeo* 2.1.14 and *LLL* 1.2.104–5, 4.1.64–85)

136–40 Shaw (*Our Theatre in the Nineties* (Standard edition, 1932) i. 180–1) describes these alternating lines as 'an effect which sets the whole scene throbbing with their absorption in one another'. In Peter Brook's production the lovers were accompanied by a guitar for ll. 128–48, underlining the formal musicality of their language.

137 **misgrafted** ill-matched, wrongly grafted (*OED*'s sole example)

139 Taylor's emendation, proposed in *N&Q* 226 (1981), p. 333, combines Q1's 'friends' and F's 'merit' (which is so otherwise unlikely as to suggest a derivation from some sort of independent manuscript). The manuscript's attempt to correct 'else it' to 'merit' was misread by F's compositor; Q1's misreading derived from 'else' in l. 137. **stood** was dependent

friends relatives, particularly those whose control over a minor's property gives them the right to make decisions about his/her marriage (see *OED sb.* 3). The notion that an individual's marriage ought not to depend on the choice of others is obviously central to this scene.

HERMIA

O hell!—to choose love by another's eyes.   140

LYSANDER

Or if there were a sympathy in choice,
War, death, or sickness did lay siege to it,
Making it momentany as a sound,
Swift as a shadow, short as any dream,
Brief as the lightning in the collied night,   145
That, in a spleen, unfolds both heaven and earth,
And, ere a man hath power to say 'Behold!',
The jaws of darkness do devour it up.
So quick bright things come to confusion.

HERMIA

If then true lovers have been ever crossed,   150
It stands as an edict in destiny.
Then let us teach our trial patience,
Because it is a customary cross,
As due to love as thoughts, and dreams, and sighs,
Wishes, and tears, poor fancy's followers.   155

LYSANDER

A good persuasion. Therefore hear me, Hermia.
I have a widow aunt, a dowager
Of great revenue, and she hath no child.
From Athens is her house remote seven leagues—

---

154 due] Q1 (dewe), Q2–F (due)   159–60] *See commentary.*

---

141 **sympathy** accord, natural agreement
143 **momentany** momentary (an archaic
    form by the date of the play)
145 **Brief as the lightning** Compare *Romeo*
    2.1.161–2, 'like the lightning which
    doth cease to be | Ere one can say it
    lightens' and Tilley L279 and Dent
    L280.11.
    collied begrimed, sooted (from 'colly'
    as 'soot').
146 **spleen** a fit of passion; the spleen was
    believed to be the organ responsible for
    outbursts of temper.
149 **quick** either an adverb (= quickly) or
    an adjective (= living)
150 **crossed** thwarted
155 **fancy's** Here 'love's' (as in 2.1.164,

4.1.162) though the word often (e.g.
5.1.25) connotes imagination and fantasy.
156 **A good persuasion** well argued ('per-
    suasion' also suggests 'doctrine')
157–8 **a dowager ... revenue** Compare ll.
    5–6 and n.
159–60 Johnson proposed reversing the
    order of the lines to make Lysander's
    logic clearer but Lysander's repeated
    'and's suggests a certain chaotic ex-
    citement.
159 **seven leagues** A league is usually
    three miles but seven leagues is a con-
    ventional formulation for 'a long way'
    (compare 'seven league boots' in fairy-
    tales).

And she respects me as her only son—   160
There, gentle Hermia, may I marry thee,
And to that place the sharp Athenian law
Cannot pursue us. If thou lov'st me then,
Steal forth thy father's house tomorrow night,
And in the wood, a league without the town,   165
Where I did meet thee once with Helena
To do observance to a morn of May,
There will I stay for thee.

HERMIA   My good Lysander,
I swear to thee by Cupid's strongest bow,
By his best arrow with the golden head,   170
By the simplicity of Venus' doves,
By that which knitteth souls and prospers loves,
And by that fire which burned the Carthage queen
When the false Trojan under sail was seen;
By all the vows that ever men have broke—   175
In number more than ever women spoke—
In that same place thou hast appointed me
Tomorrow truly will I meet with thee.

164–5 Could Shakespeare here be recalling the decision of Pyramus and
Thisbe in Golding who agreed 'To steal
out of their fathers' house and eke the
City gate' and 'at *Ninus*' Tomb to meet
without the town' (4.106–8)?

167 'The Knight's Tale' has frequent references to May Day festivities: Emelye
rises 'To doon honour to May' (l.
1047) and Arcite rises 'to doon his
observaunce to May' (l. 1500). May is
also the setting for Chaucer's *The Legend of Good Women*, one source of
'Pyramus and Thisbe'. On May Day
festivities and Maying, which could
take place at other times of year, see
Barber, pp. 18–24, 119–21, etc., and
Introduction, pp. 104–5.

170 See Marlowe's *Hero and Leander*
1.161: 'Love's arrow with the golden
head'. Golding 1.565–8 distinguishes
between Cupid's two arrows: 'That
causeth Love, is all of gold with point
full sharp and bright, | That chaseth
love is blunt, whose steel with leaden
head is dight'. Hermia's choice of
oaths is paradoxical: Cupid's arrow
was held to cause a kind of madness

(see the effect of the flower he hits
(2.1.161 ff.))

171 **simplicity** artlessness, freedom from
duplicity (*OED* 3); compare Matthew
10: 16 (Bishops' Bible), 'harmless as
the . . . Doves', and Tilley D572.
Venus' doves Doves were sacred to
Venus and pulled her chariot (she
'yokes her silver doves' to it at the end
of *Venus*, l. 1190). Since doves mate
for life they were held to exemplify
fidelity but Venus' doves were also
seen as 'an emblem for unrestrained
desire' and 'wanton . . . being means
to procure love and lust' (Olson, p.
105, and quoting A. Fraunce, *The
Third Part of the Countess of Pembroke's
Ivychurch* (1592), sig. M3ʳ).

173–4 Dido committed suicide on a pyre
as she saw Aeneas sail away from
Carthage (Virgil, *Aeneid* 4.584–5),
hardly an emblem of something that
'prospers loves' (l. 172).

175 Hermia teases Lysander with the
traditional taunt of male infidelity here
but it also prefigures his vow-breaking
in 2.2.

LYSANDER

Keep promise, love. Look, here comes Helena.
    Enter Helena

HERMIA

God speed, fair Helena. Whither away?   180

HELENA

Call you me fair? That 'fair' again unsay.
Demetrius loves your fair—O happy fair!
Your eyes are lodestars, and your tongue's sweet air
More tuneable than lark to shepherd's ear,
When wheat is green, when hawthorn buds appear.   185
Sickness is catching. O, were favour so!
Your words I catch, fair Hermia; ere I go,
My ear should catch your voice, my eye your eye,
My tongue should catch your tongue's sweet melody.
Were the world mine, Demetrius being bated,   190
The rest I'd give to be to you translated.

---

187 Your words I] QF; Your words Ide F2; Your's would I HANMER   Hermia; ere I go,]
COLLIER 1853; *Hermia, ere I go,* Q1; *Hermia ere I go,* Q2, F   191 I'd] HANMER; ile QF

179.1 **Helena** The name suggests most
strongly Helen of Troy, whose beauty
this Helena does not have, though she
is 'thought as fair as' Hermia (l. 227),
and, though the language of Demetrius
and Lysander when under the influence
of the love-juice would be entirely
appropriate to Helen of Troy, that
Helen's inconstancy contrasts with
this Helena's constancy to Demetrius.
According to North (p. 17), Theseus
raped Helen when she was very young;
Shakespeare's reading of North may
have suggested the name.

182 **your fair** your beauty
happy fair both 'fortunate beauty' and
'a lucky, beautiful person'

183 **lodestars** guiding stars which fix
lovers' looks just as navigators fix their
gaze on them
air tune, song

185 These are conventional characteristics of nature in May; 'hawthorn'
is also called 'may'.

186 **favour** both 'good looks' and 'good
will, favourable approval' (from Demetrius)

187 **Your words I** Hanmer's emendation,
'Yours would I', is widely accepted but
unnecessary. The choice is between
emending the line or reinterpreting the
punctuation in Q1: Brooks, for instance, reading 'Hermia, ere I go', has
to emend the first half of the line.
Emending the punctuation may be
held to reduce too emphatically the
end-stopping characteristic of the
play's language at this point. Helena
is complaining that Hermia's words
are the only thing she catches from
her. She goes on to enumerate what
she would like to catch before she
goes.

190 **bated** excepted

191 **translated** transformed (as Bottom
will be at 3.1.113); Helena, unlike
Bottom, positively desires 'translation'
but, by the end of the play, this
metamorphosis will prove unnecessary. In the wood Helena will be
'translated' into Hermia, as the object
of both Demetrius' and Lysander's
desire.

O, teach me how you look, and with what art
You sway the motion of Demetrius' heart.
HERMIA
I frown upon him, yet he loves me still.
HELENA
O that your frowns would teach my smiles such skill!   195
HERMIA
I give him curses, yet he gives me love.
HELENA
O that my prayers could such affection move!
HERMIA
The more I hate, the more he follows me.
HELENA
The more I love, the more he hateth me.
HERMIA
His folly, Helen, is no fault of mine.   200
HELENA
None but your beauty; would that fault were mine!
HERMIA
Take comfort. He no more shall see my face.
Lysander and myself will fly this place.
Before the time I did Lysander see
Seemed Athens as a paradise to me.   205
O then, what graces in my love do dwell,
That he hath turned a heaven unto a hell?
LYSANDER
Helen, to you our minds we will unfold.
Tomorrow night, when Phoebe doth behold
Her silver visage in the wat'ry glass,   210
Decking with liquid pearls the bladed grass—
A time that lovers' flights doth still conceal—
Through Athens' gates have we devised to steal.

200 Helen, is no fault] OXFORD; *Helena*, is no fault Q1; *Helena* is none Q2, F

200 **Helen** Oxford's emendation of the
name to its shortened form, often used
in the play, solves the metrical problem without recourse to Q2's emendation. Q1 could be left unemended if
'Helena' is elided into 'is'.
204–5 The change from paradise is only
Lysander's fault in so far as her love

for him has caused Egeus' anger and
her need to leave Athens.
209 **Phoebe** Yet another name of Luna-
Cynthia-Diana-Hecate, the multi-
named moon goddess of the play.
211 **pearls** Compare the Fairy's job at
2.1.15.

HERMIA

And in the wood where often you and I
Upon faint primrose beds were wont to lie,   215
Emptying our bosoms of their counsel sweet,
There my Lysander and myself shall meet,
And thence from Athens turn away our eyes
To seek new friends and stranger companies.
Farewell, sweet playfellow. Pray thou for us,   220
And good luck grant thee thy Demetrius.—
Keep word, Lysander. We must starve our sight
From lovers' food till morrow deep midnight.

LYSANDER

I will, my Hermia.   *Exit Hermia*
                    Helena, adieu.
As you on him, Demetrius dote on you.   *Exit*   225

HELENA

How happy some o'er other some can be!
Through Athens I am thought as fair as she.
But what of that? Demetrius thinks not so.
He will not know what all but he do know.
And as he errs, doting on Hermia's eyes,   230
So I, admiring of his qualities.
Things base and vile, holding no quantity,
Love can transpose to form and dignity.

---

216 sweet] THEOBALD; sweld QF   219 stranger companies] THEOBALD; strange companions
QF   224 *Exit Hermia*] *As in* DYCE; *after l.* 223 QF

214–20 This establishes their friendship,
  laying the basis for their quarrel in 3.2.
215 **faint** pale
219 **friends** The word may have its normal meaning but compare l. 139
  above where the strong link of 'friends'
  to freedom to marry as one chooses
  may carry over here; Hermia needs the
  right to choose her husband, something she cannot find in Athens.
  stranger companies the companion-
  ship of strangers
224 *Exit Hermia* QI's placement (after l.
  223) leaves Lysander talking to Hermia's departing back after she has
  left—possible but unlikely.
232 **Things base and vile** Helena's comments on the transforming power of

love relate, of course, to, say, Titania
and Bottom but also, more specifically,
to her love for Demetrius who
will soon be called 'vile' (2.2.113); Lysander, when he is out of love with
Hermia, will identify her as a 'vile
thing' (3.2.260).
holding no quantity having no relation
to the value love puts on them. Howard Godfrey ('Some Puns on Musical
terms in *A Midsummer Night's Dream*',
N&Q, 238 (1993), pp. 179–80) suggests a musical metaphor underlying
Helena's lines, taking 'quantity' as
'the length or duration of notes' and
'transpose' as 'changing to another
key'.

Love looks not with the eyes, but with the mind,
And therefore is winged Cupid painted blind.   235
Nor hath love's mind of any judgement taste;
Wings and no eyes figure unheedy haste.
And therefore is love said to be a child
Because in choice he is so oft beguiled.
As waggish boys in game themselves forswear,   240
So the boy Love is perjured everywhere.
For ere Demetrius looked on Hermia's eyne
He hailed down oaths that he was only mine,
And when this hail some heat from Hermia felt,
So he dissolved, and showers of oaths did melt.   245
I will go tell him of fair Hermia's flight.
Then to the wood will he tomorrow night
Pursue her, and for this intelligence
If I have thanks it is a dear expense.
But herein mean I to enrich my pain,   250
To have his sight thither and back again.   *Exit*

I.2   *Enter Quince the carpenter, and Snug the joiner, and*
          Bottom the weaver, and Flute the bellows-mender,
          and Snout the tinker, and Starveling the tailor
QUINCE Is all our company here?
BOTTOM You were best to call them generally, man by
          man, according to the scrip.

1.2.24 rest.—Yet] OXFORD; ~ₐ ~, QF; rest, yetₐ COX; ~;—~, THEOBALD

234 **Love ... mind** Love is affected by the
  mind's imagination not by the sense-
  data of the eyes.
235 **And ... blind** Erwin Panofsky shows
  that the classical tradition where Cupid
  was never blind gave way to a divided
  concept, sighted Cupid symbolizing Divine love and associated with Venus
  Coelestis and blind or blindfolded Cupid
  symbolizing the moral dangers of earth-
  ly and illicit sensuality and associated
  with Venus Vulgaris (*Studies in Icono-
  logy* (New York, 1939), pp. 95–128).
237 **figure** symbolize
240 **waggish** mischievous
  game sport, jest
242 **eyne** eyes (from Middle English

'eyen'), rare except as a rhyme-word
by the date of *Dream*, though it occurs
three more times in the play.
245 **dissolved** broke faith (punning on
  'melted')
248 **intelligence** information
249 **it is a dear expense** Both because
  Demetrius will give thanks begrudgingly
  and because the thanks will cost Helena
  dear since they are at the price of
  Demetrius' being able to follow Hermia.
1.2.2 **generally** severally; Bottom's verbal
  mistakes begin immediately.
  3 **scrip** a scrap of paper (*OED*); Bottom
  may have meant 'script' ('a piece of
  writing').

QUINCE Here is the scroll of every man's name which is
    thought fit through all Athens to play in our interlude   5
    before the Duke and the Duchess on his wedding day at
    night.

BOTTOM First, good Peter Quince, say what the play treats
    on; then read the names of the actors; and so grow to a
    point.   10

QUINCE Marry, our play is *The Most Lamentable Comedy*
    and Most Cruel Death of Pyramus and Thisbe.

BOTTOM A very good piece of work, I assure you, and a
    merry. Now, good Peter Quince, call forth your actors
    by the scroll. Masters, spread yourselves.   15

QUINCE Answer as I call you. Nick Bottom, the weaver?

BOTTOM Ready. Name what part I am for, and proceed.

QUINCE You, Nick Bottom, are set down for Pyramus.

BOTTOM What is Pyramus? A lover or a tyrant?

QUINCE A lover, that kills himself, most gallant, for love.   20

BOTTOM That will ask some tears in the true performing of
    it. If I do it, let the audience look to their eyes. I will

---

5 **interlude** play; the word was increas-
ingly less common and suggests an
outdated type of play.

8 **Quince** from 'quines' or 'quoins',
wooden wedges used by carpenters.

9–10 **grow to a point** come to a conclusion; Bottom may be punning on
Quince's name and the shape of
quoins.

11–12 *The Most ... Thisbe* The topic of
the play comes from Ovid's *Metamor-*
phoses (Golding, 4.67–201) and
Chaucer's 'The Legend of Thisbe' in
The Legend of Good Women (ll. 706–
923); its title parodies such works as
Thomas Preston's *A lamentable tragedy*
mixed full of pleasant mirth, containing
the life of Cambises king of Persia (published *c.* 1570) or *A new tragical Come-*
dy of Apius and Virginia (1575) or,
indeed, *The Most Excellent and Lament-*
able Tragedy of Romeo and Juliet.

15 **spread yourselves** Bottom is probably
objecting to their crowding round
Quince but the sight of five people
spreading out across the stage when
all will answer the roll-call is comic.

16 **Nick Bottom** A 'bottom' was the core
on which the weaver's skein of yarn
was wound; Shakespeare used it in
this sense in *Two Gentlemen* 3.2.53 (as
a verb) and *Shrew* 4.3.134–5, 'a bottom of brown thread'. Caxton, in his
translation of Virgil's *Aeneid*, had
Ariadne give Theseus a 'botome of
threde' to help him find his way
through the labyrinth. No one has yet
proved convincingly that the word
'bottom' could at this date refer to a
person's behind; if it could, then the
transformation into an ass (arse)
would seem almost a literalizing of
Bottom's name (see, for example, Annabel Patterson, *Shakespeare and the*
Popular Voice (Oxford, 1989), pp. 66–
7). See also n. to 4.1.208–11 for another proposed source of the name.
Nicholas 'was either a favourite Christian name for a weaver or a generic
appellation for a person of that trade'
(according to Halliwell who offered no
evidence for this strange assertion,
quoted New Variorum).

move storms. I will condole, in some measure. To the
rest.—Yet my chief humour is for a tyrant. I could play
Ercles rarely, or a part to tear a cat in, to make all split.   25
                    The raging rocks
                    And shivering shocks
                    Shall break the locks
                        Of prison gates,
                    And Phibbus' car   30
                    Shall shine from far
                    And make and mar
                        The foolish Fates.
This was lofty. Now, name the rest of the players.— This is
Ercles' vein, a tyrant's vein. A lover is more condoling.   35
QUINCE Francis Flute, the bellows-mender?
FLUTE Here, Peter Quince.
QUINCE Flute, you must take Thisbe on you.

25–6 split. | The] THEOBALD (split—"the); split the QF   26–33] *As verse* LEVERIDGE, JOHNSON
(*conj.* Theobald); *prose in* QF

23 **storms** Oxford (and Collier MS) conjec-
    ture 'stones' comparing Antony in
    Caesar 3.2.223–5, 'a tongue | . . . that
    should move | The stones of Rome'.
    The emendation is attractive but un-
    necessary.
    condole grieve, lament (in the appro-
    priate style for a lover)
25 **Ercles** Bottom's approximation to 'Her-
    cules'.
    tear a cat rant and bluster (*OED*'s first
    instance, though the phrase may
    already have been proverbial). Hamlet
    was offended 'to hear a robustious,
    periwig-pated fellow tear a passion to
    tatters, to very rags, to split the ears
    of the groundlings' (3.2.9–11).
    all split everything go to pieces. Ham-
    let's use suggests that 'ears' were par-
    ticularly at risk.
26–33 Shakespeare's target is the kind of
    writing in two widely separated pas-
    sages in Studley's translation of Sene-
    ca's *Hercules Oetaeus* in Thomas
    Newton, ed., *Seneca His Tenne Tragedies*
    (1581), sigs. 2B6^r and 2C5^v (first sug-
    gested by Rolfe, though he believed

Studley's work to be the exact object
of ridicule). Bottom runs the two
together seamlessly. The first is Hercules at the opening of the play:
    O Lord of Ghosts, whose fiery flash
    (That forth thy hand doth shake)
    Doth cause the trembling lodges twain
    Of Phoebus' car to quake . . .
The second comes from the Nurse
much later in the play:
    The roaring rocks have quaking stirred
    And none thereat have pushed;
    Hell gloomy gates I have brast ope
    Where grisly ghosts all hushed
    Have Stood . . .
30 **Phibbus' car** Bottom's version of the
    chariot of Phoebus Apollo the sun-god.
35 **Ercles' vein** Compare 'The twelve
    labours of *Hercules* have I terribly
    thundered on the stage', Greene's
    Groatsworth of Wit (1592), quoted
    OED, *thunder*, *v.* 3b.
37 **Flute** Suggesting the piping voice of an
    organ worked by the bellows he
    mends, appropriate to his role as
    Thisbe.

FLUTE What is Thisbe? A wandering knight?

QUINCE It is the lady that Pyramus must love.   40

FLUTE Nay, faith, let not me play a woman. I have a
beard coming.

QUINCE That's all one. You shall play it in a mask, and
you may speak as small as you will.

BOTTOM An I may hide my face, let me play Thisbe too. I'll   45
speak in a monstrous little voice: 'Thisne, Thisne!'— 'Ah
Pyramus, my lover dear, thy Thisbe dear and lady dear.'

QUINCE No, no, you must play Pyramus; and Flute, you
Thisbe.

BOTTOM Well, proceed.   50

QUINCE Robin Starveling, the tailor?

STARVELING Here, Peter Quince.

QUINCE Robin Starveling, you must play Thisbe's mother.
Tom Snout, the tinker?

SNOUT Here, Peter Quince.   55

QUINCE You, Pyramus' father; myself, Thisbe's father.

---

39 **wandering knight** a knight errant, still
a popular subject for plays from *Sir
Clyomon and Sir Clamydes* (c.1576) to
Beaumont's mockery in *The Knight of
the Burning Pestle* (?1608).

42 **beard coming** The actor playing Flute,
who is often particularly young and
unlikely to be growing a beard, often
pauses before 'coming', making it an
expression of wistful hope.

43 **mask** Women regularly wore masks to
protect their complexions or to hide
their identity (Autolycus sells 'Masks
for faces' in *Winter's Tale* 4.4.222);
though there is no suggestion that 'Pyramus and Thisbe' is to be performed
with all the actors masked, Flute's
mask is one of a series of facial disguises including Snug's as lion, Bottom's false beards for Pyramus and, of
course, the ass's head.

44 **small** thin and high-voiced

45 **An** if

46 **'Thisne, Thisne'** Perhaps Bottom's
idea of 'Pyramus' pet name for his
lady-love' (Granville Barker, p. 131) or
of her name in 'baby-talk' (Sisson, *New
Readings*, i. 125). In Reinhardt's production in Oxford in 1933, Bottom
and Quince had a running argument
throughout the play over the pronun-

ciation of the name (Styan, *Reinhardt*,
p. 59). Bottom typically demonstrates
both voices in the dialogue.

53–8 Since neither Pyramus' father nor
Thisbe's parents appear in the last act
playlet editors have suggested that
Shakespeare has not thought it all
out. The discrepancy is not noticed in
production and, in any case, like all
good experimental drama groups,
Quince's actors find that rehearsals reveal the need for rapid recasting as
Wall, Moonshine and Prologue. The
parents and their quarrel were commonly part of the French tradition of
'Pyramus and Thisbe' (see W. G. van
Emden, 'Shakespeare and the French
Pyramus and Thisbe tradition, or
Whatever happened to Robin Starveling's Part?', *Forum for Modern Language
Studies*, 11 (1975), pp. 193–204) but
Shakespeare is more likely to be recall-
ing the dramatic structure of *Romeo*
which depended on the lovers' parents.

53 **Starveling** Tailors were proverbially
thin and weak (Tilley T23, 'Nine (or
three) tailors make a man'). There is
a long theatrical tradition for Starveling to be thin, old and deaf.

54 **Snout** a nozzle or spout of a kettle
(hence mended by tinkers)

Snug the joiner, you the lion's part; and I hope here is a
play fitted.

SNUG Have you the lion's part written? Pray you, if it be,
give it me; for I am slow of study.   60

QUINCE You may do it extempore, for it is nothing but
roaring.

BOTTOM Let me play the lion too. I will roar that I will do
any man's heart good to hear me. I will roar that I will
make the Duke say 'Let him roar again; let him roar   65
again.'

QUINCE An you should do it too terribly you would fright
the Duchess and the ladies that they would shriek, and
that were enough to hang us all.

ALL THE REST That would hang us, every mother's son.   70

BOTTOM I grant you, friends, if you should fright the ladies
out of their wits they would have no more discretion but
to hang us, but I will aggravate my voice so, that I will
roar you as gently as any sucking dove. I will roar you
an 'twere any nightingale.   75

QUINCE You can play no part but Pyramus; for Pyramus is

70 ALL THE REST] *All.* QF

57 **Snug** close-fitting, as joiners' work
should be
67-8 **you . . . shriek** Probably an allusion
to or a memory of an event at a dinner
at the Scottish court on 30 August
1594 when a chariot was drawn in by
a blackamoor: 'This chariot, which
should have been drawn in by a lion,
(but because his presence might have
brought some fear to the nearest, or
that the sight of the lights and torches
might have commoved his tameness)
it was thought meet that the Moor
should supply that room' (*A True Account of the most Triumphant and Royal
Accomplishment of the Baptism of . . .
Prince Henry Frederick* in *Somer's Tracts*
(2nd edn., 1809) ii. 179) At the time
of *Dream* one Spanish company, run
by Melchor de Villalba, used an actor
dressed as a lion in a number of plays
by Lope de Vega, while another company, run by Baltasar de Pinedo, went
one step further and does seem to have
used a real lion on-stage (see Thornton
Wilder, 'Lope, Pinedo, Some Child-

Actors, and a Lion', *Romance Philology*,
7 (1953), pp. 19-25 and Sturgis E.
Leavitt, 'Lions in Early Spanish Literature and on the Spanish Stage',
Hispania, 44 (1961), pp. 272-6).
72 **no more discretion** no choice (as in a
court's discretion over sentence); Bottom's line also suggests dispara-
gingly that they would have no better
judgement than to hang them (Foakes).
73 **aggravate** Bottom's mistake for
'moderate'; compare Mistress Quickly's
identical mistake in *2 Henry IV*
2.4.158, 'aggravate your choler'.
74 **sucking dove** A confusion of 'sitting
dove' (on eggs) and 'sucking lamb',
proverbial for mildness (Tilley D573,
L34); Hallett Smith ('Bottom's Sucking Dove, "Midsummer Night's Dream"
1 ii 82-3', *N&Q* 221 (April 1976),
152-3) suggested that Shakespeare
may also be recalling an actor's mistake in saying 'Like to the harmless
lamb or sucking dove' instead of 'As
is the sucking lamb or harmless dove',
2 Henry 6 3.1.71 (noted in Richard

a sweet-faced man; a proper man as one shall see in a summer's day; a most lovely, gentlemanlike man. Therefore you must needs play Pyramus.

BOTTOM Well, I will undertake it. What beard were I best   80
to play it in?

QUINCE Why, what you will.

BOTTOM I will discharge it in either your straw-colour beard, your orange-tawny beard, your purple-in-grain beard, or your French-crown-colour beard, your perfect   85
yellow.

QUINCE Some of your French crowns have no hair at all, and then you will play bare faced. But masters, here are your parts, and I am to entreat you, request you, and desire you to con them by tomorrow night, and meet me   90
in the palace wood a mile without the town by moon-

Chamberlain, *A New Book of Mistakes* (1637), p. 51, though he attributes the line to Marlowe's *Edward II*).

76 In many productions, Quince's abrupt statement leads Bottom to throw down his part and start to walk out in a display of theatrical temperament at which Quince has to woo and flatter him back.

77–8 **in a summer's day** Proverbial; see Tilley and Dent S967.

80–6 'Bottom . . . discovers a true genius for the stage by . . . his deliberation which beard to choose among many beards, all unnatural' (Johnson). Bottom's interest in colours may reflect his trade as a weaver though Cambridge College inventories of play costumes listed numerous beards of different colours (see, e.g., Trinity College inventory for 1550, in Alan H. Nelson, ed., *Records of Early English Drama: Cambridge* (Toronto, 1989), i. 171, listing thirteen beards in six colours including four yellow ones—compare l. 89). Bottom will certainly become 'hairy about the face' (4.1.24–5) as an ass.

83 **discharge** perform

84 **orange-tawny** tan-coloured; the colour of the bill of the blackbird in Bottom's song (3.1.119); the colour often appears to have symbolized pride (Linthicum, p. 46).

purple-in-grain fast-dyed scarlet or crimson

85 **French-crown-colour** the gold colour of the *écu* or crown

87 **Some . . . all** Baldness was a common effect of syphilis, the 'French disease'.

89 **parts** Elizabethan actors' parts or cue-scripts contained only their own lines and a few words from the end of the preceding speech as a cue but without the rest of the intervening speeches, hence Flute's problems in 3.1.87–94. The cue-scripts were written on individual sheets, then glued together and rolled up to form one long continuous scroll. The only surviving Elizabethan actor's part is reproduced in W. W. Greg, *Dramatic Documents from the Elizabethan Playhouse* (Oxford, 1931) (facsimile and transcript in *Reproductions and Transcripts*; see also *Commentary*, pp. 173–87).

90 **con** learn

91 **palace wood** Quince helps to define for the audience the 'wood' (1.1.165) where Lysander and Hermia are heading, though for Lysander it was 'a league without the town' and it has now moved two miles closer to Athens. It is clearly a part of Theseus' domain, a royal forest where he will hunt in Act 4; a space between the city and whatever true wilderness lies beyond (see Anne Barton, 'Parks and Ardens', *Proc. Brit. Acad.*, 80 (1992), p. 72).

light. There will we rehearse; for if we meet in the city
we shall be dogged with company, and our devices
known. In the meantime I will draw a bill of properties
such as our play wants. I pray you fail me not.

BOTTOM We will meet, and there we may rehearse most   95
obscenely and courageously. Take pains; be perfect.
Adieu.

QUINCE At the Duke's oak we meet.

BOTTOM Enough. Hold, or cut bowstrings.   *Exeunt*   100

2.1   *Enter a Fairy at one door and Robin Goodfellow at*
       another

ROBIN

How now, spirit, whither wander you?

FAIRY

    Over hill, over dale,
    Thorough bush, thorough briar,

2.1.2–9] *Lineation as in* POPE; *divided in* QF *at* briar, | . . . fire; | . . . sphere:

94 **a bill of properties** One of the tasks
of the bookholder was to draw up the
list of all the props needed for the
performance; the sole extant Renaissance example is appended to Mass-
inger's *Believe as You List* (1631).

97 **obscenely** a mistake for 'seemly' (as
Costard in *LLL* 4.1.142, 'so smoothly
off, so obscenely, as it were, so fit') or
'obscurely' (a private place where 'ob-
scene' events may take place)
  perfect word-perfect. Wolfgang Franke
('The Logic of *Double Entendre* in *A
Midsummer Night's* Dream', *SQ* 58
(1979), p. 287) intriguingly compares
Bottom's 'Be perfect. Adieu' with St
Paul's 'Finally, brethren, farewell. Be
perfect', 2 Corinthians 13: 11—compare his use of 1 Corinthians in
4.1.207–10 and n.

100 **Hold, or cut bowstrings** The phrase
is obscure; the most likely source is
that the English longbowmen if defeated would cut their bowstrings to
prevent their use by the enemy (Charles Hertel in *The Explicator*, 33 (1975),
item 39), though see also Tilley C502
'Hold or cut codpiece point'. Carol
J. Petersen ('Bowstrings, Anyone?',

AN&Q 21 (1983), pp. 130–2) suggests
it is analogous to 'fish or cut bait' and
therefore means something like 'Hold
fast to our purpose or let someone else
have a chance'; this makes good sense
but does not square with the probable
source.

2.1.0.1–2 The doors are the ones opening
from the tiring-house on to the stage.

1–58 The scene is parallelled by and probably influenced by Lyly's *Gallathea* 1.2
where Cupid, a mischief-maker like
Robin, questions one of Diana's
nymphs about her mistress and her
quarrel with Venus. The scene opens
with Cupid asking 'Fair Nymph, are
you strayed from your company by
chance, or love you to wander solitary
on purpose?' (*Works*, ii. 434). For
Shakespeare's possible use of *Gallathea*
as source, see Introduction, p. 100–1.

2–3 The lines parallel Spenser, *The Faerie
Queene*, 6.8.32.1 (first published 1596):
'Through hils and dales, through
bushes and through breres'; Shakespeare *might* have seen Spenser's lines
in manuscript or, more probably, the
lines could simply be conventional.

Over park, over pale,
　Thorough flood, thorough fire;   5
I do wander everywhere
Swifter than the moonës sphere,
And I serve the Fairy Queen
To dew her orbs upon the green.
The cowslips tall her pensioners be;   10
In their gold coats spots you see:
Those be rubies, fairy favours;
In those freckles live their savours.
I must go seek some dewdrops here,
And hang a pearl in every cowslip's ear.   15
　Farewell, thou lob of spirits; I'll be gone.
Our Queen and all her elves come here anon.

7 moonës] STEEVENS 1778; moons QF

3–5 **Thorough** through (the spelling indicating two syllables)

4 **park** an enclosed tract of land held by royal grant for hunting (*OED*), like the 'palace wood' (1.2.94) that the fairies are in
pale an area of land enclosed by a fence or palings (*OED sb.*[1] 3)

7 **moonës** Steevens's clarification, while not strictly necessary, regularizes the metre (but see 2.1.58 for a similar metrical problem and 4.1.95 for a similar solution).
moonës sphere the transparent globe to which the moon was fixed and which moved round the earth, according to Ptolemaic astronomy

9 **orbs** circles (*OED*'s first instance), fairy-rings, circles of darker grass caused by decayed fungi

10 **pensioners** The title of Elizabeth's royal bodyguard of fifty splendidly dressed gentlemen, hence 'their gold coats' (l. 11); compare Mistress Quickly's comment, 'there has been earls, nay, which is more, pensioners', (*Merry Wives* 2.2.75–6).

11 **spots** marks in the cowslip's 'umbels or sprays of yellow scented flowers' (Foakes); compare *Cymbeline* 2.2.38–9, 'the crimson drops | I'th' bottom of a cowslip'.

12 **favours** marks of favour

13 **freckles** Compare 'the freckled cow-

slip', *Henry V* 5.2.49.
savours fragrance

15 **And . . . ear** Fashionable Elizabethan gentlemen often wore jewels in their ears. The Fairy's association of pearls and dewdrops may hark back to Pliny's belief that pearls begin as dewdrops (trans. Holland, Bk. 9 ch. 35) (Halliwell).
cowslip *Primula veris* (Rydén, p. 72)

16 **lob** country bumpkin, clown or lout (*OED sb.*[2] 2); the Fairy's use of the word suggests that Robin was to have been played by an adult actor, perhaps larger than the Fairy who was probably played by a young boy-actor. But a lob was also a particular kind of fairy of the Brownie type; Katherine Briggs advises that 'the general use of the words "hob" and "lob" is a friendly one with rustic associations' (*A Dictionary of Fairies* (1976), p. 271). Fairy lobs were at least of full mortal size and could be giants, like Lob-lie-by-the-fire who is mentioned in Beaumont's *The Knight of the Burning Pestle, c.*1608 (Briggs, *The Anatomy of Puck* (1959), p. 88), again suggesting the difference in size between Robin and the Fairy.

17 **elves** were not necessarily male but Titania's attendants were probably played by boys (see below, n. to ll. 59.1–2)

ROBIN

The King doth keep his revels here tonight.
Take heed the Queen come not within his sight,
For Oberon is passing fell and wrath   20
Because that she, as her attendant, hath
A lovely boy stol'n from an Indian king.
She never had so sweet a changeling;
And jealous Oberon would have the child
Knight of his train, to trace the forests wild.   25
But she perforce withholds the lovèd boy,
Crowns him with flowers, and makes him all her joy.
And now they never meet in grove, or green,
By fountain clear, or spangled starlight sheen,
But they do square, that all their elves for fear   30
Creep into acorn cups, and hide them there.

FAIRY

Either I mistake your shape and making quite
Or else you are that shrewd and knavish sprite
Called Robin Goodfellow. Are not you he

---

20 **passing ... wrath** extremely fierce and
angry

22 **Indian** Oberon and Titania are associated with India (e.g. ll. 69, 124). Titania's account of how she came by
the boy (ll. 122–37) is not incompatible with Robin's, since the boy's
father might reasonably imagine the
boy to have been 'stol'n' by Titania—it
depends on one's point of view.

23 **changeling** The word usually refers to
the ugly or weak child left by the
fairies in exchange for the beautiful
mortal child stealthily removed by
them; here, unusually (sole instance in
OED), it refers to the mortal boy himself. The word has three syllables here.

25 **trace** range over

29 **fountain** the source of a river (compare l. 84)

30 **square** quarrel

33 **shrewd** mischievous, malign

34 **Robin Goodfellow** and his knavery
were widely known and described in
both Elizabethan folk-lore and literature, both court and popular (see
Introduction, pp. 35–42). Though the

character is now usually known as
Puck, his name is Robin Goodfellow
(in most SDs and SPs in QF) but he
belongs to the type of hobgoblins
known as 'pucks'; hence he is properly
Robin Goodfellow the puck. His 'sur-
name' is a hopeful gesture: it is not
that he is always a good fellow but
named, propitiatingly, in the hope that
he might be willing to behave like one.

Two other plays, both probably written shortly after *Dream*, contain a
character called Robin Goodfellow; the
description of his costume there *may*
reflect the one worn in *Dream*. In *Grim
the Collier of Croydon* (*c*.1600, published 1662 in *Gratiae Theatrales*, probably
by William Haughton) Robin Goodfellow enters 'in a suit of leather close to
his body, his face and hands coloured
russet-colour, with a flail' (p. 51) and
announces a series of Robin's traditional tricks, as in *Dream* 2.1.35–57
(e.g., 'But woe betide the silly Dairy
maids, | For I shall fleet [skim] their
Cream-bowls night by night', p. 52).
Though he describes this costume as a

That frights the maidens of the villag'ry,   35
Skim milk, and sometimes labour in the quern,
And bootless make the breathless housewife churn,
And sometime make the drink to bear no barm,
Mislead night wanderers, laughing at their harm?
Those that 'hobgoblin' call you, and 'sweet puck',   40
You do their work, and they shall have good luck.
Are not you he?
ROBIN   Thou speak'st aright;
I am that merry wanderer of the night.
I jest to Oberon, and make him smile
When I a fat and bean-fed horse beguile,   45
Neighing in likeness of a filly foal;
And sometime lurk I in a gossip's bowl

35 villag'ry] Q2, F (Villagree); Villageree Q1   42–3 Thou . . . night] *As* F; *one line* Q

'transform'd disguise' (p. 52), it is similar to the one Robin offers to put on in *Wily Beguiled* (published 1606), 'I'll rather put on my flashing red nose, and my flaming face, and come wrapt in a Calf-skin and cry bo ho' (ed. W. W. Greg (Malone Society: Oxford, 1912), ll. 716–17—for Robin's cry of 'ho, ho, ho' see *Dream* 3.2.421). Elsewhere in *Wily Beguiled* he describes the costume as a 'rousing Calf-skin suit . . . like some Hob goblin or some devil' (ll. 1038–9) and as 'my devilish robes, | I mean my Christmas Calf-skin suit' (ll. 1255–6). In both these plays Robin is closely associated with hell and devils, unlike the Robin in *Dream* (but see n. to 3.1.104).

35 **villag'ry** troupe of villagers (cf. peasantry); Q2's spelling makes it clear that it has three syllables.

36 **Skim milk** steal the cream off the milk
labour in the quern 'Quern' was a variant for 'churn' and Robin's trick may have been to make the housewife's efforts to make butter fruitless, as l. 37 suggests. More often 'quern' was a handmill for grinding corn or mustard and Robin was presumably either a similarly frustrating presence or responsible for grinding corn which should not have been ground.

37 **bootless** all in vain

38 **barm** yeast; Robin stops the drink fermenting and having a frothy head (another sense of 'barm').

39 **Mislead . . . harm** One of Robin's most frequent tricks (Tilley R147, quoting Tyndale: 'led by Robin Goodfellow . . . they cannot come the right way').

41 **You . . . luck** As well as playing tricks, Robin was thought to help people by 'grinding of malt or mustard, and sweeping the house at midnight' in return for 'his mess of white bread and milk, which was his standard fee' (Scot, p. 85); he will sweep up at the end of *Dream*. In *Grim the Collier of Croydon* Robin boasts 'This half year have I lived about this Town, | Helping poor Servants to dispatch their work, | To brew and bake and other Husbandry' (p. 68).

45–57 Robin's description of himself focuses on his shape-changing, a metamorphic ability he displays throughout *Dream*.

45 **bean-fed** well-fed

46 **filly foal** female foal ('foal' can refer to either sex)

47 **gossip's bowl** Strictly a godmother's christening cup, though gossip may mean simply 'a chattering woman' here.

In very likeness of a roasted crab,
And when she drinks, against her lips I bob,
And on her withered dewlap pour the ale.   50
The wisest aunt telling the saddest tale
Sometime for three-foot stool mistaketh me.
Then slip I from her bum—down topples she,
And 'tailor' cries, and falls into a cough,
And then the whole choir hold their hips, and laugh,   55
And waxen in their mirth, and neeze, and swear
A merrier hour was never wasted there.—
But room, fairy: here comes Oberon.

FAIRY

And here my mistress. Would that he were gone.

Enter Oberon the King of Fairies at one door, with his
train, and Titania the Queen at another, with hers

---

48 **crab** crab apple, roasted to put in a
spiced winter drink

50 **dewlap** 'pendulous folds of flesh about
the human throat' like a cow's (*OED*'s
first instance of its transfer from cattle
to humans); Theseus' hounds are 'dewlapped like Thessalian bulls' (4.1.121
and n.), metamorphosing the observed
immediacy of this old woman's throat
into an Ovidian image.

51 **aunt** old woman (*OED*)

54 **tailor** Johnson remembered observing
'the custom of crying *tailor* at a sudden
fall backwards' but his association of
the cry with a tailor's squatting posture
is less likely than a derivation from
'tail' for 'bottom' (see Hilda M. Hulme,
Explorations in Shakespeare's Language
(1962), pp. 99–100).

55 **choir** company
laugh QF's spelling, 'loffe', may indicate a rustic archaic language used by
Robin here for 'waxen' and 'neeze' as
well.

56 **waxen** increase, get louder
neeze sneeze

58 **room** Pope's emendation to 'make
room' for the sake of metre is reasonable if the demands of metre are
thought to be paramount but it is unnecessary if Robin's instruction to
'stand aside' is spoken particularly ex-
pansively. 'Make room' occurs three
times elsewhere in Shakespeare; 'give

room' is also possible (compare *Romeo*
1.5.26).

59.1–2 The entrance copies, in its use of
the stage doors, the meeting of Robin
and the fairy. I have left the entrance
at the point it appears in QF but that
depends on Robin and the Fairy looking off-stage in different directions to
see the imminent arrival of their mon-
archs. On the Elizabethan stage, a
grand entry, such as this must have
been, might well have started earlier,
say after l. 57, giving everyone time
to move into patterned position without delay. If one assumes that Titania
has at least five fairies (the first fairy
and the four who attend Bottom, assuming that one of these is the same
as the Second Fairy in 2.2), Oberon is
likely to have a similar number in his
'train', necessitating at least ten extras
in this scene. If Titania's train is made
up of 'elves' (l. 17) they would probably be children (though see the possibility of their being doubled by the
actors playing the workmen, Introduction, p. 24); the long tradition of Titania's being accompanied by a whole
corps de ballet of adult women has no
authority in the text but lasted until
well into the 1950s, emphasizing a
gender division in the fairy monarch's
attendants, as in the illustration to the
play in Rowe's edition in 1709, an

OBERON

Ill met by moonlight, proud Titania.   60

TITANIA

What, jealous Oberon?—Fairies, skip hence.

I have forsworn his bed and company.

OBERON

Tarry, rash wanton. Am not I thy lord?

TITANIA

Then I must be thy lady; but I know

---

61 Fairies] FAIRY Q, THEOBALD; Fairy QF

---

illustration which also suggests the formal opposition of the two groups that might well reflect Elizabethan stage practice (see fig. 5). Such a division might also echo the play's opening if Theseus had been accompanied by male attendants and Hippolyta, as often in production, by women. While 'elves' can, in theory, be male or female, the word suggests, then as now, male fairies. Some productions have included an appearance for the changeling here (e.g. Charles Kean in 1856); Coghill, who included him in his 1945 production, comments 'he is a tremendous help to Titania to act with during her long speech about him; and he can be left howling when she goes off with Bottom Translated' (Sprague and Trewin, pp. 64–5). He did exactly that in the Reinhardt–Dieterle film (1935), played by Kenneth Anger, and looked distinctly happier to be with Oberon in the later sequences of the film, adapting his turban to imitate Oberon's headdress. In Lepage's production at the Royal National Theatre (1992), the changeling was, unusually, a baby breast-fed by Titania.

In *Merry Wives*, when Anne Page is to be disguised as the 'Fairy Queen' her mother decides 'That quaint in green she shall be loose enrobed, | With ribbons pendant flaring 'bout her head' (4.6.40–1); given the habit of Elizabethan companies of reusing costumes, it seems quite likely that Shakespeare's company could have used Titania's costume.

60 **Titania** Ovid uses the name five times in *Metamorphoses* where it refers to Diana and Circe, amongst others (see further, Introduction, p. 32); Golding never uses it, preferring 'Titan's daughter'. Elizabethan pronunciation was probably 'Tietainia', rather than the modern 'Titarnia'. Gordon Crosse, initially irritated by Oberons who pronounced the second syllable to 'rhyme with Spain' (vol. 2, p. 73), came to realise that this was the normal pronunciation (cf., e.g., vol. 2, p. 113).

61 **Oberon** In *The Book of Duke Huon of Bordeaux* (translated by Lord Berners (1533–42)), he is 'a king of the fairy' and described as 'of height but of three foot, and crooked-shouldered, but yet he hath an angelic visage' (ed. S. L. Lee (London, 1882–3), p. 63), his height being the result of a curse (p. 73); he also appears in Spenser's *Faerie Queene* (2.1.6.9 and 2.10.75.8). See also Introduction, p. 31.

61 **Fairies** Q1's 'fairy' could be defended as, for instance, an instruction to First Fairy to move away from Robin (Wells).

63 **wanton** an unmanageable, ungoverned rebellious person (*OED* 1) but also a lascivious, unchaste lewd woman (*OED* 2); Oberon appears to believe that since Titania has 'forsworn his bed' (l. 62) she must be in someone else's. Compare Titania's much gentler and perhaps correcting uses of the word at ll. 99 and 129.

63–4 **lord . . . lady** husband and wife, domination and submission

157

When thou hast stol'n away from fairyland   65
And in the shape of Corin sat all day,
Playing on pipes of corn, and versing love
To amorous Phillida. Why art thou here
Come from the farthest step of India,
But that, forsooth, the bouncing Amazon,   70
Your buskined mistress and your warrior love,
To Theseus must be wedded, and you come
To give their bed joy and prosperity?

OBERON
How canst thou thus for shame, Titania,
Glance at my credit with Hippolyta,   75
Knowing I know thy love to Theseus?
Didst not thou lead him through the glimmering night
From Perigouna whom he ravishèd,
And make him with fair Aegles break his faith,
With Ariadne and Antiopa?   80

---

78 Perigouna] WHITE; *Perigenia* QF; Perigune THEOBALD (*conj.*); Perigune POPE 1728
79 Aegles] CHAMBERS (*after* Rowe: Ægle); Eagles QF

66, 68 **Corin, Phillida** Conventional pastoral names for shepherds and shepherdesses; *The Arbour of Amorous Devices* by Nicholas Breton and others (1597), a possible source for Bottom's song (3.1.118–26), included 'A Pastoral of Phillis and Coridon' (F2ʳ–F2ᵛ). Oberon is not accused of having sex with Phillida but of wasting his time as amateur rustic poet and musician. Oberon, here, is also a shape-changer.

67 **pipes of corn** pipes made of straw

69 **step** limit (Q2, F read 'steep' which *OED* takes as 'mountain', *sb.*[1] B1)

71 **buskined** wearing knee-length boots; Spenser specifically associates 'buskins to the knee' with Diana (*Faerie Queene* 1.6.16.9) but they were also a standard part of an Amazon's costume.

75 **Glance at** allude to critically (Foakes)

78 **Perigouna** So named in North ('Perigone' in Plutarch). Theseus killed Sinnis, her father; she fled but Theseus found her hiding in a bush and 'swore by his faith he would use her gently

. . . Upon which promise she . . . lay with him, by whom she was conceived of a goodly boy' (North, p. 5). He later married her off to Deioneus.

79 **Aegles** Probably Aegle but emended here to accord with Shakespeare's probable source in North; she was a nymph who 'was loved of Theseus' (North, p. 10) and was the cause of Theseus' abandoning Ariadne on Naxos, though Plutarch distrusted the story.

80 **Ariadne** fell in love with Theseus and gave him a 'clue of thread' which enabled him to find his way out of the Cretan labyrinth after killing the Minotaur; after inheriting Crete, she fell in love with Theseus who 'made league with her . . . and concluded peace . . . between the *Athenians* and the *Cretans*' (North, pp. 9–10). She was put ashore on Cyprus by him when pregnant and seasick and abandoned by him. Different versions state she either hanged her-

TITANIA

These are the forgeries of jealousy,
And never since the middle summer's spring
Met we on hill, in dale, forest, or mead,
By pavèd fountain or by rushy brook,
Or in the beachèd margin of the sea   85
To dance our ringlets to the whistling wind,
But with thy brawls thou hast disturbed our sport.
Therefore the winds, piping to us in vain,
As in revenge have sucked up from the sea
Contagious fogs which, falling in the land,   90
Hath every pelting river made so proud
That they have overborne their continents.
The ox hath therefore stretched his yoke in vain,
The ploughman lost his sweat, and the green corn

self or was taken to Naxos, grief-stricken at his love for Aegle, though North states that 'there is no truth nor certainty' in the story (p. 10).

Antiopa An Amazon who, according to North (p. 14), was either given to Theseus by Hercules 'to honour his valiantness' or was captured by Theseus alone by being enticed on board his ship which then put to sea (the marginal note in North states she was 'ravished' by him); she was the mother of Hippolytus and was abandoned by Theseus so that he could marry Phaedra.

81 **forgeries** Is Titania lying? Theseus' involvement with these women is amply documented in Plutarch though he of course says nothing about Titania's involvement.

82 **middle summer's spring** beginning of midsummer (Steevens)

84 **pavèd fountain** a river-source 'with a pebbly bottom' (Chambers)

85 **beachèd margin** the sea's edge covered with pebbles, shingle (*OED*); compare *Timon* 5.2.101, 'the beachèd verge of the salt flood'. Shakespeare as usual prefers the spelling 'margent'.

86 **ringlets** circular dances, a fairy-ring (*OED*, quoting *Dream* and Drayton,

Quest of Cynthia (1627), 'When Fairies in their Ringlets there | Do dance their nightly rounds'). Titania is frequently linked to circles in the play (compare 'orbs' 2.1.9, 'round' 2.1.140, 'roundel' 2.2.1).

87 **brawls** clamour (*OED sb.*[1]) but also suggesting Oberon's more boisterous, circular dances (*OED sb.*[3] 2 from French 'bransles') compared with her own 'ringlets'. Mote describes 'a French brawl' in *LLL* 3.1.7–20.

88–114 Brooks suggests that Shakespeare made extensive use here of a large number of different passages in Golding's Ovid, particularly Deucalion's flood (1.313–40), the seasons (2.33–9), Ceres' curse on Sicily (5.593–604), and the plague of Aegina (7.678–702) and, less convincingly, passages from Seneca's *Medea* and *Oedipus*.

88 **piping to us in vain** Compare Matthew 11: 17 and Luke 7: 31, 'we have piped unto you and ye have not danced'.

91–2 **every...continents** The terrifying power of the rivers flooding recurred to Shakespeare as an image of disorder (compare *Hamlet* 4.5.97–8 and *Coriolanus* 3.1.247–8).

91 **pelting** paltry

92 **continents** banks

Hath rotted ere his youth attained a beard.   95
The fold stands empty in the drownèd field,
And crows are fatted with the murrain flock.
The nine men's morris is filled up with mud,
And the quaint mazes in the wanton green
For lack of tread are undistinguishable.   100
The human mortals want their winter cheer.
No night is now with hymn or carol blessed.
Therefore the moon, the governess of floods,
Pale in her anger, washes all the air,
That rheumatic diseases do abound;   105
And thorough this distemperature we see

---

97 murrain] THEOBALD 1740; murrion QF   101 cheer] HANMER (*conj.* Theobald); heere QF

---

95 **beard** Often used for 'ears of corn';
compare *Sonnets* 12.7–8, 'And sum-
mer's green all girded up in sheaves |
Borne on the bier with white and bristly beard'.
97 **murrain** (afflicted with) sheep-plague
98 **nine men's morris** A game, rather like
noughts and crosses, in which the aim
is to form lines of three by moving
across a pattern of concentric squares;
each side starts with nine pegs ('men'),
losing one each time the opponent
forms a line of three. When played
outdoors the pattern was cut in turf.
99 **quaint** elaborate, ingenious
mazes Maze-patterns were frequently
cut in turfs and were often followed by
young men as a race; W. H. Matthews
reports one 'sunk in a hollow at the
top of a hillock called "The Fairies'
Hill" ' (*Mazes and Labyrinths* (1922), p.
77) and associates another with games
on May-eve (p. 73). See also Janet
Bord, *Mazes and Labyrinths of the World*
(1976), pp. 46–58, and Penelope Reed
Doob, *The Idea of the Labyrinth from
Classical Antiquity through the Middle
Ages* (1990). Turf mazes are unicursal,
i.e. they have no false trails and are not
puzzle or multicursal mazes like, say,
the Cretan labyrinth of the Minotaur
for which Theseus needed Ariadne's
thread to find his way in and out
(though Bord points out that all rep-

resentations of the Cretan labyrinth in
the Renaissance show it as unicursal,
making Ariadne's help superfluous (p.
39)). Thomas Hill's *A most brief and
pleasant treatise, teaching how to dress,
sow, and set a garden* (1563) included
diagrams of two unicursal mazes 'as
proper adornments upon pleasure to a
garden' and suggested putting 'a proper
arbour decked with roses' in the middle
(sigs. B4^v–B5^r), just as the labyrinth of
this wood may contain Titania's rose-
canopied bower (but see 3.2.6–7 and n.).
wanton green luxuriant grass (*OED*)—
compare Oberon's use at l. 63.
101 **cheer** Q1's reading 'here' makes
sense, though weak, but Hanmer's
emendation strengthens the line,
identifying an easy misreading. Brooks
compares 'happy cheer is turn'd to
heavy chance . . . | And shepherds
wonted solace is extinct' (Spenser's
Shepheardes Calendar, November, ll.
103, 106), claiming it as a source.
Titania's following line explains her
meaning further.
103 **Therefore** Parallelling the word at l. 88.
105 **rheumatic** causing a discharge of
rheum, either dripping from eyes or
nose or, if internally, the cause of
rheumatism; accented on first syllable
106 **distemperature** 'disorder in nature'
but also the 'loss of temper' seen in
the moon's anger

The seasons alter: hoary-headed frosts
Fall in the fresh lap of the crimson rose,
And on old Hiems' thin and icy crown
An odorous chaplet of sweet summer buds   110
Is, as in mock'ry, set. The spring, the summer,
The childing autumn, angry winter change
Their wonted liveries, and the mazèd world
By their increase now knows not which is which;
And this same progeny of evils comes   115
From our debate, from our dissension—
We are their parents and original.

OBERON

Do you amend it, then. It lies in you.
Why should Titania cross her Oberon?
I do but beg a little changeling boy   120
To be my henchman.

TITANIA   Set your heart at rest.
The fairyland buys not the child of me.
His mother was a vot'ress of my order,
And in the spicèd Indian air by night
Full often hath she gossiped by my side,   125
And sat with me on Neptune's yellow sands,

---

109 thin] HALLIWELL (*conj.* Tyrwhitt); chinne QF   111 mock'ry] F; mockery Q   115 evils comes] F2; euils, | Comes QF

109 **old Hiems** winter personified as an old man, as often in Ovid (e.g. Golding 2.36–9 where he has a 'snowy frozen crown') and by Shakespeare in *LLL* 5.2.876.
109 **thin** Q1's 'chinne' produces a decidedly odd picture; 'th' and 'ch' are easily confused. The thin and scattered hairs of an old man's head are frequently referred to by Shakespeare (e.g. *Richard II* 3.2.108, 'Whitebeards have armed their thin and hairless scalps').
112 **childing** fruitful, pregnant; compare *Sonnets* 97.6, 'The teeming autumn big with rich increase' (and l. 114 below for 'increase').
    change exchange

113 **wonted** accustomed
    mazèd bewildered, terrified
114 **their increase** the produce of the seasons
116 **debate** quarrel
117 **original** origin
121 **henchman** page or squire; 'the royal henchmen or "chyldren of honor" were abolished by Queen Elizabeth in 1565' (*OED*), though nobles continued to have them.
123 **vot'ress** a woman who has taken vows (as the nuns of Diana described by Theseus in 1.1.70–4); compare Oberon's description of 'the imperial vot'ress' at l. 163.

161

Marking th'embarkèd traders on the flood,
When we have laughed to see the sails conceive
And grow big-bellied with the wanton wind,
Which she with pretty and with swimming gait   130
Following, her womb then rich with my young squire,
Would imitate, and sail upon the land
To fetch me trifles, and return again
As from a voyage, rich with merchandise.
But she, being mortal, of that boy did die;   135
And for her sake do I rear up her boy;
And for her sake I will not part with him.

OBERON

How long within this wood intend you stay?

TITANIA

Perchance till after Theseus' wedding day.
If you will patiently dance in our round,   140
And see our moonlight revels, go with us.
If not, shun me, and I will spare your haunts.

OBERON

Give me that boy and I will go with thee.

TITANIA

Not for thy fairy kingdom.—Fairies, away.
We shall chide downright if I longer stay.   145

                              Exeunt Titania and her train

OBERON

Well, go thy way. Thou shalt not from this grove
Till I torment thee for this injury.—
My gentle puck, come hither. Thou rememb'rest
Since once I sat upon a promontory

145.1 *Exeunt . . . train*] THEOBALD; *Exeunt*. QF; *Exit Tit. and Train* FAIRY Q

---

127 **embarkèd traders** merchant ships
(though *OED*'s first instance for
'traders' in this sense is 1712)
129 **wanton** sportive (compare ll. 63, 99)
130 **swimming** as though gliding through
waves or in a dance (Brooks)
131 **Following** copying
140 **round** a round dance

142 **spare** avoid (*OED v.*[1] 7b)
145 **chide** quarrel
149–57 Brooks traces a possible, though
fairly unconvincing, source for Cupid's
journey in Seneca's *Hippolytus* (especially ll. 192–203, 331–7)
149 **Since** when

And heard a mermaid on a dolphin's back   150
Uttering such dulcet and harmonious breath
That the rude sea grew civil at her song
And certain stars shot madly from their spheres
    To hear the sea-maid's music?
ROBIN   I remember.
OBERON
That very time I saw, but thou couldst not,   155
Flying between the cold moon and the earth
Cupid, all armed. A certain aim he took
At a fair vestal thronèd by the west,
And loosed his love-shaft smartly from his bow
As it should pierce a hundred thousand hearts.   160
But I might see young Cupid's fiery shaft
Quenched in the chaste beams of the wat'ry moon,
And the imperial vot'ress passèd on,

---

158 the] F; *not in* Q

150-3 There is some imprecise echo here of the legend of Arion, a singer-poet, who leaped into the sea to escape from murderous sailors and was saved by a dolphin. When Elizabeth visited Kenilworth in 1575, Leicester's spectacular entertainments included '*Arion* that excellent & famouz Muzicien . . . ryding alofte upon hiz olld freend the Dolphin, (that from hed too tayl waz a foour & twenty foot long)', a Triton like a mermaid, Proteus on a dolphin and 'a swimming Mermayd (that from top too tayl waz an eyghteen foot long)' as well as magnificent fireworks, 'with blaz of burning darts, flying too & fro, leamz of starz coruscant, streamz and hail of firie sparkes' (Robert Laneham, *A Letter* (1575), pp. 42, 40 and 16). Shakespeare *could* have known these details (even if we do not need to hypothesize that he saw them as a child). But the link between Kenilworth or the entertainment at Elvetham in 1591 (which also included a water pageant as well as an appearance by the 'Queene of *Fairy* land' who is married to '*Auberon* the *Fairy*

King' and described how 'amorous stars fall nightly in my lap' (Lyly, *Works*, i. 449-50)) and *Dream* is tenuous; neither included the 'mermaid on a dolphin's back' that Oberon describes.

153 **certain stars** an indefinite number, some particular stars; but see also l. 157 and n. The stars, like Cupid's aim, are unerring as they move in their spheres.
    spheres See 2.1.7 and n.

157 **certain** unerring

158-64 Usually taken as an allusion to Queen Elizabeth, though Wilson's doubts, for all his odd style, have not been properly considered: 'Surely the oblation of flattery is scanty—the Vestal is 'fair,' that is all—while even maiden ladies of ordinary rank are apt to be touchy about references to past courtships'; see Montrose, esp. pp. 81-2.

158 **vestal** vowed to virginity

163 **imperial** Stanley Wells has suggested that it could simply mean 'imperious' (*OED* 5b).

In maiden meditation, fancy-free.
Yet marked I where the bolt of Cupid fell.   165
It fell upon a little western flower—
Before, milk-white; now, purple with love's wound:
And maidens call it 'love-in-idleness'.
Fetch me that flower; the herb I showed thee once.
The juice of it on sleeping eyelids laid   170
Will make or man or woman madly dote
Upon the next live creature that it sees.
Fetch me this herb, and be thou here again
Ere the leviathan can swim a league.

ROBIN

I'll put a girdle round about the earth   175
In forty minutes.   *Exit*

OBERON   Having once this juice
I'll watch Titania when she is asleep,
And drop the liquor of it in her eyes.
The next thing then she waking looks upon—
Be it on lion, bear, or wolf, or bull,   180
On meddling monkey, or on busy ape—
She shall pursue it with the soul of love.
And ere I take this charm from off her sight—
As I can take it with another herb—
I'll make her render up her page to me.   185
But who comes here? I am invisible,

175–6 I'll . . . minutes] POPE; *one line in* QF   176 *Exit*] F2; *not in* QF

167 **purple** the colour of blood
168 **love-in-idleness** the pansy or hearts-ease (*OED*), *Viola tricolor* or wild pansy (Rydén, p. 77). The myth of colour change is Shakespeare's invention; in Ovid, however, the mulberry turns to purple when stained with Pyramus' blood (Golding, 4.152). St John's Wort, one of the possible plants Shakespeare may have had in mind for 'Dian's bud' in 4.1.72, has purple juice. Compare the sternly moralistic proverb 'Love is the fruit of idleness' (Dent L513.1).
170–2 Shakespeare's source here is probably Lyly's *Euphues and his England*: 'An herb there is, called Anacam-

soritis, a strange name and doubtless of a strange nature, for whosoever toucheth it, falleth in love, with the person she next seeth' (ii. 115); in Gil Polo's *Diana Enamorada* (1564), Felicia uses 'her herbs and words' to make Syrenus fall in love with Diana (translated by Bartholomew Yong, in Kennedy, p. 375). In Lyly's *Sapho and Phao* (1584), Phao knows 'no herb to make lovers sleep but Hearts-ease' (ii. 402)
174 **leviathan** a sea-monster, usually then identified as the whale; see Job 41: 31.
182 **soul** essence
186 **invisible** Henslowe's list of costumes

And I will overhear their conference.
Enter Demetrius, Helena following him

DEMETRIUS

I love thee not, therefore pursue me not.
Where is Lysander, and fair Hermia?
The one I'll slay, the other slayeth me.   190
Thou told'st me they were stol'n unto this wood,
And here am I, and wood within this wood
Because I cannot meet my Hermia.
Hence, get thee gone, and follow me no more.

HELENA

You draw me, you hard-hearted adamant,   195
But yet you draw not iron, for my heart
Is true as steel. Leave you your power to draw,

190 slay ... slayeth] THEOBALD (*conj.* Thirlby); stay ... stayeth QF

belonging to the Admiral's Men in 1598 included 'a robe for to go invisi-bell' (*Diary*, p. 325) but, while Oberon may have put on such a cloak (what-ever it may have looked like), he needed only announce his invisibility to be so. Oberons often stand aside for this and comparable scenes later in the play, giving the lovers full use of the stage, though Granville Barker's Oberon was a visible watcher, often standing between the lovers (see Dym-kowski, p. 66 and 3.2.42.1). Some Oberons have become involved in the action: in Peter Hall's production in Stratford in 1959, Helena (Vanessa Redgrave) 'tries to butt De Souza [Demetrius]. De Souza sidesteps. Red-grave falls over C. Hardy [Oberon] helps Redgrave to her feet and both move D/S. Redgrave does "a take" on Hardy, being invisible' (prompt-book). Motley's designs for George Devine's production in 1954 used a different effect: 'To make the trees, Motley had taken wire frames, covered them with gauze, and applied leaves to them, making them look like paintings. For Oberon him-self, they made a net cloak covered with leaves and painted in the same way. When he was supposed to disap-pear, he turned his back, put his arms up over his head, and the cloak spread out in the shape of a tree, so that he

became part of the scenery' (see Mi-chael Mullin and David McGuire, 'A "Purge on Prettiness": Motley's Cos-tumes for *A Midsummer Night's Dream*, Shakespeare Memorial Theatre, Strat-ford-upon-Avon, 1954', *Shakespeare Studies* (Shakespeare Soc. of Japan, Tokyo), 27 (1989), pp. 65–77).

190 **slay ... slayeth** QF's 'stay ... stayeth' can be defended though it is not clear then whether Lysander stays Demetrius by getting in the way of his love for Hermia or whether Demetrius intends to stay Lysander and is stopped by Hermia.

192 **and wood** both 'mad with anger' and 'wooed'

195–9 Brooks detects here the influence of Phaedra's grovelling pleading before Hippolytus in Seneca's *Hippolytus*, ll. 699–712.

195 **draw** like a magnet
adamant Either 'magnet loadstone' or 'a diamond-hard metal', conflated here (*OED* 4, quoting *Dream*); compare the two proverbs 'As the Adamant draws Iron' (frequently used of love and desire) and 'As hard as adamant' (Dent A31.1 and A31.2).

196–7 **But yet ... steel** Helena moves from Demetrius' magnetic and hard-hearted powers to her soft heart and then to the proverbial 'true as steel' (Tilley

And I shall have no power to follow you.
DEMETRIUS

  Do I entice you? Do I speak you fair?

  Or rather do I not in plainest truth   200

  Tell you I do not nor I cannot love you?

HELENA

  And even for that do I love you the more.

  I am your spaniel, and, Demetrius,

  The more you beat me I will fawn on you.

  Use me but as your spaniel: spurn me, strike me,   205

  Neglect me, lose me; only give me leave,

  Unworthy as I am, to follow you.

  What worser place can I beg in your love—

  And yet a place of high respect with me—

  Than to be usèd as you use your dog?   210

DEMETRIUS

  Tempt not too much the hatred of my spirit;

  For I am sick when I do look on thee.

HELENA

  And I am sick when I look not on you.

DEMETRIUS

  You do impeach your modesty too much,

  To leave the city and commit yourself   215

  Into the hands of one that loves you not;

  To trust the opportunity of night,

  And the ill counsel of a desert place,

  With the rich worth of your virginity.

HELENA

  Your virtue is my privilege, for that   220

---

201 not nor] F (not, nor); not, not Q

S840), punning on a sword as 'iron' (Demetrius may be threatening to draw his sword here). Wells finds the conceit 'somewhat strained'.

204 **The more . . . on you** Proverbial (Tilley S705); Brooks compares Lyly, *Euphues*, 'the more he is beaten the fonder he is' (i. 249) and *Euphues and his England*, 'The Spaniel that fawneth when he is beaten' (ii. 155).

206 **lose** Q1's 'loose' is ambiguously 'lose' or 'loose' when modernized.

210 Compare Tilley D514, 'To use one like a dog'.

212 **sick** nauseated

214 **impeach** call in question (*OED*)

220 **my privilege** guarantee of immunity for my actions (Foakes) because of your qualities (which she then goes on to detail)

It is not night when I do see your face.
Therefore I think I am not in the night,
Nor doth this wood lack worlds of company,
For you in my respect are all the world.
Then how can it be said I am alone,   225
When all the world is here to look on me?

DEMETRIUS

I'll run from thee, and hide me in the brakes,
And leave thee to the mercy of wild beasts.

HELENA

The wildest hath not such a heart as you.
Run when you will. The story shall be changed: 230
Apollo flies, and Daphne holds the chase.
The dove pursues the griffin; the mild hind
Makes speed to catch the tiger: bootless speed,
When cowardice pursues, and valour flies.

DEMETRIUS

I will not stay thy questions. Let me go;   235
Or if thou follow me, do not believe
But I shall do thee mischief in the wood.

HELENA

Ay, in the temple, in the town, the field,
You do me mischief. Fie, Demetrius,
Your wrongs do set a scandal on my sex.   240
We cannot fight for love as men may do;
We should be wooed, and were not made to woo.
I'll follow thee, and make a heaven of hell,
To die upon the hand I love so well.

⌈*Exit Demetrius, Helena following him*⌉

244.1 *Exit . . . him*] ROWE (*Exeunt*); *not in* Q1; *Exit.* Q2, F

227 **brakes** clumps or thickets of bushes
  or briars
231 Daphne, pursued by Apollo, was
  changed into the laurel tree (Golding,
  1.545–700).
232 **griffin** a mythical animal whose top
  half was an eagle and lower half a
  lion, notoriously ferocious
  hind a doe, particularly of red deer
233 **bootless** useless
240 **Your . . . sex** Helena complains that

Demetrius' actions force her to act in
a scandalous way.
243 **make . . . hell** Compare Hermia's
  complaint at 1.1.207.
244 **upon** by means of
244.1 *Exit . . . him* Demetrius' exit is not
  marked in Q or F; 'It is open to a
  producer to place it after line 240,
  Helena speaking the next two lines to
  herself, Demetrius stealing off while
  she does so; to leave it where it is [i.e.

OBERON

    Fare thee well, nymph. Ere he do leave this grove   245
    Thou shalt fly him, and he shall seek thy love.
        Enter Robin Goodfellow
    Hast thou the flower there? Welcome, wanderer.

ROBIN

    Ay, there it is.

OBERON   I pray thee give it me.

    I know a bank where the wild thyme blows,
    Where oxlips and the nodding violet grows,   250
    Quite overcanopied with luscious woodbine,
    With sweet musk-roses, and with eglantine.
    There sleeps Titania sometime of the night,
    Lulled in these flowers with dances and delight;
    And there the snake throws her enamelled skin,   255
    Weed wide enough to wrap a fairy in.
    And with the juice of this I'll streak her eyes,
    And make her full of hateful fantasies.
    Take thou some of it, and seek through this grove.
    A sweet Athenian lady is in love   260

246.1 *Enter . . . Goodfellow*] *after l.* 247 *in* QF (*Enter Pucke* Q1)

after l. 242 in his edition]—which allows her a loud apostrophe to the just vanished gentleman; or to place it after line 244, which implies that, having endured as much as he could, he breaks suddenly away. I prefer either 1 or 3 to 2' (Granville Barker, p. 132). Capell first placed it after l. 242.

245 **nymph** Oberon's term, in a scene full of other nymphs (e.g. Aegles, l. 79, and Daphne, l. 231), makes Helena another semi-divine being. Nymphs were often to be found inhabiting woods and looking like beautiful maidens.

250 **oxlips** Shakespeare most likely means the 'False Oxlip' (*Primula veris* x *vulgaris*), a natural hybrid of cowslip and primrose; the 'True Oxlip' (*Primula elatior*), not recognized then as a distinct species, was found only in East Anglia and was unlikely to be known to Shakespeare. The false oxlip was also known to Elizabethans as paigle, palsy-

wort or petty mullein (Rydén, pp. 72–3).

251 **woodbine** Usually 'honeysuckle' but, since at 4.1.41 it is obviously differentiated from honeysuckle, it is more likely to be convolvulus or bindweed.

252 **musk-roses** rambling roses with large fragrant flowers (*OED*); Rydén suggests it is *Rosa moschata*, cultivated in England in the 16th century, but it is more likely to be the wild native species *Rosa arvensis*.
    eglantine sweet-briar, a species of wild rose, *Rosa rubiginosa* (Rydén, p. 79), now *rosa eglanteria*; the Entertainment at Theobalds provided for Elizabeth in 1591 included 'an arbour all of eglantine' (Lyly, *Works*, i. 418).

255 **throws** casts

256 **Weed** garment (now only in 'widow's weeds')

257 **streak** smear

258 **fantasies** figments of imagination (Brooks)

With a disdainful youth. Anoint his eyes;
But do it when the next thing he espies
May be the lady. Thou shalt know the man
By the Athenian garments he hath on.
Effect it with some care, that he may prove   265
More fond on her than she upon her love;
And look thou meet me ere the first cock crow.

ROBIN
Fear not, my lord. Your servant shall do so.

Exeunt severally

2.2   *Enter Titania, Queen of Fairies, with her train*

TITANIA
Come, now a roundel and a fairy song,
Then for the third part of a minute hence:
Some to kill cankers in the musk-rose buds,
Some war with reremice for their leathern wings
To make my small elves coats, and some keep back   5
The clamorous owl, that nightly hoots and wonders
At our quaint spirits. Sing me now asleep;
Then to your offices, and let me rest.

She lies down. Fairies sing and dance

⌈FIRST FAIRY⌉
You spotted snakes with double tongue,
Thorny hedgehogs, be not seen;   10

2.2.8.1 *She lies down*] FAIRY Q, OXFORD; *not in* QF   *and dance*] This edition; *not in* QF;
fayries first Dance COX   9 FIRST FAIRY] CAPELL; *not in* QF; *and then sings* 1. COX

266 **fond on** passionately infatuated with
278.1 **severally** in different directions
2.2.1 **roundel** round dance (see 2.1.140);
    a 'rondel' is also a lyric with a refrain
    (which is what the fairies sing).
  2 The brief time suggests that the fairies
    will be rushing off at high speed but
    also that theirs is a 'diminutive world'
    (Halliwell).
  3 **cankers** canker-worms, caterpillars
    musk-rose Oberon has already associ-
    ated Titania's bower with musk-roses
    (2.1.252).
  4 **reremice** bats; Cotgrave gives 'A Batt,
    Flittermouse, Reremouse' for 'chauve-
    souris'.

  7 **quaint** strange, unusual, unfamiliar
    but also beautiful, pretty, dainty (*OED
    a.* A.I.8 and A.I.4) and 'spruce, brisk'
    (Cotgrave)
8.1 *She lies down* Henslowe lists, among
    the Admiral's Men's properties in 1598,
    'ii mose banckes' (*Diary*, p. 320); if
    Shakespeare's company had the same
    prop it would probably have been used
    in this scene.
9–30 The division of the song into a solo
    and chorus by Capell reflects Q's SP at
    l. 20 (1. Fai). F, in giving this stanza
    to 2. Fai., suggests a song for two
    soloists and chorus; F also gives 31–2
    to First Fairy. 'This song is more than

Newts and blindworms, do no wrong;
    Come not near our Fairy Queen.
⌈CHORUS⌉
    Philomel with melody,
    Sing in our sweet lullaby;
    Lulla, lulla, lullaby; lulla, lulla, lullaby.   15
        Never harm
        Nor spell nor charm
    Come our lovely lady nigh.
    So good night, with lullaby.

FIRST FAIRY
    Weaving spiders, come not here;   20
        Hence, you long-legged spinners, hence;
    Beetles black, approach not near;
        Worm nor snail do no offence.

13, 24 CHORUS] CAPELL; *not in* QF   16–17 Never . . . charm] DYCE; *one line in* QF

---

a lullaby, or even a magic lullaby; it
is a charm to ward off evils' (Seng, p.
32).

9 **double** forked

11 **blindworms** slow-worms, non-poison-
ous legless lizards, wrongly assumed to
be blind and deaf by the Greeks. Both
blindworms and newts were often
popularly thought to be dangerous (see,
for example, Edward Topsell, *The History of Serpents* (1608), pp. 212–13
and 239–40; Topsell warns that the
blindworm 'is harmless except being
provoked' and that a cow lying down
on one will die 'for the poison thereof
is very strong' (p. 240) and that if the
newt is 'moved to anger, it standeth
upon the hinder legs, and looketh directly in the face of him that hath
stirred it, and so continueth till all the
body be white, through a kind of white
humour or poison, that it swelleth outward, to harm (if it were possible) the
person that did provoke it' (p. 213)).
'Eye of newt' and 'blindworm's sting',
together with 'Adder's fork' (compare
l. 9) are ingredients of the witches'
cauldron in *Macbeth* 4.1.14, 16.

13 **Philomel** The nightingale, named after
Philomela raped by her brother-in-law
Tereus who also cut out her tongue.
Her metamorphosis is described by Ovid
(Golding, 6.511–853). She is 'like the
Fairies which | Reported are the pleas-
ant woods and water springs to haunt'
(Golding, 6.579–80) but it is not clear
why the Fairies invoke her here in
calling for her bird-form.

19 **spiders** Also thought to be poisonous;
Topsell announces that 'All Spiders are
venomous, but yet some more, and
some less' (p. 246); wild spiders that
live 'without the house abroad in the
open air' are called 'wolves and hunt-
ing-spiders' (p. 246–7). But he admits
finally that English spiders' 'biting is
poisonless, as being without venom,
procuring not the least touch of hurt
at all to any one whatsoever' (p. 272).
They may, however, be dangerous for
fairies.

21 **spinners** spiders (Cotgrave); in *Romeo*
1.4.60 Mercutio's 'long spinners' legs'
clearly belong to daddy-long-legs or
crane-flies but spiders are more likely
here.

⌈CHORUS⌉

Philomel with melody,

Sing in our sweet lullaby;   25

Lulla, lulla, lullaby; lulla, lulla, lullaby.

Never harm

Nor spell nor charm

Come our lovely lady nigh.

So good night, with lullaby.   30

Titania sleeps

SECOND FAIRY

Hence, away. Now all is well.

One aloof stand sentinel.

Exeunt all but Titania ⌈and the sentinel⌉

Enter Oberon. He drops the juice on Titania's eyelids

OBERON

What thou seest when thou dost wake,

Do it for thy true love take;

Love and languish for his sake.   35

Be it ounce, or cat, or bear,

24–30 melody . . . with lullaby.] melody, *&c.* QF   30.1 *Titania sleeps*] *Shee sleepes* F (*after l.* 32); *not in* Q   31–2 Hence . . . sentinel] *Indented* (Q1) *and italicized* (Q2, F) *as part of song*   32.1 *Exeunt . . . sentinel*] OXFORD; *Exeunt Fairies* ROWE; *not in* QF   32.2 *He . . . eyelids*] OXFORD; *and anoints her eye-lids* HANMER; *Oberon comes to her and touches her eye lids.* COX; *not in* QF

30.1 ***Titania sleeps*** Titania sleeps on stage throughout the rest of 2.2 and 3.1 until Bottom wakes her (compare the end of Act 3 and n.); in Peter Brook's production the problem of how to have her asleep on-stage without it interfering with the rest of the action was brilliantly solved by suspending her in a trapeze-hammock made of a massive scarlet feather.

31–2 **Hence . . . sentinel** These lines, in roman type in Q, as the preceding song had been, were set in italics in F, assuming them to be part of the song. They are linked to it metrically but were probably not sung.

32 **sentinel** The sentinel, in many productions kidnapped by Oberon's fairies, may have been stationed 'aloof', i.e.

on the upper stage or 'above'. Oberon is, of course, invisible to the sentinel as well as the lovers. If F's *Exit*, rather than *Exeunt*, at 2.1.268.1 is deliberate, its inclusion of 'Enter Oberon' at 2.2.32.1 may be inadvertent (compare 3.1.49.1 and n.); Oberon may, therefore, have been on-stage throughout the scene so far (Oxford).

36–7 **ounce . . . hair** 'The creatures [Oberon] cites are all noted for their ferocity and hence would be the most likely to repel, not invite, sexual overtures', leaving Titania to 'Love and languish' (l. 35) (James L. Calderwood, '*A Midsummer Night's Dream*: Anamorphism and Theseus' Dream', *SQ* 42 (1991), p. 420)

36 **ounce** lynx

> Pard, or boar with bristled hair,
> In thy eye that shall appear
> When thou wak'st, it is thy dear.
> Wake when some vile thing is near. *Exit* 40
>   *Enter Lysander and Hermia*

LYSANDER

> Fair love, you faint with wand'ring in the wood,
>   And, to speak truth, I have forgot our way.
> We'll rest us, Hermia, if you think it good,
>   And tarry for the comfort of the day.

HERMIA

> Be it so, Lysander. Find you out a bed; 45
> For I upon this bank will rest my head.
>   ⌈*She lies down*⌉

LYSANDER

> One turf shall serve as pillow for us both:
> One heart, one bed, two bosoms, and one troth.

HERMIA

> Nay, good Lysander. For my sake, my dear,
> Lie further off yet; do not lie so near. 50

LYSANDER

> O, take the sense, sweet, of my innocence!
> Love takes the meaning in love's conference—

---

40 Exit] ROWE; *not in* QF   44 comfort] Q2, F; comfor Q1   45 Be] Q2, F; Bet Q1   46.1 *She lies down*] OXFORD; *not in* QF   49 good] Q2, F; god Q1   dear,] deere, Q1 (*Bodleian*); deere Q1 (*all other copies*)

---

37 **Pard** leopard
  boar ... hair Circe changed Macareus into a boar 'rough with bristled hair' (Golding's Ovid, 14.323) in a passage where she is twice referred to as Titania (see A.D., 'Weever, Ovid and Shakespeare', *N&Q* 194 (1949), pp. 524–5).
41–2 In *Huon of Bordeaux* Geramnes warns Huon about Oberon's wood that 'such as pass that way are lost' (p. 63). Angela Carter notes that the wood 'is, of course, nowhere near Athens; ... [it] is really located somewhere in the English midlands'; she distinguishes between the 'English wood' and 'the dark necromantic forest'. Hermia and Lysander may be lost but it is only likely to be a temporary problem for,

as Carter suggests, 'an English wood, however marvellous, however metamorphic, cannot, by definition, be trackless, although it might well be formidably labyrinthine. Yet there is always a way out of a maze, and, even if you cannot find it for a while, you know that it is there' ('Overture and Incidental Music for *A Midsummer Night's Dream*', in *Black Venus* (1985), pp. 67–8).
44–5 **comfort ... so** Q1's two errors, 'comfor' and 'Bet', may be somehow interrelated.
52 **Love ... conference** when lovers talk their love means they understand each other properly

I mean that my heart unto yours is knit,
So that but one heart we can make of it.
Two bosoms interchainèd with an oath;   55
So, then, two bosoms and a single troth.
Then by your side no bed-room me deny;
For lying so, Hermia, I do not lie.

HERMIA
Lysander riddles very prettily.
Now much beshrew my manners and my pride   60
If Hermia meant to say Lysander lied.
But, gentle friend, for love and courtesy,
Lie further off, in human modesty.
Such separation as may well be said
Becomes a virtuous bachelor and a maid,   65
So far be distant; and good night, sweet friend.
Thy love ne'er alter till thy sweet life end.

LYSANDER
Amen, amen, to that fair prayer, say I;
And then end life when I end loyalty.
Here is my bed; sleep give thee all his rest.   70
        He lies down apart

HERMIA
With half that wish the wisher's eyes be pressed.
        They sleep.
        Enter Robin Goodfellow

ROBIN
Through the forest have I gone,
But Athenian found I none
On whose eyes I might approve
This flower's force in stirring love.   75
Night and silence. Who is here?

---

53 is] Q2, F; it QI   70.1 *He lies down apart*] This edition; *He lies down* OXFORD; *not in*
QF   71.1 *They sleep*] F; *not in* Q; *They lye down at a distance* FAIRY Q

55 **interchainèd** OED's first example of the
    word, perhaps coined by Shakespeare.
59 **prettily** ingeniously
60 **much beshrew** a strong curse on
74 **approve** test
76–9 Robin was not with Oberon when

he saw Helena and Demetrius and
relies on the apparent evidence of Lysander's costume, presumably a
fashionable Elizabethan gentleman's
outfit like Demetrius'.

Weeds of Athens he doth wear.
This is he my master said
Despisèd the Athenian maid—
And here the maiden, sleeping sound   80
On the dank and dirty ground.
Pretty soul, she durst not lie
Near this lack-love, this kill-courtesy.
Churl, upon thy eyes I throw
All the power this charm doth owe.   85
   He drops the juice on Lysander's eyelids
When thou wak'st, let love forbid
Sleep his seat on thy eyelid.
So, awake when I am gone.
For I must now to Oberon.   *Exit*
   Enter Demetrius and Helena, running

HELENA
Stay, though thou kill me, sweet Demetrius.   90
DEMETRIUS
I charge thee hence, and do not haunt me thus.
HELENA
O, wilt thou darkling leave me? Do not so.
DEMETRIUS
Stay, on thy peril; I alone will go.   *Exit*
HELENA
O, I am out of breath in this fond chase.
The more my prayer, the lesser is my grace.   95
Happy is Hermia, wheresoe'er she lies;
For she hath blessèd and attractive eyes.

85.1 *He . . . eyelids*] OXFORD (*after* Dyce); *not in* QF   93 *Exit*] F; *not in* Q

83 **lack-love** Shakespeare uses similar forms in *1 Henry IV* 2.4.15, 'lack-brain', and *Much Ado* 5.1.188, 'Lack-beard'.
85 **owe** own
86-7 **let . . . eyelid** may love prevent sleep from having its normal place in your eyes; may your passion make you lose sleep.
91 **haunt** run after (*OED v.* I.4), though, since the wood is 'haunted' at 3.1.99

and 3.2.5, the more ghostly sense may also be present.
92 **darkling** in the dark
94 **fond** foolish, doting (*OED a.* A.2 and A.5); compare 2.1.266 and *Twelfth Night* 2.2.33-4, 'My master loves her dearly, | And I, poor monster, fond as much on him'.
95 **The more . . . grace** the more I pray for the less I receive in return

How came her eyes so bright? Not with salt tears—
If so, my eyes are oft'ner washed than hers.
No, no; I am as ugly as a bear,   100
For beasts that meet me run away for fear.
Therefore no marvel though Demetrius
Do, as a monster, fly my presence thus.
What wicked and dissembling glass of mine
Made me compare with Hermia's sphery eyne?   105
But who is here? Lysander, on the ground?
Dead, or asleep? I see no blood, no wound.
Lysander, if you live, good sir, awake.

LYSANDER (*waking*)
And run through fire I will for thy sweet sake.
Transparent Helena, nature shows art   110
That through thy bosom makes me see thy heart.
Where is Demetrius? O, how fit a word
Is that vile name to perish on my sword!

HELENA
Do not say so, Lysander; say not so.
What though he love your Hermia? Lord, what though? 115
Yet Hermia still loves you; then be content.

LYSANDER
Content with Hermia? No, I do repent
The tedious minutes I with her have spent.
Not Hermia but Helena I love.
Who will not change a raven for a dove?   120

---

109 *waking*] ROWE; *not in* QF; *Ly. wakes* FAIRY Q

102–3 **no marvel though Demetrius | Do**
no wonder that Demetrius should
103 **as** 'as if I were' but also, perhaps,
'since he behaves like a monster or
beast'
104 **glass** mirror
105 **compare** compare myself to
sphery eyne eyes bright as the stars'
sphere
110 **Transparent** Lysander's meaning has
often appeared unclear to Helenas;
Sprague and Trewin record a tradition
of Helena 'with an air of startled modesty hastily [drawing] together the

folds of her dress' (p. 34).
nature shows art Nature displays her
magical art in making a transparent
body (unlike the normal opaque ones).
113 **vile name** See n. to 1.1.19.2.
115 **What though** what does it matter if
120 **a raven for a dove** Romeo's first sight
of Juliet makes him describe her as 'a
snowy dove trooping with crows'
(1.5.47; see also *Twelfth Night* 5.1.129).
Since Hermia is also an 'Ethiope' at
3.2.257 she was presumably intended
to be played dark-haired and also perhaps dark-complexioned.

The will of man is by his reason swayed,
And reason says you are the worthier maid.
Things growing are not ripe until their season,
So I, being young, till now ripe not to reason.
And, touching now the point of human skill,   125
Reason becomes the marshal to my will,
And leads me to your eyes, where I o'erlook
Love's stories written in love's richest book.

HELENA

Wherefore was I to this keen mock'ry born?
When at your hands did I deserve this scorn?   130
Is't not enough, is't not enough, young man,
That I did never—no, nor never can—
Deserve a sweet look from Demetrius' eye,
But you must flout my insufficiency?
Good troth, you do me wrong—good sooth, you do—   135
In such disdainful manner me to woo.
But fare you well. Perforce I must confess
I thought you lord of more true gentleness.
O, that a lady of one man refused
Should of another therefore be abused!   *Exit*   140

LYSANDER

She sees not Hermia. Hermia, sleep thou there,
And never mayst thou come Lysander near;
For as a surfeit of the sweetest things
The deepest loathing to the stomach brings,
Or as the heresies that men do leave   145

121–2 **The will … maid** As Bottom says in 3.1.136–7, 'reason and love keep little company together nowadays'. Egeus' 'will' has been a major cause of the problem in 1.1.

124 **ripe not to reason** had not matured to a pitch where I could judge rationally

125 **point** height
skill discrimination, discernment

126 **marshal** the officer charged with the ordering of guests at a banquet (*OED*)

127–8 **eyes … book** Shakespeare frequently links women's eyes and books, e.g. 'From women's eyes this doctrine I derive | ... | They are the books, the arts, the academes' *LLL* 4.3.326,

328 (see E. A. Armstrong, *Shakespeare's Imagination* (rev. edn., 1963), pp. 171–3).

127 **o'erlook** read through

128 **stories** true histories (Kittredge)

135 **Good truth … good sooth** really and truly (Brooks)

138 **gentleness** behaviour appropriate to a gentleman

143–4 **a surfeit … brings** Proverbial: see Tilley H560, 'Too much honey clogs the stomach', Proverbs 25:27 and *Romeo* 2.5.11–12, 'The sweetest honey | Is loathsome'

145–6 **as … deceive** as heresies that men renounce are most loathed by those same men who were deceived by them

Are hated most of those they did deceive,
So thou, my surfeit and my heresy,
Of all be hated, but the most of me;
And all my powers, address your love and might
To honour Helen, and to be her knight.   *Exit*   150
HERMIA (*waking*)
Help me, Lysander, help me! Do thy best
To pluck this crawling serpent from my breast!
Ay me, for pity. What a dream was here?
Lysander, look how I do quake with fear.
Methought a serpent ate my heart away,   155
And you sat smiling at his cruel prey.
Lysander—what, removed? Lysander, lord—
What, out of hearing, gone? No sound, no word?
Alack, where are you? Speak an if you hear,
Speak, of all loves. I swoon almost with fear.   160
No? Then I well perceive you are not nigh.
Either death or you I'll find immediately.   *Exit*

3.1   *Enter the clowns: Quince, Snug, Bottom, Flute,*
        Snout, and Starveling
BOTTOM Are we all met?
QUINCE Pat, pat; and here's a marvellous convenient
    place for our rehearsal. This green plot shall be our

151 waking] *After* CAPELL (*starting*); *not in* QF; *Her. wakes* FAIRY Q   155 ate] QF (eate)
3.1.0.1–2 *Quince . . . Starveling*] ROWE; *not in* QF

148 **Of . . . of** By . . . by
149 **address** direct
156 **prey** the action of preying on me
    (*OED sb.* I. 4)
160 **of all loves** for love's sake (Wells)
3.1 Oxford argues that, since Titania is
    still asleep on stage and there is there-
    fore no clear stage, the action is con-
    tinuous, a fact obscured by the
    traditional act-divisions derived from
    F. While removing the division here is
    tempting it would, I am afraid, be too
    unhelpfully confusing for users of
    other editions. In *Dream* the traditional
    act-divisions are simply editorial con-
    veniences and have little significance
    for the play's structure; moving them

seems to give them weight they should
not have. The important fact is that
the division here is felt in performance
to be no stronger than between 3.1
and 3.2 where there is a clear stage;
all the scenes in the wood flow smoothly and continuously on from each
other. See also notes at 3.2.413, 4.1.0,
5.1.361.
2 **Pat** on the dot (Kittredge)
  convenient suitable
3–4 **green   plot . . . tiring-house** The
    theatre's own stage becomes a clearing
    in the wood which becomes a stage;
    its tiring-house becomes a clump of
    hawthorn which becomes a tiring-
    house. Commentators have imagined,

stage, this hawthorn brake our tiring-house, and we
will do it in action as we will do it before the Duke.   5
BOTTOM Peter Quince?

QUINCE What sayst thou, bully Bottom?

BOTTOM There are things in this comedy of Pyramus and
Thisbe that will never please. First, Pyramus must draw
a sword to kill himself, which the ladies cannot abide.   10
How answer you that?

SNOUT By'r la'kin, a parlous fear.

STARVELING I believe we must leave the killing out, when
all is done.

BOTTOM Not a whit. I have a device to make all well. Write   15
me a prologue, and let the prologue seem to say we will
do no harm with our swords, and that Pyramus is not
killed indeed; and for the more better assurance, tell
them that I, Pyramus, am not Pyramus, but Bottom the
weaver. This will put them out of fear.   20

QUINCE Well, we will have such a prologue; and it shall be
written in eight and six.

BOTTOM No, make it two more: let it be written in eight
and eight.

SNOUT Will not the ladies be afeard of the lion?   25

STARVELING I fear it, I promise you.

for example, that 'the door might be
masked by a property-thicket' (Brooks)
but this is not only unnecessary but
also a destruction of the play's delight
in transformations, even of the stage-
space itself. By the 18th century, the
stage-floor was usually covered with a
green carpet (making Quince's line
even more directly referential) but
there is no evidence at all for the practice at the date of the play.

4 **hawthorn** Its flowers, known as 'may',
associate hawthorn particularly with
May festivals and Maying.
tiring-house the part of the theatre
behind the stage where the actors
dress and from which they come on-
stage (cf. n. to 2.1.0.1–2)

7 **bully** good friend, fine fellow (*OED sb.*[1]
I. 1)

12 **By'r la'kin** by our ladykin, by the
Virgin Mary
parlous perilous, dangerous

20 **put ... fear** free them from fear

22 **eight and six** Quince proposes the common ballad-metre of eight-syllable
lines alternating with six-syllable lines.
This proposed prologue never appears
in 5.1; Quince obviously decided not
to write it and to replace it with one
in ten-syllable lines. Foakes rightly emphasises that the play in 5.1 is 'funnier
and more engaging because we have
seen none of it before'.

23–4 **eight and eight** Bottom always veers
to excess.

25–6 See 1.2.70–1 and n.

26 **I fear it** Does Starveling mean that he
is afraid of the lion or that he is afraid
the ladies will be afraid? Actors have
played the line both ways.

BOTTOM Masters, you ought to consider with yourself, to
bring in—God shield us—a lion among ladies is a most
dreadful thing; for there is not a more fearful wild fowl
than your lion living, and we ought to look to't.   30

SNOUT Therefore another prologue must tell he is not a
lion.

BOTTOM Nay, you must name his name, and half his face
must be seen through the lion's neck, and he himself
must speak through, saying thus, or to the same defect: 35
'ladies', or 'fair ladies, I would wish you' or 'I would
request you' or 'I would entreat you not to fear, not to
tremble. My life for yours. If you think I come hither as
a lion, it were pity of my life. No, I am no such thing. I
am a man, as other men are'—and there, indeed, let   40
him name his name, and tell them plainly he is Snug
the joiner.

QUINCE Well, it shall be so; but there is two hard things:
that is, to bring the moonlight into a chamber—for you
know Pyramus and Thisbe meet by moonlight.   45

⌈SNOUT⌉ Doth the moon shine that night we play our
play?

BOTTOM A calendar, a calendar—look in the almanac,
find out moonshine, find out moonshine.
        ⌈*Enter Robin Goodfellow, invisible*⌉

46 SNOUT] CAMBRIDGE; *Sn.* QF; *Snug.* F2   49.1 *Enter . . . invisible*] F (*Enter Pucke*); *not in* Q

29 **wild fowl** Another of Bottom's mistakes though the griffin (2.1.232 and
n.), which is half-lion, is 'a crewell
fowle' in *Huon* (Cunningham).

35 **defect** effect

46 SNOUT Q1's '*Sn.*' could refer to Snug or
Snout. The ambiguity appears to result
from an overfull line; the compositor
uses *Snout* at ll. 12, 25, *Sno.* at l. 31
and *Sn.*, unambiguously, at l. 109.
F2's Snug is possible but unlikely,
though Sisson argues that 'we should
not deprive Snug of his one line in this
scene, the evidence that Shakespeare
knew his business' (*New Readings*, i.
127).

48–9 **A calendar . . . moonshine** A much

discussed passage since its reference to
the phases of the moon appears to offer
a prime piece of evidence for those
who wish to attach the first performance of *Dream* to a particular occasion fitting both this and Theseus'
comments at 1.1.2–3.

49.1 Robin's entry at this point in F may
be an error, especially since F gives
him another entry at l. 70, the point
at which he appears for the first time
in this scene in Q1. But the latter could
be inadvertent since F here directly
copies Q2 and the former may have
theatrical authority, deriving from the
manuscript F consulted to check
against Q2. F's second entry for Robin

179

QUINCE ⌈*consulting an almanac*⌉ Yes, it doth shine that   50
    night.

BOTTOM Why, then may you leave a casement of the great
    chamber window where we play open, and the moon
    may shine in at the casement.

QUINCE Ay, or else one must come in with a bush of   55
    thorns and a lantern and say he comes to disfigure, or
    to present, the person of Moonshine. Then there is an-
    other thing: we must have a wall in the great chamber;
    for Pyramus and Thisbe, says the story, did talk
    through the chink of a wall.   60

---

50 *consulting an almanac*] This edition; *with a book* OXFORD; *not in* QF   52 BOTTOM] Q2, F
(*Bot.*); *Cet.* Q1

could also mean little more than 'comes
forward' (compare F's entry for Oberon
and Robin at 3.2.344 when they have
clearly never left the stage). In a play
so full of silent spectators (Hippolyta in
1.1, Oberon and Robin frequently
throughout the play) Robin might well
enter and watch the rehearsal for a
while before speaking. Oxford imagines
theatrical business in which 'the puck
somehow comically suppl[ies] the book'
Quince consults at l. 50. In Brook's
production the fairies were on-stage
throughout the scene and 'it is a Fairy
who presents it [the calendar], his
physical presence become invisible to
their preoccupations' (Selbourne, p. 69).
Granville Barker found Robin's entry
here 'more effective' (p. 132) and in
his production Robin entered, wandered
round the stage and peered over Bottom's shoulder (Dymkowski, p. 67).
The evidence is cumulatively persuasive but I have a nagging suspicion
that 'what, a play toward?' (l. 74)
suggests that Robin has only just noticed what they are doing, unlikely if
he has been watching them for twenty
lines.

54–5 **bush of thorns** A traditional attribute of the man in the moon, sometimes
linked to Cain or to a man banished
to the moon for stealing a bundle of
thorns. In Robert Henryson's *The Testament of Cresseid* Cynthia has 'on hir
breist ane churl paintit ful evin, | Beir-

and ane bunch of thornis on his bak,
| Quhilk for his thift micht clim na nar
the hevin' (ll. 260–4). Manningham's
diary notes 'the man in the moon with
thorns on his back' at the 1601 devices at Whitehall (quoted Jonson,
Works, x. 601). In Jonson's masque of
1620 *News from the New World Discover'd in the Moone* the Factor asks
'Where? which is he? I must see his
Dog at his girdle, and the bush of
thorns at his back, ere I believe it' and
is told by the Second Herald 'Those are
stale ensigns o'th Stages man
i'th'Moon' (viii. 516–17). Starveling
has acquired a dog as well as a thorn-
bush and lantern in 5.1; compare a
seal of Edward III showing 'the crescent moon surrounding a man bearing, on a stick over his shoulder, a
bundle of thorns; he is accompanied
by a dog' (Oliver F. Emerson, 'Legends
of Cain, especially in Old and Middle
English', *PMLA* 21 (1906), p. 842;
Emerson rejects (p. 841 n. 1) the often
suggested link of the man banished to
the moon to the man executed for
gathering sticks on the sabbath (Numbers 15: 32–6)).

56 **disfigure** figure; but Quince's malapro-
pism also recalls the power of the
father over his child, according to Theseus, to 'leave the figure or disfigure
it' (1.1.51)

57 **present** personate; see the discussion
about who will 'present the Nine Worthies', *LLL* 5.1.117 ff.

SNOUT You can never bring in a wall. What say you,
Bottom?

BOTTOM Some man or other must present Wall; and let
him have some plaster, or some loam, or some roughcast about him, to signify 'wall'; and let him hold his   65
fingers thus, and through that cranny shall Pyramus
and Thisbe whisper.

QUINCE If that may be, then all is well. Come, sit down
every mother's son, and rehearse your parts. Pyramus,
you begin. When you have spoken your speech, enter   70
into that brake; and so everyone according to his cue.

ROBIN (*aside*)
What hempen homespuns have we swagg'ring here
So near the cradle of the Fairy Queen?
What, a play toward? I'll be an auditor—
An actor, too, perhaps, if I see cause.   75

QUINCE Speak, Pyramus. Thisbe, stand forth.

BOTTOM (*as Pyramus*)
Thisbe, the flowers of odious savours sweet.

---

66 and] FAIRY Q, COLLIER 1853; or QF   71 cue.] OXFORD; cue. | *Enter Robin* QF   72 *aside*]
OXFORD; *not in* QF   77, etc. BOTTOM (*as Pyramus*)] WELLS; *Pyra.* or *Py.* Q1

61 **You ... wall** Editors are prone to
argue that a wall was brought on
stage for the orchard wall in *Romeo*
2.1 and therefore that Quince's notion
of theatrical impossibility is naïve. But
it is far from clear whether a wall is
needed for the scene at all. Thomas
Garter's *Susanna* (*c*.1569) certainly
had an orchard-wall bisecting the ac-
ting-area; T. W. Craik argues that the
evidence of *Susanna* shows that the
joke 'depends, not upon the supposedly
primitive expedients of our early
drama, but upon the artisans' fantastic
circumvention of what they ought to
have been able to do' (*The Tudor Interlude* (Leicester, 1958), p. 18). If the
editors are wrong in the case of *Romeo*,
the comedy here may lie more in Bottom's comic solution than in Quince's
recognition of the problem. The possibility that *Romeo* might have had a
wall on stage may suggest it precedes
Dream.

69 **rehearse** go over, repeat; the workers

will be checking they have learned
their roles while the rehearsal is going
on (compare, for a further sense of the
word, 5.1.68)

72 **hempen** Workers' clothes were often
made of a fabric derived from hemp
and, as Robin suggests, home-made. In
Scot, Robin Goodfellow's response to
finding food and clothes put out for
him was 'What have we here? Hemton,
hamten, here will I never more tread
nor stampen' (p. 85). Brooks suggests
that 'Hemton' generated 'hempen' here.
For Robin's stamp see also 3.2.25
and n.

74 **toward** in preparation

77–80 **the flowers ... dear** There are two
textual problems here:
(1) 'So hath' in l. 79 suggests an
antecedent phrase. Oxford suggests that
'of' (l. 76) is an error for 'have', comparing *History of Lear* 24.301 but elaborate solutions to iron out the syntax
seem unnecessary to the playing of the
comedy. I take 'savours' to be a noun

QUINCE Odours, odours.

BOTTOM (*as Pyramus*) Odours savours sweet.

    So hath thy breath, my dearest Thisbe dear. 80

    But hark, a voice. Stay thou but here a while,

      And by and by I will to thee appear. *Exit*

⌈ROBIN⌉ (*aside*)

    A stranger Pyramus than e'er played here. *Exit*

FLUTE Must I speak now?

QUINCE Ay, marry must you. For you must understand he 85
goes but to see a noise that he heard, and is to come again.

FLUTE (*as Thisbe*)

    Most radiant Pyramus, most lily-white of hue,

      Of colour like the red rose on triumphant brier;

    Most bristly juvenile, and eke most lovely Jew,

---

78 Odours, odours] F; Odours, odorous Q; 'Odious'?—odorous! WILSON   79 Odours] QF;
Odorous BROOKS (*conj.* Jenkins)   83 ROBIN] F (*Puck.*); *Quin.* Q   (*aside*)] POPE; not in QF
Exit] CAPELL; *not in* QF; *Exit after him* COX   84 FLUTE] CAMBRIDGE; *Thys.* QF   87, etc. FLUTE
(*as Thisbe*)] WELLS; *Thys.* Q1   89 bristly] OXFORD; brisky QF   juvenile] Q (Iuuenall)

---

at l. 76 and a verb in Quince's corrected form.

  (2) An editor's solution to the
'odours/odious/odorous' crux depends
as much on which jokes are wanted
as on textual analysis. F's Quince exasperatedly emphasises 'odours, odours'
and Bottom gets it right at l. 78. Q's
Quince might be patiently explaining
the word and its cognates, intending
Bottom to say 'odorous' while Bottom
predictably picks up the wrong word
in the next line. If Q is corrupt, Wilson's emendation has Quince repeating Bottom's error horror-struck and
correcting it (' "Odious"?—odorous!')
while Bottom makes a new mistake,
'odours', when he tries to repeat it.
Brooks, reading 'odorous' all three
times, seems to emend too much in
search of consistency, flattening the
potentials for comedy (he discusses the
crux at length on pp. 155–8). 'Odorous' appearing somewhere here is attractive since Titania has used
'odorous' for Hiems' 'chaplet of sweet
summer buds' at 2.1.110.

77 **savours sweet** a common biblical phrase
(see for example Genesis 8: 21, 2
Corinthians 2: 15 and Ephesians 5: 2).

82 **by and by** in a moment

83 **A stranger . . . here** Robin works out
his plan to transform Bottom and
exits.

86 **see a noise** Quince, like Bottom, has a
knack of confusing his senses.

88 **triumphant** noble, magnificent; Thisbe
does not explain which parts of Pyramus are white and which are red
(compare the colour mixture at
5.1.324–9).

89 **bristly** Oxford's emendation makes
Thisbe's praise appropriately absurd:
juveniles should be beardless. 'Brisky'
is unknown elsewhere in Shakespeare
and would praise Pyramus sensibly for
his energy; 'bristly' occurs in *Venus*
620 and *Sonnets* 12.8.
   juvenile Q's spelling (Iuuenall) is the
standard Elizabethan form for 'juvenile'
(which *OED* firsts cites for 1625).
   Jew Either an abbreviation of 'juvenile'
(or possibly 'jewel') or 'a deliberately
inconsequential piece of padding'
(Wells); Costard praises Mote as 'my
incony Jew' (*LLL* 3.1.132), a phrase
which Dr Johnson describes as 'in our
author's time . . . apparently a word of
endearment'.

As true as truest horse that yet would never tire: 90
I'll meet thee, Pyramus, at Ninny's tomb.

QUINCE Ninus' tomb, man!—Why, you must not speak
that yet. That you answer to Pyramus. You speak all
your part at once, cues and all.—Pyramus, enter: your
cue is past; it is 'never tire'.   95

FLUTE O.

(*As Thisbe*) As true as truest horse that yet would never
tire.

> *Enter* ⌈*Robin Goodfellow leading*⌉ *Bottom with the
> ass-head*

BOTTOM (*as Pyramus*)

If I were fair, Thisbe, I were only thine.

QUINCE O monstrous! O strange! We are haunted. Pray,
masters; fly, masters. Help!   ⌈*The clowns all exeunt*⌉   100

97.1 *Enter Robin leading*] OXFORD (*after* Capell); *not in* QF   *Bottom . . . ass-head*] THEOBALD;
not in QF   100 *The . . . exeunt*] F (*The Clownes all Exit*); *not in* Q

91 **Ninny's** turning 'Ninus'' into 'a
fool's'; the pronunciation is often a
running joke in productions.

93–4 **You speak . . . all** Flute has conned
all the part he was given in 1.2 (see
1.2.92 and n.).

97.1 **Bottom . . . ass-head** For the sources
for Bottom's partial transformation
into an ass, see the Introduction, pp.
000–00. F's 'the Asse head' at 106.1
appears to refer to a specific company
prop. The description of the half-mask
for Snug as Lion at ll. 33–4 may indicate that the ass-head similarly
allowed 'half his face [to] be seen
through' even though the mask might
cover part of his face to make it 'marvellous hairy' (4.1.24). A half-mask is
much easier to speak through and
many productions, no matter how
ingenious and comic the mechanisms
for waggling the ass's ears or opening
its mouth, make Bottom's lines semi-
inaudible. In *Mount Tabor* (1639) Willis describes seeing *The Cradle of
Security* in the 1570s when he was a
child, in which the king fell asleep and
three ladies 'closely conveyed under
the clothes where withall he was

covered, a vizard like a swine's snout
upon his face, . . . [the ladies] then discovered his face, that the spectators
might see how they had transformed
him' (p. 111). Peter Brook's Bottom
put on a black round nose, false ears
and clogs, leaving his face fully exposed, looking rather like Mickey
Mouse.

98 **If . . . thine** The metre is defective and
the standard emendation (Cambridge)
'were fair, fair Thisbe' may be correct.
But the chaos caused by Bottom's appearance and the joke of his appearing
anything but fair make niceties of
metre irrelevant.

100 **The clowns all exeunt** F's direction
does not exclude Bottom and he could
quite reasonably exit in pursuit of
them. Most editors take F's entrance
for him at 106.1 as misplaced for 97.1
but Bottom blundering around the
stage might detract from the extraordinary power of Robin's speech
(ll. 101–6). A bemused Bottom re-
entering at 106.1 seems theatrically
effective, perhaps comically confused
and even a little sad.

ROBIN
  I'll follow you, I'll lead you about a round,
    Through bog, through bush, through brake,
      through briar.
  Sometime a horse I'll be, sometime a hound,
    A hog, a headless bear, sometime a fire,
  And neigh, and bark, and grunt, and roar, and burn,   105
  Like horse, hound, hog, bear, fire, at every turn.

                                      Exit

    ⌈ *Enter Bottom again, with the ass-head*⌉
BOTTOM Why do they run away? This is a knavery of them
to make me afeard.
    Enter Snout
SNOUT O Bottom, thou art changed. What do I see on
thee?   110
BOTTOM What do you see? You see an ass-head of your
own, do you?   ⌈ *Exit Snout*⌉
    Enter Quince

106.1 *Enter . . . head*] OXFORD; *Enter Piramus with the Asse head.* F; *not in* Q   112 *Exit
Snout*] DYCE; *Exit* CAPELL (*at l.* 110); *not in* QF

101 **a round** both 'a round dance' and 'in
a roundabout route'
102–4 **Through bog . . . fire** Robin's lines
echo the Fairy at 2.1.3–5 who wanders 'thorough bush, thorough briar,
| . . . thorough fire', though where the
fairy wanders over hill and dale, Robin
will lead the workers through bog and
brake (presumably the one that was
their 'tiring-house' at l. 4).
103–4 **Sometime . . . fire** Robin has already
commented on his ability as a shape-
changer at 2.1.46–53. Thomas Keight-
ley (*The Fairy Mythology*, revised edn.,
1850) recorded that an Irish boy believed that 'Pookas . . . were wicked-
minded, black-looking, bad things, that
would come in the *form of wild colts*' (p.
371); even something as apparently in-
nocuous as Robin's transformation into
a horse may have diabolic overtones.
104 **headless bear** The headlessness of the
bear is significant. Percy Simpson suggested a link to the kind of events
described in a pamphlet of 1614, *A
Miracle of Miracles* ('The "Headless

Bear" in Shakespeare and Burton', in
his *Studies in Elizabethan Drama* (Oxford, 1955), pp. 89–94). But the
pamphlet was in fact first published in
1584 as *A true and most Dreadfull discourse of a woman possessed with the
Devill*: the woman's husband described
seeing 'a thing come to the bed, much
like unto a Bear, but it had no head
nor no tail, half a yard in length and
half a yard in height' (sigs. A6ʳ–A6ᵛ);
it hauled the woman out of bed, rolled
her round the room and down the
stairs. This clear association of Robin
with the attested activities of the devil
reflects the diabolic origins of pucks
(see Introduction, figs. 8 and 9 for the
title-pages of the pamphlets showing
the headless bear).
111–12 **You see . . . your own** Proverbial
('a fool's head of your own', Tilley
F519, A388). Bottom ironically
identifies his own metamorphosis before anyone else but there is no suggestion here that he knows what has
happened to him.

QUINCE Bless thee, Bottom, bless thee. Thou art translated.

                  Exit

BOTTOM I see their knavery. This is to make an ass of me,
 to fright me, if they could; but I will not stir from this   115
 place, do what they can. I will walk up and down here,
 and I will sing, that they shall hear I am not afraid.
 (*Sings*)

    The ousel cock so black of hue,
     With orange-tawny bill;
    The throstle with his note so true,   120
     The wren with little quill.

TITANIA (*waking*)

What angel wakes me from my flow'ry bed?

BOTTOM (*sings*)

    The finch, the sparrow, and the lark,
     The plainsong cuckoo grey,
    Whose note full many a man doth mark,   125
     And dares not answer 'Nay'—

for indeed, who would set his wit to so foolish a bird?

113.1 *Exit*] Q; *Exeunt* COX 117.1 *Sings*] COX (*he sings*), POPE; *not in* QF 122 *waking*]
ROWE; *not in* QF; *Queen of Fairy wakes and looks upon him* COX 123 *sings*] POPE (*combined
with SD to 122* [*waking*] *in error*); *not in* QF

113.1 *Exit* Cox, in giving 'Exeunt' here
and giving no exit for Snout allows for
stage business such as Quince's drag-
ging out Snout who has been rooted
to the spot in horror; QF do not indicate when Snout leaves the stage.

114 **make . . . of me** Proverbial; see Dent
A379.1.

117 **I will sing** Weavers seem to have
been famous for singing; Falstaff announces 'I would I were a weaver—I
could sing psalms, or anything' (*1
Henry IV* 2.5.132–3).

118 **ousel** cock-blackbird, *Turdus merula*.
Bottom's song may be a parody of a
stanza of Richard Edwards's 'A poem
of a maid forsaken' (in Nicholas Breton
and others, *The Arbour of Amorous Devices* (1597), sigs. A4ᵛ–B1ʳ); 'The
Lark, the Thrush and Nightingale, |
The Linnets sweet, and eke the Turtles
true, | The chattering Pie, the Jay, and
eke the Quail, | The Thrustle-Cock
that was so black of hue'.

119 **orange-tawny** Bottom is right about
the colour but may have had it on his
mind from his discussion of beards at
1.2.87.

120 **throstle** thrush, often specifically the
song-thrush, *Turdus philomelos*

121 **little quill** small pipe, thin voice

122 **What . . . bed?** Titania's line seems a
comic parody of Hieronimo's much-
quoted line in Kyd's *The Spanish Tragedy* 'What outcries pluck me from my
naked bed?' (2.5.1) when he enters to
find his son's murdered corpse.

124 **plainsong** because its melody is as
simple as church plainchant; compare
'to keep just plainsong | Our chanters
shall be the Cuckoo' (John Skelton,
'Phillip Sparrow' in *Pithy, Pleasant and
Profitable Works* (1568), sig. S4ʳ).

127 Bottom adapts the proverb 'Do not
set your wit against a fool's' (Tilley
W547).
 set his wit to use his intelligence to
answer

Who would give a bird the lie, though he cry 'Cuckoo'
never so?

TITANIA

I pray thee, gentle mortal, sing again.   130
Mine ear is much enamoured of thy note;
So is mine eye enthrallèd to thy shape;
And thy fair virtue's force perforce doth move me
On the first view to say, to swear, I love thee.

BOTTOM Methinks, mistress, you should have little reason   135
for that. And yet, to say the truth, reason and love keep
little company together nowadays—the more the pity
that some honest neighbours will not make them
friends. Nay, I can gleek upon occasion.

TITANIA

Thou art as wise as thou art beautiful.   140

BOTTOM Not so, neither; but if I had wit enough to get out
of this wood, I have enough to serve mine own turn.

TITANIA

Out of this wood do not desire to go.
Thou shalt remain here, whether thou wilt or no.
I am a spirit of no common rate: 145
The summer still doth tend upon my state;
And I do love thee. Therefore go with me.
I'll give thee fairies to attend on thee,
And they shall fetch thee jewels from the deep,
And sing while thou on pressèd flowers dost sleep;   150
And I will purge thy mortal grossness so
That thou shalt like an airy spirit go.
Peaseblossom, Cobweb, Mote, and Mustardseed!

---

142 own] Q2, F; owe Q1   153 Mote] QF (*Moth*)

---

128 **'Cuckoo'** The cuckoo was thought to
be saying 'cuckold', 'Unpleasing to a
married ear' (*LLL* 5.2.887).

133 **thy fair virtue's force** the power of
your excellent qualities (Wells)

139 **gleek** make satiric jests

142 **wood** 'forest', of course, but also
'madness, state of confusion'; compare
Demetrius at 2.1.192.

145 **rate** value

151 **mortal grossness** materiality as a

mortal (Brooks)

153 F's compositor probably misread the
line as part of the SD and hence added
four more fairies to the entrance.
Mote QF's 'Moth' could be either an
insect or a speck of dust. Shakespeare's
unequivocal references to moths are
uncomplimentary (*Merchant* 2.9.78
and *Othello* 1.3.256). The character in
LLL is clearly 'Mote' (see John Kerrigan's edition of *LLL* (New Penguin Shake-

*Enter four fairies: Peaseblossom, Cobweb, Mote, and
    Mustardseed*

A FAIRY
    Ready.
ANOTHER And I.
ANOTHER   And I.
ANOTHER   And I.
⌈ALL FOUR⌉   Where shall we go?
TITANIA
    Be kind and courteous to this gentleman.   155
    Hop in his walks, and gambol in his eyes.
    Feed him with apricots and dewberries,
    With purple grapes, green figs, and mulberries;
    The honeybags steal from the humble-bees,
    And for night tapers crop their waxen thighs   160
    And light them at the fiery glow-worms' eyes
    To have my love to bed, and to arise;

153.1-2 *Enter . . . Mustardseed*] *Enter foure Fairyes* Q; *Enter Pease-blossome, Cobweb, Moth,
Mustard-seede, and four Fairies* F (*omitting l.* 154) 154 A FAIRY . . . ANOTHER . . . ANOTHER . . .
ANOTHER . . . ALL FOUR] OXFORD; *Fairies.* Q1; *Fai.* Q2, F. ROWE *divided the line between four fairies;*
CAPELL *gave* 'Where shall we go?' *to all.* DYCE *assigned the speeches to the names of the
fairies in the order of Titania's summons.*

speare (1982), pp. 160-1)—I am unconvinced by George Hibbard's contrary argument in his edition of *LLL*
(Oxford, 1990)). Motes and cobwebs
are similarly insubstantial; motes and
mustardseeds are equivalently minute
in the Bible (e.g. Matthew 7: 3-5 and
Luke 6: 41-2 (motes), Matthew 13:
31-2 (mustardseed)). The echo of the
word at 5.1.313 seems to support the
case for 'mote'. It was probably pronounced with a short 'o' as 'mot' (see
Fausto Cercignani, *Shakespeare's Works
and Elizabethan Pronunciation* (Oxford,
1981), p. 120).

154 **Ready . . . go?** White's distribution of
the line to the four fairies in the order
of Titania's summons is temptingly
neat; I would assume that they speak
in the same sequence at ll. 166-9.
157 **dewberries** usually 'blackberries' but
possibly 'dwarf-mulberries' which Halliwell claimed were called dewberries

in Warwickshire; neither is a cultivated fruit like the others in Titania's
list. Rydén (p. 87) identifies them as
Rubus caesius.
161 **glow-worms' eyes** Q1's 'Glow-wor-
mes' could be singular or plural. Dr
Johnson complained that the lights in
a glow-worm were in its tail not its
eyes but T. P. Harrison points out
('Shakespeare's Glowworms', *SQ* 22
(1971), pp. 395-6) that Shakespeare
is referring not to the English glow-
worms (*Lampyris noctiluca*) about which
Johnson was right but to the exotic
Cucuius, much larger than the English
form and frequently described in reports from the West Indies as having
very strong lights in its eyes.
162 **To . . . arise** Bottom is to have a royal
couchée and levée as a royal lover; if
Titania is thinking of having sex with
Bottom, then 'arise' will carry suggestions of 'have an erection'.

And pluck the wings from painted butterflies
To fan the moonbeams from his sleeping eyes.
Nod to him, elves, and do him courtesies.   165

A FAIRY Hail, mortal.

⌈ANOTHER⌉ Hail.

ANOTHER Hail.

ANOTHER Hail.

BOTTOM I cry your worships mercy, heartily.—I beseech   170
your worship's name.

COBWEB Cobweb.

BOTTOM I shall desire you of more acquaintance, good
Master Cobweb. If I cut my finger, I shall make bold
with you.—Your name, honest gentleman?   175

PEASEBLOSSOM Peaseblossom.

BOTTOM I pray you commend me to Mistress Squash, your
mother, and to Master Peascod, your father. Good Master Peaseblossom, I shall desire you of more acquaintance, too.—Your name, I beseech you, sir?   180

MUSTARDSEED Mustardseed.

BOTTOM Good Master Mustardseed, I know your patience
well. That same cowardly giantlike ox-beef hath devoured many a gentleman of your house. I promise you
your kindred hath made my eyes water ere now. I desire   185
you of more acquaintance, good Master Mustardseed.

TITANIA (*to the Fairies*)

Come, wait upon him, lead him to my bower.
    The moon, methinks, looks with a wat'ry eye,

---

166 A FAIRY] OXFORD; 1 *Fai.* QF   166–7 mortal. | ⌈ANOTHER⌉ Hail.] CAPELL (mortal! 2. Hail!);
mortall, haile. QF   168–9 ANOTHER . . . ANOTHER] OXFORD; 2 *Fai.* . . . 3 *Fai.* QF; 3 . . . . 4.
CAPELL   186 you of] DYCE; you QF   187 *to the Fairies*] OXFORD; *not in* QF

---

174 **If I . . . finger** Cobwebs were often
used as a plaster and a styptic to stop
bleeding.

175 **honest gentleman** my good sir

177 **Squash** an unripe pea-pod (first instance in *OED*); see *Twelfth Night*
1.5.152, 'as a squash is before 'tis a
peascod'.

178 **Peascod** pea-pod; the peascod was a
popular remedy for love-sickness (Lou
Agnes Reynolds and Paul Sawyer, 'Folk
Medicine and the Four Fairies of *A*

Midsummer Night's Dream', SQ 10
(1959), p. 518: 'if either lover were
jilted, the pain of the lost love was
eased by rubbing the whole body with
the hay of the pea-plant').

182 **patience** suffering

185 **your . . . now** Bottom's eyes wept in
sympathy or smarting with the effect
of the mustard; mustardseed was also
used as a medicinal plaster.

188 **The moon . . . eye** The moon was
held to be the mother of dew: 'Also

And when she weeps, weeps every little flower,
　　Lamenting some enforcèd chastity.   190
Tie up my love's tongue; bring him silently.   *Exeunt*

3.2   *Enter Oberon, King of Fairies*
OBERON

I wonder if Titania be awaked,
Then what it was that next came in her eye,
Which she must dote on in extremity.
　　Enter Robin Goodfellow
Here comes my messenger. How now, mad spirit?
What nightrule now about this haunted grove?   5
ROBIN

My mistress with a monster is in love,
Near to her close and consecrated bower.

191 love's] POPE; louers QF   *Exeunt*] FAIRY Q, ROWE; *Exit.* QF
　3.2.0.1 *Enter . . . Fairies*] F (*Enter King of Pharies, solus*); *Enter King of* Fairies, *and* Robin
goodfellow. Q   3.1 *Enter Robin Goodfellow*] F (*Enter Pucke.*); *not in* Q   6 love,] QF; ~.
ROWE   7 bower.] Q1; ~. Q2

the Moon gathereth dew in the air, for
she printeth the virtue of her moisture
in the air, . . . and gendereth dew in
the utter part thereof' (S. Bateman,
Batman upon Bartholome (1582), VIII.
29 (sig. 2A1ᵛ)).

190 **enforcèd chastity** 'chastity violated by
force' (Diana was patroness of chastity
and the moon-goddess) but also, more
probably since Titania's thoughts are
running on bed, 'someone forced to be
a virgin' (the threat hanging over Hermia). Louis Zufosky in *Bottom: On Shakespeare* (Austin, 1963), p. 85, is more
emphatic: '*Enforced* means here *compelled, involuntary* and not *violated* as
the glossary profanes'; he compares
Merchant 5.1.240, 'Portia, forgive me
this enforcèd wrong'.

191 **Tie . . . tongue** To stop him braying.
Wells suggests that Bottom may 'be
making involuntary asinine noises'.

3.2.1–40 A recapitulation of the action in
the wood so far. Its expository style is
common at the mid-point of a Shakespeare play. In modern productions with
an interval the second half starts here.

3 **extremity** extravagant behaviour (*OED*
5), extreme of experience

5 **nightrule** disorders of the night, the
inverted order of night-time (*OED*, *rule*,
sb. 13c), but the word could also be a
form of 'night-revel', linking Oberon's
question to Robin's earlier words to
the fairy, 'The King doth keep his revels here tonight' (2.1.18) (see Helge
Kökeritz, 'Shakespeare's nightrule',
Language, 18 (1942), pp. 40–4).

6–7 **My . . . bower** Homer Swander has
pointed out that nearly all editors re-
ject Q's punctuation at this point, replacing the comma after 'love' with a
full stop and the full stop after 'bower'
with a comma ('Editors vs. A Text: The
Scripted Geography of *A Midsummer
Night's Dream*', *Studies in Philology*, 87
(1990), pp. 83–108), thereby assuming that her meeting with Bottom took
place near her bower and that the
bower and the bank are the same place.
But the bank where Titania slept is
nowhere directly referred to as a bower
(though it is 'overcanopied' (2.1.251)
with climbing flowers like a bower).
Oberon's 'bower' (4.1.60) is explicitly

While she was in her dull and sleeping hour
A crew of patches, rude mechanicals
That work for bread upon Athenian stalls,   10
Were met together to rehearse a play
Intended for great Theseus' nuptial day.
The shallowest thickskin of that barren sort,
Who Pyramus presented in their sport,
Forsook his scene and entered in a brake,   15
When I did him at this advantage take.
An ass's nole I fixèd on his head.
Anon his Thisbe must be answerèd,
And forth my mimic comes. When they him spy—
As wild geese that the creeping fowler eye,   20
Or russet-pated choughs, many in sort,
Rising and cawing at the gun's report,
Sever themselves and madly sweep the sky—
So, at his sight, away his fellows fly,
And at our stamp here o'er and o'er one falls.   25
He 'Murder' cries, and help from Athens calls.
Their sense thus weak, lost with their fears thus strong,

---

19 mimic] F (Mimmick); Minnick Q1; Minnock Q2

'in fairyland' and Titania has instructed her fairies to lead Bottom 'to
my bower' (3.1.187). The difference is
between leading Bottom to the bank
(visibly present on stage) and leading
him to fairyland (a mysterious place
often referred to but never seen in the
play). F's punctuation, with a comma
at the end of both lines, does not clarify the matter and there is no good
reason to emend Q here. It makes, as
Swander argues at length, a substantial difference to Bottom's experiences
if he has gone to fairyland and returned (see n. to 4.2.40).

7 **close** secluded

8 **patches** clowns, fools; see 4.1.207
and n.
rude mechanicals rough working-men
13 **barren sort** dull-witted, unimaginative
crew
17 **nole** head, noddle

19 **mimic** actor (the common sense of 'im-
personator' is here only in so far as
Bottom is such a bad actor as to be a
kind of parody)
21 **russet-pated choughs, many in sort**
a large flock of jackdaws with dull-
coloured heads. 'Russet' covers a range
of drab colours from reddish-brown to
near black; jackdaws' heads are grey.
23 **Sever** scatter
25 **our stamp** Robin Goodfellow traditionally stamped (see Scot, quoted at n. to
3.1.72). Johnson conjectured 'stump',
quoting a parallel moment in Drayton's
Nimphidia, The Court of Fayrie (1625),
a poem indebted to *Dream*, when a
fairy's charms against Hob make him
fall in briars and 'A stump doth trip
him'. But 'senseless things' only 'begin
to do them wrong' at l. 28. Could 'our
stamp' mean that Robin and Bottom
made sounds like an ass's hooves?

Made senseless things begin to do them wrong.
For briers and thorns at their apparel snatch;
Some sleeves, some hats—from yielders all things catch.   30
I led them on in this distracted fear,
And left sweet Pyramus translated there;
When in that moment, so it came to pass,
Titania waked and straightway loved an ass.

OBERON

This falls out better than I could devise.   35
But hast thou yet latched the Athenian's eyes
With the love juice, as I did bid thee do?

ROBIN

I took him sleeping—that is finished, too—
And the Athenian woman by his side,
That when he waked of force she must be eyed.   40

Enter Demetrius and Hermia

OBERON

Stand close. This is the same Athenian.

ROBIN

This is the woman, but not this the man.

⌈*They stand apart*⌉

DEMETRIUS

O, why rebuke you him that loves you so?
Lay breath so bitter on your bitter foe.

HERMIA

Now I but chide, but I should use thee worse;   45
For thou, I fear, hast given me cause to curse.
If thou hast slain Lysander in his sleep,
Being o'er shoes in blood, plunge in the deep,
And kill me too.

42.1 *They stand apart*] COLLIER 1853; *not in* QF   48-9] *As* ROWE 1714; *one line* QF

---

30 **from . . . catch** everything catches at
the timid
36 **latched** possibly 'moistened' (*OED*,
leach, *v.*² 1) but more probably
'caught, snared'
41 **Stand close** stand aside secretly
43-81 Demetrius' use of 'you' to Hermia
is clearly adoring and respectful. Fur-

ness's suggestion that her use of 'thou'
is contemptuous is unlikely, given her
use of 'thou' to Lysander at 1.1.169 ff.
48 Proverbial (Tilley S379, 'over shoes,
over boots', and S380, 'To be over
shoes'): having waded in so far, wade
in further.

The sun was not so true unto the day 50
As he to me. Would he have stolen away
From sleeping Hermia? I'll believe as soon
This whole earth may be bored, and that the moon
May through the centre creep, and so displease
Her brother's noontide with th'Antipodes. 55
It cannot be but thou hast murdered him.
So should a murderer look: so dead, so grim.

DEMETRIUS
So should the murdered look, and so should I,
Pierced through the heart with your stern cruelty.
Yet you, the murderer, look as bright, as clear 60
As yonder Venus in her glimmering sphere.

HERMIA
What's this to my Lysander? Where is he?
Ah, good Demetrius, wilt thou give him me?

DEMETRIUS
I had rather give his carcass to my hounds.

HERMIA
Out, dog; out, cur. Thou driv'st me past the bounds 65
Of maiden's patience. Hast thou slain him then?
Henceforth be never numbered among men.
O, once tell true; tell true, even for my sake.
Durst thou have looked upon him being awake,
And hast thou killed him sleeping? O brave touch! 70
Could not a worm, an adder do so much?
An adder did it, for with doubler tongue
Than thine, thou serpent, never adder stung.

---

53 **whole** complete and solid (compare *Macbeth*, 'whole as the marble', 3.4.21)

54 **centre** mid-point
displease annoy the sun by bringing night to the opposite side of the world at midday. Wells compares the cosmic disorder described by Titania at 2.1.81–114.

56 **but** other than that

57, 60 **murderer** (two syllables here)

57 **dead** deadly

61 **Venus** The planet Venus is the evening star but she is also the goddess of love. The play is still dominated by the influence of Venus and her attendant Cupid (see also l. 107 below).
sphere orbit (see 2.1.7 and n.)

70 **brave touch** fine stroke

71–3 **Could ... stung** The elements of Hermia's dream surface; see Introduction, p. 14.

71 **worm** snake

72 **doubler** more deceitful and more forked

DEMETRIUS

You spend your passion on a misprised mood.
I am not guilty of Lysander's blood,   75
Nor is he dead, for aught that I can tell.

HERMIA

I pray thee, tell me then that he is well.

DEMETRIUS

And if I could, what should I get therefor?

HERMIA

A privilege never to see me more;
And from thy hated presence part I so.   80
See me no more, whether he be dead or no.   *Exit*

DEMETRIUS

There is no following her in this fierce vein.
Here therefore for a while I will remain.
So sorrow's heaviness doth heavier grow
For debt that bankrupt sleep doth sorrow owe,   85
Which now in some slight measure it will pay,
If for his tender here I make some stay.
      He lies down and sleeps

OBERON (*to Robin*)

What hast thou done? Thou hast mistaken quite,
And laid the love juice on some true love's sight.
Of thy misprision must perforce ensue   90
Some true love turned, and not a false turned true.

ROBIN

Then fate o'errules, that, one man holding troth,
A million fail, confounding oath on oath.

OBERON

About the wood go swifter than the wind,

---

80 so] POPE; *not in* QF   80–1] As POPE; Q1 *divides at* more   85 sleep] ROWE; slippe QF
87.1 *and sleeps*] REYNOLDS, DYCE; *not in* QF   88 *to Robin*] OXFORD; *not in* Q1

74 **spend** waste
  misprised mood mistaken anger
78 **therefor** for that
87 **tender** Sleep's offer in discharge of a
  debt (*OED sb.*² 1b), continuing the
  legal language of l. 85.
87.1 QF's SD is imperative (Q *Ly doune*),
  suggesting a playhouse instruction,
though the source of Q in foul papers
would argue against that.
90 **misprision** mistake (also at *LLL* 4.3.96)
92–3 In that case fate has taken over
  control, since for each man who is
  true in love a million fail, breaking
  oath after oath.

And Helena of Athens look thou find.   95
All fancy-sick she is, and pale of cheer
With sighs of love that costs the fresh blood dear.
By some illusion see thou bring her here.
I'll charm his eyes against she do appear.

ROBIN
I go, I go. Look how I go,   100
Swifter than arrow from the Tartar's bow.   *Exit*

OBERON
   Flower of this purple dye,
   Hit with Cupid's archery,
   Sink in apple of his eye.
      He drops the juice on Demetrius' eyelids
   When his love he doth espy,   105
   Let her shine as gloriously
   As the Venus of the sky.
   When thou wak'st, if she be by,
   Beg of her for remedy.
      Enter Robin Goodfellow

ROBIN
   Captain of our fairy band,   110
   Helena is here at hand,
   And the youth mistook by me,
   Pleading for a lover's fee.
   Shall we their fond pageant see?

---

101 *Exit*] Q2, F; *not in* Q1   104.1 *He . . . eyelids*] OXFORD (*after* Dyce); *Anoints* Demetrius*'s
eyes* HANMER (*after l.* 102); *not in* QF

96 **fancy-sick** love-sick
   cheer face
97 **sighs . . . dear** Sighs were held to use
   up blood (compare 'blood-consuming
   sighs', *2 Henry VI* 3.2.61).
99 **against** ready for when
100 **I go . . . I go** Leslie French, Robin to
   Gielgud's Oberon at the Old Vic in
   1929, 'cried enthusiastically, "I go, I
   go . . . ", then, as Oberon turned away,
   paused with a spoilt-child intonation:
   "*Look* how I go!" ' (Sprague and
   Trewin, p. 69).
101 **the Tartar's bow** The oriental bow
   was particularly powerful. The source

is probably Golding's Ovid (10.687, 'as
swift as arrow from a Turkey bow');
'Tartar' could be used for any part of
Central Asia including Turkey. In
Romeo 'a Tartar's painted bow of lath'
is associated with 'Cupid hoodwinked
with a scarf' (1.4.4–5); compare
Dream 1.1.235, 'And therefore is
winged Cupid painted blind', and
3.2.103.
104 **apple** pupil
105–9 **When . . . remedy** On the different
   effect of the juice when applied to
   Demetrius see Introduction, pp. 66–8.
114 **fond pageant** foolish spectacle or

Lord, what fools these mortals be!   115
OBERON
    Stand aside. The noise they make
    Will cause Demetrius to awake.
ROBIN
        Then will two at once woo one.
        That must needs be sport alone;
        And those things do best please me   120
        That befall prepost'rously.
            ⌈*They stand apart.*⌉
            Enter Helena, Lysander ⌈*following her*⌉
LYSANDER
    Why should you think that I should woo in scorn?
        Scorn and derision never come in tears.
    Look when I vow, I weep; and vows so born,
        In their nativity all truth appears.   125
    How can these things in me seem scorn to you,
    Bearing the badge of faith to prove them true?
HELENA
    You do advance your cunning more and more,
        When truth kills truth—O devilish holy fray!
    These vows are Hermia's. Will you give her o'er?   130
        Weigh oath with oath, and you will nothing weigh.
    Your vows to her and me put in two scales
    Will even weigh, and both as light as tales.
LYSANDER
    I had no judgement when to her I swore.

121.1 *They ... apart*] COLLIER 1853; *not in* QF   121.2 *Enter ... her*] OXFORD; *Enter* Lysander, *and* Helena QF

scene, a kind of play watched by Oberon and Robin as on-stage audience

119 **alone** 'on its own' or, possibly,
'unique'; in *Wily Beguiled* (printed
1606), Robin Goodfellow cries delight-
edly 'Why this will be sport alone' (ed.
W. W. Greg (Malone Society; Oxford,
1912), l. 543).
121 **prepost'rously** back to front
124 **Look when** whenever

124–5 **vows ... appears** when vows are
born out of weeping, nothing but truth
appears in their birth
127 **badge of faith** tears are the mark
(worn by servants) of his truthfulness
129 **truth kills truth** his vows to Hermia
deny his protestations to Helena (or
vice versa)
    devilish holy one holy vow destroyed
diabolically by a false one
133 **tales** fictions, lies

HELENA

Nor none, in my mind, now you give her o'er.   135

LYSANDER

Demetrius loves her, and he loves not you.

DEMETRIUS (*waking*)

O Helen, goddess, nymph, perfect, divine!
To what, my love, shall I compare thine eyne?
Crystal is muddy. O, how ripe in show
Thy lips, those kissing cherries, tempting grow!   140
That pure congealèd white—high Taurus' snow,
Fanned with the eastern wind—turns to a crow
When thou hold'st up thy hand. O, let me kiss
This princess of pure white, this seal of bliss!

HELENA

O spite! O hell! I see you all are bent   145
To set against me for your merriment.
If you were civil, and knew courtesy,
You would not do me thus much injury.
Can you not hate me—as I know you do—
But you must join in souls to mock me too?   150
If you were men, as men you are in show,
You would not use a gentle lady so,

---

137 *waking*] *Awa.* F (*at end of l.* 136); *not in* Q

136 **you** Oxford follows earlier suggestions and posits a lost line for Helena
at this point, completing the couplet
and waking Demetrius. Lysander and
Helena have been part of an elaborate
poetic structure from l. 122, alternating six-line stanzas, then sharing a
couplet (ll. 134–5). The sudden waking of Demetrius seems to me more
theatrical in that the poetic form does
not end neatly. Instead, Lysander's
naming of Demetrius seems enough to
wake him; it is as if he is conjured into
the scene by his name (neither Lysander nor Helena has had the slightest
idea he is there).

137–44 **O Helen . . . bliss** Demetrius' language here elevates Helena to the
status of Helen of Troy, a semi-divine,
perfectly beautiful woman.

139 **ripe** red and full

141–4 **That . . . bliss** White skin was always highly prized but here it is comically exaggerated.

141 **Taurus** A range of mountains in Turkey. John Studley's translation of Seneca's *Hippolytus* mentions 'on top of
Taurus hill | The wat'ry snows' which
melt but they are also mentioned in
Golding's Ovid (2.275).

144 **seal** when she takes his hand and
agrees to marry him

147 **courtesy** good manners

148 **do . . . injury** insult me so much

150 **join in souls** unite; editors often
emend 'souls' to a mocking word (e.g.
Hanmer's 'flouts', Johnson's 'scorns'
or 'scoffs') but emendation seems unnecessary.

152 **gentle** noble, as well as mild and kind

To vow and swear and superpraise my parts
When I am sure you hate me with your hearts.
You both are rivals and love Hermia,   155
And now both rivals to mock Helena.
A trim exploit, a manly enterprise:
To conjure tears up in a poor maid's eyes
With your derision. None of noble sort
Would so offend a virgin, and extort   160
A poor soul's patience, all to make you sport.

LYSANDER
You are unkind, Demetrius. Be not so.
For you love Hermia; this you know I know.
And here with all good will, with all my heart,
In Hermia's love I yield you up my part;   165
And yours of Helena to me bequeath,
Whom I do love, and will do till my death.

HELENA
Never did mockers waste more idle breath.

DEMETRIUS
Lysander, keep thy Hermia. I will none.
If e'er I loved her, all that love is gone.   170
My heart to her but as guestwise sojourned
And now to Helen is it home returned,
There to remain.

LYSANDER   Helen, it is not so.

DEMETRIUS
Disparage not the faith thou dost not know,
Lest to thy peril thou aby it dear.   175

        Enter Hermia

Look where thy love comes; yonder is thy dear.

HERMIA
Dark night, that from the eye his function takes,
The ear more quick of apprehension makes.
Wherein it doth impair the seeing sense,

---

153 **parts** qualities
157 **trim** fine
158 **conjure** create as if by magic
171 **sojourned** travelled (though *OED*'s
   only instance is 1608), stayed with on

a visit
175 **aby it dear** pay dearly for it
178 **apprehension** grasp, suggesting a
   physical action; compare 5.1.5 and
   5.1.19 and n.

197

It pays the hearing double recompense.   180
Thou art not by mine eye, Lysander, found;
Mine ear, I thank it, brought me to thy sound.
But why unkindly didst thou leave me so?

LYSANDER

Why should he stay whom love doth press to go?

HERMIA

What love could press Lysander from my side?   185

LYSANDER

Lysander's love, that would not let him bide:
Fair Helena, who more engilds the night
Than all yon fiery O's and eyes of light.
Why seek'st thou me? Could not this make thee know
The hate I bare thee made me leave thee so?   190

HERMIA

You speak not as you think. It cannot be.

HELENA

Lo, she is one of this confederacy.
Now I perceive they have conjoined all three
To fashion this false sport in spite of me.
Injurious Hermia, most ungrateful maid,   195
Have you conspired, have you with these contrived
To bait me with this foul derision?
Is all the counsel that we two have shared—
The sisters' vows, the hours that we have spent
When we have chid the hasty-footed time   200
For parting us—O, is all quite forgot?
All schooldays' friendship, childhood innocence?
We, Hermia, like two artifical gods

---

201 quite forgot] OXFORD; forgot QF

---

188 **O's and eyes** stars; 'oes' were round
spangles used to ornament a dress to
make it glitter. 'Eyes' puns on 'I's.

192–4 **Lo . . . me** Oxford marks these lines
as an aside; they may be but need not
be. Helena is perfectly capable of ad-
dressing her reasoning out of the mystery to the others on-stage.

194 **in spite of me** to spite me

197 **bait** persecute

201 **quite forgot** There have been numerous suggestions to restore the metre. I
prefer Oxford's conjecture, unless 'O'
is taken to cover the missing syllable;
'quite' and 'forget' are combined ten
times elsewhere in Shakespeare.

203 **artificial** highly skilled in art (*OED a.*
6b)

Have with our needles created both one flower,
Both on one sampler, sitting on one cushion,   205
Both warbling of one song, both in one key,
As if our hands, our sides, voices, and minds
Had been incorporate. So we grew together,
Like to a double cherry: seeming parted,
But yet an union in partition,   210
Two lovely berries moulded on one stem.
So, with two seeming bodies but one heart,
Two of the first—like coats in heraldry,
Due but to one and crownèd with one crest.
And will you rend our ancient love asunder,   215
To join with men in scorning your poor friend?
It is not friendly, 'tis not maidenly.
Our sex as well as I may chide you for it,
Though I alone do feel the injury.

HERMIA
I am amazèd at your passionate words.   220
I scorn you not. It seems that you scorn me.
HELENA
Have you not set Lysander, as in scorn,
To follow me, and praise my eyes and face?
And made your other love, Demetrius—
Who even but now did spurn me with his foot—   225

---

213 like] THEOBALD (*conj.* Folks); life QF   220 passionate] F; *not in* Q

204 **needles** one syllable, pronounced 'neelds'
206 **both in one key** Obviously two people singing the same song should be in the same key, but Helena is emphasizing their total harmony.
208 **Had been incorporate** had turned into one body; 'incorporate' is trisyllabic here.
212 **with ... heart** Compare Dent B503.1, 'One soul (heart, mind) in Bodies twain'—a proverbial definition of friendship.
213–14 **Two ... crest** 'Coats' are heraldic 'coats of arms'. 'Of the first' is a technical heraldic term for the first colour or metal referred to in a description of a coat of arms; the 'bodies' are Hele-

na's colour 'of the first' and the body's 'one heart' is the crest, punning on 'hart', a common heraldic crest, 'due but to one' since a coat of arms is granted to a single individual. 'Partition' (l. 210) is also a heraldic term for the definition of a shield and initiates the transition to this image.
220 **passionate** F's addition of 'passionate' may be the result of its consulting its manuscript authority; compare the similar incomprehension in 'what means this passionate discourse', *2 Henry VI* 1.1.101. The word has two syllables.
225 **Who ... foot** As she asked him to do at 2.1.204–5.

To call me goddess, nymph, divine, and rare,
Precious, celestial? Wherefore speaks he this
To her he hates? And wherefore doth Lysander
Deny your love, so rich within his soul,
And tender me, forsooth, affection,   230
But by your setting on, by your consent?
What though I be not so in grace as you,
So hung upon with love, so fortunate,
But miserable most, to love unloved—
This you should pity rather than despise.   235

HERMIA
I understand not what you mean by this.

HELENA
Ay, do. Persever, counterfeit sad looks,
Make mouths upon me when I turn my back,
Wink each at other, hold the sweet jest up.
This sport well carried shall be chronicled.   240
If you have any pity, grace, or manners,
You would not make me such an argument.
But fare ye well. 'Tis partly my own fault,
Which death or absence soon shall remedy.

LYSANDER
Stay, gentle Helena, hear my excuse,   245
My love, my life, my soul, fair Helena.

HELENA
O excellent!

HERMIA (*to Lysander*) Sweet, do not scorn her so.

DEMETRIUS (*to Lysander*)
If she cannot entreat I can compel.

LYSANDER
Thou canst compel no more than she entreat.

---

237 Ay, do.] Q2, F (I, do.); I‸ do Q1   247 *to Lysander*] WELLS; *not in* QF   248 *to Lysander*]
OXFORD; *not in* QF

237 **Ay, do**. Q1's reading, 'I do.', is   238 **Make mouths upon** scorn, mock
possible, Helena meaning that she un-   239 **Wink each at other** tip each other the
derstands perfectly well what is going   wink
on, even if Hermia 'pretends' not to,   **hold . . . up** keep it up
before she turns on the other 'conspir-   240 **carried** managed
ators'.   242 **argument** topic, object (of mockery)
sad serious

Thy threats have no more strength than her weak   250
    prayers.—
Helen, I love thee; by my life I do.
I swear by that which I will lose for thee
To prove him false that says I love thee not.

DEMETRIUS (*to Helena*)

I say I love thee more than he can do.

LYSANDER

If thou say so, withdraw, and prove it too.   255

DEMETRIUS

Quick, come.

HERMIA   Lysander, whereto tends all this?
   ⌈ *She holds him* ⌉

LYSANDER

Away, you Ethiope.

DEMETRIUS   No, no, sir, yield.
Seem to break loose, take on as you would follow,
But yet come not. You are a tame man; go.

LYSANDER (*to Hermia*)

Hang off, thou cat, thou burr; vile thing, let loose,   260

---

250 prayers] THEOBALD; praise QF   254 *to Helena*] OXFORD; *not in* QF   256.1 *She ... him*]
This edition; *not in* QF   257 No, no, sir, yield] OXFORD; No, no: heele Q1; No, no, hee'l
Q2; No, no, Sir, F   260 *to Hermia*] OXFORD; *not in* QF

250 **prayers** Theobald's emendation pro-
    vides an antithesis to 'threats'.
256.1 **She holds him** Since Lysander (at
    l. 261) turns Hermia into a serpent, as
    in her dream (2.2.155), she might
    here hold him as the serpent held her;
    see Introduction, pp. 15–16.
257 **Ethiope** blackamoor; another refer-
    ence to Hermia's dark complexion.
257–8 **No ... loose** This textual crux is
    brilliantly analysed by Gary Taylor, 'A
    Crux in *A Midsummer Night's Dream*',
    N&Q 230 (1985), pp. 47–9. Q1's
    'heele | Seeme' produces a highly im-
    probable enjambment, if 'heele' is
    'he'll', and, in any case, leaves the line
    a foot short. Q2's reading is possible
    but F's replacement of Q2's 'hee'l'
    with 'Sir' is unlikely to be compositor-
    ial guesswork. 'Seem to break loose' is
    plainly a mocking instruction to Ly-
    sander only to appear to be trying to

break Hermia's grip on him, so as to
have an excuse not to fight Demetrius;
it parallels 'take on as you would follow', (that is, 'behave as if you wanted
to follow me'). Any emendation of
'heele' will work best if the whole of
Demetrius' speech is directed to Lysander. Unfortunately there are no contemporary examples for 'heel' as an
instruction to a dog to come to heel.
Taylor's emendation, 'No, no, sir,
yield', corrects the metre by incorporating F's 'Sir' as an incomplete correction derived from manuscript and
construes 'heele' as a perfectly easy
misreading of 'yeeld'. 'Yield' is Demetrius' mocking suggestion to Lysander to
give up struggling to get free of Hermia,
as he is presumably trying to do.
259 **go** off with you, go on
260 **burr** burdock heads, proverbial for
    sticking (Tilley B724)

Or I will shake thee from me like a serpent.

HERMIA

Why are you grown so rude? What change is this,
Sweet love?

LYSANDER   Thy love? Out, tawny Tartar, out;
Out, loathèd med'cine; O hated potion, hence.

HERMIA

Do you not jest?   265

HELENA   Yes, sooth, and so do you.

LYSANDER

Demetrius, I will keep my word with thee.

DEMETRIUS

I would I had your bond, for I perceive
A weak bond holds you. I'll not trust your word.

LYSANDER

What, should I hurt her, strike her, kill her dead?
Although I hate her, I'll not harm her so.   270

HERMIA

What, can you do me greater harm than hate?
Hate me—wherefore? O me, what news, my love?
Am not I Hermia? Are not you Lysander?
I am as fair now as I was erewhile.
Since night you loved me, yet since night you left me.   275
Why then, you left me—O, the gods forbid—
In earnest, shall I say?

LYSANDER   Ay, by my life,
And never did desire to see thee more.
Therefore be out of hope, of question, doubt.
Be certain, nothing truer; 'tis no jest   280
That I do hate thee and love Helena.

279 doubt] POPE; of doubt QF

261 **Or . . . serpent** Compare Acts 28: 5
    where St Paul 'shook off the beast
    ["viper" in Bishops' Bible] into the fire'.
263 **tawny** tanned, swarthy; compare
    Cleopatra's 'tawny front', *Antony* 1.1.6.
    Tartar See l. 101 and n.
264 **med'cine . . . potion** Both could refer
    to poisons.

267–8 **bond . . . bond** (a) pledge (b) bind-
    ing tie
    be out of hope abandon hope
279 **of hope . . . doubt** For Pope's emen-
    dation, compare Helena's 'Ay, in the
    temple, in the town, the field'
    (2.1.238).

HERMIA (*to Helena*)

  O me, you juggler, you canker blossom,

  You thief of love—what, have you come by night

  And stol'n my love's heart from him?

HELENA   Fine, i'faith.

  Have you no modesty, no maiden shame,   285

  No touch of bashfulness? What, will you tear

  Impatient answers from my gentle tongue?

  Fie, fie, you counterfeit, you puppet, you!

HERMIA

  Puppet? Why so? Ay, that way goes the game.

  Now I perceive that she hath made compare   290

  Between our statures; she hath urged her height,

  And with her personage, her tall personage,

  Her height, forsooth, she hath prevailed with him—

  And are you grown so high in his esteem

  Because I am so dwarfish and so low?   295

  How low am I, thou painted maypole? Speak,

  How low am I? I am not yet so low

  But that my nails can reach unto thine eyes.

HELENA

  I pray you, though you mock me, gentlemen,

  Let her not hurt me. I was never curst.   300

  I have no gift at all in shrewishness.

  I am a right maid for my cowardice.

---

282 *to Helena*] BROOKS (*after* O me,); *not in* QF   299 gentlemen] Q2, F; gentleman Q1

282 **juggler** trickster (three syllables here)
  canker blossom a grub that kills blossom; compare 'cankers in the muskrose buds', 2.2.3.
283-4 **You thief... from him?** Hermia's accusation is strikingly like Egeus' of Lysander in 1.1; both Lysander and Helena are accused of stealing love by night.
288 **puppet** The argument over height appears in Lyly's *Endimion* (3.34). The different heights of the two boy actors is used again in *As You Like It* to contrast Rosalind and Celia.
289 **Why so?** could be punctuated 'Why,

so!' (Theobald, *subs.*) but I prefer a Hermia who takes a moment to make the mental leap from understanding a 'puppet' as a 'counterfeit' human to its being a comment on her size.
292 **personage** a person of rank and stature (*OED*)
296 **painted maypole** A double insult: a tall, skinny person (Tilley M778) but 'painted' is also the standard insult against a woman who uses cosmetics (first usage in this sense in *OED*).
300 **curst** shrewish
302 **right** proper

Let her not strike me. You perhaps may think
Because she is something lower than myself
That I can match her—

HERMIA   Lower? Hark again.   305

HELENA

Good Hermia, do not be so bitter with me.
I evermore did love you, Hermia,
Did ever keep your counsels, never wronged you—
Save that in love unto Demetrius
I told him of your stealth unto this wood.   310
He followed you; for love I followed him.
But he hath chid me hence, and threatened me
To strike me, spurn me, nay, to kill me too.
And now, so you will let me quiet go,
To Athens will I bear my folly back,   315
And follow you no further. Let me go.
You see how simple and how fond I am.

HERMIA

Why, get you gone. Who is't that hinders you?

HELENA

A foolish heart that I leave here behind.

HERMIA

What, with Lysander?

HELENA   With Demetrius.   320

LYSANDER

Be not afraid; she shall not harm thee, Helena.

DEMETRIUS

No, sir, she shall not, though you take her part.

HELENA

O, when she is angry she is keen and shrewd.
She was a vixen when she went to school,
And though she be but little, she is fierce.   325

---

305 **Lower?** Again, as at l. 289, the punctuation could as easily be an exclamation mark (a furious shriek) as a question.
310 **stealth** stealing away (*OED* 3)
312 **chid me hence** tried to drive me away by scolding
323 **shrewd** malicious. Helena's image of Hermia changes from the image of perfect childhood friendship at ll. 198–214.

HERMIA

   'Little' again? Nothing but 'low' and 'little'?—

   Why will you suffer her to flout me thus?

   Let me come to her.

LYSANDER   Get you gone, you dwarf,

   You *minimus* of hind'ring knot-grass made,

   You bead, you acorn.

DEMETRIUS   You are too officious   330

   In her behalf that scorns your services.

   Let her alone. Speak not of Helena.

   Take not her part. For if thou dost intend

   Never so little show of love to her,

   Thou shalt aby it.

LYSANDER   Now she holds me not.   335

   Now follow, if thou dar'st, to try whose right,

   Of thine or mine, is most in Helena.

DEMETRIUS

   Follow? Nay, I'll go with thee, cheek by jowl.

               Exeunt Lysander and Demetrius

HERMIA

   You, mistress, all this coil is long of you.

   Nay, go not back.

HELENA   I will not trust you, I,   340

   Nor longer stay in your curst company.

   Your hands than mine are quicker for a fray;

   My legs are longer, though, to run away.   *Exit*

HERMIA

   I am amazed, and know not what to say.   *Exit*

    ⌈ *Oberon and Robin Goodfellow come forward* ⌉

OBERON

   This is thy negligence. Still thou mistak'st,   345

---

326 but] Q2, F; hut Q1   338.1 *Exeunt . . . Demetrius*] F (*Exit . . .*); *Exit.* Q2;   *not in*
Q1   343 *Exit*] CAPELL; *not in* Q; *Exeunt.* F (*omitting l.*344)   344 *Exit*]] CAPELL; *Exeunt.*
Q   344.1 *Oberon . . . forward*] WELLS (*subs.*); *Enter Oberon and Pucke* F; *not in* Q

---

329 *minimus* extremely small creature;
   italicized as a Latin word in Q1
   knot-grass a common creeping weed,
   Polygonum aviculare, an infusion of
   which was supposed to stunt growth
   (*OED*)

335 **aby** pay dearly for (see 3.2.175)
338 **cheek by jowl** Proverbial (Tilley
   C263).
339 **all . . . you** all this to-do is your fault
345 **Still** continually

Or else committ'st thy knaveries wilfully.
ROBIN
Believe me, king of shadows, I mistook.
Did not you tell me I should know the man
By the Athenian garments he had on?
And so far blameless proves my enterprise   350
That I have 'nointed an Athenian's eyes;
And so far am I glad it so did sort
As this their jangling I esteem a sport.
OBERON
Thou seest these lovers seek a place to fight.
Hie therefore, Robin, overcast the night;   355
The starry welkin cover thou anon
With drooping fog as black as Acheron,
And lead these testy rivals so astray
As one come not within another's way.
Like to Lysander sometime frame thy tongue,   360
Then stir Demetrius up with bitter wrong;
And sometime rail thou like Demetrius,
And from each other look thou lead them thus
Till o'er their brows death-counterfeiting sleep
With leaden legs and batty wings doth creep.   365
Then crush this herb into Lysander's eye,
Whose liquor hath this virtuous property:
To take from thence all error with his might,
And make his eyeballs roll with wonted sight.
When they next wake, all this derision   370
Shall seem a dream and fruitless vision,
And back to Athens shall the lovers wend
With league whose date till death shall never end.

---

350 **so far** at least to this extent
352 **sort** turn out
353 **jangling** discord
355 **Hie** go, hasten
355–7 **night . . . Acheron** Compare Mar-
     lowe, *Hero and Leander* (1598), 1.189,
     'Night, deep-drench'd in misty Ache-
     ron'.
356 **welkin** sky
357 **Acheron** one of the four rivers of
     Hades

359 **As** so that
364 **death-counterfeiting sleep** Proverbial;
     Tilley S527.
365 **batty** bat-like
367 **virtuous** efficacious, potent
368 **his** its
370–1 Compare Robin's similar sugges-
     tion in his epilogue that the audience
     could treat the whole play like this
     (5.1.416–22).
373 **date** period of duration

Whiles I in this affair do thee employ,
I'll to my queen and beg her Indian boy;   375
And then I will her charmèd eye release
From monster's view, and all things shall be peace.

ROBIN

My fairy lord, this must be done with haste,
For night's swift dragons cut the clouds full fast,
And yonder shines Aurora's harbinger,   380
At whose approach ghosts, wand'ring here and there,
Troop home to churchyards; damnèd spirits all
That in cross-ways and floods have burial
Already to their wormy beds are gone,
For fear lest day should look their shames upon.   385
They wilfully themselves exiled from light,
And must for aye consort with black-browed night.

OBERON

But we are spirits of another sort.
I with the morning's love have oft made sport,
And like a forester the groves may tread   390
Even till the eastern gate, all fiery red,
Opening on Neptune with fair blessèd beams

---

386 exiled] ALEXANDER (*conj*. Thirlby); exile Q; dxile F

---

379 **night's swift dragons** Compare Marlowe's *Hero and Leander*, 1.108 where
the moon has 'yawning dragons draw
her thirling car', and *Troilus* 5.9.17,
Cymbeline 2.2.48.

380 **Aurora's harbinger** the morning star,
herald of the dawn

381–4 **At . . . gone** Robin distinguishes
between 'ghosts wandering' ('walking
spirits') who are now leaving, and
'damnèd spirits' who have already
gone (Brooks).

383 **in . . . burial** The bodies of suicides,
who were automatically damned, were
buried in unconsecrated ground, particularly at cross-roads; those who
drowned themselves were still in the
sea ('floods') unless the bodies had
been recovered.

386–7 **They . . . night** Some editors argue
that these lines belong to Oberon, 'a

forceful rejoinder to [Robin's] merely
descriptive lines' (Jenkins in Brooks)
but the emphatic change from Robin's
horror to Oberon's reassurance is surely right.

386 **exiled** F's 'dxile' is a bungled correction of Q's 'exile'; their permanent
night-time existence is a consequence
of their decision to choose exile.

387 **consort** keep (bad) company
black-browed night Compare *Romeo*
3.2.20.

389 **I . . . sport** Oberon could mean either
'I have hunted with Cephalus, Auro-
ra's lover' (for Cephalus see 5.1.197
and n.) or 'I have dallied with Aurora';
he certainly means that he does not
have to vanish before dawn.

390 **forester** His job was to preserve the
game in woods and to keep watch for
poachers.

Turns into yellow gold his salt green streams.
But notwithstanding, haste, make no delay;
We may effect this business yet ere day.   *Exit*   395

ROBIN

Up and down, up and down,
I will lead them up and down.
I am feared in field and town.
Goblin, lead them up and down.
Here comes one.   400

     Enter Lysander

LYSANDER

Where art thou, proud Demetrius? Speak thou now.

ROBIN

Here, villain, drawn and ready. Where art thou?

LYSANDER

I will be with thee straight.

ROBIN   Follow me then.
To plainer ground.

                 ⌈*Exit Lysander*⌉

     Enter Demetrius

DEMETRIUS   Lysander, speak again.
Thou runaway, thou coward, art thou fled?   405
Speak! In some bush? Where dost thou hide thy head?
ROBIN ⌈*shifting place*⌉

Thou coward, art thou bragging to the stars,

---

395 *Exit*] ROWE; *not in* QF   396–9] *Divided as in* POPE; *two lines in* Q1, *divided after* Up . . . down: 403–4 Follow . . . ground] THEOBALD; *one line in* QF   404 Exit Lysander] THEOBALD (*subs.*); *not in* QF; *Leads* Lysander *out, and returns.* FAIRY Q   406 Speak! In some bush?] CAPELL (~. ~?); ~ₐ ~. QF   407, etc. shifting place] OXFORD; F (*shifting places*) *after l.* 418 *only*; *not in* Q

399 **Goblin** Robin himself
400 Oberon has instructed Robin to pro-
    duce fog (ll. 355–7) and in modern
    productions the stage usually starts to
    fill up with dry ice at this point, un-
    necessarily (Wells); after Oberon's exit
    at l. 395, Granville Barker's prompt-
    book, emphasizing the theatricality of
    the realization of Oberon's orders, has
    Robin moved downstage and 'motion
    for lights to go down. Then up to cloth
    [, bend] down and raise cloth as it
    ascends' (quoted by Dymkowski, p.

68). In the Reinhardt–Dieterle film
    (1935) the fog was breathed out from
    Robin's own mouth.
402 **drawn** with drawn sword
404 *Exit Lysander* The exit is not strictly
    necessary but things might be a bit *too*
    confusing if Robin mimics Lysander's
    voice with an on-stage Lysander who
    ignores the sound of Demetrius' and
    'his' voices, though this would not be
    particularly problematic within the
    conventions of Elizabethan staging.
407, etc. *shifting place* In F the SD *shifting*

Telling the bushes that thou look'st for wars,
And wilt not come? Come, recreant; come, thou child,
I'll whip thee with a rod. He is defiled   410
That draws a sword on thee.
DEMETRIUS ⌈*shifting place*⌉   Yea, art thou there?
ROBIN ⌈*shifting place*⌉
    Follow my voice; we'll try no manhood here.   *Exeunt*
        ⌈*Enter Lysander*⌉

LYSANDER

He goes before me, and still dares me on;
When I come where he calls, then he is gone.
The villain is much lighter heeled than I;   415
I followed fast, but faster he did fly,
That fallen am I in dark uneven way,
And here will rest me.
        He lies down
                    Come, thou gentle day;
For if but once thou show me thy grey light,

412.1 *Enter Lysander*] THEOBALD (*subs.*); *not in* QF; *Enter* Lysander. *He leads him in* FAIRY Q
418 *He lies down*] *lye down* F (*at end of line*); *not in* Q

places appears at l. 416; it probably derives from the prompt-book and indicated that Robin dodges about the stage in this scene (he is 'shifting every place' at l. 424), while Demetrius and Lysander move around, trying to follow him. Given that Robin is presumably *not* moving at l. 416, Oxford proposes that its appearance in the prompt-book, near the middle of the section of toing and fro-ing, might have been a marginal direction with a long line or bracket, originating, perhaps, as Wilson suggested, from the need of the book-holder to note the 'careful and probably frequent rehearsal' all this stage business required. Oxford distributes the SD very frequently from l. 403 (eight times in all); I have been slightly more restrained, using it to indicate the more necessary shifts, while accepting that in production the movement might well have occurred more often.

412.1 *Enter Lysander* Oxford, noting the

clear stage here (the first since the opening of 3.2), begins a new scene (Scene 6 or 3.3) which runs to the end of 4.1, arguing that the new scene helps 'the ease with which an audience accepts the subsequent wearied surrender of Lysander and Demetrius' by suggesting a gap of time and place. But the audience would not have had any way of noticing a new scene and interpreting the break as representing a passage of time unless there were a sizeable time-gap at this point, a gap which would seem undesirable in its disruption of the action. Since the action either side of l. 413 is remarkably similar, something Shakespeare never does across scenes, and since in Elizabethan performance the action would here surely have been continuous as usual, I have reverted to the traditional lack of division (see also 3.2.464 and n.).

417 **fallen am I in** I have got into

I'll find Demetrius, and revenge this spite.   *He sleeps*   420
    Enter Robin Goodfellow and Demetrius
ROBIN ⌈*shifting place*⌉

  Ho, ho, ho, coward, why com'st thou not?
DEMETRIUS

  Abide me if thou dar'st, for well I wot
  Thou runn'st before me, shifting every place,
  And dar'st not stand nor look me in the face.
  Where art thou now?
ROBIN ⌈*shifting place*⌉   Come hither, I am here.   425
DEMETRIUS

  Nay, then thou mock'st me. Thou shalt buy this dear
  If ever I thy face by daylight see.
  Now go thy way. Faintness constraineth me
  To measure out my length on this cold bed.
     He lies down
  By day's approach look to be visited.   *He sleeps*   430
     Enter Helena

HELENA

  O weary night, O long and tedious night,
    Abate thy hours; shine comforts from the east
  That I may back to Athens by daylight
    From these that my poor company detest;
  And sleep, that sometimes shuts up sorrow's eye,   435
  Steal me a while from mine own company.
     She lies down and sleeps

ROBIN

  Yet but three? Come one more,

420, 430 *He sleeps*] FAIRY Q (*Sleeps*), CAPELL (*subs.*); *not in* QF   420.1 *Enter*] F; *not in* Q
426 shalt] Q2, F; shat Q1   429.1 *He lies down*] CAPELL (*subs.*); F4 (*subs., after l.* 430);
not in QF   430 *He sleeps*] CAPELL; *not in* QF   436.1 *She . . . sleeps*] DYCE (*subs.*); *Sleepe.* QF

---

420 **spite** bad turn
421 **Ho, ho, ho** This could be spoken in Lysander's voice but it was also Robin's own traditional mocking laugh and is probably in his own voice here (compare his 'Ho, ho, ho, my Masters' in *Grim the Collier of Croydon*, p. 67). Gordon Crosse commented

'Puck is an English spirit in an English wood, & his laugh should be a deep Ho Ho Ho' (Drury Lane, January 1925, vol. 9, p. 50)
424 **stand** stand still
432 **Abate thy hours** make the time shorter
434 **detest** repudiate

Two of both kinds makes up four.
  ⌈*Enter Hermia*⌉
Here she comes, curst and sad.
Cupid is a knavish lad   440
Thus to make poor females mad.

HERMIA

Never so weary, never so in woe,
  Bedabbled with the dew, and torn with briers,
I can no further crawl, no further go.
  My legs can keep no pace with my desires.   445
Here will I rest me till the break of day.
    She lies down
Heavens shield Lysander, if they mean a fray.
    She sleeps

ROBIN   On the ground
               Sleep sound.
               I'll apply   450
               To your eye,
            Gentle lover, remedy.
    He drops the juice on Lysander's eyelids
             When thou wak'st
             Thou tak'st
             True delight   455
             In the sight
          Of thy former lady's eye,
      And the country proverb known,
      That every man should take his own,
      In your waking shall be shown.   460

438.1 *Enter Hermia*] *after l. 440* Q2, F; *not in* Q1   446.1 *She lies down*] CAPELL (*subs.*);
ROWE (*after l. 447*); *not in* QF   447.1 *She sleeps*] FAIRY Q (*Sleeps*), CAPELL (*subs.*); *not in* QF
448–52] *Divided as in* WARBURTON; *two lines in* Q1 *divided at* sound: 451 To] ROWE; *not*
in QF   452.1 *He . . . eyelids*] ROWE (*subs.*); *not in* QF   453–7] *Divided as in* WARBURTON;
two lines in Q1 *divided at* tak'st

452.1 **He . . . eyelids** The fact that Demetrius stays under the influence of the
first drug troubles many commentators
but since its effect on him has been
different he does not need 'curing'; see
Introduction, pp. 66–8. Gordon Crosse
noted that, in a production by Ben
Greet in August 1899, Robin 'anointed Demetrius' eyes as well as Lysander's with the antidote' (vol. 2,
p. 88).

> Jack shall have Jill,
> Naught shall go ill,
> The man shall have his mare again,
> And all shall be well.   *Exit*

4.1   *Enter Titania, Queen of Fairies, and Bottom with the ass-head, and fairies: Peaseblossom, Cobweb, Mote, and Mustardseed*

TITANIA (*to Bottom*)
  Come, sit thee down upon this flow'ry bed,

461–2] *Divided as in* JOHNSON; *one line in* QF   463–4] *Divided as in* COLLIER; *one line in* QF
464 *Exit*] ROWE; *not in* Q; *They sleepe all the Act* F

4.1.   0.1 *and Bottom*] ROWE; *and Clowne* QF   *with the ass-head*] OXFORD; *not in* QF
0.2–3 *fairies . . . Mustardseed*] OXFORD; Faieries: *and the king behinde them* QF   1 *to Bottom*]
OXFORD; *not in* QF

461 Proverbial (Tilley A164, 'All shall be well and Jack shall have Jill'; M209, 'Let every man have his own'); reversed in *LLL* 5.2.861, 'Jack hath not Jill'.

463–4 Another proverb (Tilley A153, 'All is well and the man has his mare again').

464 F's direction here (*They sleepe all the Act*) certainly indicates the continuity of the scene from here through the whole of 4.1 (see above n. to l. 412.1). F's SD, placed at 4.1.100, '*Sleepers Lye still*', is another reminder that they are still asleep on-stage (not that they should lie without moving—see 4.1.101.2). F's act-division here is theatrically meaningless and one which modern productions never have to face; the play's natural single interval is at the end of 3.1 (see n. to 3.2.1–40). Foakes argues that F's '*the Act*', usually taken to mean 'the interval between the acts' or 'music played between the acts' (a meaning it certainly did have in the period, in relation to performances at private theatres), here means a unit of drama in the modern sense, comparing *All is True* Epilogue 3, 'And sleep an act or two' (which is however *OED*'s first instance in this sense) and entries for payments by the act in Henslowe's *Diary*. The source may well have been prompt-book and have

preceded the heavy act-division created by F's editors' inclusion of an emphatic *Actus Quartus* between rules. But Foakes's argument does not face up to F's use of 'all', '*all the Act*', since the lovers are on-stage asleep for approximately one hundred lines, a segment of the play which is not conceivably an 'act' in any sense. For that reason, I understand the SD in F to indicate the interval between acts. The importance of the lack of a clear stage at this point is to alert us to the onward flow of the action: the sequence from the beginning of 2.1 to the end of 4.1 moves with extraordinary connectedness until the play leaves the wood for the return to Athens.

4.1.0.1–3 *Enter . . . Mustardseed* QF give Oberon an entrance at the beginning of this scene (*and the king behinde them*); this was undoubtedly Shakespeare's first intention and almost all editions follow it. But F also has Oberon enter at l. 44. Like the case of 3.1.49.1 where I have argued cautiously for the theatrical advantages and possibilities from following F with an early entrance for Robin, F's later entrance for Oberon in this scene seems a legitimate theatrical decision and is likely to derive from the prompt-book authority F used. It is also, however, parallelled by F's direction at

While I thy amiable cheeks do coy,
And stick musk-roses in thy sleek smooth head,
And kiss thy fair large ears, my gentle joy.

BOTTOM Where's Peaseblossom? 5

PEASEBLOSSOM Ready.

BOTTOM Scratch my head, Peaseblossom. Where's
Monsieur Cobweb?

COBWEB Ready.

BOTTOM Monsieur Cobweb, good monsieur, get you your 10
weapons in your hand and kill me a red-hipped humble-
bee on the top of a thistle; and, good monsieur, bring
me the honeybag. Do not fret yourself too much in the
action, monsieur; and, good monsieur, have a care the

5, etc. BOTTOM] ROWE; *Clo.* QF

3.2.344, '*Enter Oberon and Pucke*', when they come forward, never having left the stage; if this parallel is significant it would tend to justify the presence of Oberon on-stage from the start of the scene. Oxford points out that Oberon's previous encounter with Titania is structurally parallel to F's form here if Oberon enters at l. 44: in both Titania dismisses her train and falls asleep; Oberon then enters and applies the magic juice. This type of structural parallel is certainly used frequently by Shakespeare throughout his career. In isolating the Titania/Bottom scene from Oberon's gaze it allows their relationship its full innocence (see Introduction, pp. 72–3), less practicable in Q's version which comes closer to making the audience share something prying and voyeuristic in the husband's watching, the cuckold peeping at his wife and her lover. F's Oberon has completed his revenge offstage in the brutal, taunting manifestation of male power and triumph he describes at 4.1.47–62. Q's version displaces the significance of this description through its emphasis on the continued fascination the sight of Bottom and Titania has for Oberon. The play is of course full of silent spectators but Oberon's silence in Q seems un-

usually gnomic; there is nothing in his subsequent behaviour to define his response to seeing Titania entwined around Bottom. Oberon's first words, 'Welcome, good Robin' (l. 45), however, tend to support Q's staging; 'welcome' is most commonly used by Shakespeare as a word of greeting from a character already on stage to one arriving. The editorial decision is finely balanced; readers or directors can make their choices. The difference between the two versions of the scene is, none the less, substantial. From here to l. 198 the stage is remarkably full with unnoted sleepers; productions always have the problem of how to accommodate four sleeping lovers alongside Bottom, Titania and her train and, later, Bottom asleep while the stage is occupied by the lovers, Hippolyta, Theseus and his train.

2 **coy** caress (*OED* v.[1] 2); the term is from falconry but Jason 'coyed' the 'dangling dewlaps' of bulls he had tamed in Golding's Ovid (7.161)—compare 'dewlapped' at l. 121.

3 **musk-roses** Their third appearance in the wood (compare 2.1.252, 2.2.3).

6–7 **Monsieur** For Bottom the fairies become French or Italian gentlemen (see 'Cavaliery', l. 22 and n.).

honeybag break not. I would be loath to have you over-   15
flowen with a honeybag, signor.   ⌈*Exit Cobweb*⌉
Where's Monsieur Mustardseed?

MUSTARDSEED Ready.

BOTTOM Give me your neaf, Monsieur Mustardseed. Pray
you, leave your courtesy, good monsieur.   20

MUSTARDSEED What's your will?

BOTTOM Nothing, good monsieur, but to help Cavaliery
Peaseblossom to scratch. I must to the barber's, monsieur, for methinks I am marvellous hairy about the
face; and I am such a tender ass, if my hair do but tickle   25
me I must scratch.

TITANIA

What, wilt thou hear some music, my sweet love?

BOTTOM I have a reasonable good ear in music. Let's have
the tongs and the bones.
        ⌈*Rural music*⌉

---

16 *Exit Cobweb*] OXFORD; *not in* QF   22 Cavaliery] QF (Caualery)   23 Peaseblossom] RANN;
Cobwebbe QF   24 marvellous] Q (maruailes)   29.1 *Rural music*] *Musicke Tongs, Rurall
Musicke* F; *not in* Q

---

16 **Exit Cobweb** One would expect Titania's obedient fairies to follow Bottom's
orders immediately.

19 **neaf** fist

20 **leave your courtesy** stop bowing; Mustardseed is politely respectful, as Titania had ordered (3.1.156 and 166),
but Bottom wishes to be friendly and
shake his hand. Brooks compares 'remember thy courtesy . . . apparel thy
head' (*LLL* 5.1.93–4) but it seems unlikely that Mustardseed has a hat to
doff and the fairy's action is more likely to parallel the bowing of 3.1.

22 **Cavaliery** cavaliero, a gentleman gallant (from Italian *cavaliere*)

23 **Peaseblossom** Q's Cobweb is a mistake—though attractive for its alliteration—since Cobweb has been sent on
a mission and Peaseblossom is already
engaged in scratching.

23–5 **I must . . . the face** It is tempting to
find an echo in this passage of the
story of Midas whose ass's ears were
revealed to all by his barber's uncon-
trollable urge to gossip.

29 **the tongs and the bones** Tongs were
struck with a key; bones (or knackers)
were clappers rattled together between
the fingers. They made crude music,
here associated with rustic country
music. Inigo Jones included costume
designs for 'A Man with Knackers and
Bells' and 'A Man with Tongs and
Key' for *Britannia Triumphans* (1637)
(see Stephen Orgel and Roy Strong,
*Inigo Jones: The Theatre of the Stuart
Court* (1973), figs. 347 and 348, p.
686).

29.1 **Rural music** Titania's next line
might seem to deny Bottom his music
but F's SD for music from the tongs,
if not bones, is likely to have prompt-
book authority, the 'Rurall Musicke'
obviously accompanying the tongs.
The whole scene is built up out of a
brilliant series of contrasting musics
(the 'still music' of 82.1, the dance
music of 85.1 and the horns of 101.3
and 137.2), each of which is powerfully and resonantly symbolic; Bottom's rough music is the first.

TITANIA

Or say, sweet love, what thou desir'st to eat.   30

BOTTOM Truly, a peck of provender. I could munch your
    good dry oats. Methinks I have a great desire to a bottle
    of hay. Good hay, sweet hay, hath no fellow.

TITANIA

I have a venturous fairy that shall seek
    The squirrel's hoard, and fetch thee off new nuts.   35

BOTTOM I had rather have a handful or two of dried peas.
    But I pray you, let none of your people stir me. I have an
    exposition of sleep come upon me.

TITANIA

Sleep thou, and I will wind thee in my arms.
    Fairies, be gone, and be always away.   *Exeunt Fairies*   40
    So doth the woodbine the sweet honeysuckle
    Gently entwist; the female ivy so

34–5] *Divided as in* HANMER; *divided in* Q1 *at* hoard,   35 thee off] OXFORD; thee QF; thee
thence HANMER   40 always] QF (alwaies); all ways THEOBALD   40 *Exeunt Fairies*] CAPELL;
not in QF

Granville Barker, who placed it after
the fairies' exit at l. 40, commented
on 'the pleasing, fantastic irony in
little Titania and her monster being
lulled to sleep by the distant sound of
the tongs and the bones; it would
make a properly dramatic contrast to
the 'still music' for which she calls a
moment later, her hand in Oberon's
again. A producer might, without
offence, venture on the effect. (But
Oberon, by the way, had better stop
the noise with a disgusted gesture before he begins to speak)' (p. 110).

32 **bottle** bundle, truss, sufficient for one
    feed

33 **hay** The word suggests an opportunity
    for the actor to bray like an ass.
    hath no fellow is unmatched (Dent
    F181.1)

35 **thee off** ll. 34–5 are incorrectly divided
    in Q1 and turned into three short lines
    in Q2, F; they are also metrically de-
    fective. Hanmer's emendation, 'thee
    thence', was widely accepted but Ox-
    ford points out that Shakespeare never
    uses 'fetch thence'; its solution, 'fetch

thee off', underlines the need for a
venturous fairy since 'fetch off' could
mean 'bring out of a difficulty, deliver,
rescue' (*OED v.* 16a).

38 **exposition of** Bottom means 'disposi-
    tion to'.

40 **always**   Theobald's   emendation,
    usually accepted, has Titania sending
    the fairies off in all different directions;
    it seems more likely she is ordering
    them to go away and stay away so
    that she can be alone with Bottom.

41 **woodbine** bindweed or convolvulus
    (compare 2.1.251 and n.); Wells
    (p. 152) quotes Martin Gardner, *The
    Ambidextrous Universe* (1967, p. 65),
    'The honeysuckle . . . always twines in
    a left-handed helix. The bindweed fam-
    ily . . . always twines in a right-handed
    helix . . . When plants of opposite han-
    dedness coil round each other, they
    produce a hopeless tangle. The mixed-
    up violent left-right embrace of the
    bindweed and honeysuckle . . . has long
    fascinated English poets'.

42–3 **the female . . . elm** The conventional
    proverb places the wife as a vine em-
    bracing the husband as elm (Tilley

Enrings the barky fingers of the elm.
O how I love thee, how I dote on thee!
      They sleep.
      Enter Robin Goodfellow ⌈ and Oberon, meeting⌉

OBERON

Welcome, good Robin. Seest thou this sweet sight?   45
Her dotage now I do begin to pity,
For meeting her of late behind the wood,
Seeking sweet favours for this hateful fool,
I did upbraid her and fall out with her,
For she his hairy temples then had rounded   50
With coronet of fresh and fragrant flowers,
And that same dew which sometime on the buds
Was wont to swell like round and orient pearls
Stood now within the pretty flow'rets' eyes,
Like tears that did their own disgrace bewail.   55
When I had at my pleasure taunted her,

44.1 *They sleep*] CAPELL; *not in* QF   44.2 *and Oberon meeting*] OXFORD; *and Oberon* F; *not in* Q; *Oberon approaches Enter Pug.* COX

V61, 'The vine embraces the elm',
Psalms 128:3, Golding's Ovid 14.755–
63, all derived from practical vinicul-
ture) is altered here (see Peter Demetz,
'The Elm and the Vine: Notes Toward
the History of a Marriage Topos',
PMLA 73 (1958), pp. 521–32).
Shakespeare uses the traditional version in *Errors* 2.2.177, 'Thou art an
elm, my husband; I a vine' and contrasts it with 'Usurping ivy, brier, or
idle moss' (l. 181). Titania becomes ivy
here perhaps because the love is adulterous (though Bottom is the usurper
and hence should be the ivy in the
pattern suggested by *Errors*).

46 **dotage** foolish loving
48 **favours** flowers as love-tokens
    hateful fool Oberon's terms are surpris-
    ingly strong, his hatred for Bottom,
    who has, at least to some extent,
    usurped his position as husband, sur-
    facing in his speech. But his attempt
    to demean Bottom, as in his elaborate
    image of the disgrace of the flowers
    that crown him (l. 55), is rarely effec-

tive for an audience which tends to
find the physical presence of Bottom
sufficient to offset Oberon's anger.
51 **With ... flowers** Compare Golding's
    Ovid, 'with a crown of fresh and fra-
    grant flowers' (2.33) and Spenser, *She-
    pheardes Calendar*, 'fragrant flowers . . .
    dewed with teares' (December, ll. 109,
    112) and 'the kindlye dewe drops from
    the higher tree, | And wets the little
    plants' (November, ll. 31–2). Titania's
    decorating Bottom with a 'coronet'
    transforms her treatment of the
    changeling: according to Robin, she
    'Crowns him with flowers' (2.1.27).
54 **flow'rets'** 'Flouret] a diminutive for a
    little floure' (E.K.'s gloss to November,
    l. 83, in Spenser's *Shepheardes Calen-
    dar*).
56–7 **When ... patience** Oberon's view of
    the correct relation of husband and
    wife is reasserted brutally in the con-
    trast between his taunting and her
    meek submission as much as in his
    success in being given the changeling.
    Unlike their on-stage quarrel in 2.1,
    this time it is Oberon who has taken

And she in mild terms begged my patience,
I then did ask of her her changeling child,
Which straight she gave me, and her fairy sent
To bear him to my bower in fairyland.   60
And now I have the boy, I will undo
This hateful imperfection of her eyes.
And, gentle puck, take this transformèd scalp
From off the head of this Athenian swain,
That he, awaking when the other do,   65
May all to Athens back again repair,
And think no more of this night's accidents
But as the fierce vexation of a dream.
But first I will release the Fairy Queen.
    He drops the juice on Titania's eyelids
Be as thou wast wont to be,   70
See as thou wast wont to see.
Dian's bud o'er Cupid's flower
Hath such force and blessèd power.

69.1 *He . . . eyelids*] *after* CAPELL; *not in* QF   72 o'er] THEOBALD (*conj.* Thirlby); *or* QF

---

the opportunity to speak at length, taunting her 'at my pleasure' (l. 56). His sadism is offset by her drug-induced mildness and our realization that the spell has made her give up so easily the boy of whose significance she spoke so movingly in 2.1.

60 **my bower** Contrasted with Titania's (3.1.187 and 3.2.7 and n.).

62 **hateful** Titania's distorted vision that has led to her love for Bottom is hateful to Oberon, as he had predicted at 2.1.258 ('hateful fantasies'); compare l. 48 above and her recognition, when she is behaving with due submissiveness to her lord, that she now 'loathe[s]' Bottom (l. 78)

68 **vexation** affliction; Foakes compares Ecclesiastes 2: 17, 'all is vanity and vexation of spirit'.

72 **Dian's bud** Oberon's restorative drug is never precisely identified; suggestions include (a) *Artemisia vulgaris* (Rydén, p. 76) also known as Mugwort

(Artemis was one of Diana's names); though it was mostly used as a cure for women's diseases and menstrual pains, it was commonly used at midsummer festivals and its other name, St John's plant, explicitly links it to St John's eve, another name for midsummer night; (b) *Vitex agnus-castus* or the vitex tree (which in *The Flower and the Leaf*, a poem then included in editions of Chaucer, is carried by 'Diana, the goddesse of chastitie . . . for because she a maiden is' (ll. 473–4)), though since the reason it was used by 'Athenian Matrons . . . desirous to keepe themselves chaste' was that it dried up 'the seed of generation' (Gerard, p. 1388) it does not seem helpful in the context of marriage; (c) an amalgam of white water-lily (used against lustful desires), euphrasia (known as eyebright, recommended by Gerard for taking away 'the darkness and dimness of the eyes', p. 663), and spurge (two of these euphorbias are also

Now, my Titania, wake you, my sweet queen.

TITANIA (*waking*)

My Oberon, what visions have I seen!   75

Methought I was enamoured of an ass.

OBERON

There lies your love.

TITANIA   How came these things to pass?

O, how mine eyes do loathe his visage now!

OBERON

Silence a while.—Robin, take off this head.—

Titania, music call, and strike more dead   80

Than common sleep of all these five the sense.

TITANIA

Music, ho—music such as charmeth sleep.

⌈*Still music*⌉

ROBIN (*taking the ass-head off Bottom*)

Now when thou wak'st with thine own fool's eyes peep.

OBERON

Sound music.

⌈*The music changes*⌉

Come, my queen, take hands with me,

---

75 *waking*] WELLS (*wakes*); *not in* QF; *She rises* FAIRY Q   81 *sleep . . . five*] THEOBALD (*conj.*
Thirlby); *sleepe: of all these, fine* QF   82 ho] Q2, F; howe Q1   82.1 *Still music*] THEOBALD;
Musick still F; *not in* Q   83 *taking . . . Bottom*] WILSON (*subs.*); *not in* QF; *he puls off his
asses head* COX   84 *The music changes*] OXFORD (*conj.* Wilson); *not in* QF

---

known as Virgin Mary's Nipple which,
like all euphorbias, produces a milky
juice; it was only collected on St John's
eve (= midsummer night)); see Marion
Cohen ' "Dian's Bud" in *A Midsummer
Night's Dream*, IV i 72', *N&Q* 228
(1983), pp. 118–20 and Charlotte
F. Otten, ' "Dian's Bud" in *A Midsummer Night's Dream* IV.i.72', *N&Q* 233
(1988), p. 466. What is far more important than a precise botanical
identification is the transition here
from the power of Cupid and Venus to
the dominance of Diana—see Introduction, pp. 32–3.

75 **My Oberon** Compare Hippolyta's 'my

Theseus' at 5.1.1.

81 **five** the four lovers and Bottom

82.1 **Still music** F's *Musick still* cannot be
an instruction to the music to stop (it
has not yet started). 'Still music' is
associated with the supernatural and
sleep at, for example, the entrance of
Hymen in *As You Like It* 5.4.105.1. In
Two Noble Kinsmen 5.3.0.1 still music
is played by recorders. J. S. Manifold
(*The Music in English Drama* (1956),
pp. 97–8) argues that still music was
always soft recorder music, but see
also Christopher Welch, *Six Lectures on
the Recorder* (Oxford, 1911), p. 131 n.
2 for a more sceptical view.

And rock the ground whereon these sleepers be.   85
    Oberon and Titania dance
Now thou and I are new in amity,
And will tomorrow midnight solemnly
Dance in Duke Theseus' house, triumphantly,
And bless it to all fair prosperity.
There shall the pairs of faithful lovers be   90
Wedded with Theseus, all in jollity.

ROBIN

    Fairy King, attend and mark.
    I do hear the morning lark.

OBERON

    Then, my queen, in silence sad
    Trip we after nightës shade.   95
    We the globe can compass soon,
    Swifter than the wand'ring moon.

TITANIA

    Come, my lord, and in our flight
    Tell me how it came this night

85.1 *Oberon . . . dance*] WILSON (*subs.*); *not in* QF   95 nightës] OXFORD; nights Q1; the nights Q2, F

---

85 **rock** The earth itself becomes the sleepers' cradle and the Fairies' power to make the earth and weather destructive through their dissension is, in Oberon's single word 'rock', transformed into a benign, soothing natural magic swaying the ground.

85.1 The dance moves the play powerfully towards a new movement of reunion and reconciliation, symbolizing the newly orthodox harmony and hierarchy between Oberon and Titania, husband and wife, king and queen, and the play's new sense of chastity as marriage rather than virginity. Sir John Davies's poem *Orchestra* (written 1594), the greatest Elizabethan expression of the power of the dance, describes marriage and dance:

If they whom sacred Love hath linked in one,
Do as they dance, in all their course of life,

Never shall burning grief nor bitter moan,
Nor factious difference, nor unkind strife,
Arise betwixt the husband and the wife.
  For whether forth or back, or round he go,
  As the man doth, so must the woman do.

(stanza 111, in *Poems*, ed. Robert Krueger (Oxford, 1975, pp. 119–20). As usual the orthodoxy of female compliance in the pattern of order is emphasized.

87 **solemnly** with serious festive ceremonies

88 **triumphantly** as at a triumph (compare 1.1.19, 'with pomp, with triumph, and with revelling')

89 **prosperity** As promised at 2.1.73.

94 **sad** sober

95 **nightës** Compare 2.1.7 and n.

That I sleeping here was found   100
With these mortals on the ground.

> *Exeunt Oberon, Titania, and Robin*
> *Goodfellow. The sleepers lie still*
> *Wind horns within. Enter Theseus with Egeus,*
> *Hippolyta, and all his train*

THESEUS

Go, one of you, find out the forester,
For now our observation is performed;
And since we have the vanguard of the day,
My love shall hear the music of my hounds.   105

101.2 *The . . . still*] *Sleepers Lye still* F (*after l.* 100); *not in* Q   101.3 *Wind horns within*]
F (*Winde Hornes*); *Winde horne* Q1 (*after l.* 101.4, *traine*)   101.3–4 *with Egeus, Hippolyta*]
F; *not in* Q   104 vanguard] QF (vaward)

101.1–4 There is no gap between the exit
of Oberon and Titania and the entrance of Theseus and Hippolyta, a fact
which has suggested to some critics
that the two pairs of roles could not
be doubled (see, most recently, T. J.
King, *Casting Shakespeare's Plays* (Cambridge, 1992), Tables 46 and 47), but
Peter Brook's production showed that
the actors simply by turning upstage
and then walking back downstage can
define the metamorphosis perfectly
easily, indeed magically.

101.3–4 *Wind . . . train* Theseus was particularly fond of hunting. In Chaucer
he 'for to hunten is so desirus, | And
namely at the grete hert in May, |
That in his bed ther daweth hym no
day | That he nys clad, and redy for
to ryde | With hunte and horn and
houndes hym bisyde' (Chaucer, 'The
Knight's Tale', ll. 1674–8). For
Chaucer's Theseus, hunting is his
pleasure now the war is over: 'For
after Mars he serveth now Dyane' (l.
1682). The hunt is strongly associated
with Diana as huntress and goddess of
chastity and links to the new view of
chastity the play is beginning to take,
see Introduction, p. 33.

101.3 *Wind* blow. Granville Barker recommends that 'the winding of horns
. . . should be quite elaborately sym-
phonic. This is Shakespeare's picturing

of sunrise' (p. 110); that might smack
of Mendelssohn, though there is, of
course, much elaborate and brilliant
Elizabethan music for brass consort.
The horns are an instrument clearly
associated with Diana, goddess of the
hunt, now clearly in the ascendant in
the play's theomachia.

102 **forester** See 3.2.390 and n.; Theseus' use of a word that Oberon has
used to describe himself suggests to
Patrick Stewart, who played Oberon in
the RSC's 1977 production, 'a shim-
mering sense of these two figures, Theseus and Oberon, having contact in
the forest—that there has been a time
when Oberon, as a forester, has met
and associated with Theseus' (quoted
Warren, p. 25).

103 **observation** observance of the rites of
May (compare 1.1.167)

104 **vanguard** the foremost part of the
army, here applied to the early part of
the day

105 **the music of my hounds** The Elizabethan concern for the music of the
pack's cry is described in Gervase
Markham, *Country Contentments* (1615):
'If you would have your kennel for
sweetness of cry, then you must com-
pound it of some large dogs, that have
deep, solemn mouths and are swift in
spending, which must (as it were) bear
the bass in the consort; then a double

Uncouple in the western valley; let them go.
Dispatch, I say, and find the forester.   *Exit one*
We will, fair Queen, up to the mountain's top,
And mark the musical confusion
Of hounds and echo in conjunction.   110
HIPPOLYTA
I was with Hercules and Cadmus once
When in a wood of Crete they bayed the bear
With hounds of Sparta. Never did I hear
Such gallant chiding; for besides the groves,
The skies, the fountains, every region near   115
Seemed all one mutual cry. I never heard

---

107 *Exit one*] DYCE (*subs.*); *not in* QF   116 Seemed] F2; Seeme QF

---

number of roaring and loud ringing
mouths, which must bear the counter-
tenor; then some hollow, plain, sweet
mouths, which must bear the mean or
middle part; and so with these three
parts of music you shall make your cry
perfect' (p. 7). Markham emphasizes
that the mixture is not simply to make
sure the cry is musical but also because 'these hounds thus mixed do run
just and even together and not hang
off loose one from another . . . and if
amongst these you cast in a couple or
two of small slinging beagles, which
as small trebles may warble amongst
them, the cry will be a great deal the
sweeter' (pp. 7–8). He goes on to make
other recommendations for the loud-
ness or depth of the cry.

106 **Uncouple** Hounds were leashed in
pairs and unfastened for the beginning
of the hunt.

111 **with Hercules** North associated The-
seus and Hercules in an expedition
against the Amazons (see n. to 2.1.80);
Cadmus was the legendary founder of
Thebes and has no classical link with
Theseus or Hippolyta.

112–13 **Crete . . . Sparta** Both famous for
their hounds (Golding's Ovid has a pair
of hounds 'that had a sire of *Crete*, |
And dam of *Sparta*', 3.267–8). Theseus

is linked to Crete as the location of the
labyrinth of the Minotaur which he
killed.

112 **bayed** drove to bay with barking
hounds

bear Hanmer's proposed emendation
to 'boar' links this to the Calydonian
boar which Theseus hunted (in North
and Golding) and which Shakespeare
calls 'the boar of Thessaly' in *Antony*
4.14.2. But bears were hunted by
Adonis (*Venus* 883–4). Shakespeare is
unlikely to have been particular about
the precise location of bears for hunting. Both animals have already been
mentioned in the play ('bear, | Pard,
or boar', 2.2.36–7).

114 **chiding** yelping

115 **fountains** echoing fountains, an odd
concept, occur in Propertius' *Elegies*
20.49–50 (Theobald); Laneham describes the 'pastime delectabl' of the
hunting which was part of Elizabeth's
entertainment at Kenilworth in 1575,
including its spectacular mixture of
sounds: 'the earning of the hoounds in
continuauns of their crie, . . . the blast-
ing of hornz, the halloing & hewing of
the huntsmen, with the excellent Echoz
between whilez from the woods and
waters in valleiz resounding' (*A Letter*,
p. 17).

116 **mutual** common

So musical a discord, such sweet thunder.

THESEUS

My hounds are bred out of the Spartan kind,
So flewed, so sanded; and their heads are hung
With ears that sweep away the morning dew,   120
Crook-kneed, and dewlapped like Thessalian bulls,
Slow in pursuit, but matched in mouth like bells,
Each under each. A cry more tuneable
Was never holla'd to nor cheered with horn
In Crete, in Sparta, nor in Thessaly.   125
Judge when you hear. But soft: what nymphs are these?

EGEUS

My lord, this is my daughter here asleep,
And this Lysander; this Demetrius is;
This Helena, old Nedar's Helena.
I wonder of their being here together.   130

THESEUS

No doubt they rose up early to observe
The rite of May, and, hearing our intent,
Came here in grace of our solemnity.
But speak, Egeus: is not this the day
That Hermia should give answer of her choice?   135

EGEUS It is, my lord.

THESEUS

Go bid the huntsmen wake them with their horns.
⌈*Exit one*⌉

127 this is] Q2, F; this QI   132 rite] POPE; right QF   137.1 *Exit one*] OXFORD; *not in* QF
137.2 *Shout ... up*] This edition; *Shoute within: they all start vp. Winde hornes.* Q; *Hornes
and they wake. Shout within, they all start vp* F

117 **So ... discord** The creation of harmony from disharmony, *concordia dis-
cors*, is wondered at by Theseus at
5.1.60, 'How shall we find the concord
of this discord?'
119 **flewed** with large hanging chaps; one
of Jason's hounds in Golding's Ovid was
a 'large flewed hound' (3.269)
sanded sandy-coloured
121 **dewlapped ... bulls** Brooks points out
that in Golding (7.161) Jason has tamed
bulls and 'Their dangling dewlaps with
his hand he coyed' as, at the beginning

of this scene, Titania 'coyed' the cheeks
of her tame animal, Bottom (4.1.2).
But the dewlaps have also metamorphosed from the 'withered dewlap' of
the old woman Robin tricks (2.1.50).
122 **matched ... bells** See l. 105 and n.
123 **cry** pack
tuneable melodious
132 **The rite of May** Compare Lysander's
description of the wood at 1.1.165-7.
133 **in ... solemnity** in honour of our
marriage ceremony

⌈ *Shout within:* 'Wind horns'. *The lovers wake.*
  Wind horns. They all start up⌉
Good morrow, friends. Saint Valentine is past.
Begin these wood-birds but to couple now?
LYSANDER
  Pardon, my lord.
    The lovers kneel
THESEUS   I pray you all stand up.   140
    The lovers stand
(*To Demetrius and Lysander*) I know you two are rival
  enemies.
How comes this gentle concord in the world,
That hatred is so far from jealousy
To sleep by hate, and fear no enmity?
LYSANDER
  My lord, I shall reply amazèdly,   145

---

140 *The lovers kneel*] CAPELL (*subs.*); *not in* QF   140.1–141 *The ... Lysander*] OXFORD; *not in* QF

137.2–3 It is clear that the SDs in Q and F refer to two different off-stage events, a shout and the sound of horns. The shout which must have preceded the horns is, I have assumed, Theseus' order relayed to the huntsmen who are the horn-players. Equally clearly, F envisages two different on-stage events: the lovers wake and then start up. I have produced an SD which combines these four events into a sequence which may appear too logical: the off-stage order wakes the lovers who then leap up, startled, at the sound of the horns. The lovers, of course, have no idea that they have all four fallen asleep so close to each other; their amazement is as much at finding each other there as at the sight of the court out hunting.

138–9 Birds were traditionally held to choose their mates on St Valentine's Day, 14 February. See Tilley S66. While this suggests the tradition of St Valentine's Day inaugurating a permanent relationship, as the lovers may assume, there is the tradition of St Valentine's Day marking a mock-betrothal, a marriage for a day with the

partners chosen by lots (Laroque, pp. 105–7), and the tradition of a woman being obliged to take as her valentine the first man she sees, a practice with strong resonances for *A Midsummer Night's Dream* (see, for example, though later, Mrs Pepys keeping her hands over her eyes to make sure she did not see the painters working in the house (Pepys's *Diary*, iii. 28–9 and x. 377–8)). St Valentine's Day was always an opportunity for festivities with strong sexual overtones. See also Ophelia's song, suggesting that the festival gave women a rare degree of power to take a sexual initiative (*Hamlet* 4.5.47–65).

139 **couple** (a) join in marriage (*OED v.* 3), as the lovers will go on to do; (b) have sexual intercourse (*OED v.* 4, quoting this passage), as the lovers may appear to have been doing overnight in the wood, following common practice on St Valentine's Day; (c) to join in pairs like dogs (*OED v.* 1; compare Theseus' use of 'uncouple' at l. 106)

143 **jealousy** mistrust

Half sleep, half waking. But as yet, I swear,
I cannot truly say how I came here,
But as I think—for truly would I speak,
And, now I do bethink me, so it is—
I came with Hermia hither. Our intent   150
Was to be gone from Athens where we might,
Without the peril of the Athenian law—
EGEUS (*to Theseus*)
Enough, enough, my lord, you have enough.
I beg the law, the law upon his head.—
They would have stol'n away, they would, Demetrius,   155
Thereby to have defeated you and me—
You of your wife, and me of my consent,
Of my consent that she should be your wife.
DEMETRIUS (*to Theseus*)
My lord, fair Helen told me of their stealth,
Of this their purpose hither to this wood,   160
And I in fury hither followed them,
Fair Helena in fancy following me.
But, my good lord, I wot not by what power—
But by some power it is—my love to Hermia,
Melted as the snow, seems to me now   165
As the remembrance of an idle gaud
Which in my childhood I did dote upon,
And all the faith, the virtue of my heart,
The object and the pleasure of mine eye
Is only Helena. To her, my lord,   170
Was I betrothed ere I see Hermia.
But like in sickness did I loathe this food;

153, 159 *to Theseus*] OXFORD; *not in* QF   164–6] *Divided as in* POPE; Q1 *divides at* love |
... snow]   172 But‸] Q2, F; ~, Q1   in sickness] STEEVENS–REED 1793 (*proposed, according
to Halliwell, in 'The Student', Oxford,* 1750); a sickness QF

146 **sleep** Probably an aphetic form of
    'asleep' though it might be a noun
    (Wright compares 'He speaks plain
    cannon', *King John* 2.1.463).
152 **Without** beyond the reach of
156 **defeated** defrauded, cheated
162 **fancy** love
163 **wot** know
166 **idle gaud** worthless ornament (com-

pare 1.1.33)
168 **all ... heart** Demetrius identifies his
    fidelity, newly found, as the particular
    quality, 'virtue', of his heart.
171 **see** saw; an archaic past tense (com-
    pare Shallow in *2 Henry IV* 3.2.28–9,
    'I see him break Scoggin's head')
172 **But ... sickness** QF's reading is only
    defensible if, as Capell argued, 'a sick-

But, as in health come to my natural taste,
Now I do wish it, love it, long for it,
And will for evermore be true to it.   175
THESEUS
Fair lovers, you are fortunately met.
Of this discourse we more will hear anon.—
Egeus, I will overbear your will,
For in the temple by and by with us
These couples shall eternally be knit.—   180
And, for the morning now is something worn,
Our purposed hunting shall be set aside.
Away with us to Athens. Three and three,
We'll hold a feast in great solemnity.
Come, Hippolyta.   185
                    Exit Duke Theseus with Hippolyta, Egeus,
                                       and all his train

DEMETRIUS
These things seem small and undistinguishable,
Like far-off mountains turnèd into clouds.
HERMIA
Methinks I see these things with parted eye,

184–5] *Divided as in* Q2; *one line in* Q1   185.1–2 *Exit . . . train*] F (*Exit Duke and Lords.*);
not in Q1; *Exit.* Q2

ness' stands for 'a sick man' (a Shakespearian form of abstract for con-
crete, though this one is unknown).
Oxford's emendation is simple and
probable and avoids the need to emend
'But' in l. 173.

178 **Egeus . . . your will** Theseus asserts
his power over Egeus (and also over
Athenian law) with generosity but also
with a full awareness of his power, not
least to add to the glory of his own
wedding-day.
184 **solemnity** Compare 1.1.11, 4.1.87,
5.1.361–2.
186 **undistinguishable** At 2.1.100 Titania
has spoken of the overgrown mazes
that have become 'undistinguishable';
now the word is taken over by Demetrius, after the mazes the lovers have

trod in the wood, to describe 'these
things'. But are 'these things' the experiences in the wood or the strangeness of the encounter with Theseus
and the new relationships in the waking, dawn world? Hermia uses the
same phrase at l. 188. 'Undistinguishable', an awkward mouthful of a word
for an actor, appears to have been
coined by Shakespeare (first recorded
use in *OED*, next recorded use is by
Milton in 1645); he uses it in no other
play (a point Adrian Poole drew to my
attention). The lovers' wonder here (ll.
186–97), in its beautifully tentative
language, produced from Britten the
finest passage of his opera, *A Midsummer Night's Dream* (1960).
188 **parted** divided, with the eyes out of
focus

When everything seems double.

HELENA   So methinks,
And I have found Demetrius like a jewel,   190
Mine own and not mine own.

DEMETRIUS   It seems to me
That yet we sleep, we dream. Do not you think
The Duke was here and bid us follow him?

HERMIA
Yea, and my father.

HELENA   And Hippolyta.

LYSANDER
And he did bid us follow to the temple.   195

DEMETRIUS
Why then, we are awake. Let's follow him,
And by the way let us recount our dreams.

                                        Exeunt the lovers

      Bottom wakes

BOTTOM When my cue comes, call me, and I will answer.
My next is 'most fair Pyramus'. Heigh-ho. Peter Quince?
Flute the bellows-mender? Snout the tinker? Starveling?   200

---

190 found] Q2, F; fonnd Q1   191 It] F; Are you sure | That we are awake? It Q
196–7] *As in* ROWE 1714; *prose in* QF   197 let us] Q2, F; lets Q1   197.1 *Exeunt the
lovers*] F (*Exit Louers.*); *Exit.* Q2; *not in* Q1   197.2 *Bottom wakes*] F; *not in* Q; *After a
while Bottome wakes* COX

---

190 **like a jewel** Demetrius is like a jewel
she has found: she claims him unsure
whether he may belong to someone
else.

191 **Mine . . . me** F's excision of Q's 'Are
you sure | That we are awake?' re-
stores the corrupt metre. Editors have
emended Q's sentence to the same end
(e.g. 'That we are yet awake' or 'That
we are well awake') but F's omission
still needs explanation. Compositorial
excision is unlikely since the line is far
from nonsensical. F's authority, probably prompt-book, must have cut the
line. Oxford suggests, a little extra-
vagantly, that Q1's sentence 'bears all
the hallmarks of a first shot abandoned
currente calamo'; I think it unlikely that
Shakespeare's first drafts were unme-
trical.

197 **And . . . dreams** Recounting dreams,
as the lovers do both to each other
and, later, to Theseus and Hippolyta,
is for many theorists a crucial part of
the transforming experience of dreaming: 'Intimates who tell each other
their dreams seek, I believe, to enhance
their self-conceptions by making each
other witnesses of aspects of themselves
which have not become assimilated
into their waking selves but which are,
they hope, emergent' (Charles Rycroft,
The Innocence of Dreams (1979), p. 56).

197.2 **Bottom wakes** Cox's SD, '*After a
while Bottome wakes*', suggests the
necessary pause before the audience is
allowed to realise that there is one
sleeper still left on stage.

199 **Heigh-ho** A yawn with a hint of an
ass's 'hee-haw' (Wells).

God's my life! Stolen hence, and left me asleep?—I have
had a most rare vision. I have had a dream past the wit
of man to say what dream it was. Man is but an ass if he
go about to expound this dream. Methought I was—
there is no man can tell what. Methought I was, and   205
methought I had—but man is but a patched fool if he
will offer to say what methought I had. The eye of man
hath not heard, the ear of man hath not seen, man's
hand is not able to taste, his tongue to conceive, nor his
heart to report what my dream was. I will get Peter   210
Quince to write a ballad of this dream. It shall be called

204 to expound] Q2, F; expound Q1   206 a patched fool] F; patcht a foole Q   211 ballad]
QF (Ballet)

202 **vision** Used by Oberon at 3.2.371,
Titania at 4.1.75 and, in the epilogue,
by Robin at 5.1.417; see Introduction,
pp. 3–21.

203 Compare Chaucer, *The Book of the
Duchess*, 'Me mette so ynly swete a
sweven [dream], | So wonderful, that
never yit | Y trowe no man had the
wyt | To konne wel my sweven rede'
(ll. 276–9, suggested by David G. Hale,
'Bottom's Dream and Chaucer', *SQ* 36
(1985), pp. 219–20).

204 **go about** should try

205 **Methought I was** In Reinhardt's
outdoor production in Oxford in 1933
this passage 'began with a nervous
groping, to see if the long snout and the
long ears were still there; then a quic-
kening of gesture, a nervous laughter;
a sudden cut to silence; a fifty-yard
run to the pond; a look at the reflection in the water; a scream of relief;
and a jubilant dance off through the
trees towards Athens' (Styan, *Reinhardt*, p. 59); the same business was
preserved in his film version in 1935.

206–8 **but man ... I had** Possibly a distant echo of 2 Corinthians 12: 1–6,
esp. v. 4: 'How that he was caught up
into paradise, and heard unspeakable
words, which it is not lawful for a man
to utter'.

207 **a patched fool** a fool wearing motley
or parti-coloured coat. Cardinal Wol-
sey's fool was named Patch. The Italian word 'pazzo' is defined by Florio

as 'a fool, a patch, a mad-man' in
Queen Anna's New World of Words
(1611). Q1's reading, 'patcht a foole'
is possible: 'a fool clumsily put
together'.

208–11 **The eye ... was** A corruption of
1 Corinthians 2: 9–10: 'the eye hath
not seen, and the ear hath not heard,
neither have entered into the heart of
man, the things which God hath prepared for them that love him. But God
hath revealed them unto us by his
spirit: For the spirit searcheth all
things, yea the deep things of God'
(Bishops' Bible, 1568). In the Geneva
Bible (1557) and other early English
Bibles, the final phrase reads 'yea, the
bottom of God's secrets'; Thomas B.
Stroup has suggested over-emphatic-
ally that the final phrase is *the* source
of Bottom's name ('Bottom's Name
and His Epiphany', *SQ* 29 (1978), pp.
79–82; see also Robert F. Willson, Jr.,
'God's Secrets and Bottom's Name: A
Reply', *SQ* 30 (1979), pp. 407–8 for
a sensible response). The passage here
would certainly have summoned up
the following verse in the Bible as a
distant echo and hence possibly the
phrase as it had appeared in earlier
Bibles; see also on Bottom's vision,
Introduction, pp. 82–4. Bottom and
company are prone to confuse the senses; compare 3.1.85, 5.1.191–2.

211 **ballad** A topical narrative set to a
popular tune, printed as a broadsheet,

'Bottom's Dream', because it hath no bottom, and I will
sing it in the latter end of a play, before the Duke. Per-
adventure, to make it the more gracious, I shall sing it
at her death.   *Exit*   215

4.2   *Enter Quince, Flute, Snout, and Starveling*
QUINCE Have you sent to Bottom's house? Is he come
   home yet?
STARVELING He cannot be heard of. Out of doubt he is
   transported.
FLUTE If he come not, then the play is marred. It goes not   5
   forward. Doth it?
QUINCE It is not possible. You have not a man in all
   Athens able to discharge Pyramus but he.
FLUTE No, he hath simply the best wit of any handicraft-
   man in Athens.   10
QUINCE Yea, and the best person, too; and he is a very
   paramour for a sweet voice.
FLUTE You must say 'paragon'. A paramour is, God bless
   us, a thing of naught.
      Enter Snug the joiner
SNUG Masters, the Duke is coming from the temple, and   15
   there is two or three lords and ladies more married. If
   our sport had gone forward we had all been made men.

---

215 *Exit*] Q2, F; *not in* Q1
4.2.0.1 *Flute*] ROWE 1714; Flute, Thisby QF   *Snout, and Starveling*] F; *and the rabble* Q
3 STARVELING] F; *Flut.* Q   5, etc. FLUTE] COX, ROWE 1714; *Thys.* QF

and widely sold as a means of com-
municating new songs and tabloid-style
news stories (compare Autolycus's bal-
lads in *Winter's Tale* 4.4.260–306).

213 **hath no bottom** (a) has no foundation
   in reality (b) is unfathomably profound—but see also n. to ll. 208–11
   above (c) has no yarn out of which it
   could be woven (see n. to 1.2.16)
214 **a play** 'our play' is a possible emendation but Bottom's mind is still confused
215 **her death** presumably Thisbe's
4.2.0.1 Q's SD 'and the rabble' has distinct authorial traces as does the use

of *Thys.* as SP for Flute.
3 STARVELING F's source for this correction
   is presumably prompt-book.
4 **transported** Starveling may mean
   'translated, transformed', but the effect
   is that Bottom has been conveyed from
   one realm to another or that he is
   enraptured.
9 **wit** intellect
11 **person** appearance, presence
14 **a thing of naught** something immoral
   or wicked (much stronger than our
   'naughty')
17 **we . . . made men** our fortunes would
   have been made

FLUTE O sweet bully Bottom! Thus hath he lost sixpence a
day during his life. He could not have scaped sixpence a
day. An the Duke had not given him sixpence a day for   20
playing Pyramus, I'll be hanged. He would have
deserved it. Sixpence a day in Pyramus, or nothing.

    Enter Bottom

BOTTOM Where are these lads? Where are these hearts?

QUINCE Bottom! O most courageous day! O most happy
hour!   25

BOTTOM Masters, I am to discourse wonders; but ask me
not what. For if I tell you, I am no true Athenian. I will
tell you everything right as it fell out.

QUINCE Let us hear, sweet Bottom.

BOTTOM Not a word of me. All that I will tell you is that   30
the Duke hath dined. Get your apparel together, good
strings to your beards, new ribbons to your pumps.
Meet presently at the palace; every man look o'er his
part. For the short and the long is, our play is preferred.
In any case let Thisbe have clean linen, and let not him   35
that plays the lion pare his nails, for they shall hang out
for the lion's claws. And, most dear actors, eat no
onions nor garlic, for we are to utter sweet breath, and
I do not doubt but to hear them say it is a sweet comedy.
No more words. Away, go, away!   40

                                  Exeunt

27 no] F; *not* Q   40.1 *Exeunt*] F; *not in* Q

18 **bully** See 3.1.7 and n.
19-20 **sixpence a day** The daily wages of
the most skilled craftsmen varied between sixpence and ninepence (see
Shakespeare's England, i. 331).
20 **An** if
23 **hearts** good fellows (compare supposed
sailors' slang 'me hearties')
24 **courageous** splendid, brave (Foakes
compares Miranda's 'O brave new
world', *Tempest* 5.1.186)
32 **strings** to tie the false beards on
pumps light low-soled shoes, hence associated with comedy—unlike the
high-soled tragic shoes—but 'their
presence in Bottom's 'Pyramus and
Thisbe' is unexplainable, unless they

were used as part of the parody, or, as
the usual footwear of Bottom's fellows,
were not changed'; the 'new ribbons'
were to tie the shoes, not simply dec-
oration (Linthicum, pp. 253-4).
33 **presently** immediately
34 **preferred** recommended, chosen; Bottom could mean that their play is on
the 'select list' (Wilson) but no audience would take it that way. Though
their play is not chosen by Theseus
until 5.1.76 the audience has not the
slightest doubt that it will be; critics
who argue differently have a fine sense
of logic and reality and little awareness
of how dramatic plots work.
40 **No ... away!** Henry Morley offers a

5.1   *Enter Theseus, Hippolyta,* ⌈*Egeus*⌉, *and attendant*
            lords

HIPPOLYTA

'Tis strange, my Theseus, that these lovers speak of.

THESEUS

More strange than true. I never may believe

These antique fables, nor these fairy toys.

Lovers and madmen have such seething brains,

Such shaping fantasies, that apprehend   5

5.1.0.1 *Egeus*] F; *not in* Q   1.0.1–1.0.2 *attendant Lords*] F (*his Lords*); Philostrate Q
5–6] *Divided as in* THEOBALD; QF *divide at* More

---

brilliant description of Samuel Phelps
as Bottom in 1853: 'Quite masterly
was the delivery by Mr Phelps of the
speech of Bottom on awakening. He
was still a man subdued, but subdued
by the sudden plunge into a state of
unfathomable wonder. His dream clings
about him, he cannot sever the real
from the unreal, and still we are made
to feel that his reality itself is but a
fiction. The preoccupation continues to
be manifest during [4.2], and his parting 'No more words; away; go away',
was in the tone of a man who had
lived with spirits and was not yet perfectly returned into the flesh' (*The Journal of a London Playgoer* (1891),
pp. 60–1).

5.1.0.1–84 For a fuller discussion of the
textual problems of these lines, the
evidence for and significance of Shakespeare's two revisions of the passage, see Appendix, pp. 257–68.

0.1 *Egeus* In Q Egeus is not named to
appear after 4.1. In F he takes over
Philostrate's lines and becomes, in
effect, Theseus' Master of Revels,
marking his inclusion in the reconciliation and harmony of the end of the
play. Q does not include any attendant
lords, making the scene far more private. See Appendix, pp. 265–8.

2 Compare Tilley S914 'It is no more
strange than true'—Theseus would
have done better to follow the
proverb's normal form.

2–3 Brooks compares the opening of Act

5 of Lyly's *Endimion*: '*Eumenides* hath
told such strange tales as I may well
wonder at them, but neuer believe
them' (iii. 63).

3 **antique** 'old' but also punning on
'antic' meaning 'grotesque'. While 'antique' has strong links to the ancient
world—'antique fables' are classical
myths, the world which Theseus mocks
but to which he himself belongs—'antic'
suggests a world of performance, the
theatrical context of a play which this
Theseus will watch but also the one in
which he is a character.

fairy toys idle tales about fairies; Theseus's rational dismissal of fairies is, at
the least, misguided in *Dream*.

4 **seething** boiling

5 **fantasies** extravagant fancies, imagination

apprehend 'apprehend' has the basic
sense of 'grasp, seize' (compare 'apprehension', 3.2.178 and n.) but also
'feel emotionally' (*OED v.* 7) and 'see'
(*OED v.* 8). It is often glossed as 'conceive' but *OED* (*v.* 9) gives 1639 for
its first example in this sense. Bacon,
in the dedication of *The Advancement of
Learning* (*Works*, ed. J. Spedding *et al.*
(1857), iii. 262), praised the King for
having a 'composition of understanding
admirable, being able to compass and
comprehend the greatest matters, and
nevertheless to touch and apprehend
the least, whereas it should seem an
impossibility in nature for the same
instrument to make itself fit for great
and small works'. Graham Bradshaw

More than cool reason ever comprehends.
The lunatic, the lover, and the poet
Are of imagination all compact.
One sees more devils than vast hell can hold:
That is the madman. The lover, all as frantic,   10
Sees Helen's beauty in a brow of Egypt.
The poet's eye, in a fine frenzy rolling,
Doth glance from heaven to earth, from earth to heaven,
And as imagination bodies forth
The forms of things unknown, the poet's pen   15
Turns them to shapes, and gives to airy nothing
A local habitation and a name.

6–8] *Divided as in* Q2, F; *two lines in* Q1 *divided at* lunatic   12–14] *Divided as in* ROWE;
QF *divide at* glance | . . . as   14–15] *Divided as in* ROWE 1714; QF *divide at* things   15–18]
Divided as in ROWE 1714; QF *divide at* shapes, | . . . habitation |

argues that '*comprehending* evidently involves a fuller (comprehensive) grasping of a difficult meaning or idea, while *apprehending* involves a predominantly sensory or sympathetic perception, and emphasises that kind of responsive quickness' (*Shakespeare's Scepticism* (Brighton, 1987), pp. 40–1). Compare also John Dee's comment in his preface to a translation of Euclid (1570): 'Things supernatural are immaterial, simple, indivisible, incorruptible, and unchangeable. Things natural are material, compounded, divisible, corruptible, and changeable. Things supernatural are of the mind only comprehended; things natural of the sense exterior are able to be perceived' (quoted Herbert, p. 91).

6 **comprehends** understands; Bradshaw, p. 40, suggests that Theseus uses the word ironically at l. 20 in relation to a product of fantasy.

11 **Helen's** Primarily Helen of Troy but also the play's Helen(a).
   brow of Egypt a dark-skinned face, like a gypsy; 'gypsy' was a corruption of 'Egyptian'. The phrase suggests Hermia's dark complexion; Hermia has been called an 'Ethiope' (3.2.257) and a 'tawny Tartar' (3.2.263 and n.) by Lysander and rejected by him for Helen(a) while Demetrius rejected Helena for Hermia.

12–17 Compare the very first line of Golding's Ovid as Ovid describes his aim in *Metamorphoses*: 'Of shapes transformed to bodies strange, I purpose to entreat'; Ovid's Latin is even closer: '*In nova fert animus mutatas dicere formas | Corpora*', 'My mind bids me tell of forms turned into new shapes'. Sir Philip Sidney, in *An Apology for Poetry*, separates the work of the poet from other arts in relation to nature: 'Only the poet, . . . lifted up with the vigour of his own invention, doth grow in effect into another nature, in making things either better than Nature bringeth forth, or, quite anew, forms such as never were in Nature, . . . not enclosed within the narrow warrant of [Nature's] gifts, but freely ranging only within the zodiac of his own wit' (ed. Geoffrey Shepherd (1965), p. 100).

12 **fine frenzy** Poets were thought to be divinely inspired and hence mad; the concept, derived from Plato's *Ion* and *Phaedrus* was, as *furor poeticus*, widely praised in the Renaissance—Theseus is more mocking.

14 **bodies forth** embodies

231

Such tricks hath strong imagination
That if it would but apprehend some joy
It comprehends some bringer of that joy;   20
Or in the night, imagining some fear,
How easy is a bush supposed a bear!

HIPPOLYTA

But all the story of the night told over,
And all their minds transfigured so together,
More witnesseth than fancy's images,   25
And grows to something of great constancy;
But howsoever, strange and admirable.

> *Enter the lovers: Lysander, Demetrius, Hermia, and*
> *Helena*

THESEUS

Here come the lovers, full of joy and mirth.
Joy, gentle friends, joy and fresh days of love
Accompany your hearts.

LYSANDER   More than to us   30
Wait in your royal walks, your board, your bed.

THESEUS

Come now, what masques, what dances shall we have
To wear away this long age of three hours
Between our after-supper and bed-time?

29–30] *Divided as in* F2; *QF divide at* days   30–1 More . . . bed!] *Divided as in* F2; *prose in* QF   33–6] *Divided as in* Q2; *three lines in* Q1 *divided at* Between | . . . manager | 34 our] F; Or Q

18–20 In Act 4 of Lyly's *Campaspe*, Apelles turns Campaspe's portrait into a reality: it 'will cause me to embrace thy shadow continually in mine arms, of the which by strong imagination I will make a substance' (ii. 348) (Brooks).

19–20 **apprehend . . . comprehends** Compare 5–6 and nn.; 'comprehends' here suggests 'includes, extrapolates' or 'assumes' as well as 'understands'.

21 **some fear** something to be afraid of

22 **How . . . bear** Proverbial (Tilley B737, B738). Demetrius took a bush for Lysander at 3.2.405–6; bears have been mentioned nine times in the play so

far. Proverbial folk wisdom crowns Theseus' argument.

26 **something** Answering Theseus's 'airy nothing' at l. 16.
constancy 'fidelity' as well as 'assuredness, consistency'. The story of the night has created the new firmness of love and marriage; see Introduction, pp. 68–9.

27 **admirable** to be wondered at

32 **masques** spectacular court entertainments often with masked dancers

34 **our** Q1 probably misread the contraction 'o'' as 'or'.
after-supper dessert served after supper, not the same as 'rere-supper' served 'when it was time to go to rest

Where is our usual manager of mirth?   35
What revels are in hand? Is there no play
To ease the anguish of a torturing hour?
Call Egeus.
⌈EGEUS⌉   Here, mighty Theseus.
THESEUS
Say, what abridgement have you for this evening?
What masque, what music? How shall we beguile   40
The lazy time if not with some delight?
⌈EGEUS⌉ (*giving Lysander a paper*)
There is a brief how many sports are ripe.
Make choice of which your highness will see first.
⌈LYSANDER⌉ (*reads*)
'The battle with the centaurs, to be sung
By an Athenian eunuch to the harp.'   45
THESEUS
We'll none of that. That have I told my love
In glory of my kinsman Hercules.

---

38 Egeus] F; *Philostrate* Q   38, etc. EGEUS] F (*Ege.*); *Philostrate.* Q   42 *giving . . . paper*]
This edition (*Giving a paper* THEOBALD); *not in* QF   44 LYSANDER] F; *The.* Q   44, 48, 52,
56 *reads*] THEOBALD; *not in* Q   46, 50, 54, 58 THESEUS] F; *not in* Q

. . . the nobility, gentry, and students
do ordinarily go . . . to supper between
five and six at afternoon' (William
Harrison, 'An historical description of
the Island of Britain' in Holinshed's
Chronicles (1587), ii. 170–1).

35–6 **manager . . . revels** Foakes compares
the title of Sir Edmund Tilney, Queen
Elizabeth's Master of the Revels, who
was responsible for selecting plays for
court performance and therefore had
the play 'rehearsed' to him, as Egeus
has done (l. 68 and n.).

38 **Egeus** See n. to 5.1.0.1 and Appendix
for discussion of the replacement of
Philostrate by Egeus here.

39 **abridgement** 'something to make the
time seem short' but also, possibly, 'a
shortened version of a longer play'

41 **lazy** sluggish

42 *giving . . . paper* In Q the titles of the
plays and the comments on them (ll.
44–60) are all one speech for Theseus.

F turns this into an exchange between
Lysander and Theseus (see Appendix)
and I have therefore included an SD
for Egeus to hand the scroll with the
list of titles to his new son-in-law Lysander, a gesture of reconciliation and
a mark of the new family harmony.
brief summary, list

44–5 **The battle with the centaurs** is told
by Nestor in Golding's Ovid (12.236–
599); Theseus modestly says nothing
of his part in the battle. Since the
carnage took place at a wedding-feast
it is also hardly an appropriate subject
for these revels. Of the four entertainments offered to Theseus, no fewer
than three are based on Ovid's *Metamorphoses*.

47 **kinsman** 'they were near kinsmen,
being cousins removed by the mother's
side' (North, p. 4).
Hercules 'The fame and glory of *Hercules*' noble deeds, had long before secretly set [Theseus'] heart on fire, so

⌈LYSANDER⌉ (*reads*)

   'The riot of the tipsy bacchanals

   Tearing the Thracian singer in their rage.'

THESEUS

   That is an old device, and it was played   50

   When I from Thebes came last a conqueror.

⌈LYSANDER⌉ (*reads*)

   'The thrice-three muses mourning for the death

   Of learning, late deceased in beggary.'

THESEUS

   That is some satire, keen and critical,

   Not sorting with a nuptial ceremony.   55

⌈LYSANDER⌉ (*reads*)

   'A tedious brief scene of young Pyramus

   And his love Thisbe: very tragical mirth.'

THESEUS

   'Merry' *and* 'tragical'? 'Tedious' *and* 'brief'?—

   That is, hot ice and wondrous strange black snow.

48, 52, 56 LYSANDER] F; *not in* Q   58–60] *Divided as in* THEOBALD; Q1 *divides at* ice, | . . . concord |; F *prints as prose*   59 strange black] CAPELL (*conj.* Upton); strange QF

that he made reckoning of none other but him, and lovingly hearkened unto those . . . which had seen him, and been in his company, when he had said or done any thing worthy of memory' (North, p. 4).

48–9 **The riot . . . rage** The poet Orpheus was torn to pieces by a drunken crowd ('rout') of women followers of Bacchus (in Golding's Ovid, 11.1–93).

50 **device** show; in *LLL* 5.2.656 Armado describes the Nine Worthies as a 'device'.

51 **When . . . conqueror** At the opening of Chaucer's 'The Knight's Tale', Theseus returns to Athens in triumph with two Theban prisoners, Palamon and Arcite.

52–3 The link of poverty and learning was proverbial (Tilley M1316). Robert Greene, dramatist and scholar, had died in poverty in 1592 and these lines have often been held to be a topical reference to his death, though there are others to whom it could equally well apply, if indeed it applies specifi-

cally to anyone. Spenser's poem 'The Tears of the Muses', published in *Complaints* (1591), is a complaint, not a satire, admittedly, but it does have five of the muses referring to learning as a victim to be mourned. James P. Bednarz argues that this and other passages in *Dream* are a deliberate attack on Spenser, not least for his mockery of the public theatres in 'The Tears of the Muses' (ll. 192–4) ('Imitations of Spenser in *A Midsummer Night's Dream*', *Renaissance Drama*, 14 (1983), pp. 79–102).

54 **critical** censorious

55 **sorting with** appropriate to

56–7 **A tedious . . . mirth** Compare 1.2.11–12 and n.; this version of the play's title is closer to the title of Preston's *Cambyses, A lamentable tragedy mixed full of pleasant mirth*. Falstaff, when he has to 'speak in passion', pretending to be King Henry IV, 'will do it in King Cambyses' vein' (*1 Henry IV* 2.5.389–90).

59 **strange black snow** QF's 'strange snow' has been explained as meaning

How shall we find the concord of this discord?   60
⌈EGEUS⌉
A play there is, my lord, some ten words long,
Which is as 'brief' as I have known a play;
But by ten words, my lord, it is too long,
Which makes it 'tedious', for in all the play
There is not one word apt, one player fitted.   65
And 'tragical', my noble lord, it is,
For Pyramus therein doth kill himself;
Which when I saw rehearsed, I must confess,
Made mine eyes water; but more merry tears
The passion of loud laughter never shed.   70
THESEUS What are they that do play it?
⌈EGEUS⌉
Hard-handed men that work in Athens here,
Which never laboured in their minds till now,
And now have toiled their unbreathed memories
With this same play against your nuptial.   75
THESEUS
And we will hear it.
⌈EGEUS⌉   No, my noble lord,

66–70] *Divided as in* F2; Q1 *divides at* Pyramus | . . . saw | . . . water | . . . laughter |
76 EGEUS] OXFORD; *Phi.* QF   76–8] *Divided as in* ROWE 1714; *two lines in* Q1 *divided at* it

'snow no less wondrously unnatural'
(Kittredge, followed by Brooks). Oxford
argues at length that the passage suggests contrasts (tedious/brief, merry/
tragical, hot/ice, etc.) and that Shakespeare frequently uses 'snow' in such
contrasts. 'Wondrous' is always two
syllables in Shakespeare's verse and
hence the line is a syllable short.
'Black', frequently used by Shakespeare for oxymoronic contrasts, is a
fine proposed emendation.

68 **when I saw rehearsed** Egeus has not
been attending rehearsals like that in
the wood; plays offered for performance at court were performed ('rehearsed' or 'recited' according to the
accounts) before the Master of the Revels so that he could make a choice of
an appropriate play for performance.
The chosen play would be further 're-

hearsed' so that it could be censored
for court performance (see E. K. Chambers, *The Elizabethan Stage* (Oxford,
1923), i. 223–4).

70 **passion** any strong feeling; Wells com-
pares 'idle merriment— | A passion
hateful to my purposes' (*King John*
3.3.46–7).

74 **toiled** taxed
   unbreathed unpractised, unexercised

75 **against** in preparation for

76 EGEUS QF give the speech to Philostrate
but in F this becomes Philostrate's only
speech in the scene. His sudden intervention seems odd and discordant, re-
minding the audience of his role in 1.1
and that Egeus has taken over his job.
F is likely to have failed to have
changed one of the SPs in Q2 in making the changes for the restaged scene
(see Appendix).

It is not for you. I have heard it over,
And it is nothing, nothing in the world,
Unless you can find sport in their intents
Extremely stretched, and conned with cruel pain   80
To do you service.
THESEUS   I will hear that play;
For never anything can be amiss
When simpleness and duty tender it.
Go, bring them in; and take your places, ladies.
                                        Exit ⌈Egeus⌉
HIPPOLYTA
I love not to see wretchedness o'ercharged,   85
And duty in his service perishing.
THESEUS
Why, gentle sweet, you shall see no such thing.
HIPPOLYTA
He says they can do nothing in this kind.
THESEUS
The kinder we, to give them thanks for nothing.
Our sport shall be to take what they mistake,   90
And what poor duty cannot do,
Noble respect takes it in might, not merit.
Where I have come, great clerks have purposèd
To greet me with premeditated welcomes,
Where I have seen them shiver and look pale,   95
Make periods in the midst of sentences,

81–3 I . . . it] *Divided as in* ROWE 1714; *two lines in* Q1 *divided at* anything   84 ladies.]
Q; COX *adds* They take their seates.   84.1 *Exit ⌈Egeus⌉*] OXFORD; *not in* QF; *Exit Phil.* POPE
91–2 And . . . merit] THEOBALD; Q1 *divides at* respect

79 **intents** both 'endeavours' and 'the
subject or theme in a discourse' (*OED,
intent, sb. 7*); both the play and the
workmen's efforts are fully stretched.
80 **conned** studied, learnt, pored over
83 **simpleness** artless sincerity (Kittredge)
85 **wretchedness o'ercharged** people of
low ability and low rank overburdened
92 **Noble respect** generous, aristocratic
consideration
takes . . . merit accepts it, not at its
actual value, but in terms of what they
can do

93–9 This often happened to Queen Elizabeth: at Warwick in 1572 she reassured the Recorder who stopped dead
from fright; at Norwich in 1578 she
praised the Latin speech of a nervous
schoolmaster as 'the best that ever I
heard' (J. Nichol, *The Progresses and
Public Processions of Queen Elizabeth*
(1788), vol. 1, 'The Queen's progress,
1571', pp. 23 and 26).
93 **great clerks** distinguished scholars
96 **Make periods** come to a full stop; for
Quince's periods see ll. 108–17.

Throttle their practised accent in their fears,
And in conclusion dumbly have broke off,
Not paying me a welcome. Trust me, sweet,
Out of this silence yet I picked a welcome,   100
And in the modesty of fearful duty
I read as much as from the rattling tongue
Of saucy and audacious eloquence.
Love, therefore, and tongue-tied simplicity
In least speak most, to my capacity.   105
        Enter ⌈Egeus⌉
⌈EGEUS⌉
So please your grace, the Prologue is addressed.
THESEUS Let him approach.
        ⌈*Flourish trumpets.*⌉ *Enter ⌈Quince as⌉ the Prologue*
⌈QUINCE⌉ *(as Prologue)*
If we offend, it is with our good will.
    That you should think, we come not to offend
But with good will. To show our simple skill,   110
    That is the true beginning of our end.
Consider then we come but in despite.
    We do not come as minding to content you,
Our true intent is. All for your delight

105.1 *Enter* ⌈*Egeus*⌉] OXFORD; *not in* QF; *Enter Philostrate* CAPELL *(subs.)*; *Enter* Philomon (POPE)   107, 205, etc. THESEUS] *Duk.* Q1   107.1 *Flourish trumpets*] F (*Flor. Trum.*); *not in* Q   *Enter . . . Prologue*] F (*Enter the Prologue. Quince.*); *Enter the Prologue.* Q

101 **modesty** deference
  fearful frightened, timid
104–5 **Love . . . capacity** Compare Tilley
  L165, T416.
105 **to my capacity** as far as I can judge,
  in my reckoning
106 **addressed** 'ready to begin' but also
  'made ready with the proper costume'
  (*OED, address, v.* 4). Foakes compares
  Pericles 7[= 2.4].98 where the knights
  are to dance, 'Ev'n in your armours,
  as you are addressed'.
107.1 **Flourish trumpets** Dekker refers to
  the prologue giving 'the trumpets their
  cue, that he's upon point to enter'
  (*Gull's Hornbook* (1609), ch. 6, cited
  by Cunningham).
108–17 Quince's nervous mispunctuation

may have been influenced by Matthew
Merrygreek's mischievous intentional
mispunctuation of the 'hero's' letter in
Nicholas Udall's *Ralph Roister Doister*
(*c.*1533, printed *c.*1566), 3.4; a similar trick occurs in Barnabe Riche's
Farewell to Military Profession (1581)
which was one of Shakespeare's sources
for *Twelfth Night*. Quinces have varied
between non-stop panic, an increasing
panic inducing the mistakes after a
good start, and horrified amazement at
the meaningless speech he finds himself making.
110 **But** except (Quince); on the contrary
  (correctly punctuated)
112 **in despite** in contempt (Quince); to
  vex you (correctly)

We are not here. That you should here repent you   115
The actors are at hand; and by their show
You shall know all that you are like to know.
THESEUS This fellow doth not stand upon points.
LYSANDER He hath rid his prologue like a rough colt: he
knows not the stop. A good moral, my lord: it is not   120
enough to speak, but to speak true.
HIPPOLYTA Indeed, he hath played on this prologue like a
child on a recorder: a sound, but not in government.
THESEUS His speech was like a tangled chain: nothing im-
paired, but all disordered. Who is next?   125

  Enter ⌈with a trumpeter before them⌉ Bottom as
  Pyramus, Flute as Thisbe, Snout as Wall, Starveling as
  Moonshine, and Snug as Lion, for the dumb show
⌈QUINCE⌉ (*as Prologue*)
 Gentles, perchance you wonder at this show,
  But wonder on, till truth make all things plain.
 This man is Pyramus, if you would know;
  This beauteous lady Thisbe is, certain.
 This man with lime and roughcast doth present   130
  Wall, that vile wall which did these lovers sunder;

125.1 *with a trumpeter before them*] OXFORD; *Tawyer with a trumpet before them.* F; *not in*
Q   125.1–3 *Bottom . . . show*] WELLS (*subs.*); *Enter* Pyramus, *and* Thisby, *and* Wall, *and*
Mooneshine, *and* Lyon Q   126 QUINCE (*as Prologue*)] *Prologue* QF

---

116 **show** appearance; but also the dumbshow that accompanies the second
part of the prologue (ll. 126–50); compare Ophelia's description of the
dumbshow as a 'show' in *Hamlet*
3.2.133, 136.
118 **stand upon points** care about punctuation; trouble about details. As Andrews notes, the on-stage audience
from this point on switches to prose to
offset the workers' verse all the more
emphatically.
120 **stop** full stop; the sudden checking of
a horse at full gallop so that it rears
up
123 **in government** under control
125.1 *a trumpeter* F refers to *Tawyer* who
was William Tawyer, 'Mr Heminges
man' according to the record of his

burial at St Saviour's, Southwark, in
June 1625 (John Heminges was an
actor-sharer in the King's Men, Shakespeare's company); the note clearly
relates to a revival of the play.
127 **till . . . plain** Proverbial; compare
'Truth will come to light' (Tilley
T591).
129 **certain** The accent on the second syllable is archaic by this time; I. Tomson
in 'A New Sonet of Pyramus and
Thisbe' (in Clement Robinson and
others, *A Handful of Pleasant Delights*
(1584)), uses the same archaic stress
for the same reason, to provide a
rhyme (Bullough, i. 410; see also Kenneth Muir, *The Sources of Shakespeare's
Plays* (1977), p. 72); compare Quince's
use of the archaic 'hight' at l. 138.

And through Wall's chink, poor souls, they are
  content
To whisper; at the which let no man wonder.
This man, with lantern, dog, and bush of thorn,
  Presenteth Moonshine. For if you will know,   135
By moonshine did these lovers think no scorn
  To meet at Ninus' tomb, there, there to woo.
This grizzly beast, which 'Lion' hight by name,
  The trusty Thisbe coming first by night
Did scare away, or rather did affright;   140
And as she fled, her mantle she did fall,
  Which Lion vile with bloody mouth did stain.
Anon comes Pyramus, sweet youth and tall,
  And finds his trusty Thisbe's mantle slain;
Whereat with blade—with bloody, blameful blade—   145
  He bravely broached his boiling bloody breast;
And Thisbe, tarrying in mulberry shade,
  His dagger drew and died. For all the rest,
Let Lion, Moonshine, Wall, and lovers twain
At large discourse, while here they do remain.   150
        ⌈*Exeunt all the clowns but Snout as Wall*⌉
THESEUS I wonder if the lion be to speak.
DEMETRIUS No wonder, my lord: one lion may when
many asses do.

150.1 *Exeunt . . . Wall*] F (*Exit all but Wall.*); *Exit Lyon, Thisby, and* Mooneshine QF (*after*
l. 153)

---

134 **This . . . thorn** See 3.1.54–5 and n.
  Starveling's dog may have been and
  usually is a stuffed animal though
  Lance's dog Crab was real in *Two
  Gentlemen* 2.3 and 4.4.
138–40 **This . . . affright** The rhyme
  scheme makes this stanza defective,
  lacking a line to rhyme with 'name'
  in l. 138 but the sense shows no gap.
  Is it Shakespeare's error or Quince's?
140 **did** Muir suggests that Quince's repeated use of 'did' here (four times in
  three lines) is picked up from its 'desperate prevalence' as an auxiliary in
  Golding (*Shakespeare's Sources*, p. 70).
143 **tall** brave, handsome

144 **mantle** Thisbe 'let hir mantle fall' in
  Golding's Ovid (4.125).
145–6 **Whereat . . . breast**   Shakespeare
  mocks the alliterative style of old plays.
146 **broached** pierced, usually used of
  tapping a cask or barrel
  boiling bloody breast The Calydonian
  boar in Golding's Ovid (8.478) has a
  'boiling breast' but it seems likely that
  Shakespeare's joke depends on his having read Ovid in Latin where Pyramus
  '*ferventi moriens e vulnere traxit*',
  'dying, he drew [his sword] from the
  boiling wound' (Golding has 'bleeding').
150 **At large** at length

⌈SNOUT⌉ (*as Wall*)

In this same interlude it doth befall
That I, one Snout by name, present a wall;   155
And such a wall as I would have you think
That had in it a crannied hole or chink,
Through which the lovers Pyramus and Thisbe
Did whisper often, very secretly.
This loam, this roughcast, and this stone doth show   160
That I am that same wall; the truth is so.
And this the cranny is, right and sinister,
Through which the fearful lovers are to whisper.

THESEUS Would you desire lime and hair to speak better?
DEMETRIUS It is the wittiest partition that ever I heard   165
    discourse, my lord.

        Enter Bottom as Pyramus

THESEUS Pyramus draws near the wall. Silence.
BOTTOM (*as Pyramus*)

O grim-looked night, O night with hue so black,
    O night which ever art when day is not;
O night, O night, alack, alack, alack,   170
    I fear my Thisbe's promise is forgot.

---

154 SNOUT (*as Wall*)] WELLS; *Wall.* QF   155 Snout] F; *Flute* Q   166.1 *Enter . . . Pyramus*]
Enter Pyramus F (*after l.* 167); *not in* Q   168, etc. BOTTOM (*as Pyramus*)] WELLS; *Py. (and variants)* QF

---

154 SNOUT Q's *Flute* is obviously an error.
  interlude play; compare 1.2.5 and n.
157-9 In Golding the lovers 'talk together
  secretly' through a 'cranny' (4.83 and
  87).
160 Wall has acquired stone to go with
  the loam and roughcast of 3.1.63-4
  and 5.1.130; he may be more than a
  little overburdened.
162 **sinister** left, accented on the second
  syllable as usual in the period
163 **whisper** The half-rhyme is a comically limp conclusion to Wall's speech;
  Wall may try to produce a better
  rhyme with 'whisisper' (Sprague and
  Trewin, p. 67).
164 **hair** Used to bind the plaster in building walls and perhaps yet another object carried by Wall.

165 **wittiest** cleverest
  partition 'wall' but also 'section of a
  book'; in Cicero's *Topica* the definition
  of something which can be partitioned
  is preceded by a discussion of a wall
  (Baldwin, ii. 110).
168-74 For Bottom's repeated cries of 'O'
  compare Gascoigne's translation of Euripides' *Jocasta* (1566), 'O wife, O
  mother, O both woeful names, | O
  woeful mother, and O woeful wife'
  (*The Posies*, ed. John W Cunliffe (Cambridge, 1907), p. 322) and Nurse's
  uncomic distress over the 'dead' body
  of Juliet, 'O woe! O woeful, woeful,
  woeful day! | Most lamentable day!
  Most woeful day | That ever, ever, I
  did yet behold! | O day, O day, O day,
  O hateful day', *Romeo* 4.4.80-3.

And thou, O wall, O sweet, O lovely wall,
  That stand'st between her father's ground and mine,
Thou wall, O wall, O sweet and lovely wall,
  Show me thy chink, to blink through with mine eyne.   175
    Wall shows his chink
Thanks, courteous wall. Jove shield thee well for this.
  But what see I? No Thisbe do I see.
O wicked wall, through whom I see no bliss,
  Cursed be thy stones for thus deceiving me.
THESEUS The wall methinks, being sensible, should curse   180
again.
BOTTOM (*to Theseus*) No, in truth, sir, he should not.
  'Deceiving me' is Thisbe's cue. She is to enter now,
  and I am to spy her through the wall. You shall see,
  it will fall pat as I told you.   185
    Enter Flute as Thisbe
Yonder she comes.
FLUTE (*as Thisbe*)
O wall, full often hast thou heard my moans
  For parting my fair Pyramus and me.
My cherry lips have often kissed thy stones,
  Thy stones with lime and hair knit up in thee.   190

175.1 *Wall . . . chink*] CAPELL (*Wall holds up his fingers*); *not in* QF   182 *to Theseus*] OXFORD;
not in QF   182–5] *As in* POPE; QF *prints as verse*; Q1 *divides at* is | . . . spy | . . . fall |
185.1 *Enter . . . Thisbe*] *Enter Thisby* Q1 (*after* comes, *l.* 186); *Enter Thisbie* F (*after* fall.,
l. 185)   187, etc. FLUTE (*as Thisbe*)] WELLS; *This.* QF   190 up in thee] F; *now againe* Q

172–9 Ovid's lovers also talk directly to
the wall, for example, 'O thou envious
wall (they said) why let'st thou lovers
thus?' (Golding 4.91), as do Chaucer's,
'Alas, thow wikkede wal!' (*The Legend
of Good Women*, l. 756). The extent of
Bottom's gratitude at l. 176 will depend on how quickly Wall remembers
to show his chink.

175.1 **Wall . . . chink** QF do not give a
direction; Capell's direction assumes,
as do most editors, that Wall's chink
is the one suggested by Bottom at
3.1.64–5 ('and let him hold his fingers
thus'). But the probable jokes on
'stones' (l. 189 and n.) and 'hole' (l.
200 and n.) may mean that Wall

stands with his legs astride and the
lovers talk between his legs, releasing
a bawdy dimension in the language
and requiring them to bend down
(which is comically awkward). See
Thomas Clayton's elaborate analysis,
' "Fie what a question's that if thou
wert near a lewd interpreter": The Wall
Scene in *A Midsummer Night's Dream*',
ShStuds 7 (1974), pp. 101–13.

180 **being sensible** having feelings
181 **again** back, in return
189 **stones** Punning on the meaning 'tes-
ticles'; Oxford points out that 'knit'
can mean 'geld, castrate' (*OED v.* 12).
190 **up in thee** Q1's 'now againe' is nonsensical; F's correction is likely to have

---

BOTTOM (*as Pyramus*)

   I see a voice. Now will I to the chink

      To spy an I can hear my Thisbe's face.

   Thisbe?

FLUTE (*as Thisbe*) My love—thou art my love, I think.

BOTTOM (*as Pyramus*)

     Think what thou wilt, I am thy lover's grace,

   And like Lemander am I trusty still.   195

FLUTE (*as Thisbe*)

   And I like Helen, till the fates me kill.

BOTTOM (*as Pyramus*)

   Not Shafalus to Procrus was so true.

FLUTE (*as Thisbe*)

   As Shafalus to Procrus, I to you.

BOTTOM (*as Pyramus*)

   O kiss me through the hole of this vile wall.

192–3] *Divided as in* ROWE 1714; Q1 *divides at* Thysby?   190 love—thou art] HANMER (~!
~ ~ˌ); ~ˌ ~ ~, QF;   ~, ~ ~ˌ COX

been from prompt-book to restore the rhyme.

191 **I see a voice** Compare 3.1.85, 4.1.208–11 and 5.1.345–6.

193 Q1's punctuation, 'My loue thou art, my loue I thinke', may represent another of the workmen having trouble with punctuation.

194 **Think . . . wilt** A commonplace; compare Tilley T27, T28.
   thy lover's grace indeed your lover; Bottom's line is a comic parallel to such conventional phrases as 'my lord's grace'.

195 **Lemander** Bottom's stab at Leander but also echoing 'Lysander' (Alexander, another name for Paris, the lover of Helen of Troy). Leander drowned swimming the Hellespont to visit his lover Hero (see Marlowe's *Hero and Leander*).

196 **Helen** Flute means Hero but Helen 'logically' follows 'Lemander' as a mistaken form of Alexander as Paris. Helen was, of course, not at all faithful. But 'Helen' also suggests the play's

'Helena' who was constant as Hero but never as unfaithful as Helen or Lysander–Lemander.

197 **Shafalus . . . Procrus** Bottom's error for Cephalus and Procris. Shakespeare may be thinking of the myth that Cephalus, abducted by Aurora, remained faithful to his wife, Procris, and was returned to her (see 3.2.389 and n.). But he might have been remembering the part of the myth that interested Ovid (see Golding's Ovid, 7.874–1117): Cephalus wrongly accused his wife of being unfaithful and, later, she, hearing a report that he was unfaithful, rushed to find him and was accidentally killed by him using a javelin that could not miss its target. This latter myth, of faithful spouse mistaken for being unfaithful, would be potent here and also has connections with the myth of Diana and Actaeon so powerfully present in the play; see also I. Lavin, 'Cephalus and Procris: Transformations of an Ovidian Myth', *JWCI* 17 (1954), pp. 260–87.

FLUTE (*as Thisbe*)

   I kiss the wall's hole, not your lips at all.   200

BOTTOM (*as Pyramus*)

   Wilt thou at Ninny's tomb meet me straightway?

FLUTE (*as Thisbe*)

   Tide life, tide death, I come without delay.

                  Exeunt Bottom and Flute severally

SNOUT (*as Wall*)

   Thus have I, Wall, my part dischargèd so;

   And being done, thus Wall away doth go.   *Exit*

THESEUS Now is the wall down between the two   205
   neighbours.

DEMETRIUS No remedy, my lord, when walls are so wilful
   to hear without warning.

HIPPOLYTA This is the silliest stuff that ever I heard.

THESEUS The best in this kind are but shadows, and the   210
   worst are no worse if imagination amend them.

202.1 *Exeunt . . . severally*] OXFORD (*after* Dyce); *not in* QF; *Exeunt* Pyramus *and* Thisbe *several ways* FAIRY Q   204 *Exit*] F (*Exit Clow.*); *not in* Q   205 wall] COLLIER 1853; Moon Q; morall F; Mural POPE; mure all HANMER; mure BROOKS; LAMPE (The *Wall* is down) downe] F; used Q   209, etc. HIPPOLYTA] *Dutch.* Q

200 **hole** Depending on the nature of the Wall's cranny (see n. to l. 175.1), this could mean 'arse-hole'.

201 **Ninny's** Bottom repeats Flute's error at 3.1.91 though Quince got it right at 5.1.137; Flute is wrong again at l. 257—is Quince heard exasperatedly correcting it from the prompter's seat?

202 **Tide . . . death** come life, come death

204 It is possible that F's 'Exit Clow.' refers to all three clowns but it seems likely that Pyramus and Thisbe, Bottom and Flute, have already left the stage.

205 **wall down** This is a famous textual crux and I offer no solution. Q's 'Moon used' is obviously nonsense and F's version, 'morall downe', is not much better. It seems sensible to keep F's 'downe', since emendations based on 'used' seem forced and 'downe' is likely to derive from F's independent authority; Brooks's argument that 'used' is an acceptable misreading of 'rased', his emendation, is not convincing. F's

'morall' could conceivably be a misreading of a bungled attempt to delete 'Moon' and write in 'Wall'. Pope's 'Mural' was probably already archaic by the date of *Dream*. 'Mure', Brooks's reading for 'Moon', is Shakespearian (*2 Henry IV* 4.3.119) but would be unlikely to be a misreading of 'Moon'. However no emendation is entirely convincing and 'wall' seems rather weak in context.

207–8 **walls . . . hear** From the proverb 'walls have ears' (Tilley W19), though this wall has shown no particular signs of having them; productions often make play of Wall's deafness or over-careful listening in order to justify the line.

207 **wilful** 'forward' but also 'willing' (*OED a.*[1] 3)

210 **shadows** Compare Robin's epilogue (5.1.414–20) and his description of Oberon as 'king of shadows' at 3.2.347. While the description of performers as shadows is conventional,

HIPPOLYTA It must be your imagination, then, and not
  theirs.
THESEUS If we imagine no worse of them than they of
  themselves, they may pass for excellent men. Here   215
  come two noble beasts in: a man and a lion.
> *Enter Snug as Lion, and Starveling as Moonshine with*
> *a lantern, thorn bush, and dog*
SNUG (*as Lion*)
  You, ladies, you whose gentle hearts do fear
    The smallest monstrous mouse that creeps on floor,
  May now perchance both quake and tremble here
    When lion rough in wildest rage doth roar.   220
  Then know that I as Snug the joiner am
  A lion fell, nor else no lion's dam;
  For if I should as Lion come in strife
  Into this place, 'twere pity on my life.
THESEUS A very gentle beast, and of a good conscience.   225
DEMETRIUS The very best at a beast, my lord, that e'er I
  saw.
LYSANDER This lion is a very fox for his valour.
THESEUS True, and a goose for his discretion.
DEMETRIUS Not so, my lord, for his valour cannot carry   230
  his discretion, and the fox carries the goose.

---

216 beasts in:] ROWE 1714 (~ˌ ~,); ~, ~ˌ QF; ~ˌ ~, COX   216.1–2 *Enter . . . dog*] OXFORD;
Enter Lyon, and Moone-shine. Q   217, etc. SNUG (*as Lion*)] WELLS; *Lyon* QF

<table>
<tr><td>

the discussion between Truth and
Poetry in the prologue to *The True
Tragedy of Richard the Third* (1594)
seems particularly potent here: '*Truth.*
. . . what makes thou upon a stage? |
Poetry. Shadows. | *Truth.* Then will I
add bodies to the shadows. | Therefore
depart and give Truth leave | To show
her pageant' (ed. W. W. Greg (Malone
Society; Oxford, 1929), ll. 8–12).

218 **monstrous** because a mouse is a ter-
  rifying monster to the 'ladies'
221–2 **I as . . . dam** He is a cruel lion in
  so far as he is Snug but he is not in
  any other way a lion's 'dam', female
  parent. Thisbe is frightened by a lion-

</td><td>

ess in Golding's Ovid 4.120.
226 **best at a beast** The two words could
  be pronounced similarly enough to
  make the pun work; Sisson found
  exactly this pun on the name of a
  Captain Best in a 1595 Chancery de-
  position (*New Readings*, i. 133).
228–33 The lion was famous for its va-
  lour (Tilley L308), the fox for cunning,
  'discretion' (F645, F647, F656 (fox
  and geese) and F659 (fox and lion))
  and the goose for stupidity (G346,
  G348); compare also L319, 'If the
  lion's skin cannot the fox's shall'). The
  joke is complicated, confusing and la-
  boured; it is abandoned by Theseus at
  l. 233.

</td></tr>
</table>

THESEUS His discretion, I am sure, cannot carry his valour, for the goose carries not the fox. It is well. Leave it
to his discretion, and let us listen to the moon.

STARVELING (*as Moonshine*)

This lantern doth the hornèd moon present—   235

DEMETRIUS He should have worn the horns on his head.

THESEUS He is no crescent, and his horns are invisible
within the circumference.

STARVELING (*as Moonshine*)

This lantern doth the hornèd moon present,
Myself the man i'th' moon do seem to be—   240

THESEUS This is the greatest error of all the rest: the man
should be put into the lantern. How is it else the man
i'th' moon?

DEMETRIUS He dares not come there for the candle; for
you see it is already in snuff.   245

HIPPOLYTA I am aweary of this moon. Would he would
change.

THESEUS It appears by his small light of discretion that he
is in the wane; but yet in courtesy, in all reason, we
must stay the time.   250

LYSANDER Proceed, Moon.

STARVELING All that I have to say is to tell you that the
lantern is the moon, I the man i'th' moon, this thorn
bush my thorn bush, and this dog my dog.

235, etc. STARVELING (*as Moonshine*)] WELLS; *Moone* QF   252 STARVELING] WELLS; *Moon* QF

235 **lantern** Modernisation here obscures
a joke; a 'lanthorne' (Q's spelling from
this point on) was made of thin sheets
of horn and eases the pun on 'horned'.

236 **He ... head** like a cuckold; an over-
used joke (Tilley H625)

237 **crescent** a waxing, growing moon;
Starveling is presumably thin

241–2 **the man ... lantern** The joke is all
the better for Starveling's thinness.

245 **in snuff** needing to be snuffed like a
candle, angry ('to take in snuff' meant
'to take offence', see Tilley S598 and

1 *Henry IV* 1.3.40); Starvelings often
appear nervous but the comment suggests that he is angry and eventually
gives up in furious disgust.

246–7 **I am ... change** As Theseus had
felt at the opening of the play.

248 **It ... discretion** Theseus feebly returns to the 'discretion' joke.

249 **in all reason** as is only reasonable

252–4 **All ... dog** Starveling, under the
hail of mockery, gives up verse and
provides a prose summary.

DEMETRIUS Why, all these should be in the lantern, for all   255
   these are in the moon. But silence; here comes Thisbe.
     Enter Flute as Thisbe
FLUTE (*as Thisbe*)
  This is old Ninny's tomb. Where is my love?
SNUG (*as Lion*) O.
     Lion roars. Thisbe drops her mantle and runs off
DEMETRIUS Well roared, Lion.
THESEUS Well run, Thisbe.   260
HIPPOLYTA Well shone, Moon.—Truly, the moon shines
   with a good grace.
     Lion worries Thisbe's mantle
THESEUS Well moused, Lion.
DEMETRIUS And then came Pyramus.
     ⌈*Enter Bottom as Pyramus*⌉
LYSANDER And so the lion vanished.   ⌈*Exit Lion*⌉   265
BOTTOM (*as Pyramus*)
  Sweet moon, I thank thee for thy sunny beams.
   I thank thee, moon, for shining now so bright;
  For by thy gracious, golden glittering gleams
    I trust to take of truest Thisbe sight.
     But stay, O spite!   270
     But mark, poor knight,

256.1 *Enter ... Thisbe*] WELLS; *Enter Thisby* QF   257–8] *Divided as in* F; *one line in* Q
258.1 *Lion ... off*] BROOKS (*subs.*); *The Lion roares, Thisby runs off* F; *not in* Q; Lion roars.
Thisbe *drops her Veil, runs off.* LAMPE   262.1 *Lion ... mantle*] CAPELL (*subs., after l.* 264);
not in QF   264.1 *Enter ... Pyramus*] WELLS; *Enter* Pyramus QF (*after l.* 265)   265 *Exit
Lion*] OXFORD; *not in* QF; *after l.* 263 CAPELL   268 gleams] STAUNTON (*conj.* Knight); beames
QF   270–1, 273–4, 279–0] *Divided as in* FAIRY Q, POPE; *each one line in* QF

---

259 **Well roared, Lion** What Bottom had
   envisioned of his own performance as
   Lion in 1.2 ('I will make the Duke say
   'Let him roar again' ') now comes true
   for Snug.
263 **moused** Lion has been playing with
   the mantle like a cat with a mouse.
   Foakes suggests that Theseus is also
   implying that Lion's roars are rather
   close to a mouse's squeaks.
268 **gleams** The emendation 'improves'
   the alliteration while avoiding the
   repetition of 'beams' from l. 267 in QF.

270–81 Bottom speaks in a variant of the
   'eight and six' metre which Quince
   was going to use for the prologue
   (3.1.22 and n.). Shakespeare may have
   found a source for it in Tomson's 'A
   New Sonnet of Pyramus and Thisbe':
   'In Babylon, | not long agone, | a
   noble Prince did dwell, | whose
   daughter bright, | dimmed each one's
   sight, | so far she did excel' (in Bul-
   lough, i. 409; see also Muir, *Shakespeare's Sources*, pp. 70–1).

What dreadful dole is here?
   Eyes, do you see?
   How can it be?
O dainty duck, O dear!   275
   Thy mantle good,
   What, stained with blood?
Approach, ye furies fell.
   O fates, come, come,
   Cut thread and thrum,   280
Quail, crush, conclude, and quell.
THESEUS This passion, and the death of a dear friend,
   would go near to make a man look sad.
HIPPOLYTA Beshrew my heart, but I pity the man.
BOTTOM (*as Pyramus*)
O wherefore, nature, didst thou lions frame,   285
   Since lion vile hath here deflowered my dear?—
Which is—no, no, which *was*—the fairest dame

276–7] *Divided as in* POPE; *one line in* QF

---

272 **dole** cause for sorrow
278 **furies** the goddesses, usually three
(Tisiphone, Megaera and Alecto), who
left their home Tartarus to hound
the guilty and exact vengeance. In
Chaucer's 'Knight's Tale', the appearance of 'a furie infernal' startles Arcite's horse, throwing and killing him
(l. 2684–5) and they often turned up
in Seneca's tragedies and English plays
derived from them.
279 **fates** the goddesses Clotho, Lachesis
and Atropos who, respectively, spun,
drew out and cut the thread of life
280 **thread and thrum** 'threads' were the
warp, extending lengthways on the
loom; the 'thrum' is the tufted end of
the threads left attached to the loom
when the warp of the finished piece of
cloth is cut off. Bottom's language, of
course, recalls his trade, as if Bottom
has characteristically rewritten his
own part.
281 **Quail** destroy
   quell kill
286 **deflowered** Presumably Bottom
means 'devoured' but the suggestion

of rape and of flowers hovers significantly here: if Pyramus' and Thisbe's
blood in Ovid metamorphoses the mulberry to a 'deep dark purple colour'
(4.152), the colour of blood, then in
Dream the change of colour of a flower
to purple has already happened to love-
in-idleness, caused, in Oberon's words,
by 'love's wound' (2.1.167) which
suggests the bleeding caused by the
rupture of the hymen, the deflowering.
From the very beginning of the play
the question of whether virgins will be
deflowered in marriage or will be
forced to remain chaste by becoming
nuns has been at issue; the bleeding
of 'love's wound' for Hippolyta, Hermia, and Helena lies just beyond the
end of the play. In the Reinhardt–
Dieterle film (1935), Joe E. Brown as
Flute carried an enormous fake flower
so that he could be 'de-flowered'.
287 **no . . . was** Sometimes played as Bottom prompting himself without
Quince's help but it is perhaps better
as Pyramus' aghast realization that
Thisbe is no more.

That lived, that loved, that liked, that looked with
    cheer.
  Come tears, confound;
  Out sword, and wound   290
The pap of Pyramus.
  Ay, that left pap,
  Where heart doth hop.
Thus die I: thus, thus, thus.
  He stabs himself
  Now am I dead,   295
  Now am I fled,
My soul is in the sky.
  Tongue, lose thy light;
  Moon, take thy flight.   ⌐*Exit Moonshine*⌐
Now die, die, die, die, die.   *He dies*   300
DEMETRIUS No die but an ace for him; for he is but one.
LYSANDER Less than an ace, man, for he is dead; he is
  nothing.
THESEUS With the help of a surgeon he might yet recover
  and prove an ass.   305
HIPPOLYTA How chance Moonshine is gone before Thisbe
  comes back and finds her lover?
THESEUS She will find him by starlight.
   ⌐*Enter Flute as Thisbe*⌐
Here she comes, and her passion ends the play.

289–90, 292–3, 295–7, 298–9] *Divided as in* FAIRY Q, JOHNSON; *each one line in* QF   294.1
He stabs himself] DYCE; *not in* QF   299 *Exit Moonshine*] CAPELL (*after l.* 300); *not in* QF; COX
(*after l.* 299)   300 *He dies*] THEOBALD 1740; *not in* QF   305 prove] Q2, F; yet prooue Q1
306 before] ROWE; ~? QF   308.1 *Enter . . . Thisbe*] *Enter Thisby* F (*after l.* 307); *not in* Q

---

291 **pap** Usually used of a woman's breast
and hence comic in its application here
but Biron comments of the King in
love, 'sweet Cupid, thou hast thumped
him with thy birdbolt under the left
pap' (*LLL* 4.3.21–2).

293 **heart doth hop** 'hop' sounds ridiculous but for its strong sense of 'dance'
(*OED v.* 2) here compare Herod, 'O,
my harte hoppis for joie', in *The York
Plays*, ed. Richard Beadle (1982), p.
275.

298 **Tongue** A mistake for 'eye'.

301 **die** one of a pair of dice
  ace the side of a die with a single spot,
  the lowest throw with a die

302 **ace** punning on 'ass'; 'ace' could be
pronounced with a short 'a' (Kökeritz,
p. 89). As so often in their comments,
the on-stage spectators convey, una-
wares, echoes of the experiences in the
wood.

309 **passion** passionate speech, suffering
(compare 3.2.74, 5.1.70 and 282)

HIPPOLYTA Methinks she should not use a long one for   310
    such a Pyramus. I hope she will be brief.
DEMETRIUS A mote will turn the balance which Pyramus,
    which Thisbe, is the better—he for a man, God warrant
    us; she for a woman, God bless us.
LYSANDER She hath spied him already with those sweet   315
    eyes.
DEMETRIUS And thus she means, videlicet:
FLUTE (*as Thisbe*)
      Asleep, my love?
      What, dead, my dove?
    O Pyramus, arise.   320
      Speak, speak. Quite dumb?
      Dead, dead? A tomb
    Must cover thy sweet eyes.
      These lily lips,
      This cherry nose,   325
    These yellow cowslip cheeks
      Are gone, are gone.
      Lovers, make moan.
    His eyes were green as leeks.
      O sisters three,   330
      Come, come to me

---

313 warrant] Q (warnd)   318–19, 321–2, 327–8, 330–1, 333–4, 336–7, 339–40]
Divided as in FAIRY Q, POPE; *each one line in* QF   324–5] *Divided as in* THEOBALD; *one line in* QF

312 **mote** An echo of the name of Tita-
    nia's fairy.
313–14 **he . . . us** Omitted from F, pres-
    umably as a result of the 1606 statute
    against profanity and blasphemy in
    plays
313 **warrant** preserve
317 **means** (a) signifies (b) laments (*OED
    v.*² 1) (c) states a grievance or formal
    complaint (*OED v.*² 3, a legal term
    leading to 'videlicet', 'as you may see')
324–29 Instead of confusing the senses
    Flute this time confuses colours. 'Lily'
    and 'cherry' would be more appropri-
    ate to a heroine than hero; 'yellow
    cowslip' is simply irrelevant. Brooks
    compares a speech in Lyly's *Endimion*

praising one 'whose nose shall throw
more beams from it then the fiery Car-
buncle! . . . And whose lips might compare with silver for the paleness!' (iii.
70–1); Chaucer's Sir Thopas is praised
for his 'semely nose' (l. 1919).
326 **cowslip** Compare 2.1.10 and 2.1.15.
329 **green as leeks** Proverbial (Tilley
    L176); here nonsensical applied to
    eyes, even though Paris is praised for
    his eye 'so green, so quick, so fair' in
    Romeo 3.5.220.
330–5 Compare the prologue to *Cam-
    byses*, 'when sisters three had wrought
    to shear his vital thread' (l. 17).
330 **sisters three** The fates; see l. 279 and
    n.

With hands as pale as milk.
  Lay them in gore,
  Since you have shore
With shears his thread of silk.   335
  Tongue, not a word.
  Come, trusty sword,
Come, blade, my breast imbrue.
  She stabs herself
And farewell friends,
  Thus Thisbe ends.   340
Adieu, adieu, adieu.   *She dies*

THESEUS Moonshine and Lion are left to bury the dead.
DEMETRIUS Ay, and Wall too.
⌈BOTTOM⌉ No, I assure you, the wall is down that parted
    their fathers. Will it please you to see the epilogue or to   345
    hear a bergamask dance between two of our company?
        ⌈*Bottom and Flute stand up*⌉

338.1 *She stabs herself*] DYCE; *not in* QF   341 *She dies*] THEOBALD 1740; *not in* QF
344 BOTTOM] F; *Lyon.* Q

---

332 **as pale as milk** Proverbial for a lady's
  skin (Tilley M391).
334 **shore** for 'shorn'; a comic rhyme
338 **imbrue** pierce (*OED* 3b)
338.1 ***She stabs herself*** A comment in
  Edward Sharpham's *The Fleire* (1607)
  may refer to the stage-business here,
  'Faith like *Thisbe* in the play, a has
  almost killed himself with the scab-
  bard' (sig. D2ᵛ), suggesting a version
  of the common piece of business here
  where Flute cannot find the sword, for
  example because Bottom is lying on it;
  the Flute for the RSC's production at
  Stratford in 1989 found a new joke by
  speaking his stage directions, a logical
  extension of his earlier problem with
  cues.
342 **left** left alive
344 BOTTOM Q1's *Lion* is a mistake picked
  up perhaps from l. 342. Snug is off-
  stage and the speech is unmistakably
  in Bottom's style.
344–5 **the wall . . . fathers** Bottom's line
  suggests reconciliation between the
  two families, a problem that never
  arises in the play as performed, what-

ever its importance in the play the
workmen began rehearsing (see
1.2.54–9 and n.) or in *Romeo* (see
Ernest Schanzer, 'A Midsummer Night's
Dream and *Romeo and Juliet*', *N&Q* 197
(1955), pp. 13–14).
346 **bergamask** Usually identified as a
comic, clownish rustic dance, named
after the people of Bergamo, in Northern
Italy, commonly ridiculed as clowns;
there are Elizabethan keyboard pieces
by John Bull and Anthony Holborne to
accompany 'bergomasks'. However,
Walter Sorell ('Shakespeare and the
Dance', *SQ* 8 (1957), p. 383) identifies
it as the Italian country dance, 'a
round dance of couples in which
dancers execute little entrechats after
every sixth or ninth step', a description
which suggests a much more ordered
dance and certainly not a comic one.
But Thomas Morley, in *A Plaine and
Easie Introduction to Practicall Musicke*
(1597), p. 180, describes songs called
'Justinianas', written 'in the *Bergama-
sca* language' as 'a wanton and rude
kind of music' named after a courtesan

THESEUS No epilogue, I pray you; for your play needs no
excuse. Never excuse; for when the players are all dead
there need none to be blamed. Marry, if he that writ it
had played Pyramus and hanged himself in Thisbe's   350
garter it would have been a fine tragedy; and so it is,
truly, and very notably discharged. But come, your bergamask. Let your epilogue alone.

⌈*Bottom and Flute*⌉ *dance a bergamask, then exeunt*

347.1 *Bottom . . . up*] This edition; *not in* QF   353.1 *Bottom . . . exeunt*] OXFORD; *not in* QF

of Bergamo. If Bottom is offering a
song as well as a dance then his suggestion that Theseus might 'hear a
bergamask dance' is accurate, rather
than yet another example of the workers' confusion of the senses. Andrew
J. Sabol compares bergamasks to morris dances and notes that a morris
dance celebrates the wedding at the
end of Munday's *John a Kent and John
a Cumber* as the bergamask is part of
the nuptial celebrations here (*Four
Hundred Songs and Dances from the
Stuart Masques* (Providence, 1978), p.
594). Wilson suggests that the bergamask is 'the antimasque, introductory
to the dance and song of the fairies'.
It is certainly both a peasant dance
and the only dance called for in the
play not to be danced by the fairies.
Could it have been accompanied by the
tongs and the bones (see 4.1.29 and
n.), as Brissenden suggests (*Shakespeare
and the Dance* (1981), p. 45)? In Granville Barker's production (1914), the
dance was, according to *The Times* review, 'right Warwickshire, the acme of
the clumsy grotesque with vigorous
kickings in that part of the anatomy
meant for kicks' (quoted Dymkowski,
p. 76).

347.1 ***Bottom . . . up*** Bottom and Flute
obviously have to stand up at some
point but the choice of putting the SD
here, rather than, for example, at l.
344, is arbitrary.

350–1 **hanged . . . garter** 'To hang him-
self in his own garters' was proverbial
(Tilley G42); Falstaff tells Prince Harry
'Hang thyself in thine own heir-appar-

ent garters', *1 Henry IV* 2.2.43.

353.1 This SD, following Oxford, is the
logical solution on the evidence available since two are to dance the bergamask and only Bottom and Flute are
on stage. Since Bottom was most probably originally played by Will Kemp,
famous for his dancing, it seems very
likely he was one of the dancers here.
Most editors bring all the cast back and
have any two of them dance; most
productions bring all the cast back and
have *all* of them dance. QF are no help
here but it does seem likely that the
on-stage spectators would applaud and
that the whole company would come
back to take a bow. In Alexandru
Darie's production for the Comedy
Theatre of Bucharest (seen in England
in 1991), Theseus threw the workers
a purse of money as payment but they,
having been painfully aware of the
court's insulting comments throughout
their performance, left it lying on the
ground, staring proudly back at Theseus, dignified in their silent reply to
his contempt. Some other productions
have shown aristocratic rudeness in
extreme forms: in the Reinhardt—
Dieterle film, for example, the workers
went off to prepare for their dance and,
in the meantime, the courtiers sneaked
off to bed; as the workers burst back
on in a jubilant dance they were
stopped dead in their tracks by the
sight of an empty hall before them; in
John Hancock's San Francisco production of 1966, masked armed guards
forced the workers back from the departing court.

The iron tongue of midnight hath told twelve.
Lovers, to bed; 'tis almost fairy time.   355
I fear we shall outsleep the coming morn
As much as we this night have overwatched.
This palpable-gross play hath well beguiled
The heavy gait of night. Sweet friends, to bed.
A fortnight hold we this solemnity   360
In nightly revels and new jollity.   *Exeunt*
     Enter Robin Goodfellow with a broom

ROBIN

Now the hungry lion roars,
     And the wolf behowls the moon,
Whilst the heavy ploughman snores,
     All with weary task fordone.   365
Now the wasted brands do glow
     Whilst the screech-owl, screeching loud,
Puts the wretch that lies in woe
     In remembrance of a shroud.

361.1 *with a broom*] COLLIER 1853 (*with a broom on his shoulder*); *not in* QF   362 lion]
ROWE; Lyons QF   363 behowls] THEOBALD (*conj.* Warburton); beholds QF

354 **iron tongue** the bell's clapper; King
John speaks of 'the midnight bell' with
'his iron tongue and brazen mouth',
(*King John* 3.3.37–8).
     told counted, punning on 'tolled'
355 **fairy time** Theseus, whose scepticism
about 'fairy toys' (5.1.3) suggests that
his comment here may be a gentle
joke, appears to accept that it is restricted to the hours from midnight to
dawn; Oberon has argued differently
(3.2.388–93).
357 **overwatched** stayed up beyond our
period of watch duty
358 **palpable-gross** obviously rough and
ready
359 **heavy gait** slow walk, sluggish passage
361.1 **Enter . . . broom** Oxford marks a
new scene (5.2) here with the clear
stage but the action is self-evidently
continuous and any hint of a break
would ruin the effect of Robin's entrance.
362 **the hungry lion roars** This lion is

distinctly unlike Snug.
363 **behowls** Unknown elsewhere in
Shakespeare but the emendation is
entirely convincing; compare *As You
Like It* 5.2.104–5, 'like the howling of
Irish wolves against the moon'.
364 **heavy** with weariness
365 **fordone** tired out
366 **wasted brands** burnt-out logs
367 **screech-owl** traditionally a bird of ill-
omen. In *Epithalamion* (1595) Spenser
prays 'Let not the shriech Oule, nor
the Storke be heard: | . . . | Nor
damned ghosts cald up with mighty
spels' (ll. 345, 347); Robin, whose
blunt statement here warns of the
presence of the type of ill-omens Spenser fears, belongs with another group
Spenser names, 'Ne let the Pouke, nor
other evill sprights, | . . . | Ne let hob
Goblins, names whose sence we see
not, | Fray us with things that be not'
(ll. 341, 343–4). The whole of *Dream*
may belong with Spenser's 'deluding
dreames' (l. 338).

Now it is the time of night   370
   That the graves, all gaping wide,
Every one lets forth his sprite
   In the churchway paths to glide;
And we fairies that do run
   By the triple Hecate's team   375
From the presence of the sun,
   Following a darkness like a dream,
Now are frolic. Not a mouse
Shall disturb this hallowed house.
I am sent with broom before   380
To sweep the dust behind the door.
   Enter Oberon and Titania, King and Queen of Fairies,
   with all their train

OBERON

Through the house give glimmering light.

---

374 we] Q (wee)   382.1 *Oberon and Titania*] OXFORD; *not in* QF

370–3 Ghosts were held to walk from midnight to dawn; compare 3.2.380–2.

375 **triple Hecate's** Golding's Ovid talks of 'triple Hecate' (7.136) but the phrase is not original to him (see James Sledd, 'A Note on the Use of Renaissance Dictionaries', *Modern Philology*, 49 (1951), pp. 10–15); the goddess was named Hecate or Proserpina in Hades, Diana on earth and Luna, Cynthia or Phoebe in heaven. The word has two syllables here.
   team the dragons pulling her chariot; see 3.2.379.

378 **frolic** frolicsome, merry

380 **with broom** Robin was often described carrying a broom (see also fig. 4, the title-page to *Robin Good-Fellow, His Mad Pranks* (1628)). In Jonson's masque *Love Restored* (1612), Robin describes himself as 'he that sweeps the hearth, and the house clean, riddles for the country maids, and does all their other drudgery'; trying to get admittance to the masque he 'stuck to this shape you see me in, of mine own, with my broom, and my candles' (vii. 378, 381).

381 **dust** There is a superstitious association of dirt with wealth that may be echoed here; Holinshed records a story of Alice Kettle sweeping the dirt towards her son's house with the words 'To the house of William my Sonne, Hie all the wealth of Kilkennie towne' (quoted by Iona Opie and Moira Tatem, eds., *A Dictionary of Superstitions* (Oxford, 1989), s.v. Dirt). But Robin may just be helpfully cleaning up.

382 **glimmering light** As Wilson suggests, the fairies probably have candles or tapers in headbands; in *Merry Wives* the pretended fairies in 5.5 wear 'rounds of waxen tapers on their heads' (4.4.50). The device leaves their hands free here for a round dance, 'Hand in hand' (l. 390). These lights echo and transform the lights which Titania's fairies were instructed to use to light Bottom to her bed (3.1.160–2). 'Glimmering' has appeared twice before in *A Midsummer Night's Dream* (at 2.1.77 and 3.2.61); Shakespeare uses the word nowhere else. The 'glimmering night' which has accompanied Theseus's previous desertions has now become the 'glimmering light' that blesses his marriage bed. (Adrian Poole drew my attention

By the dead and drowsy fire
Every elf and fairy sprite
   Hop as light as bird from briar,   385
And this ditty after me
Sing, and dance it trippingly.

TITANIA

First rehearse your song by rote,
To each word a warbling note.
Hand in hand with fairy grace   390
Will we sing and bless this place.
   ⌈ *The song. The fairies dance* ⌉

OBERON

Now until the break of day
Through this house each fairy stray.
To the best bride bed will we,
Which by us shall blessèd be,   395
And the issue there create
Ever shall be fortunate.
So shall all the couples three
Ever true in loving be,

387–8] *Divided as in* ROWE 1714; *one line in* QF   391.1 *The song*] F (*centred over ll.*
392–413 *which is italicized, omitting SP* OBERON); *not in* Q   *The fairies dance*] CAPELL (*subs.*);
not in QF

to Shakespeare's intriguing use of the
word here.)

388 **rehearse** repeat; John Caird's production (RSC, Stratford, 1989) made a
great deal of comic business out of
taking 'rehearse' in its modern sense
with the fairies holding a rehearsal
that was all too necessary. See also
5.1.68 and n.: the rehearsal of 'Pyramus and Thisbe' that has been
presented to Egeus before it can be
presented to a duke becomes rehearsal
of the fairy song in the presence of the
fairy rulers.

390–1 **Hand . . . place** Alan Brissenden
suggests that Titania is describing a
round dance of blessing or a carole
(*Shakespeare and the Dance* (1981),
p. 45); if that was recognizably the
case it would link to the 'carols' that
Titania describes 'human mortals'

wanting (2.1.101–2).

392–413 F heads these lines '*The Song*'
and indents and italicizes them without a SP. Q1 gives them to Oberon and
prints them in roman as a speech.
They could have been the words of the
song but this seems unlikely; most
probably the song is simply missing
and F's compositor probably misinter-
preted the added SD 'The Song' from
the prompt-book as relating to the following speech. The missing song was
presumably for Oberon and the fairies
as chorus; 'after me | Sing' (ll. 386–7)
suggests as much. Granville Barker
(1914) used the song for the wedding
of Theseus and Hippolyta that opens
Two Noble Kinsmen (1.1.1–24), a lyric
with strong connections to *A Midsummer Night's Dream*.

394 **best bride bed** that of Theseus and
Hippolyta

And the blots of nature's hand   400
Shall not in their issue stand.
Never mole, harelip, nor scar,
Nor mark prodigious such as are
Despisèd in nativity
Shall upon their children be.   405
With this field-dew consecrate
Every fairy take his gait
And each several chamber bless
Through this palace with sweet peace;
And the owner of it blessed   410
Ever shall in safety rest.
Trip away, make no stay,
Meet me all by break of day.
                        Exeunt all but Robin Goodfellow

ROBIN

If we shadows have offended,
Think but this, and all is mended: 415
That you have but slumbered here,

410–11 *As* STAUNTON *(conj.* Singer); *reversed in* QF   413 *Exeunt . . . Goodfellow*] CAPELL
(subs.); Exeunt Q; *not in* F

---

403 **mark prodigious** ominous birthmark
406 **field-dew   consecrate** consecrated
field-dew, 'fairy holy-water' (Dyce).
Foakes compares the task of Titania's
fairies to 'dew her orbs' (2.1.9) and
Belarius' invocation 'The benediction of
these covering heavens | Fall on their
heads like dew' (*Cymbeline* 5.6.351–2).
As Barber points out, 'fertilizing and
beneficent virtue are in festival custom
persistently attributed to dew gathered
on May mornings' (p. 139).
407 **gait** way
410–11 **And . . . rest** Transposed in QF,
ruining the sense.
413 *Exeunt . . . Goodfellow The Times*'s review of Granville Barker's production
described the transition to the epilogue:
'In the end the golden fairies play hide-
and-seek round the columns of Theseus's palace. Gradually their numbers
dwindle. At last only one, a girl, is
left—the last patch of gold to fade from

sight'; then the curtain fell and Robin
spoke the epilogue in front of it.
414–29 Robin speaks the play's epilogue,
offering the kind of excuses that Theseus had suggested were unnecessary
(5.1.349–51).
414 **shadows** Robin has called the fairies
'shadows' at 3.2.347 (see also
5.1.210); E. K. begins his sceptical
gloss on 'frendly Faeries' in Spenser's
Shepheardes Calendar (n. to June, l. 25),
'the opinion of Faeries and elfes is very
old, and yet sticketh very religiously
in the myndes of some. But . . . there
be no such thinges, nor yet the sha-
dowes of the things'.
416–19 Compare the prologue to Lyly's
The Woman in the Moon 'If many faults
escape her discourse, | Remember all
is but a Poet's dream' (iii. 241). Robin's
solution to the possibility of offending
places the answer in the hands of the
audience's perception of its experience;

While these visions did appear;
And this weak and idle theme,
No more yielding but a dream,
Gentles, do not reprehend.   420
If you pardon, we will mend.
And as I am an honest puck,
If we have unearnèd luck
Now to 'scape the serpent's tongue,
We will make amends ere long,   425
Else the puck a liar call.
So, good night unto you all.
Give me your hands, if we be friends,
And Robin shall restore amends.   *Exit*

429 *Exit*] ROWE (*Exeunt omnes*); *not in* QF

Peter Quince's prologue (5.1.108–17),
however punctuated, places the
answer in the actors' intentions: 'If we
offend, it is with our good will'.

419 **No more yielding but** providing nothing more than
420 **Gentles** Quince had addressed his
audience in the same way (l. 126).
421 **mend** do better
424 **the serpent's tongue** 'be[ing] dismissed with hisses' (Johnson); compare *LLL*, 'if any of the audience hiss,

you may cry "Well done, Hercules,
now thou crushest the snake!" '
(5.1.131–3) but see also the serpent of
Hermia's dream (2.2.152) and her description of Demetrius, 'with doubler
tongue | Than thine, thou serpent,
never adder stung' (3.2.72–3).
428 **Give . . . hands** Robin invites ap-
plause; in Peter Brook's production the
cast left the stage to shake hands with
the audience.
429 **restore amends** give satisfaction in
return

SHAKESPEARE'S REVISIONS OF ACT 5

SHAKESPEARE revised the opening of Act 5 twice. The mislined speeches in Q1 suggest that he revised the passage during composition; the variants between Q1 and F suggest a second stage of his thinking about this crucial passage. My edition has followed F for this passage but in this appendix I want to set out the section's different states, more clearly than can be done in the collational apparatus, presenting the evidence for revision and considering some of the implications.

1. *From draft to Q1*

In Q1 there are a number of demonstrably mislined passages in lines 1–84. In the course of subsequent editing the mislineations were progressively and rapidly straightened out and the flow of regular verse restored. By Rowe 1714 the passage's true lineation was effectively restored. There was little difficulty in recognizing that a passage like the following represents four lines of verse mislined as three—I mark the natural verse divisions with an oblique:

> Such shaping fantasies, that apprehend / more
> Than cool reason ever comprehends. / The lunatic,
> The lover, and the poet / are of imagination all compact.

Passages mislined in such ways are, of course, common throughout the early printed texts of Shakespeare. But John Dover Wilson noted that the removal of the mislined passages throughout these eighty-four lines left a scene that was both regularly lined and entirely coherent. In Theseus' speech on the imagination the irregular lines are all concerned with the poet's imagination; the removal of these passages left a duller but complete and intelligible speech about the lunatic and the lover.[1]

Similarly the mislined lines which expand on the discussion of the paradoxes of the title of the workmen's play, particularly Philostrate's description of his reaction to watching a rehearsal (ll. 66–70), neither affect the communication of essential information nor disrupt the flow of the dialogue if removed. Wilson explained the additional lines about the rehearsal as being 'needed to endow Philostrate with laughter, tears, and life' (p. 84). But this explanation may be less

---

[1] Wilson, pp. 80–6.

significant than the passage's anticipation of the tension between the on-stage audience's reaction to the performance of 'Pyramus and Thisbe' as comic and the opposing seriousness both in the playlet's matter and the performers' manner. But the nub of his argument, that the mislined passages can be construed as additional, is undeniable.

Wilson went on to argue that the mislined verse constitutes Shakespeare's insertions and additions to a previously drafted passage (p. 85). Wilson's argument has been seriously challenged only by Hazelton Spencer[1] who quibbled over some of the passages Wilson identified as additions, found some of the remainder unacceptable on the grounds, for example, that Theseus' behaviour was too 'cavalier' (p. 25), and argued that the 'original' draft Wilson created was a stripped-down acting version by the company.[2]

For Wilson the levels of revision he found in this passage were part of a colossal theory of layers of revision throughout the play, an argument clearly untenable and now long discarded. It is one thing to show convincingly that the passage has been revised, that the first draft was accompanied by a series of insertions, but it is impossible to show when the revision was done; as Brooks comments, 'an inspired afterthought may come to an author after five minutes just as well as after four years' (p. xi). Nonetheless Robert K. Turner's extensive analysis of the printing of Q1 showed that there was likely to have been some disturbance in the copy for this passage: the compositor varied the number of lines of type on each page in gathering G, the gathering in which these lines appear (35 elsewhere but 34 on G1^r and G2^v and 32 on G2^r),[3] and his hypothesis that this is likely to indicate problems in the compositor's copy is entirely reasonable.

While most of the additions are straightforward, Shakespeare's perception that Theseus' comments on two forms of fantasy, madness and love, could be extended into *a* view—powerful and persuasive, however inadequate and partial—of the poet's imagination is clearly important, given the centrality of these lines to so much consideration of the play in particular and what is assumed to be Shakespeare's attitude towards poetry in general. Almost every critic writing on the play treats the speech at length.

[1] Hazelton Spencer, 'A Nice Derangement: The Irregular Verse-Lining in "A Midsummer Night's Dream" Act v, Sc. i, ll.1–84', *MLR* 25 (1930), pp. 23–9; see also Leo Kirschbaum, 'Shakespeare's Hypothetical Marginal Additions', *MLN* 61 (1946), pp. 44–9, for a counter-argument from rhetorical form.

[2] See also Wilson's reply, *MLR* 25 (1930), pp. 29–31.

[3] Robert K. Turner, Jr., 'Printing Methods and Textual Problems in *A Midsummer Night's Dream* Q1' *SB* 15 (1962), p. 51.

I offer here a modernized text of Q1 with the mislined passages left unregularised, juxtaposed with a hypothetical reconstruction of the text before Shakespeare inserted the passages that confused the compositor. My version differs in some decisions from the two versions previously offered.[1] Wilson, for instance, marks all of l. 55 as an insertion, thereby giving Philostrate's comments on tedious and brief no antecedent; Oxford at the same point removes the two half-lines, 'very tragical mirth'. | Merry and "tragical" ', without justification except, I presume, the neat way in which Shakespeare's insertion of Philostrate's comments on merry and tragical is accompanied by his insertion of Theseus' use of the words. Others may make other decisions but the major choices are clear.

[1] By Wilson, pp. 80–2, and Oxford, pp. 375–6.

A. Q1 LINED AS PRINTED

Enter Theseus, Hippolyta and Philostrate
HIPPOLYTA
'Tis strange, my Theseus, that these lovers speak of.
THESEUS
More strange than true. I never may believe
These antique fables, nor these fairy toys.
Lovers and mad men have such seething brains,
Such shaping fantasies, that apprehend more   5
Than cool reason ever comprehends. The lunatic,
The lover, and the poet are of imagination all compact.
One sees more devils than vast hell can hold:
That is the madman. The lover, all as frantic,
Sees Helen's beauty in a brow of Egypt.   10
The poet's eye, in a fine frenzy rolling, doth glance
From heaven to earth, from earth to heaven, and as
Imagination bodies forth the forms of things
Unknown, the poet's pen turns them to shapes,
And gives to airy nothing a local habitation   15
And a name. Such tricks hath strong imagination
That if it would but apprehend some joy
It comprehends some bringer of that joy;
Or in the night, imagining some fear,
How easy is a bush supposed a bear!   20
HIPPOLYTA
But all the story of the night told over,
And all their minds transfigured so together,
More witnesseth than fancy's images,
And grows to something of great constancy;
But howsoever, strange and admirable.   25
Enter the lovers: Lysander, Demetrius, Hermia and Helena
THESEUS
Here come the lovers, full of joy and mirth.
Joy, gentle friends, joy and fresh days
Of love accompany your hearts.
LYSANDER
More than to us wait in your royal walks, your board,
     your bed.
THESEUS
Come now, what masques, what dances shall we have   30
To wear away this long age of three hours between
Our after-supper and bed-time? Where is our usual manager
Of mirth? What revels are in hand? Is there no play

B. HYPOTHESIZED ORIGINAL VERSION

Enter Theseus, Hippolyta, and Philostrate

HIPPOLYTA

'Tis strange, my Theseus, that these lovers speak of.

THESEUS

More strange than true. I never may believe
These antique fables, nor these fairy toys.
Lovers and mad men have such seething brains.
One sees more devils than vast hell can hold: 5
That is the madman. The lover, all as frantic,
Sees Helen's beauty in a brow of Egypt.

Such tricks hath strong imagination
That if it would but apprehend some joy
It comprehends some bringer of that joy;   10
Or in the night, imagining some fear,
How easy is a bush supposed a bear!

HIPPOLYTA

But all the story of the night told over,
And all their minds transfigured so together,
More witnesseth than fancy's images,   15
And grows to something of great constancy;
But howsoever, strange and admirable.

Enter the lovers: Lysander, Demetrius, Hermia, and Helena

THESEUS

Here come the lovers, full of joy and mirth.

Come now, what masques, what dances shall we have

To ease the anguish of a torturing hour? Call Philostrate.
PHILOSTRATE
 Here mighty Theseus.   35
THESEUS
 Say, what abridgement have you for this evening?
 What masque, what music? How shall we beguile
 The lazy time if not with some delight?
PHILOSTRATE
 There is a brief how many sports are ripe.
 Make choice of which your highness will see first.   40
THESEUS
 'The battle with the centaurs, to be sung
 By an Athenian eunuch to the harp.'
 We'll none of that. That have I told my love
 In glory of my kinsman Hercules.
 'The riot of the tipsy Bacchanals   45
 Tearing the Thracian singer in their rage.'
 That is an old device, and it was played
 When I from Thebes came last a conqueror.
 'The thrice-three Muses mourning for the death
 Of learning, late deceased in beggary.'   50
 That is some satire, keen and critical,
 Not sorting with a nuptial ceremony.
 'A tedious brief scene of young Pyramus
 And his love Thisbe; very tragical mirth.'
 Merry and 'tragical'? 'Tedious' and 'brief'? That is hot ice 55
 And wondrous strange snow. How shall we find the
     concord
 Of this discord?
PHILOSTRATE
 A play there is, my lord, sme ten words long,
 Which is as 'brief' as I have known a play;
 But by ten words, my lord, it is too long,   60
 Which makes it 'tedious', for in all the play
 There is not one word apt, one player fitted.
 And 'tragical', my noble lord, it is. For Pyramus
 Therein doth kill himself. Which when I saw
 Rehearsed, I must confess, made my eyes water;   65
 But more merry tears the passion of loud laughter
 Never shed.
THESEUS
 What are they that do play it?
PHILOSTRATE
 Hard-handed men that work in Athens here,

To ease the anguish of a torturing hour?   20
Call Philostrate.

PHILOSTRATE

           Here mighty Theseus.

THESEUS

Say, what abridgement have you for this evening?
What masque, what music? How shall we beguile
The lazy time if not with some delight?

PHILOSTRATE

There is a brief how many sports are ripe.   25
Make choice of which your highness will see first.

THESEUS

'The battle with the centaurs, to be sung
By an Athenian eunuch to the harp.'
We'll none of that. That have I told my love
In glory of my kinsman Hercules.   30
'The riot of the tipsy Bacchanals
Tearing the Thracian singer in their rage.'
That is an old device, and it was played
When I from Thebes came last a conqueror.
'The thrice-three Muses mourning for the death   35
Of learning, late deceased in beggary.'
That is some satire, keen and critical,
Not sorting with a nuptial ceremony.
'A tedious brief scene of young Pyramus
And his love Thisbe: very tragical mirth.'   40
Merry and 'tragical'? 'Tedious' and 'brief'?

PHILOSTRATE

A play there is, my lord, some ten words long,
Which is as 'brief' as I have known a play;
But by ten words, my lord, it is too long,
Which makes it 'tedious'; for in all the play   45
There is not one word apt, one player fitted.

THESEUS

What are they that do play it?

PHILOSTRATE

Hard-handed men that work in Athens here,

Which never laboured in their minds till now,
And now have toiled their unbreathed memories   70
With this same play against your nuptial.

THESEUS

And we will hear it.

PHILOSTRATE

No, my noble lord, it is not for you. I have heard
It over, and it is nothing, nothing in the world,
Unless you can find sport in their intents   75
Extremely stretched and conned with cruel pain
To do you service.

THESEUS

I will hear that play; for never anything
Can be amiss when simpleness and duty tender it.
Go, bring them in; and take your places, ladies.   80

Exit Philostrate

HIPPOLYTA

I love not to see wretchedness o'ercharged
And duty in his service perishing.

Which never laboured in their minds till now,
And now have toiled their unbreathed memories   50
With this same play against your nuptial.

THESEUS

And we will hear it.

PHILOSTRATE

                    No, my noble lord.

THESEUS

Go, bring them in; and take your places, ladies.

                                        Exit Philostrate

HIPPOLYTA

I love not to see wretchedness o'ercharged
And duty in his service perishing.   55

2. *From Q1 to F*

There are two major variants between Q1 and F in this passage: the
speeches given to Philostrate in Q1 are, with one exception, reassigned to Egeus in F and the titles of the entertainments available
that evening are reassigned from Theseus to Lysander, with Theseus
still responding with his comments on the offerings. In both cases
the only changes are to the distribution of the speeches; the words
spoken remain unchanged.

The latter change is simple. While some commentators have worried why Lysander should be given the task, whether Philostrate has
had his place usurped or has turned away in a huff, and whether
the hierarchies and niceties of court behaviour have been disrupted,
the dialogue certainly works more effectively when split between
Lysander and Theseus, involving one more character in the action.
The decision may have been Shakespeare's or might have originated
in the company after their experience of playing the scene as originally written and printed; there is no evidence in the variant itself to
suggest which might be the source. If, however, the other change
can be credibly argued to be Shakespeare's, then the incorporation
of Lysander into the scene might fairly be seen as authorial. Grace
Ioppolo has pointed out that there is a possible connection between
this change and the mislined passage making Lysander 'the spokes-

man for the four lovers' in Q1 (l. 29 above)[1], but I see no reason to assume that this suggests that the changes between Q1 and F were made at the same time as the hypothesized changes preceding the Q1 state of the text. It is perfectly reasonable to imagine Shakespeare first perceiving that the lovers might well respond to Theseus' acknowledgement of their arrival and then realizing subsequently that Lysander would therefore make a good interlocutor for the discussion of the entertainments; this is more probable than the over-elaborate notion of the compositor for Q1 misreading already present speech-prefixes for Lysander's reading the titles.

It is the decision to include Egeus that is more complex and intriguing. It seems obvious that the one speech still given to Philostrate in F, lines 76–80, is a result of compositorial error, especially as the speech-prefix is at the head of a page (sig. O2^v). We can reasonably assume that the Folio version was intended to turn Philostrate into a mute in this scene, if indeed he is on stage at all.

The conventional argument has been that this was a company response to a doubling possibility: as Foakes puts it, since Philostrate does not speak in Act 1, 'the substitution here, doing away with one speaking-part, was a natural economy for an acting company' (p. 141). The only recent attempt to produce a doubling chart for the play[2] creates a scheme in which Philostrate is doubled by the actor playing Robin and Egeus by the actor playing Quince, a scheme that Peter Brook used in his production. It is obviously suggestive to double Theseus' Master of the Revels in Q, Philostrate, and Robin, who fulfils a similar function for Oberon. But such a scheme means that the elimination of Philostrate in F does not save an actor at all: since F's Egeus is on stage at the same time as Quince in Act 5 the two roles cannot be doubled. Though F's Egeus can also play Robin I cannot find a double for Quince that would save on an actor. I have tried out a number of other doubling schemes, none of which enable the company to economize on speaking actors by substituting Egeus for Philostrate in Act 5.

In the absence of an evident theatrical reason for the change, one is left to turn to other reasons, as the elimination of Philostrate, who becomes simply a name invoked in Act 1, focuses attention on Egeus. Q1 simply excludes Egeus from Act 5, from the creation of a social order which in the power it accords Theseus current criticism might well identify as patriarchal,[3] a patriarchy created, oddly

[1] Grace Ioppolo, *Shakespeare Revised* (Cambridge, Mass., 1991), p. 113.

[2] William A. Ringler, Jr., 'The Number of Actors in Shakespeare's Early Plays', in G. E. Bentley, ed., *The Seventeenth-Century Stage* (Chicago, 1968), p. 132.   [3] See, for example, Montrose, p. 67.

enough, by denying a father's rights. When Theseus announces to Egeus that 'I will overbear your will' (4.1.178), he displaces the law of Athens by replacing a father's right to choose by a daughter's right. When a critic writes that F's version 'all sweetness and light—concludes a play different from the one in which Hermia learns that gaining a husband has been purchased at the cost of losing a father',[1] he assumes that Egeus' silence is defiant and that Egeus ought to be absent in Act 5 as in Q1. Q1's omission of an entrance anywhere in the act for Egeus or for any group of attendant lords that might include the missing father becomes purposeful and deliberate. Q1's marking of entrances is not so complete that I could feel confident in such an assumption.

Many productions, even while using Q1's distribution of speeches, have felt duty bound to include attendant lords to fill out Theseus' court and have accommodated Egeus amongst them, making him mute but acquiescent. John Caird's production for the RSC in 1989 had Egeus persuaded to join the dance with Hermia, reconciled though silent. Reynolds in 1816 was so anxious about the position Egeus faces in Act 4 that he included lengthy speeches showing Egeus's dilemma before the sleeping lovers are discovered:

> and, ah! for her sake, and for mine,
> 'Pray Heaven she chuse Demetrius for her lord!—
> He hath my sacred pledge; my honour's bound! (p. 54)

Much as this Egeus would wish otherwise, he is forced to 'beg the law' since 'a parent's sacred word is pledg'd' (p. 55). Reynolds's Hermia asks Egeus for forgiveness which he willingly gives, calling down blessings on all, while neatly shifting some of the blame to Demetrius:

> and for thee, Demetrius
> The busy phantoms of thy brain dispers'd,
> May all be happiness and love! (p. 55)

Productions have, in effect, needed a father at the end of the play even though Shakespeare gives Egeus no lines in Q1 nor allows any other character a reference to him. Harley Granville Barker, in fact, needed two fathers, including a mute but identified Nedar, Helena's father, in his Act 5.[2]

While the Philostrate who is instructed to organize revels in Act 1 might most easily be seen as Theseus' 'usual manager of mirth' (5.1.35), audiences are unlikely to object if Egeus proves to be the

---

[1] George Walton Williams, reviewing the Oxford edition, *Cahiers Elisabéthains*, 35 (1989), p. 107.

[2] See Trevor Griffiths, 'Tradition and Innovation in Harley Granville Barker's *A Midsummer Night's Dream*', *TN* 30 (1976), p. 83.

person at court who fulfils that role, as in Bill Alexander's 1986 RSC production. F's text allows Egeus' incorporation in the Athenian society at the end of the play to be visible. It does not, however, prescribe his attitude.[1] Egeus may be truculent, obstinate or irritable.[2] His silence towards his daughter and her new husband and theirs to him may be significant in its cold-shouldering but it could equally be because there is no need for words. Productions which have Egeus reconciled to his daughter do not seem to need words to show that reconciliation.

The brief to which Egeus refers and which lists the revels becomes distinctly significant since it is Lysander who reads it. McGuire considers a number of ways in which Lysander might come to be holding it, snatching it, for example, from Egeus as he snatched his daughter, or being given it by Theseus who thereby marks his part in the transfer of the possession of Hermia from Egeus to Lysander, from father to husband. But it might simply indicate that Egeus is happy to let Lysander take on his role, marking his acceptance of his new son-in-law by giving him the brief to read. Either way the presence of Egeus in Act 5 seems rich with dramatic possibilities mostly indecipherable in his silence.

But it is clear in one particular respect. In 4.1 Egeus, finding the lovers asleep, demanded the immediate application of Athenian law, only to find that his will was overridden by Theseus. His response in the scene is silent, whether acquiescent or defiant. In Act 5, in F's version, Egeus does everything he can to persuade Theseus not to choose 'Pyramus and Thisbe'. Again Theseus simply overrules him; again he must leave the stage silent. He will return to announce, perhaps begrudgingly or with a different air of 'don't say I didn't warn you', 'So please your grace, the Prologue is addressed' (l. 106). If 'Pyramus and Thisbe' is, as I have argued in the Introduction (p. 93), a warning of what might have been, then the two moments are drawn even closer together. Theseus silences Egeus twice: once to produce a marriage; once to allow the comic presentation of a tragic version of the same narrative, a version no less fierce than what would in effect have happened if Egeus' will had not been overruled the first time in Act 4. The perception and invocation of that pattern seems to me distinctly Shakespearian.

---

[1] See Barbara Hodgdon, 'Gaining a Father: the Role of Egeus in the Quarto and the Folio', *RES*, NS 37 (1986), pp. 534–42 and Philip C. McGuire, 'Egeus and the Implications of Silence', in Marvin and Ruth Thompson, eds., *Shakespeare and the Sense of Performance* (Newark, Del., 1989), pp. 103–15 and his 'Intentions, Options, and Greatness: An Example from *A Midsummer Night's Dream*' in Sidney Homan, ed., *Shakespeare and the Triple Play* (Lewisburg, 1988), pp. 177–86. [2] McGuire, 'Egeus', p. 110.

INDEX

The index covers words glossed in the commentary, a very selective group of authors, and all productions of *A Midsummer Night's Dream* referred to in the introduction, commentary, and appendix. It does not include proverbial allusions or biblical references. References to illustrations are italicized.

abate, 3.2.432
abridgement, 5.1.39
aby, 3.2.335
aby it dear, 3.2.175
ace, 5.1.301; 5.1.303
Acheron, 3.2.357
adamant, 2.1.195
address, 2.2.149
addressed, 5.1.106
admirable, 5.1.27
Aegles, 2.1.79
after-supper, 5.1.34
again, 5.1.181
against, 3.2.99; 5.1.75
aggravate, 1.2.73
air, 1.1.183
Alexander, Bill, p. 98; Appendix
All is True, 3.2.464
alone, 3.2.119
an, 1.2.45; 4.2.20
Antiopa, 2.1.80
antique, 5.1.3
Antony and Cleopatra, 3.2.263
apple, 3.2.104
apprehend, 5.1.5; 5.1.19–20
apprehension, 3.2.178
approve, 2.2.74
argument, 3.2.242
Ariadne, 2.1.80
arm, 1.1.117
Artemidorus, pp. 5–7
artificial, 3.2.203
as, 3.2.359
as well derived, 1.1.99
as well possessed, 1.1.100
As You Like It, 4.1.82.1; 5.1.363
at large, 5.1.150
aunt, 2.1.51
Aurora's harbinger, 3.2.380
avouch, 1.1.106
aye, 1.1.90

bait, 3.2.197
ballad, 4.1.211
barm, 2.1.38
barren sort, 3.2.13
bated, 1.1.190
batty, 3.2.365
bayed, 4.1.112
be it so, 1.1.39
be out of hope, 3.2.267–8
beachèd margin, 2.1.85
bean-fed, 2.1.45
Benson, Frank, pp. 25, 66
bergamask, 5.1.346
beteem, 1.1.131
bill of properties, 1.2.94
blindworms, 2.2.11
blood, 1.1.135
bodies forth, 5.1.14
bond, 3.2.267–8
bootless, 2.1.37; 2.1.233
bottle, 4.1.32
bottom, hath no, 4.1.213
Bottom, 1.2.16
brakes, 2.1.227
brave touch, 3.2.70
brawls, 2.1.87
Britten, Benjamin, p. 108; 4.1.186
broached 5.11.146
Brook, Peter, pp. 24, 72–3, 96–7, 108, *109*; 1.1.136–40; 2.2.30.1; 3.1.97.1; 4.1.101.1–4; 5.1.428; Appendix
bully, 3.1.7; 4.2.18
burr, 3.2.260
buskined, 2.1.71
but, 3.2.56; 5.1.110
by and by, 3.1.82
By'r la'kin, 3.1.12

Caird, John, 5.1.388; Appendix
cankers, 2.2.3

American Literature

British and Irish Literature

Children's Literature

Classics and Ancient Literature

Colonial Literature

Eastern Literature

European Literature

History

Medieval Literature

Oxford English Drama

Poetry

Philosophy

Politics

Religion

The Oxford Shakespeare